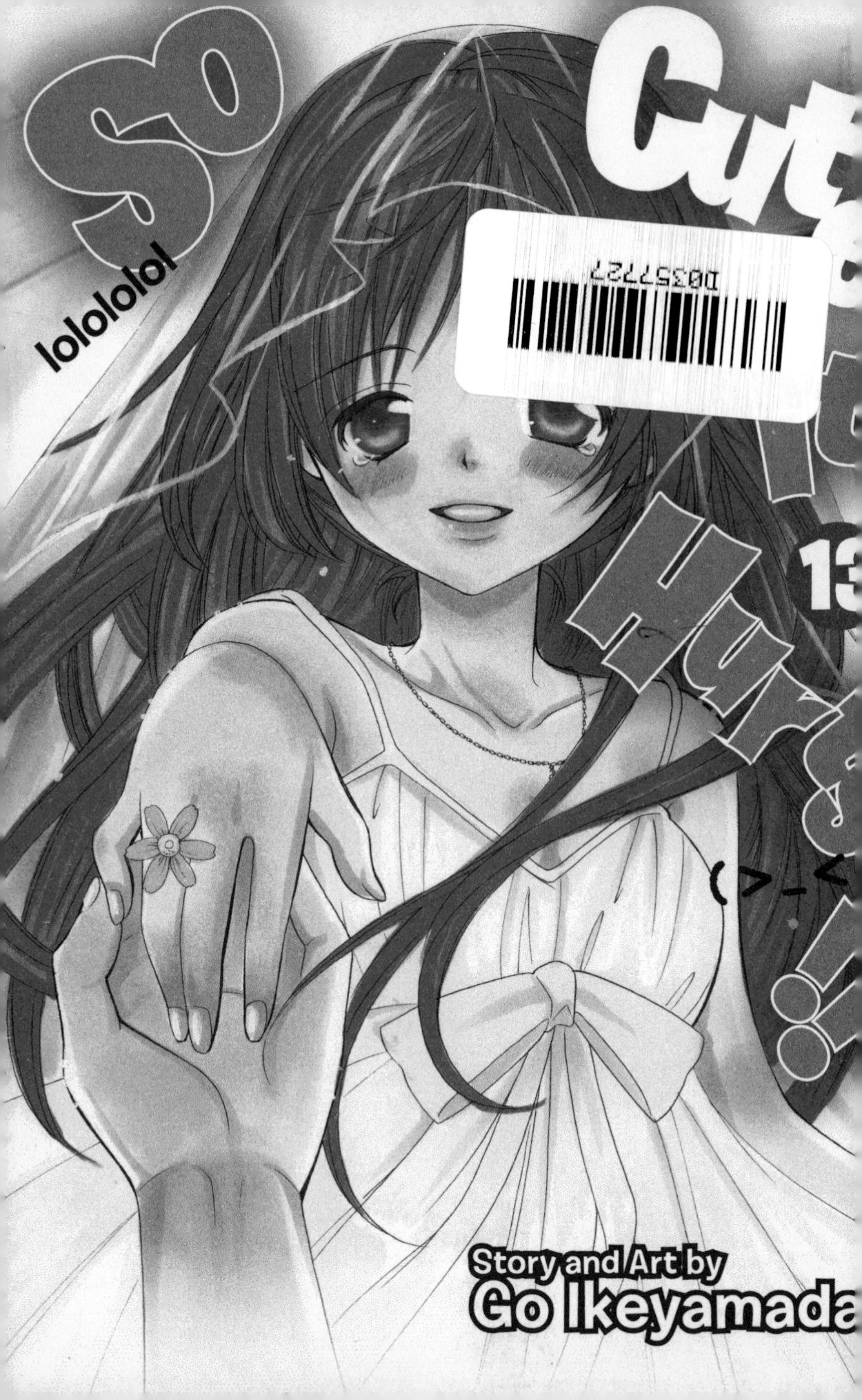
So
lolololol
13
(>_<
Story and Art by
Go Ikeyamada

CHARACTERS

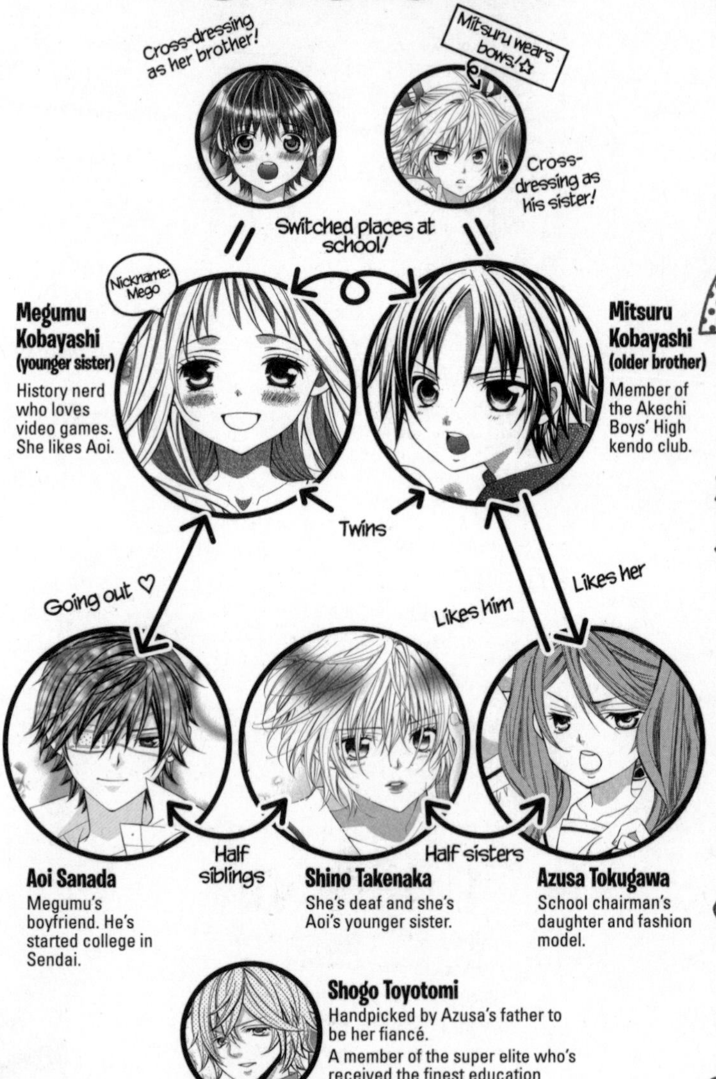

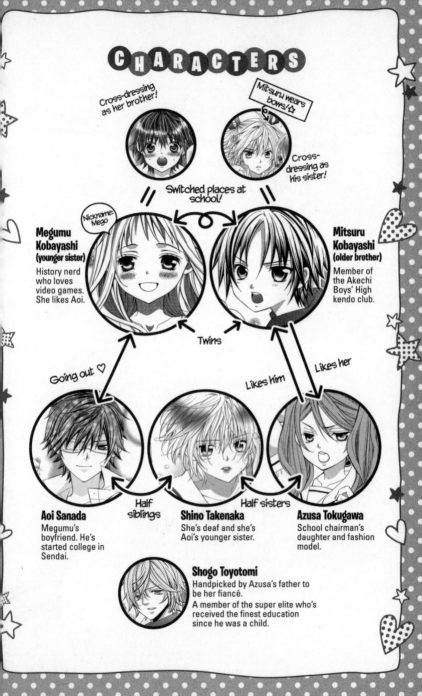

Cross-dressing as her brother!
Mitsuru wears bows!☆
Cross-dressing as his sister!
Switched places at school!
Nickname: Mego
Megumu Kobayashi (younger sister)
History nerd who loves video games. She likes Aoi.
Mitsuru Kobayashi (older brother)
Member of the Akechi Boys' High kendo club.
Twins
Going out ♡
Likes him
Likes her
Half siblings
Half sisters
Aoi Sanada
Megumu's boyfriend. He's started college in Sendai.
Shino Takenaka
She's deaf and she's Aoi's younger sister.
Azusa Tokugawa
School chairman's daughter and fashion model.
Shogo Toyotomi
Handpicked by Azusa's father to be her fiancé.
A member of the super elite who's received the finest education since he was a child.

STORY

★ Mitsuru and Megumu are twins. One day they switch places and go to each other's school for a week! That's when Megumu falls in love with Aoi. They begin a long-distance relationship when Aoi goes to Sendai for college, but their hearts are still strongly bound. When Megumu's father meets Aoi in Sendai, he approves of Aoi going out with his daughter after he witnesses Aoi sacrificing himself to protect Megumu.

★ Meanwhile, Mitsuru and Azusa have become attracted to each other. Mitsuru asks Azusa to marry him after he finds out how hurt and alone she's been because she felt like her parents never loved her. Azusa accepts Mitsuru's proposal, but her father schemes to separate them since he doesn't approve of their relationship.

★ Shogo and Azusa's engagement is announced on TV and Azusa goes to see her father to protest, but she ends up walking right into a press conference about her supposed engagement! Mitsuru then tells the press that he's Azusa's fiancé too. He declares that he'll score better than Shogo on the next national pre-exam and that Azusa's father will accept their engagement if he beats Shogo.

★ One night, Mitsuru and Megumu have a dream where black hands attack Aoi. Megumu feels like she'll regret it if she doesn't become one with Aoi now, and they sleep together. However, she still feels uneasy...

CONTENTS

So Cute It Hurts!! (˘‾˘)

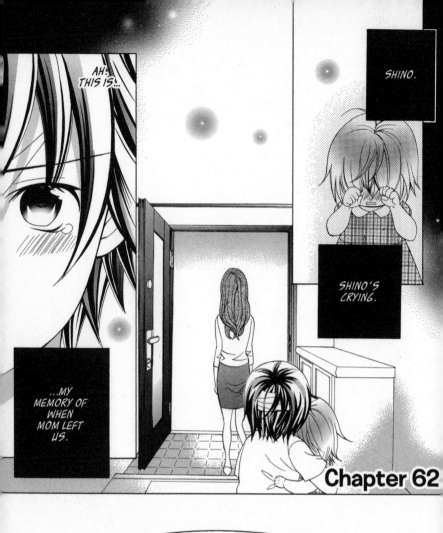

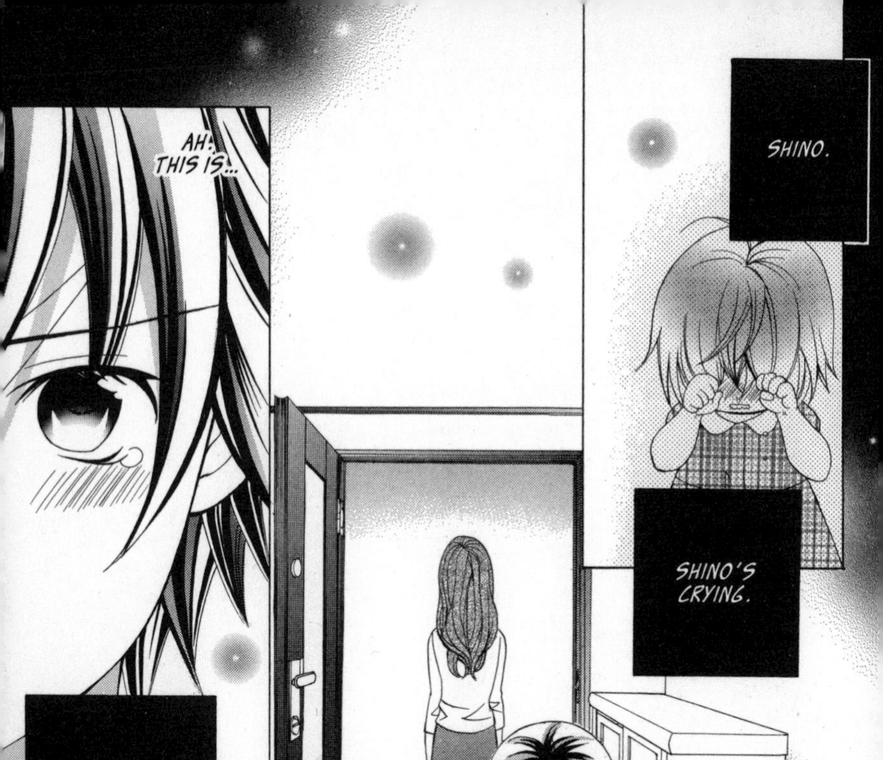
SHINO.
SHINO'S CRYING.
AH! THIS IS...
...MY MEMORY OF WHEN MOM LEFT US.
Chapter 62

NICE TO MEET YOU AND HELLO. I'M GO IKEYAMADA. THANK YOU FOR PICKING UP MY 56TH BOOK!! THIS IS VOLUME 13 OF *SO CUTE IT HURTS!!* THERE'S A SHOCKING PLOT DEVELOPMENT IN THIS VOLUME. I'M SURE PEOPLE WILL HAVE ALL SORTS OF REACTIONS TO IT, BUT I DREW IT WITH ALL MY HEART, AND I'M READY TO LISTEN TO YOUR THOUGHTS. THE SERIES WILL SOON END IN THE MAGAZINE, BUT PLEASE KEEP READING. I'LL DO MY VERY BEST UNTIL THE VERY END. (>_<)

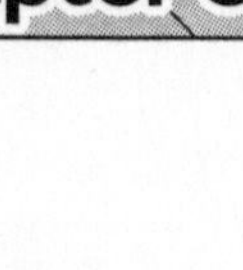

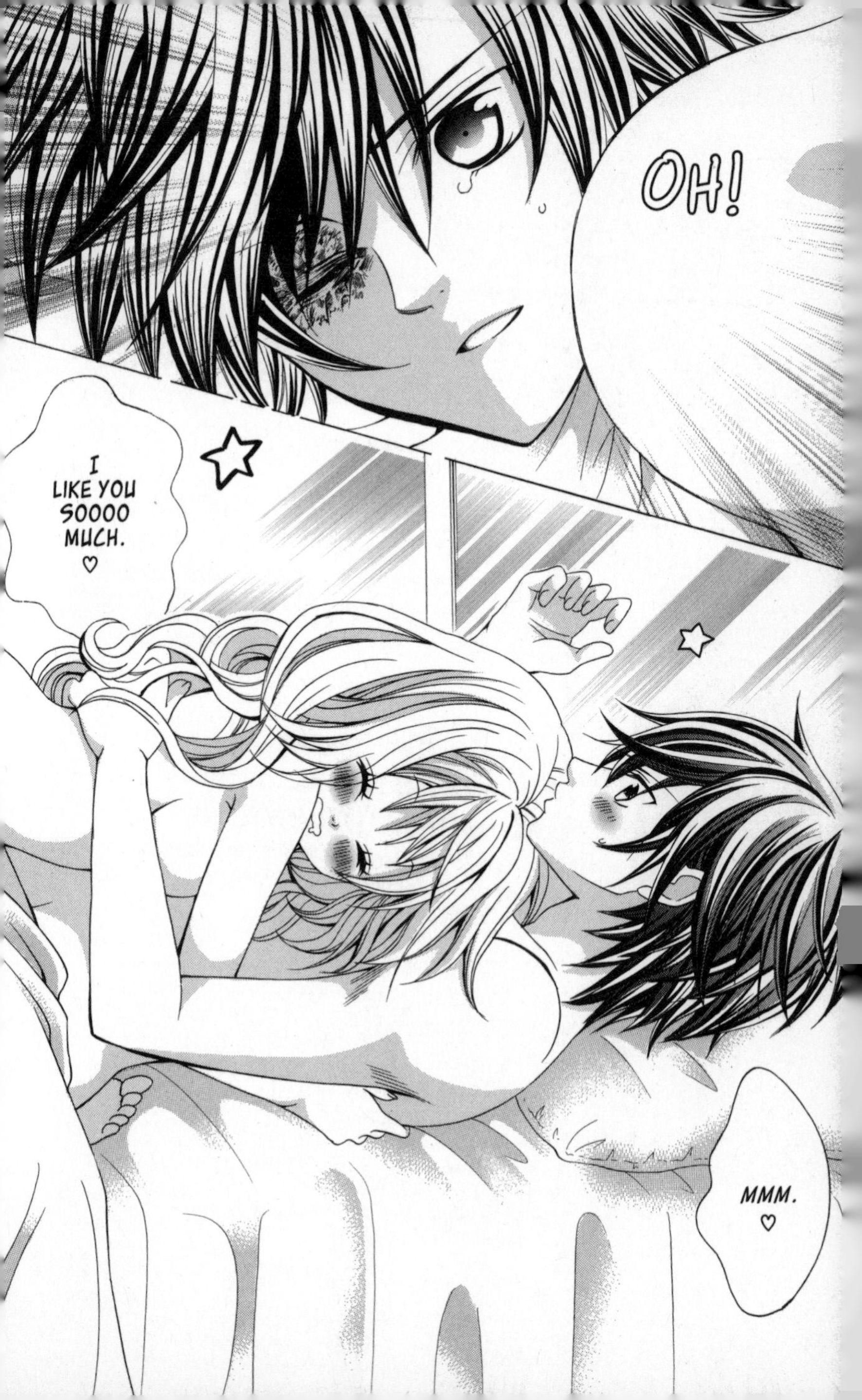
OH!
I LIKE YOU SOOOO MUCH. ♡
MMM. ♡

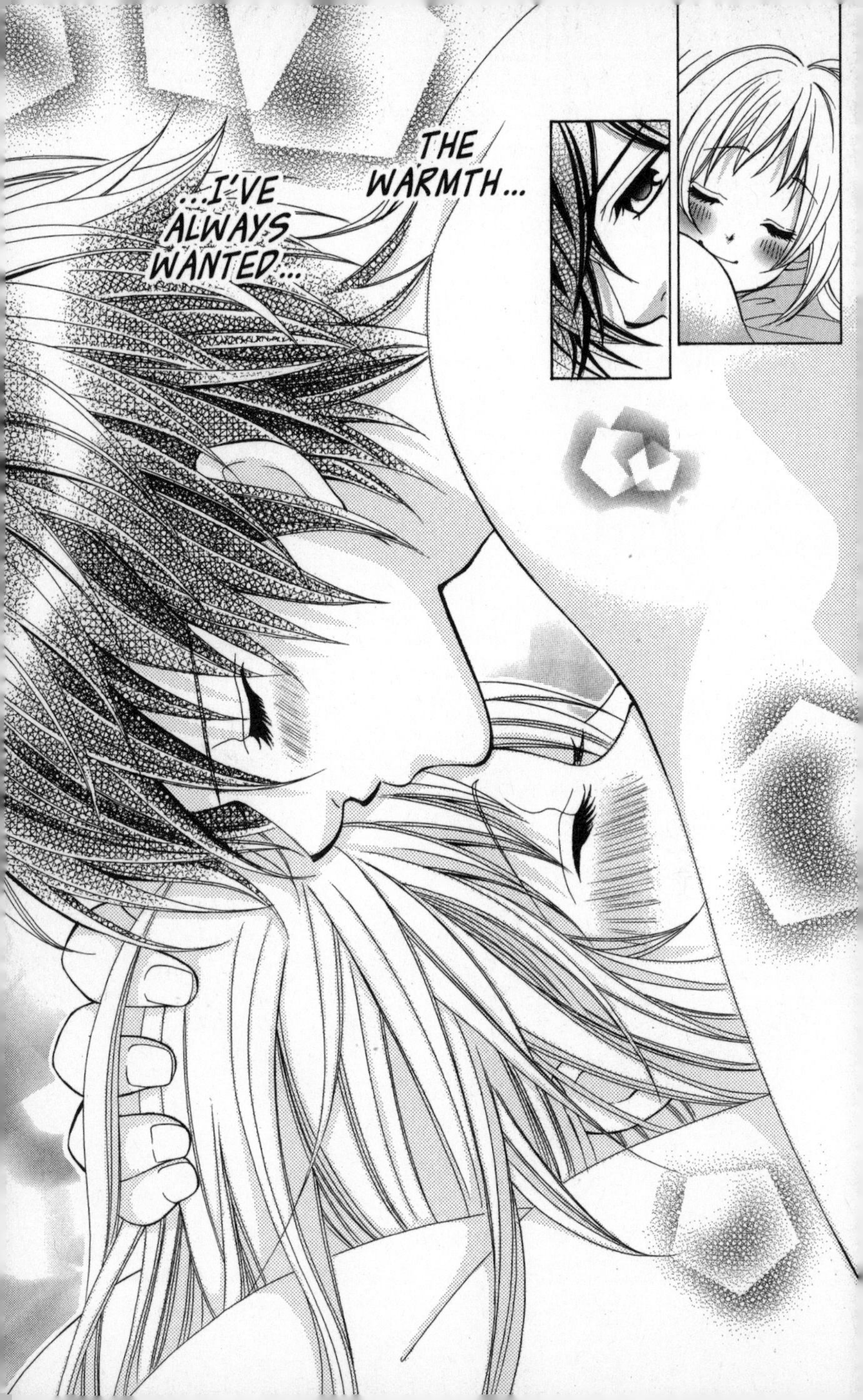
THE WARMTH...
...I'VE ALWAYS WANTED...

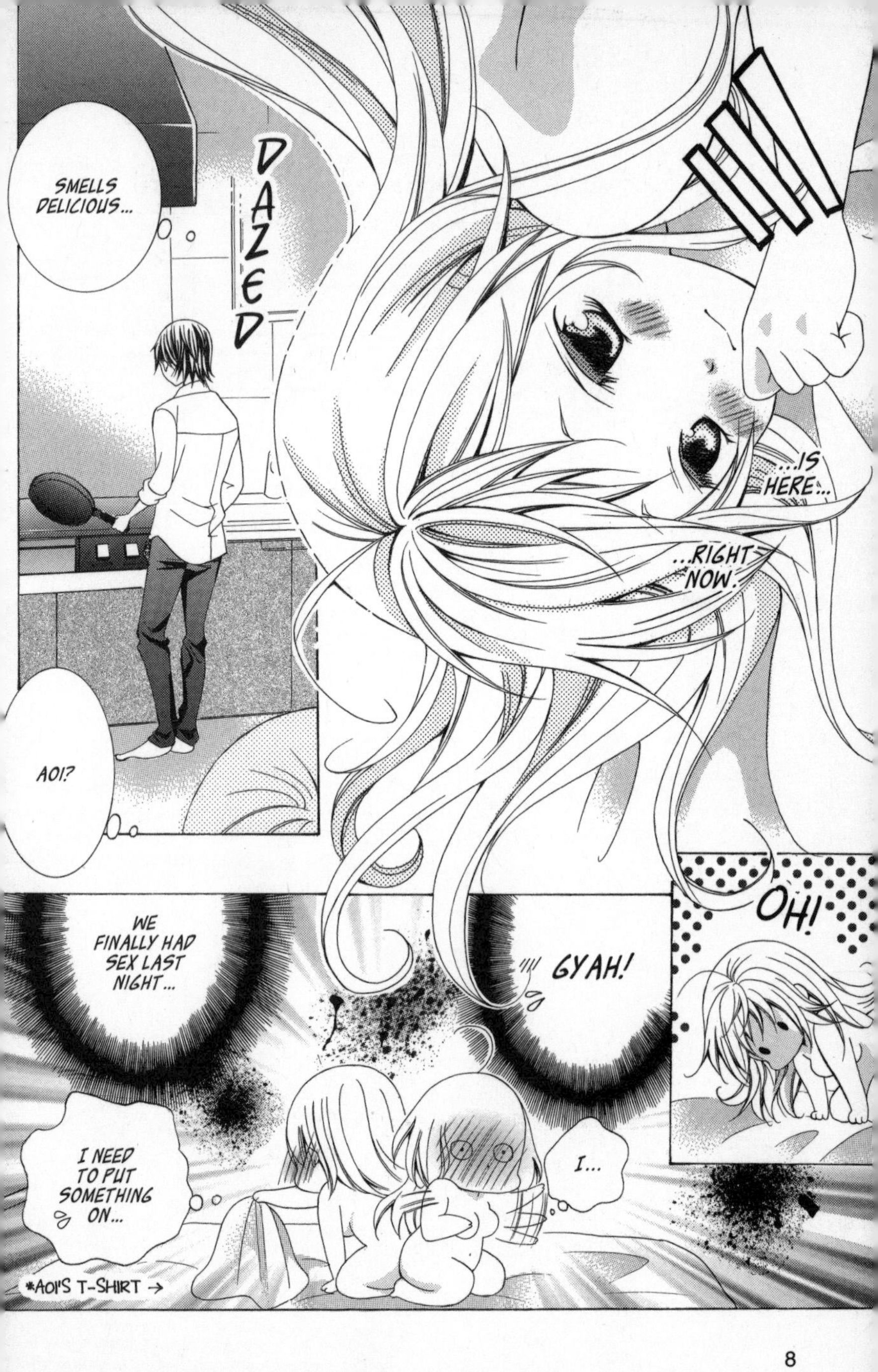
DAZED
SMELLS DELICIOUS...
AOI?
...IS HERE...
...RIGHT NOW.
OH!
GYAH!
I...
WE FINALLY HAD SEX LAST NIGHT...
I NEED TO PUT SOMETHING ON...
*AOI'S T-SHIRT →

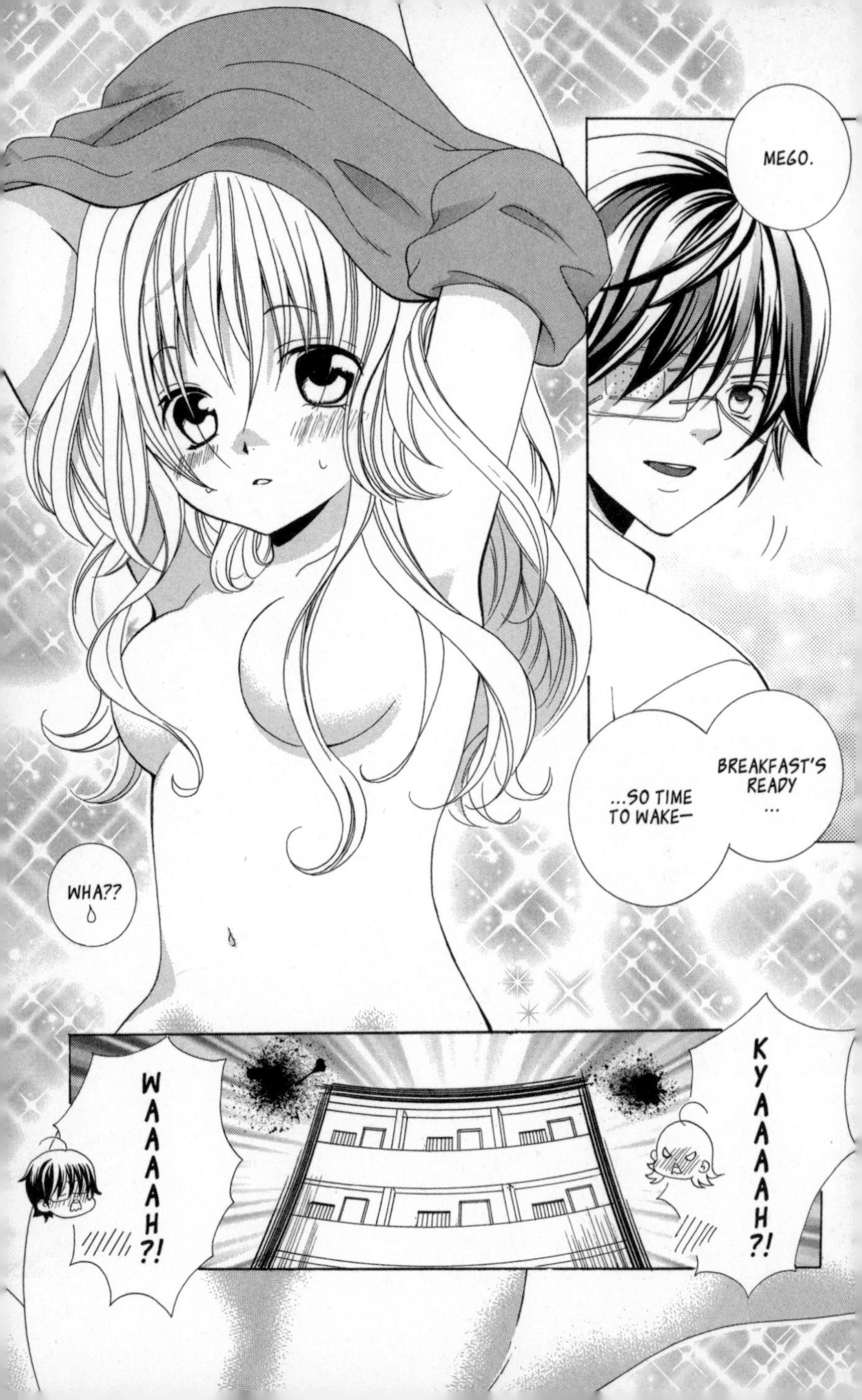
MEGO.
BREAKFAST'S READY ...
...SO TIME TO WAKE—
WHA??
KYAAAAH?!
WAAAAH?!

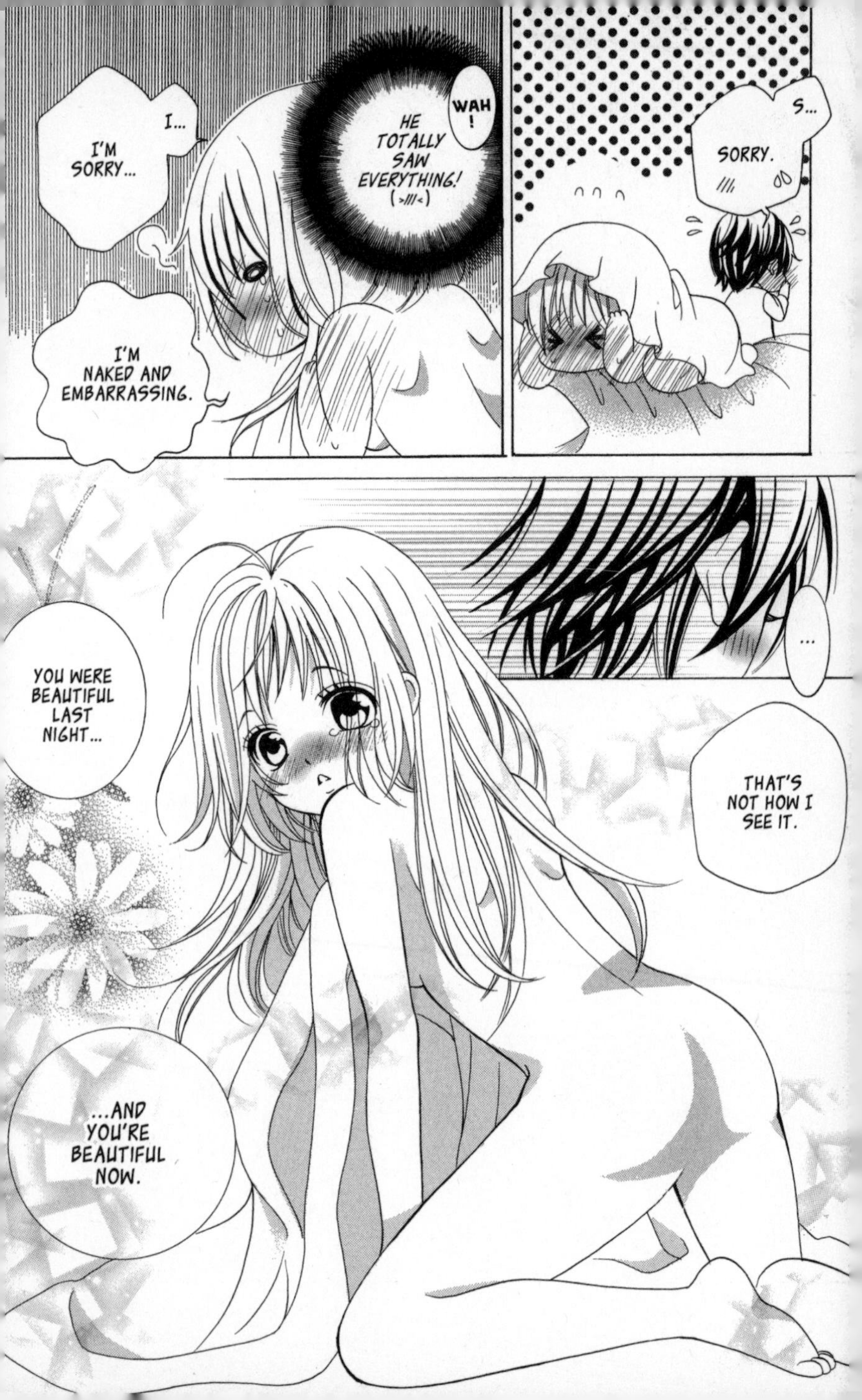
S...
SORRY.
WAH!
HE TOTALLY SAW EVERYTHING! (>///<)
I...
I'M SORRY...
I'M NAKED AND EMBARRASSING.
...
THAT'S NOT HOW I SEE IT.
YOU WERE BEAUTIFUL LAST NIGHT...
...AND YOU'RE BEAUTIFUL NOW.

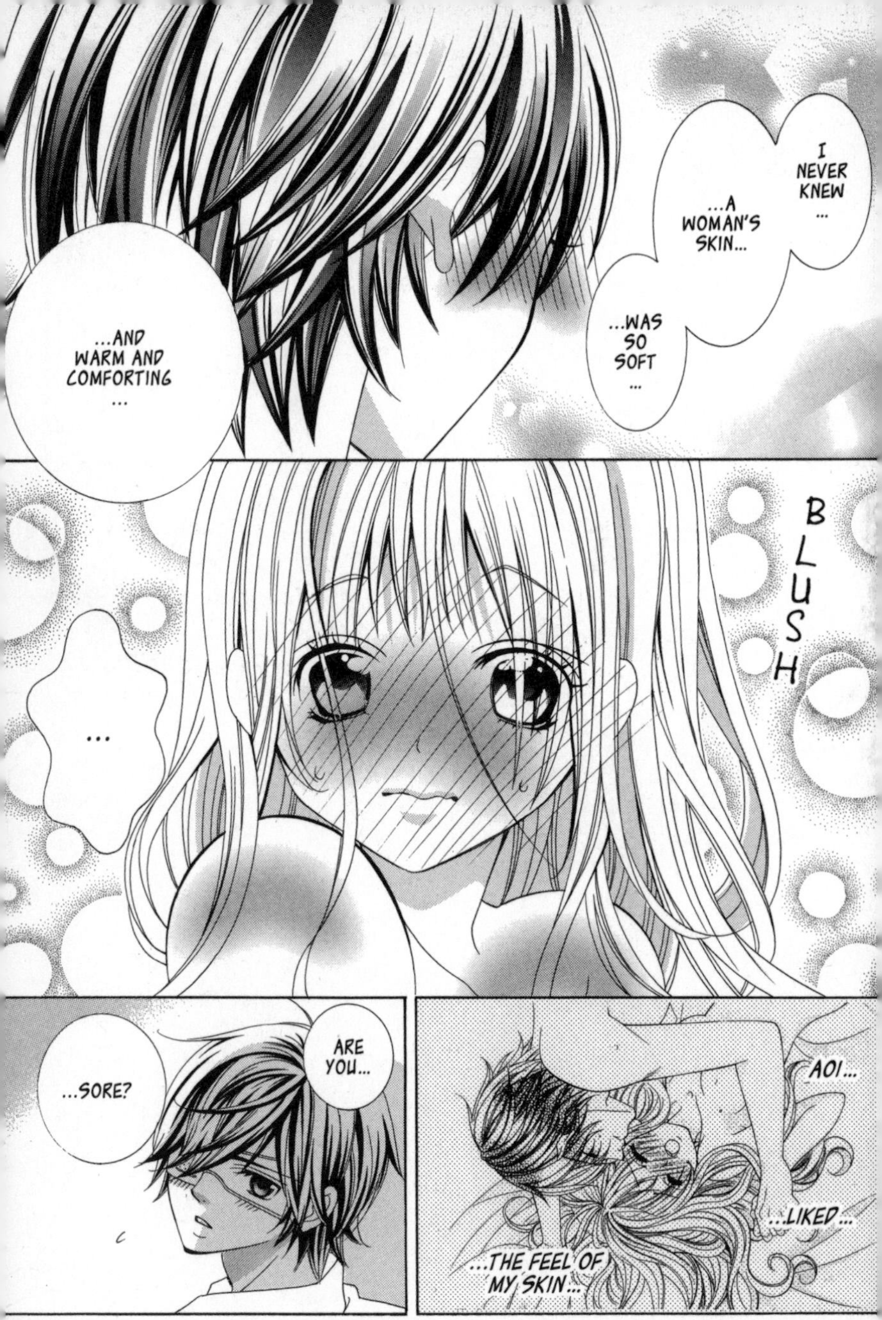
I NEVER KNEW...
...A WOMAN'S SKIN...
...WAS SO SOFT...
...AND WARM AND COMFORTING...
BLUSH
...
AOI...
...LIKED...
...THE FEEL OF MY SKIN...
ARE YOU...
...SORE?

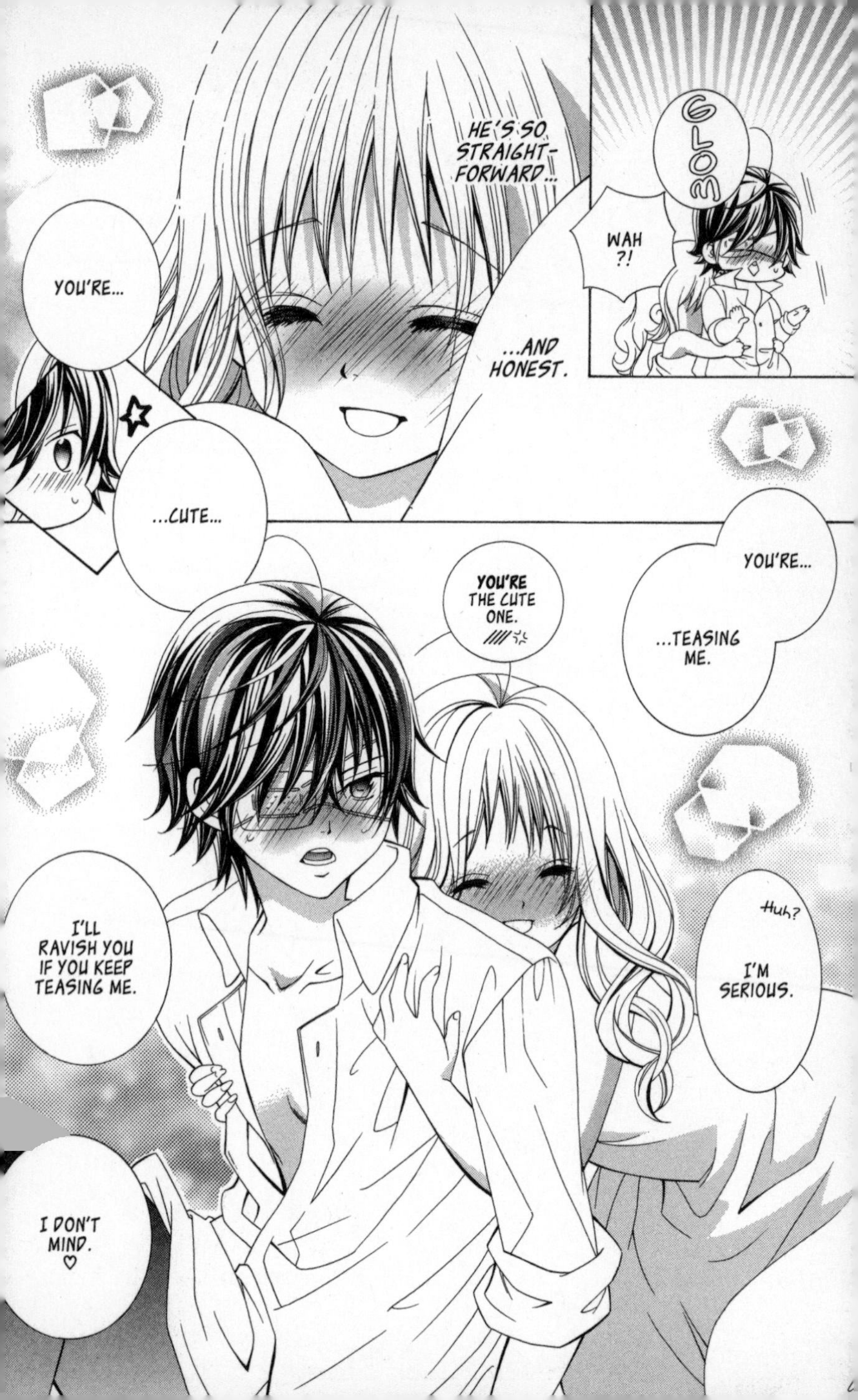
GLOMP
WAH?!
HE'S SO STRAIGHT-FORWARD...
...AND HONEST.
YOU'RE...
...CUTE...
YOU'RE...
...TEASING ME.
YOU'RE THE CUTE ONE.
Huh?
I'M SERIOUS.
I'LL RAVISH YOU IF YOU KEEP TEASING ME.
I DON'T MIND. ♡

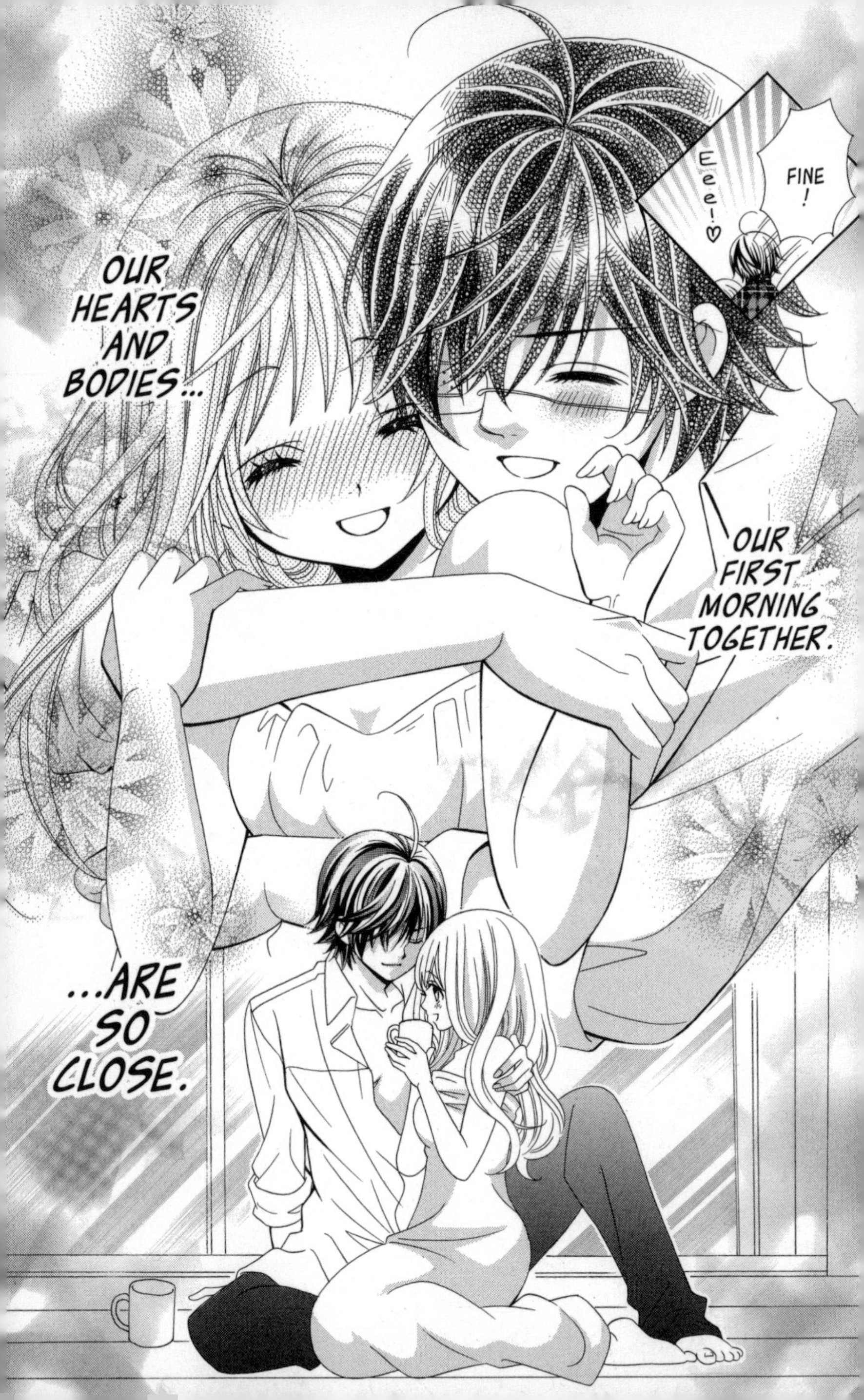
FINE!
Eee!♥
OUR FIRST MORNING TOGETHER.
OUR HEARTS AND BODIES...
...ARE SO CLOSE.

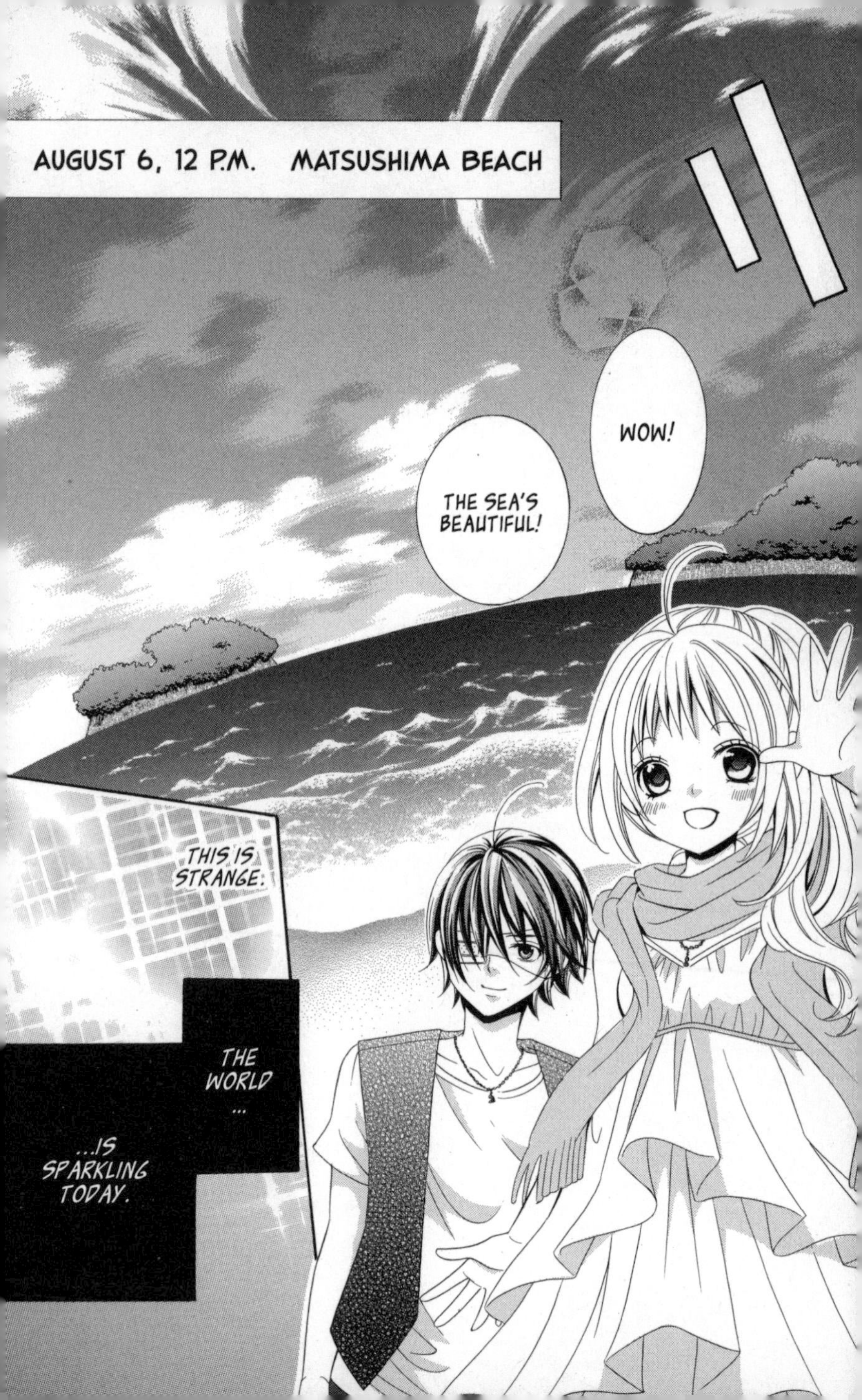
AUGUST 6, 12 P.M. MATSUSHIMA BEACH
WOW!
THE SEA'S BEAUTIFUL!
THIS IS STRANGE.
THE WORLD ...
...IS SPARKLING TODAY.

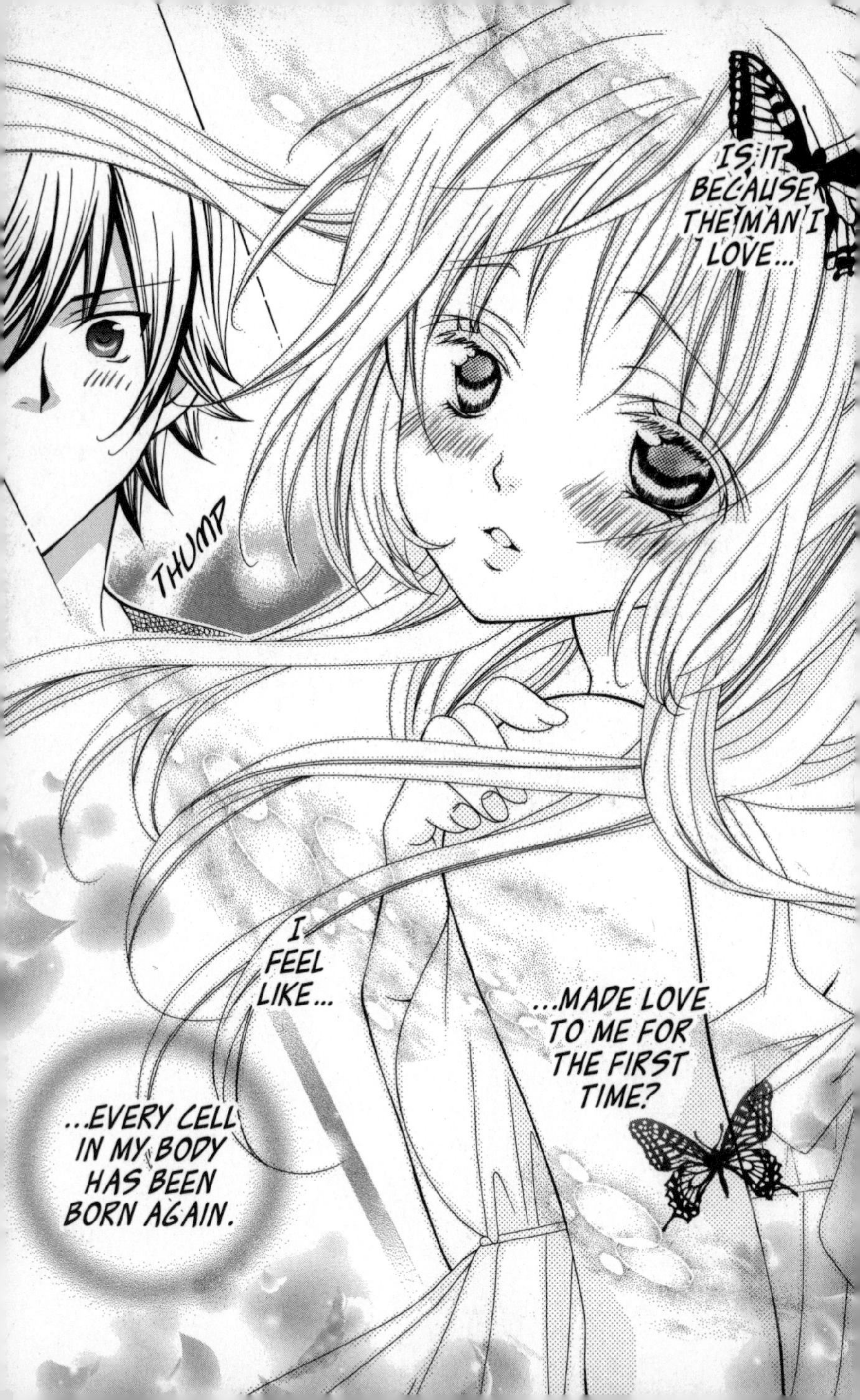
IS IT BECAUSE THE MAN I LOVE...
THUMP
...MADE LOVE TO ME FOR THE FIRST TIME?
I FEEL LIKE...
...EVERY CELL IN MY BODY HAS BEEN BORN AGAIN.

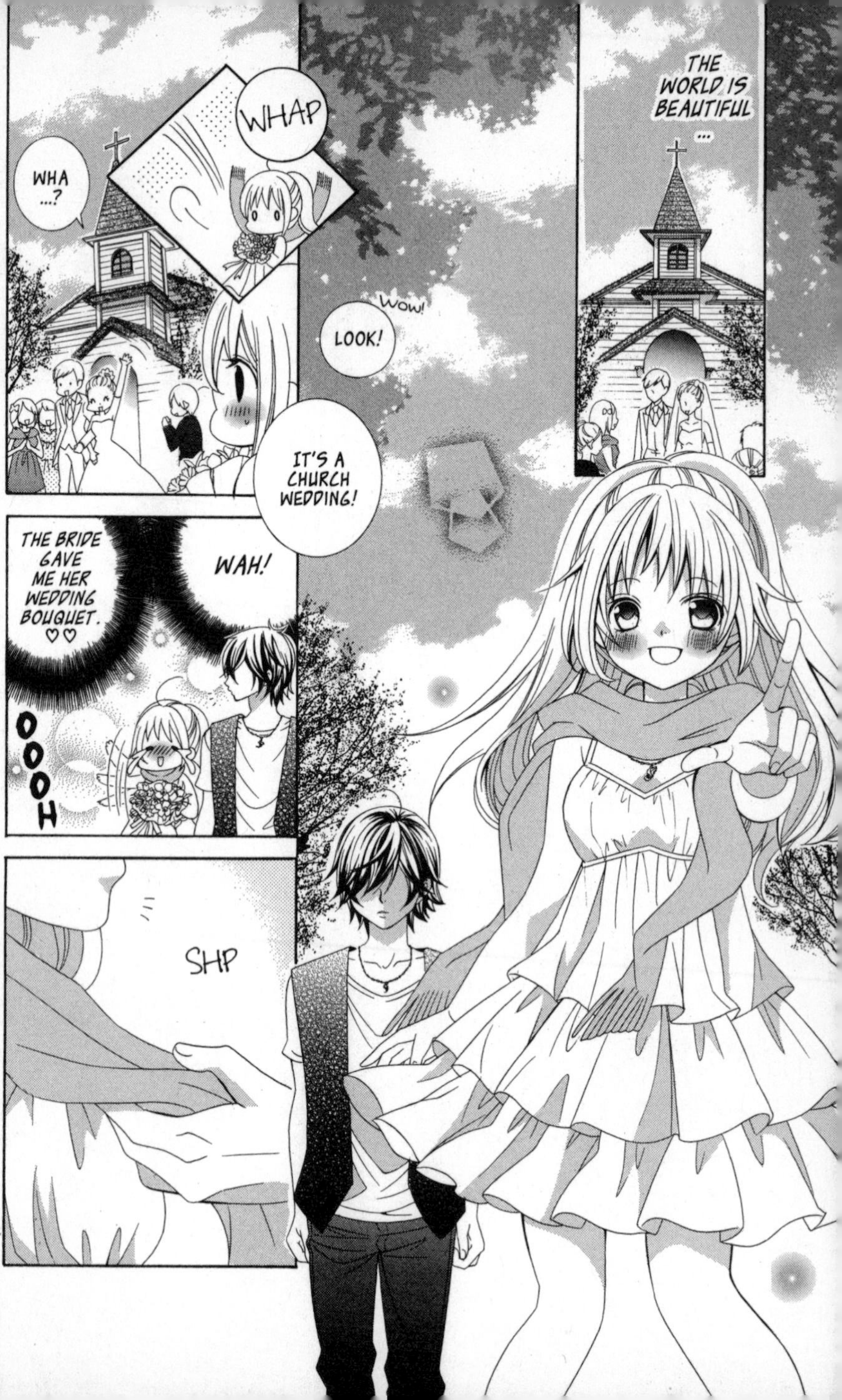

THE WORLD IS BEAUTIFUL...
WOW!
LOOK!
IT'S A CHURCH WEDDING!
WHAP
WHA ...?
WAH!
THE BRIDE GAVE ME HER WEDDING BOUQUET. ♡♡
OOOH
SHP

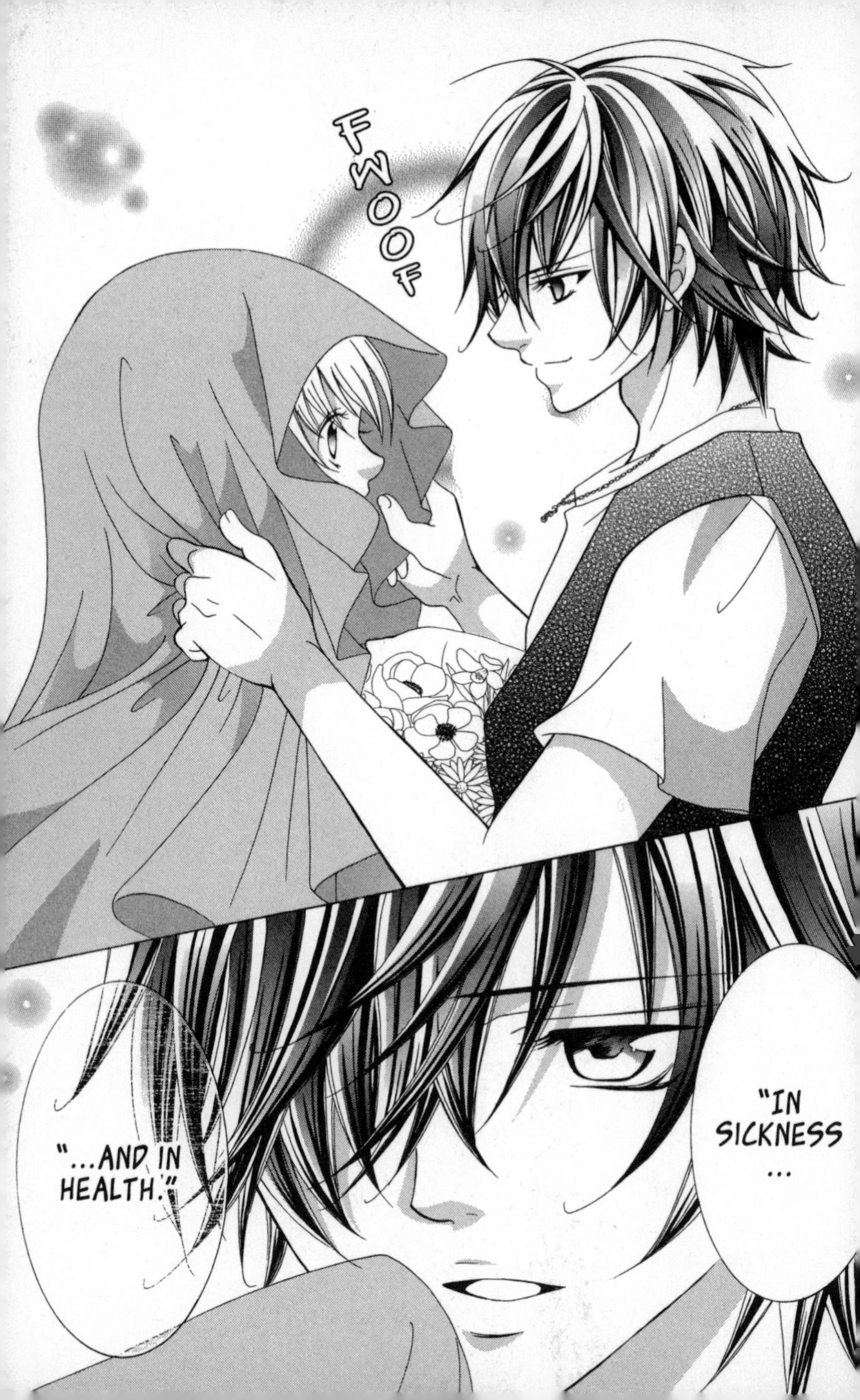
FWOOF
"IN SICKNESS ...
"...AND IN HEALTH."

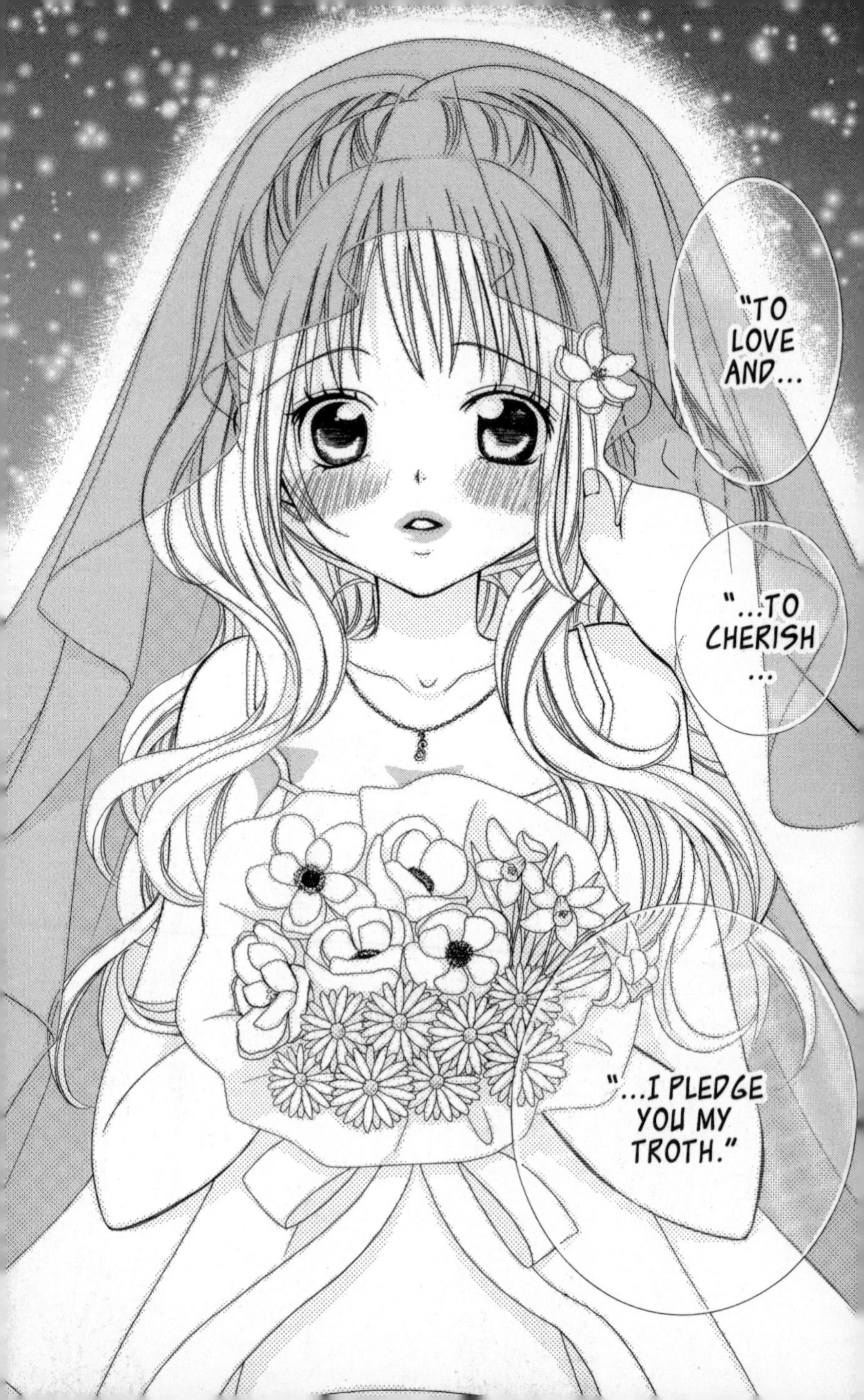
"TO LOVE AND...
"...TO CHERISH ...
"...I PLEDGE YOU MY TROTH."

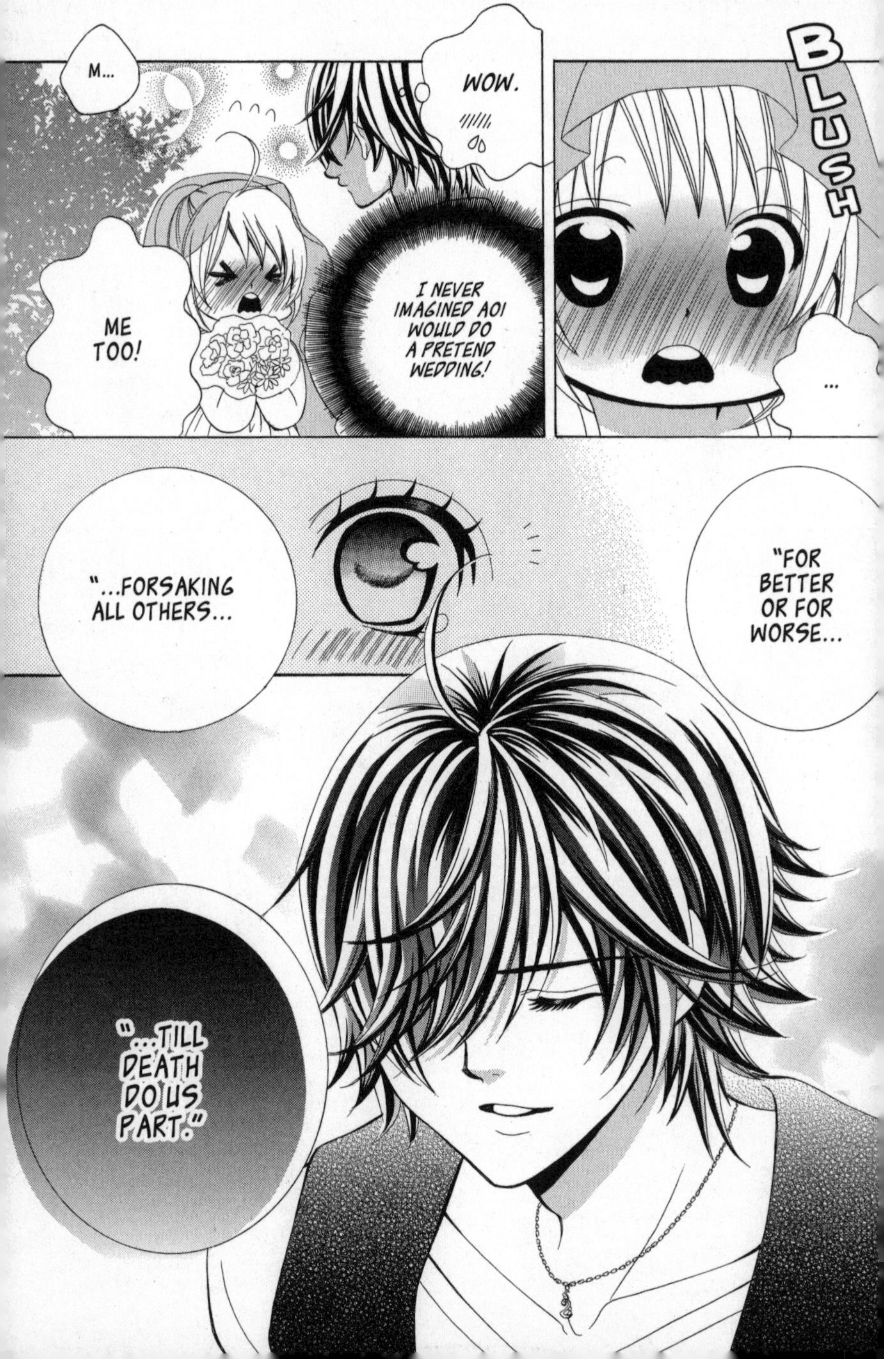
BLUSH
...
WOW.
M...
I NEVER IMAGINED AOI WOULD DO A PRETEND WEDDING!
ME TOO!
"FOR BETTER OR FOR WORSE...
"...FORSAKING ALL OTHERS...
"...TILL DEATH DO US PART."

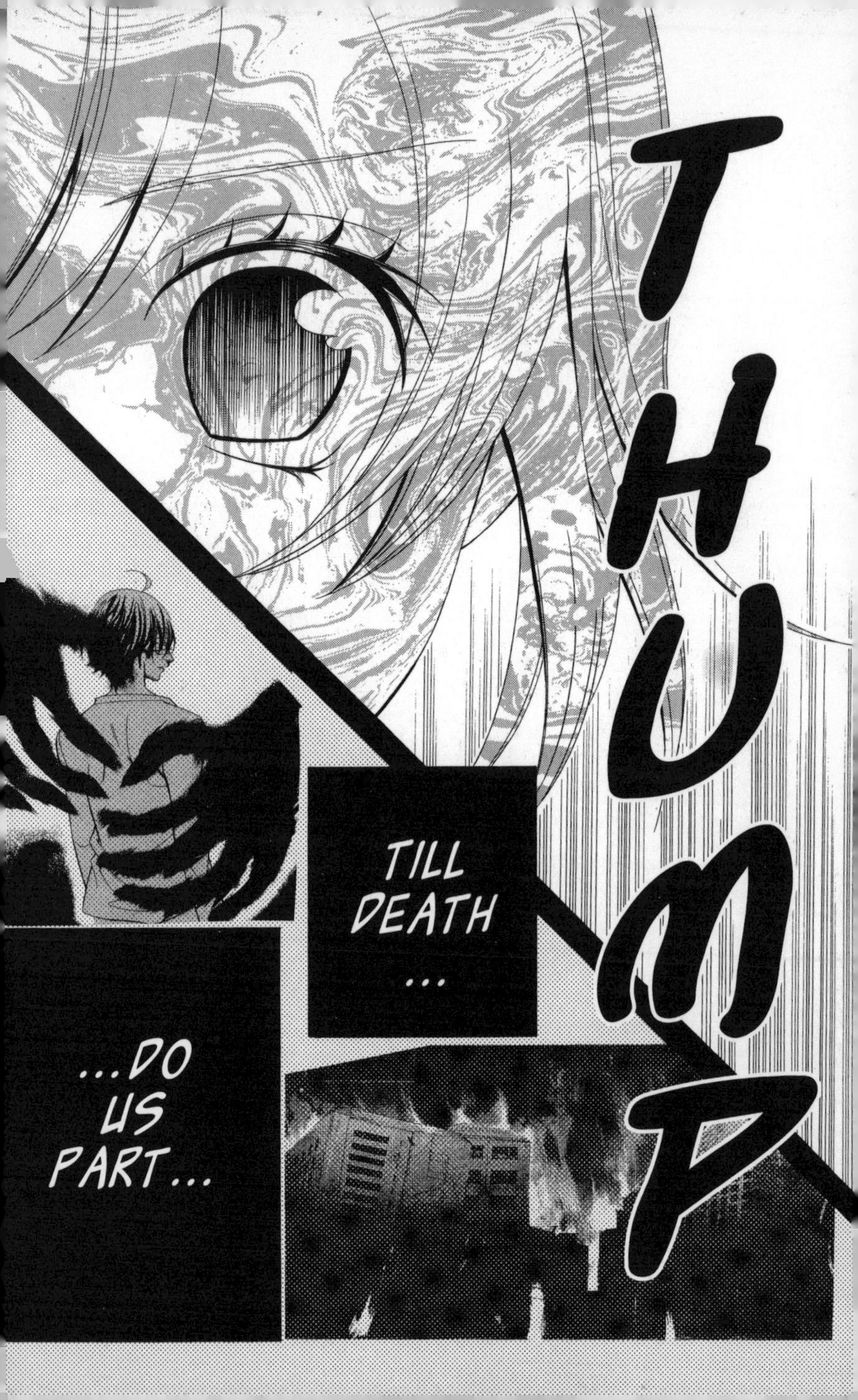
THUMP
TILL DEATH ...
...DO US PART...

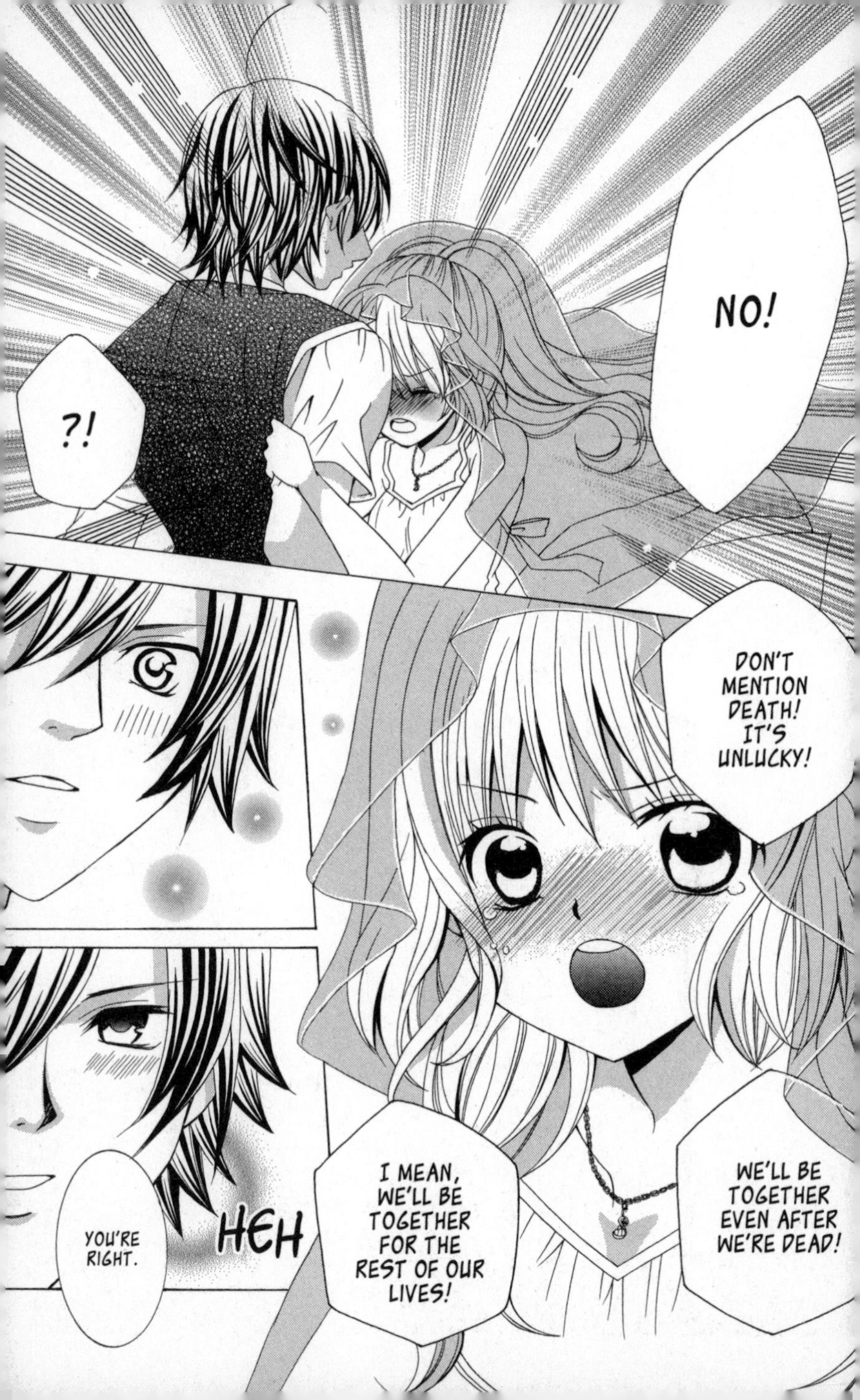
NO!
?!
DON'T MENTION DEATH! IT'S UNLUCKY!
WE'LL BE TOGETHER EVEN AFTER WE'RE DEAD!
I MEAN, WE'LL BE TOGETHER FOR THE REST OF OUR LIVES!
HEH
YOU'RE RIGHT.

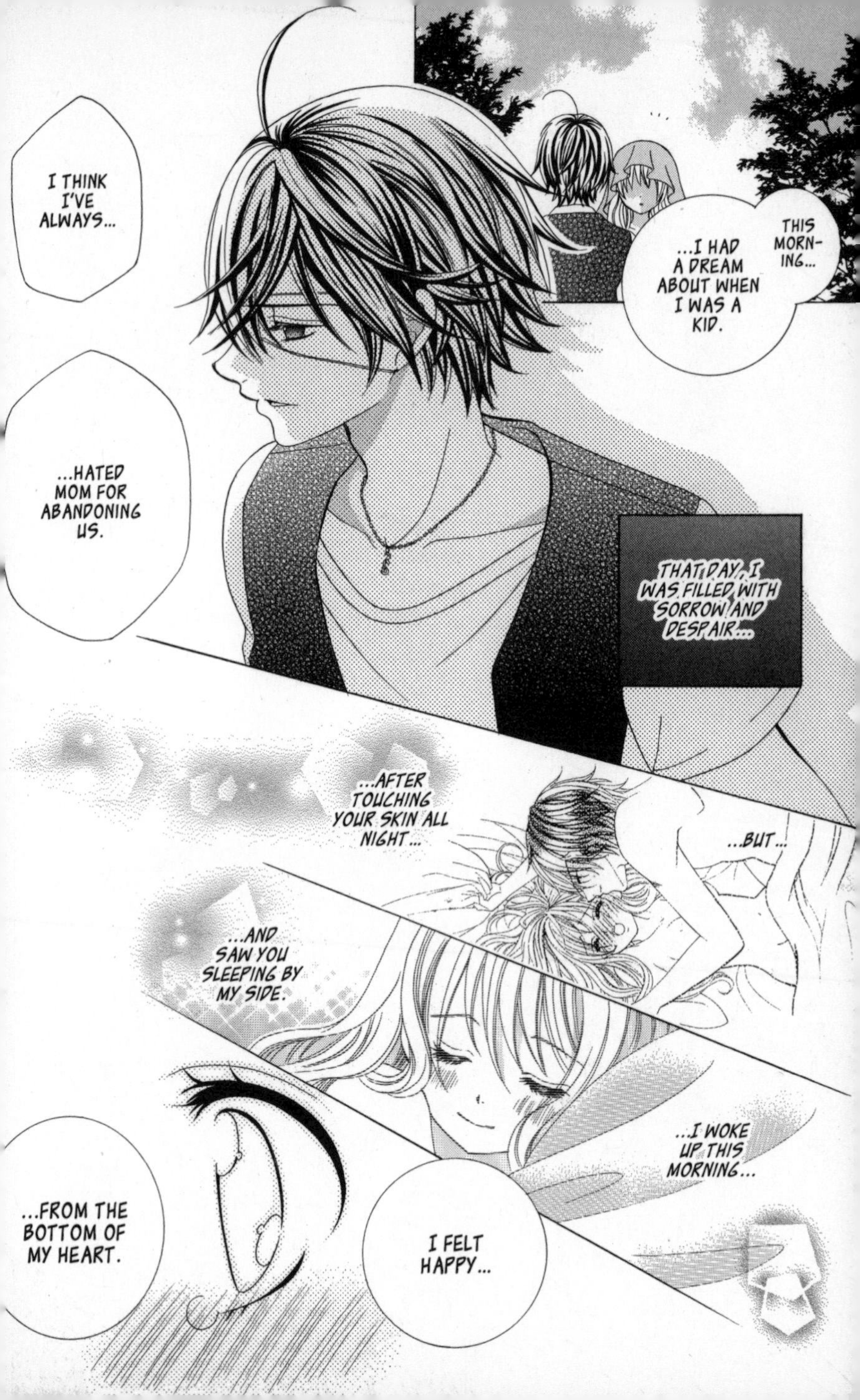
...
THIS MORNING...
...I HAD A DREAM ABOUT WHEN I WAS A KID.
I THINK I'VE ALWAYS...
...HATED MOM FOR ABANDONING US.
THAT DAY, I WAS FILLED WITH SORROW AND DESPAIR...
...BUT...
...AFTER TOUCHING YOUR SKIN ALL NIGHT...
...I WOKE UP THIS MORNING...
...AND SAW YOU SLEEPING BY MY SIDE.
I FELT HAPPY...
...FROM THE BOTTOM OF MY HEART.

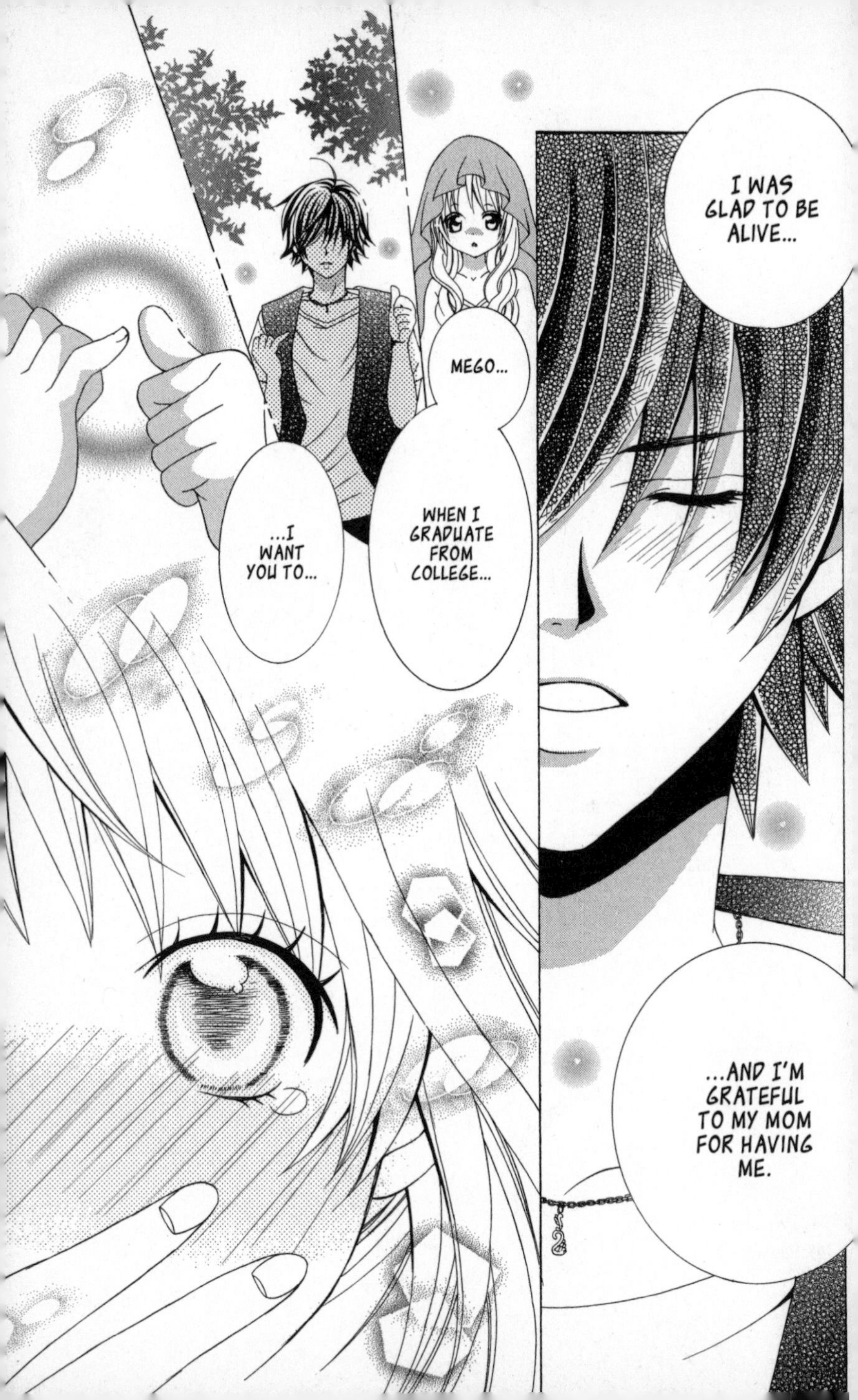
I WAS GLAD TO BE ALIVE...
...AND I'M GRATEFUL TO MY MOM FOR HAVING ME.
MEGO...
WHEN I GRADUATE FROM COLLEGE...
...I WANT YOU TO...

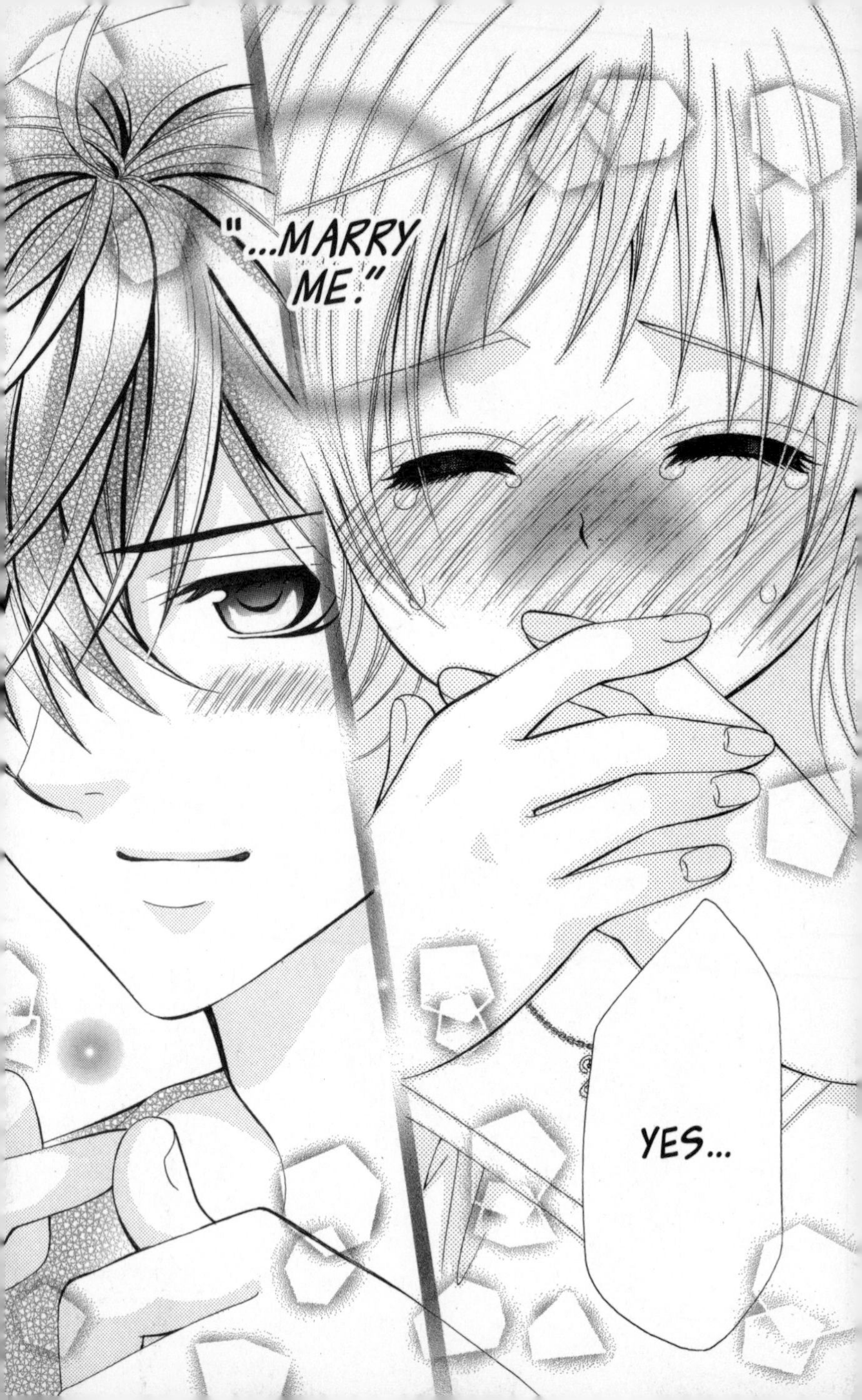
"...MARRY ME."
YES...

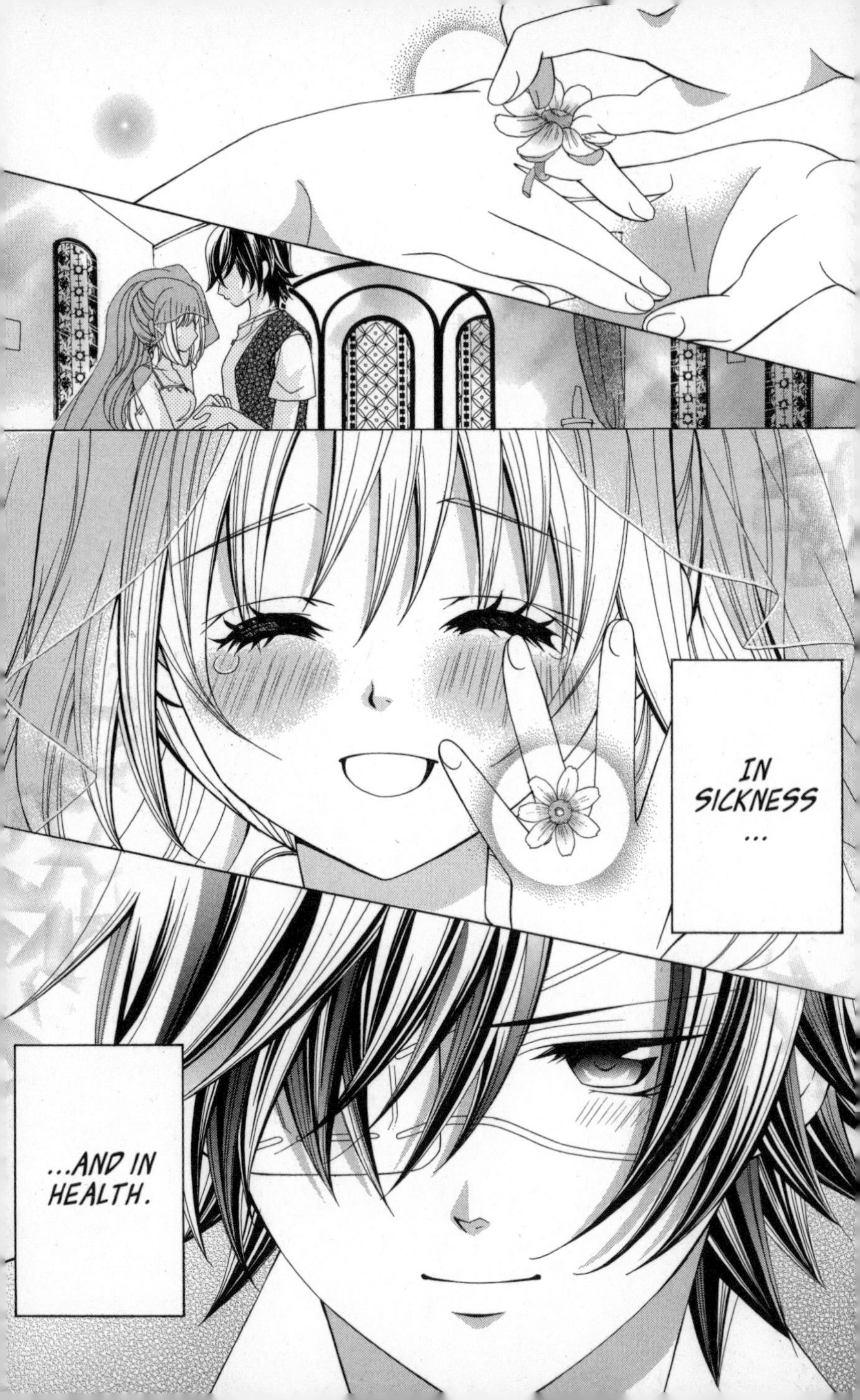
IN SICKNESS ...
...AND IN HEALTH.

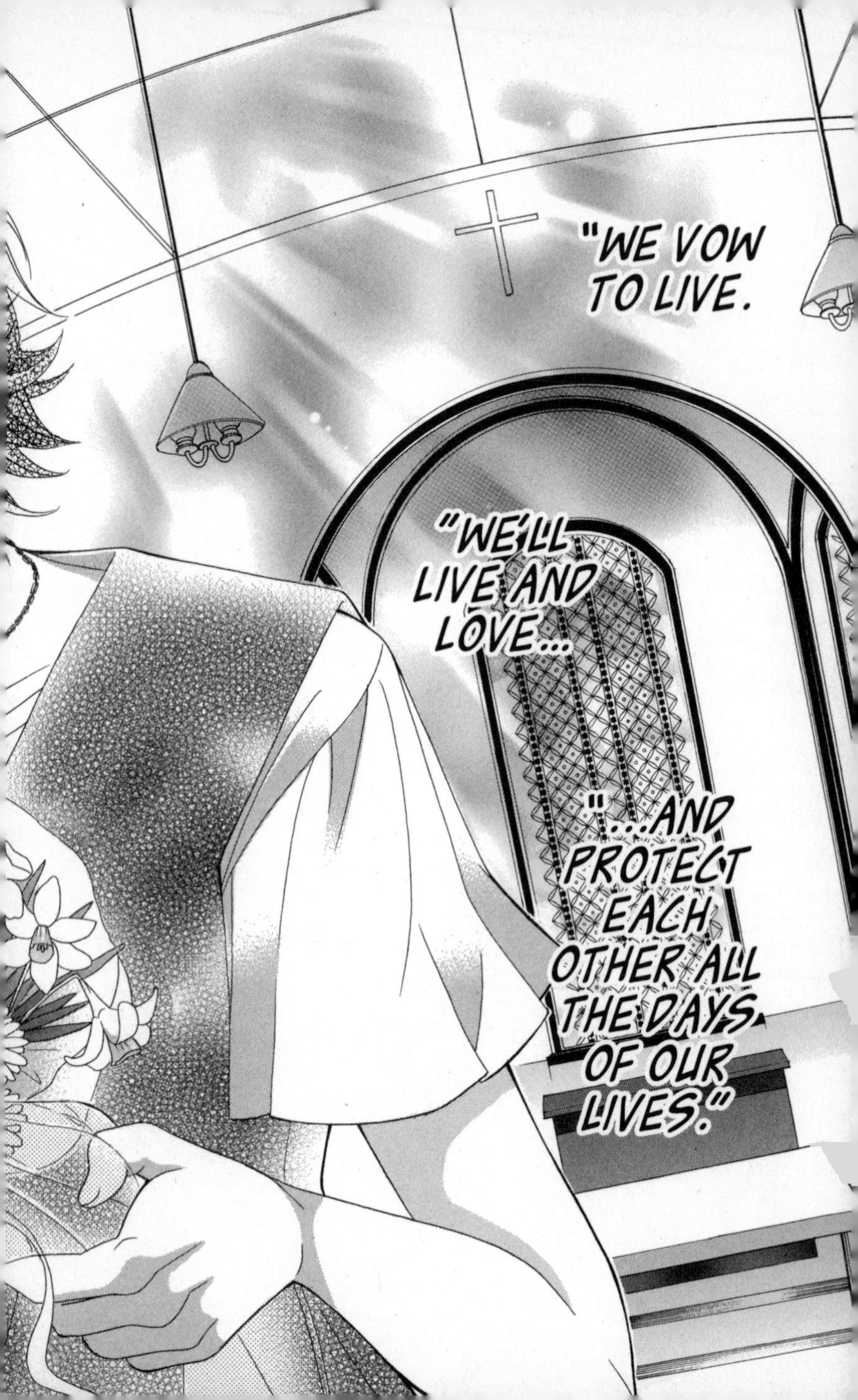
"WE VOW TO LIVE.
"WE'LL LIVE AND LOVE...
"...AND PROTECT EACH OTHER ALL THE DAYS OF OUR LIVES."

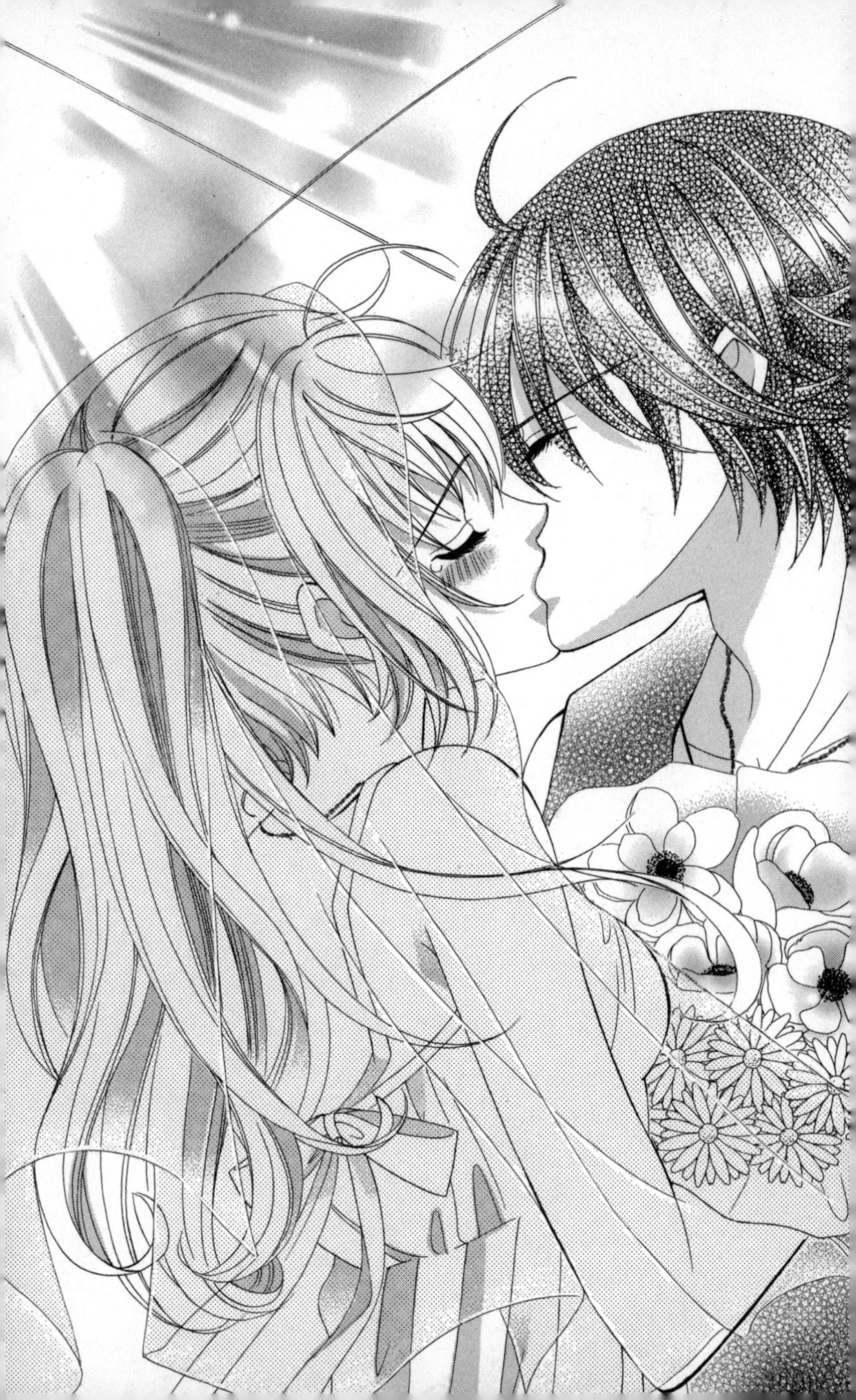

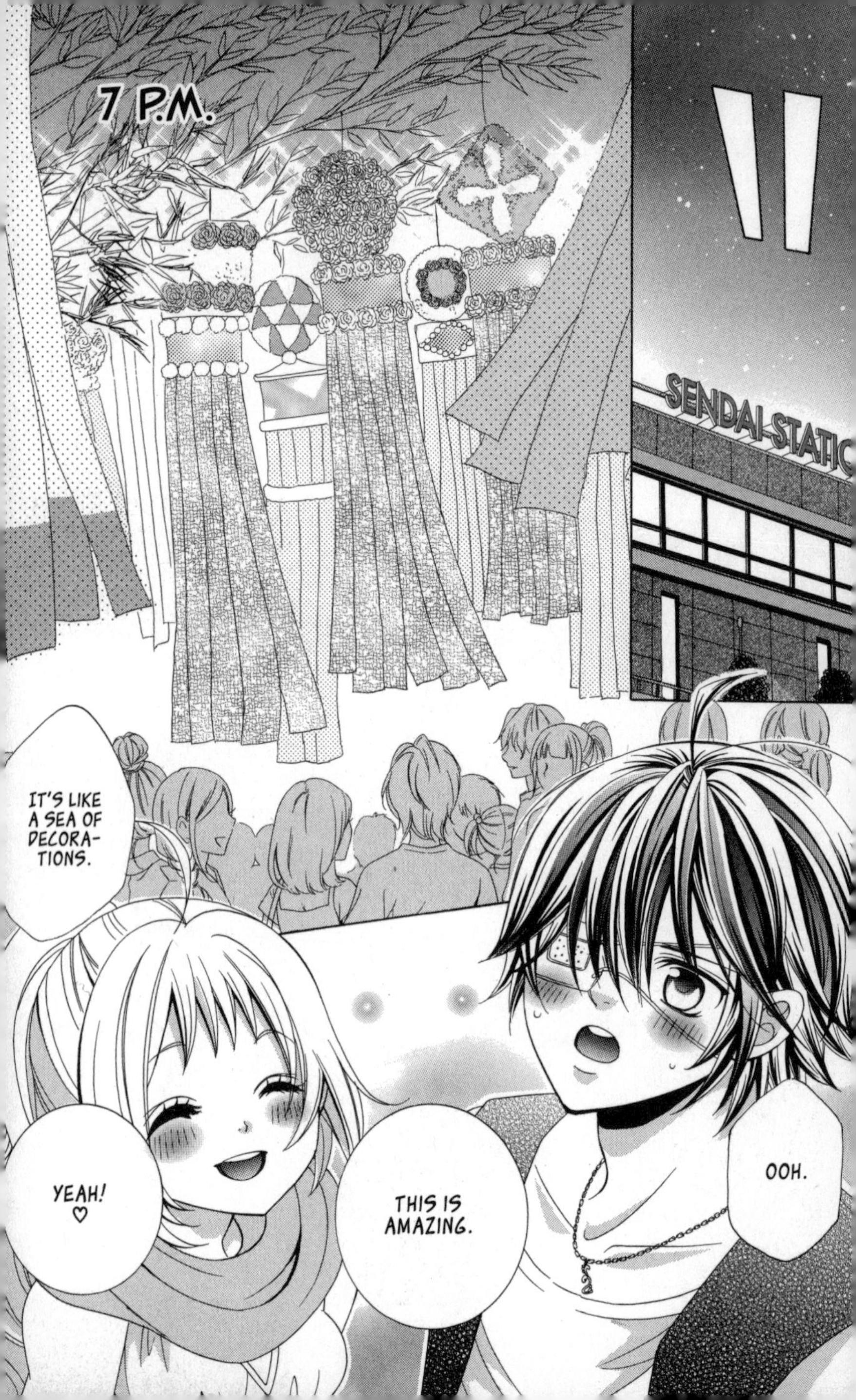
7 P.M.
SENDAI STATIC
OOH.
THIS IS AMAZING.
IT'S LIKE A SEA OF DECORATIONS.
YEAH! ♡

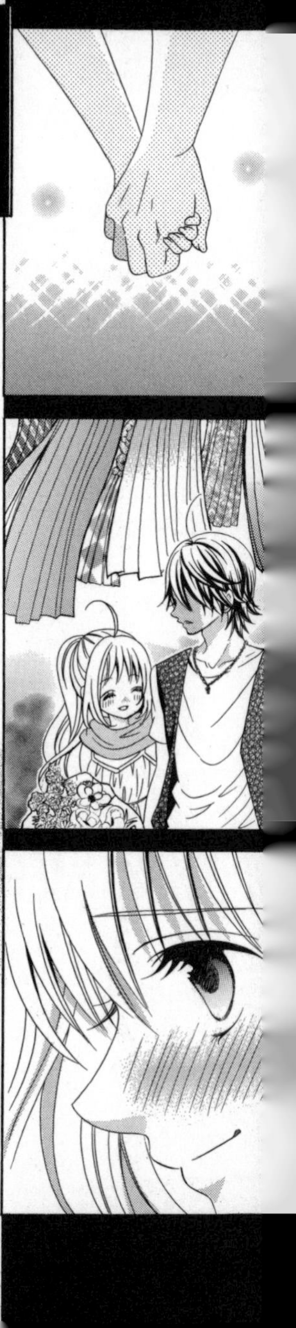

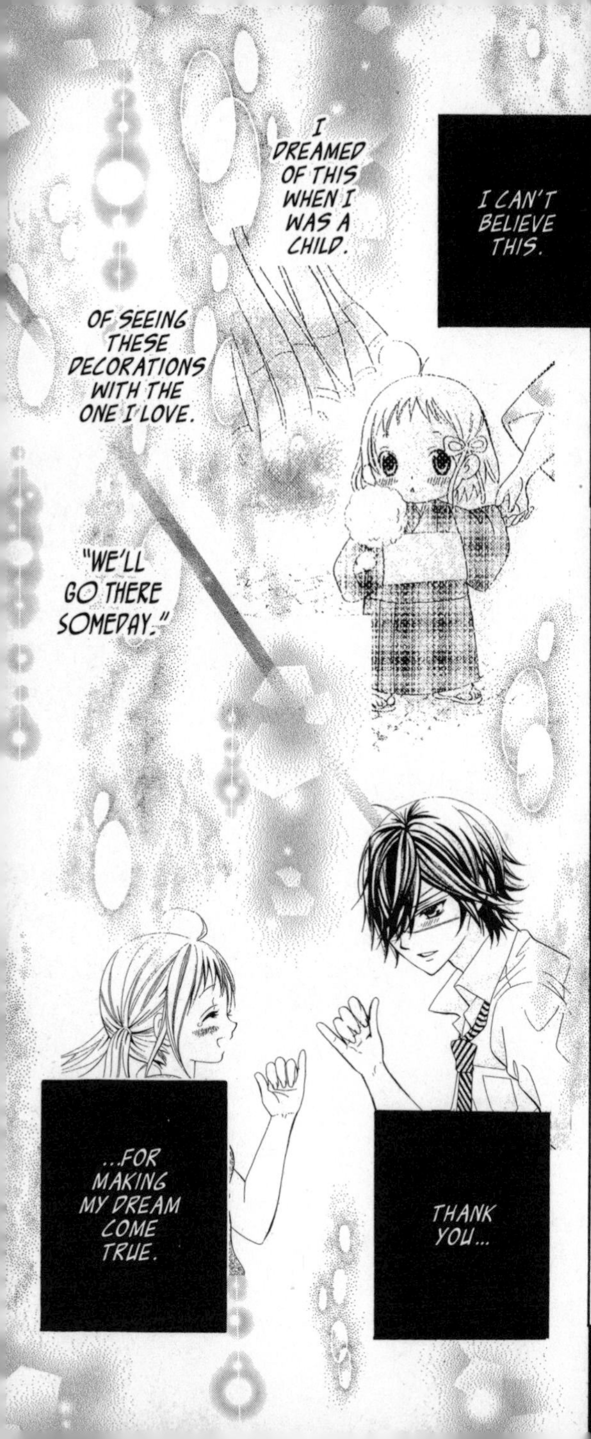
I CAN'T BELIEVE THIS.
I DREAMED OF THIS WHEN I WAS A CHILD.
OF SEEING THESE DECORATIONS WITH THE ONE I LOVE.
"WE'LL GO THERE SOMEDAY."
THANK YOU...
...FOR MAKING MY DREAM COME TRUE.

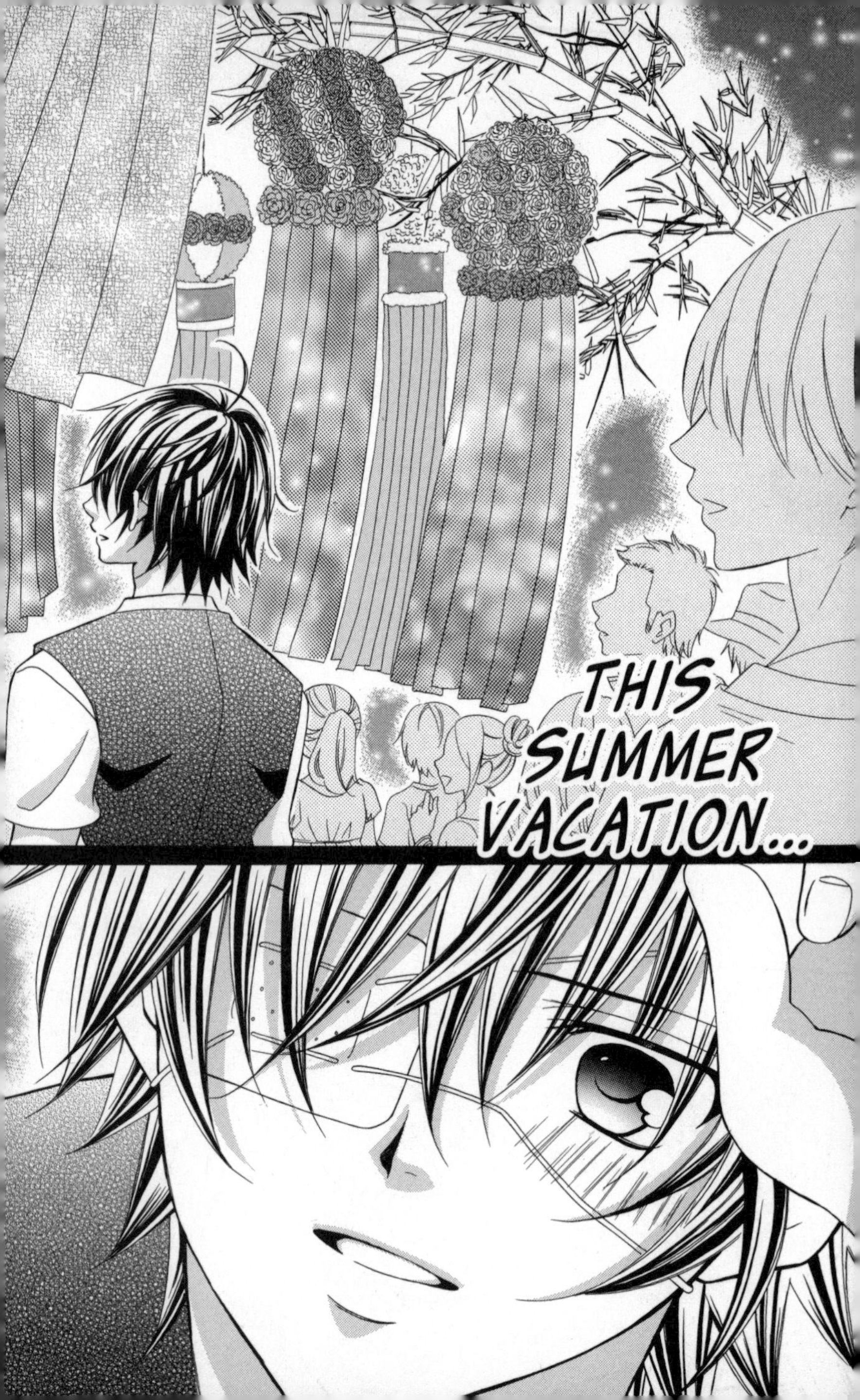
THIS SUMMER VACATION...

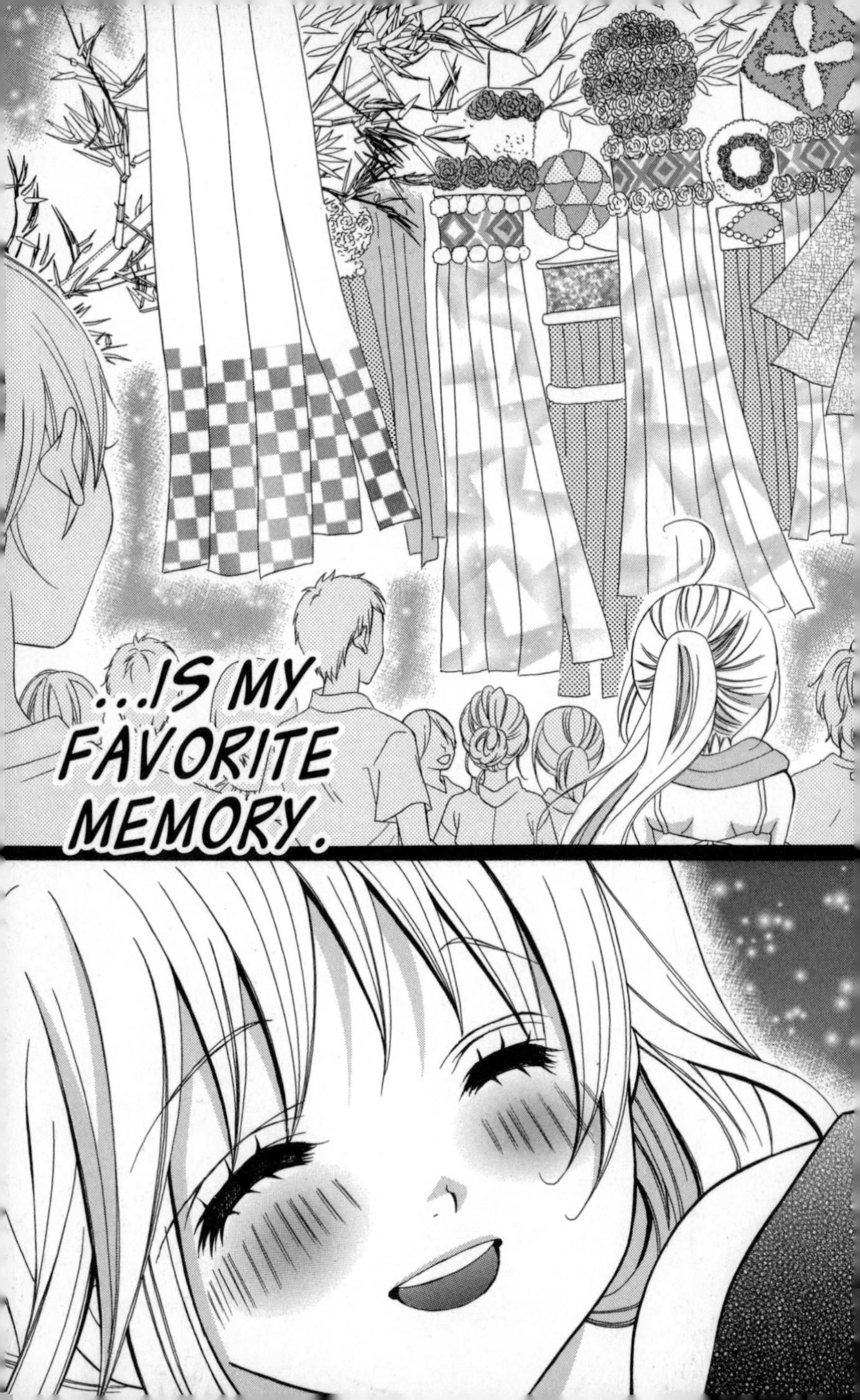
...IS MY FAVORITE MEMORY.

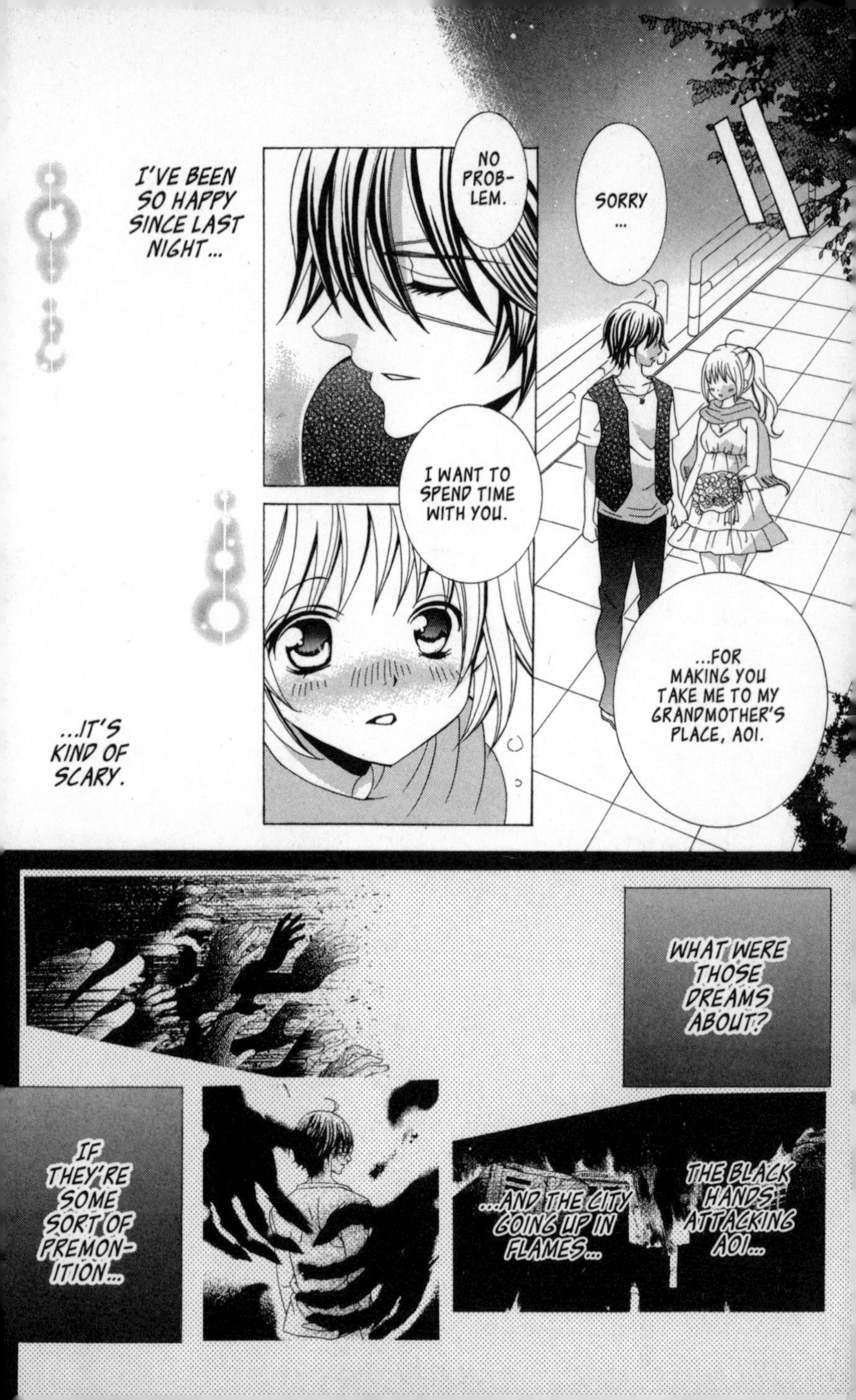
SORRY...
...FOR MAKING YOU TAKE ME TO MY GRANDMOTHER'S PLACE, AOI.
NO PROB-LEM.
I WANT TO SPEND TIME WITH YOU.
I'VE BEEN SO HAPPY SINCE LAST NIGHT...
...IT'S KIND OF SCARY.
WHAT WERE THOSE DREAMS ABOUT?
THE BLACK HANDS ATTACKING AOI...
...AND THE CITY GOING UP IN FLAMES...
IF THEY'RE SOME SORT OF PREMON-ITION...

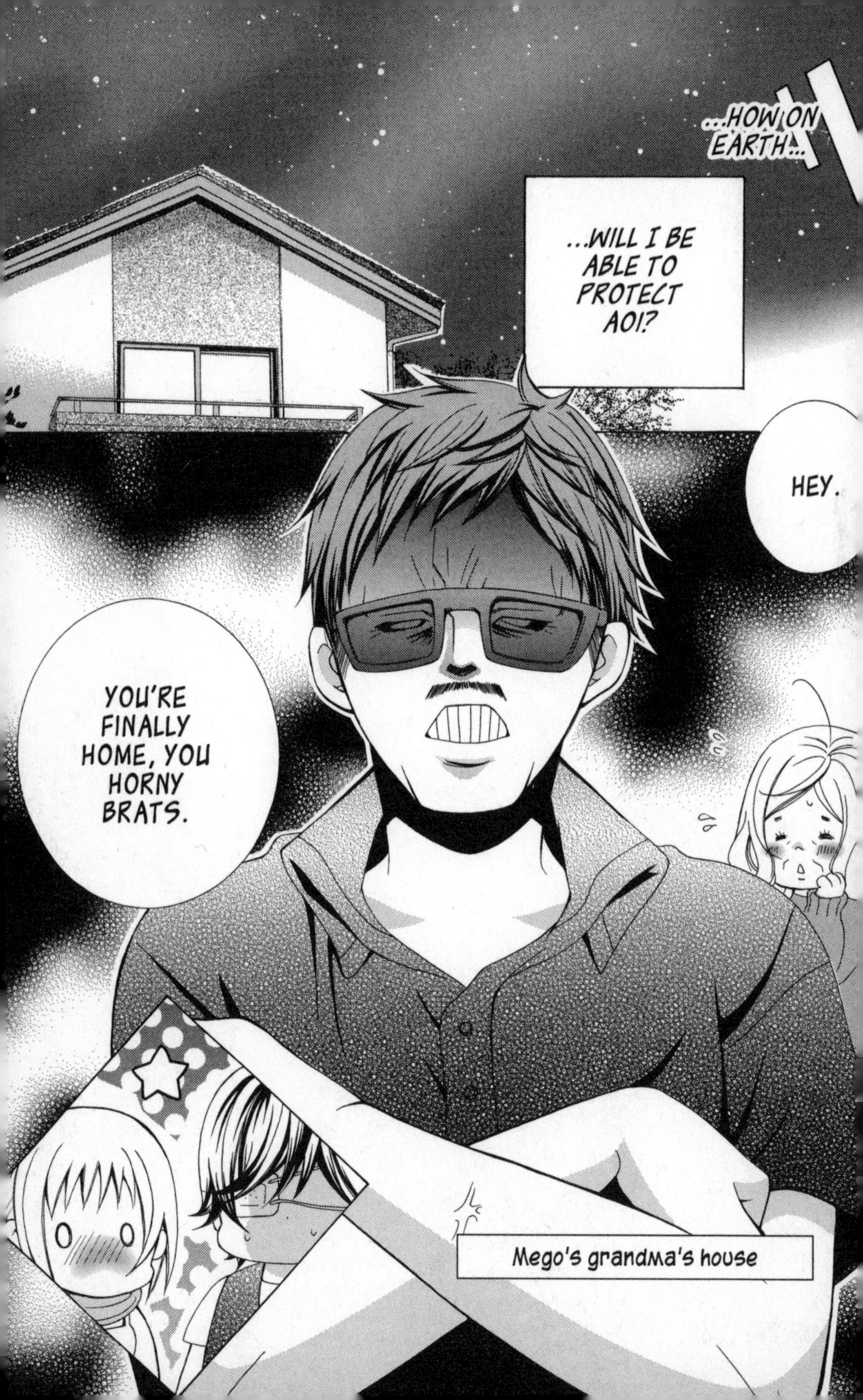
...HOW ON EARTH...
...WILL I BE ABLE TO PROTECT AOI?
HEY.
YOU'RE FINALLY HOME, YOU HORNY BRATS.
Mego's grandma's house

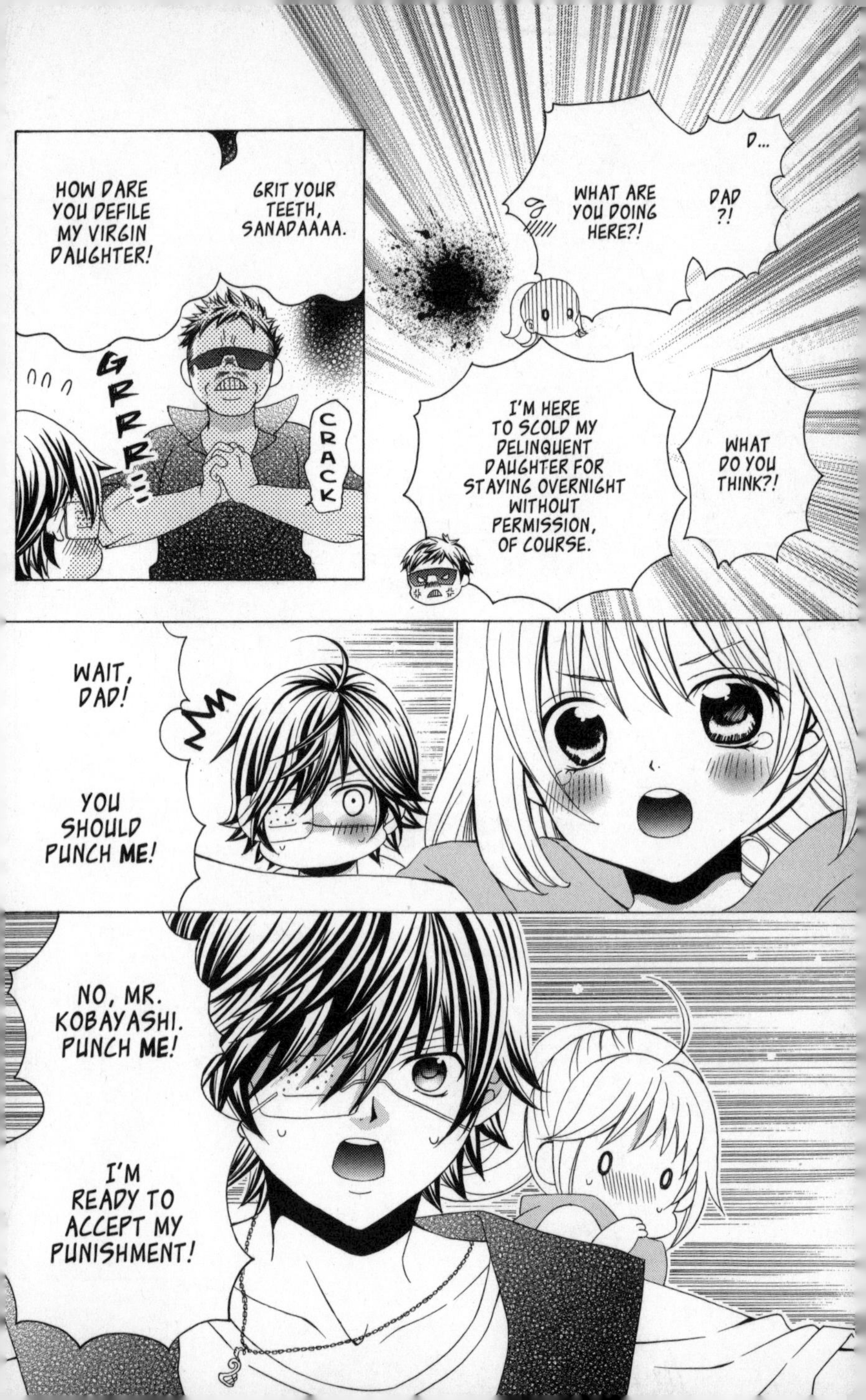
D...
DAD?!
WHAT ARE YOU DOING HERE?!
WHAT DO YOU THINK?!
I'M HERE TO SCOLD MY DELINQUENT DAUGHTER FOR STAYING OVERNIGHT WITHOUT PERMISSION, OF COURSE.
GRIT YOUR TEETH, SANADAAAA.
HOW DARE YOU DEFILE MY VIRGIN DAUGHTER!
CRACK
GRRRR
WAIT, DAD!
YOU SHOULD PUNCH ME!
NO, MR. KOBAYASHI. PUNCH ME!
I'M READY TO ACCEPT MY PUNISHMENT!

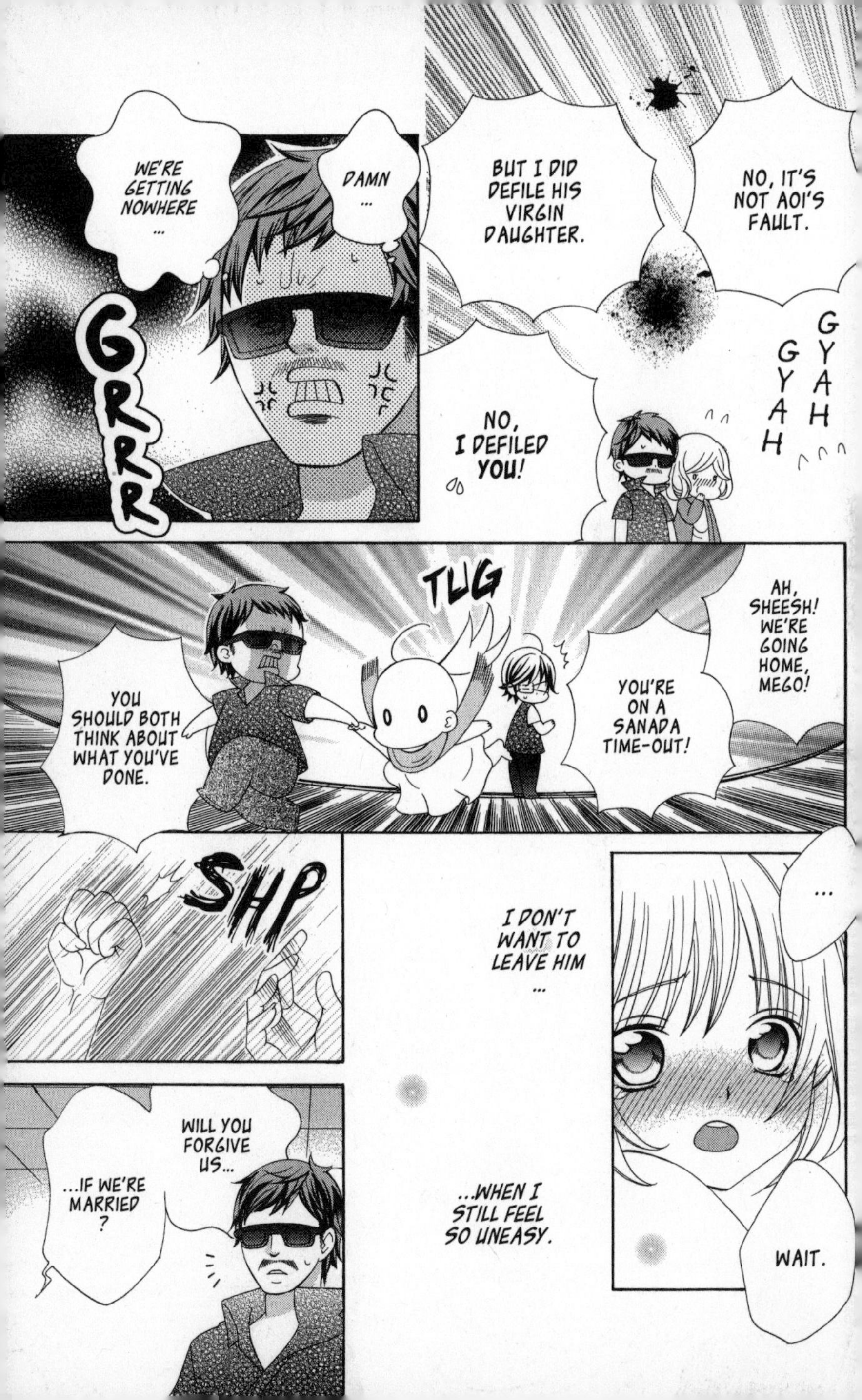
NO, IT'S NOT AOI'S FAULT.
BUT I DID DEFILE HIS VIRGIN DAUGHTER.
GYAH GYAH
GYAH
NO, I DEFILED YOU!
DAMN ...
WE'RE GETTING NOWHERE ...
GRRR
TUG
AH, SHEESH! WE'RE GOING HOME, MEGO!
YOU'RE ON A SANADA TIME-OUT!
YOU SHOULD BOTH THINK ABOUT WHAT YOU'VE DONE.
...
WAIT.
I DON'T WANT TO LEAVE HIM ...
...WHEN I STILL FEEL SO UNEASY.
SHP
WILL YOU FORGIVE US...
...IF WE'RE MARRIED ?

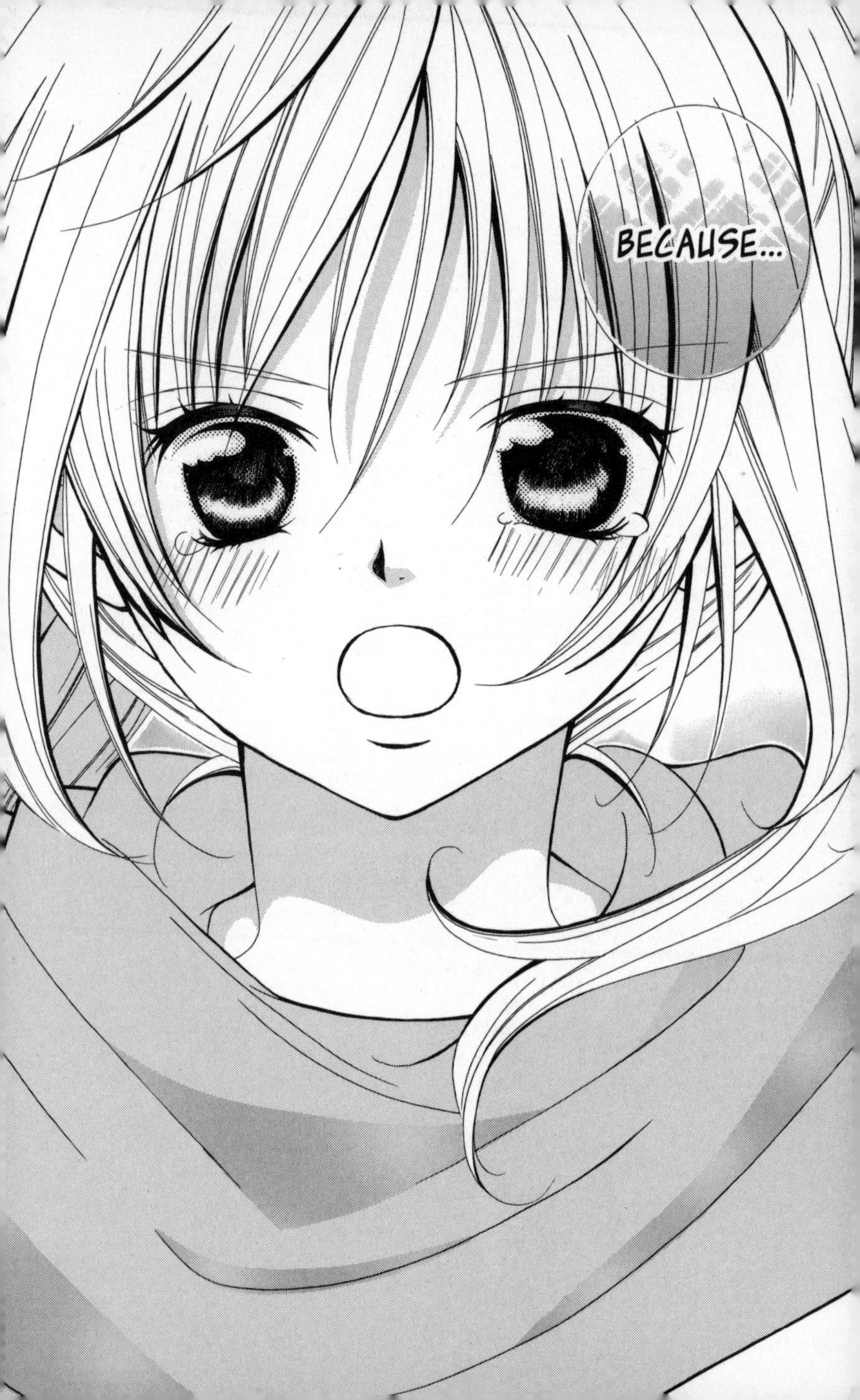
BECAUSE...

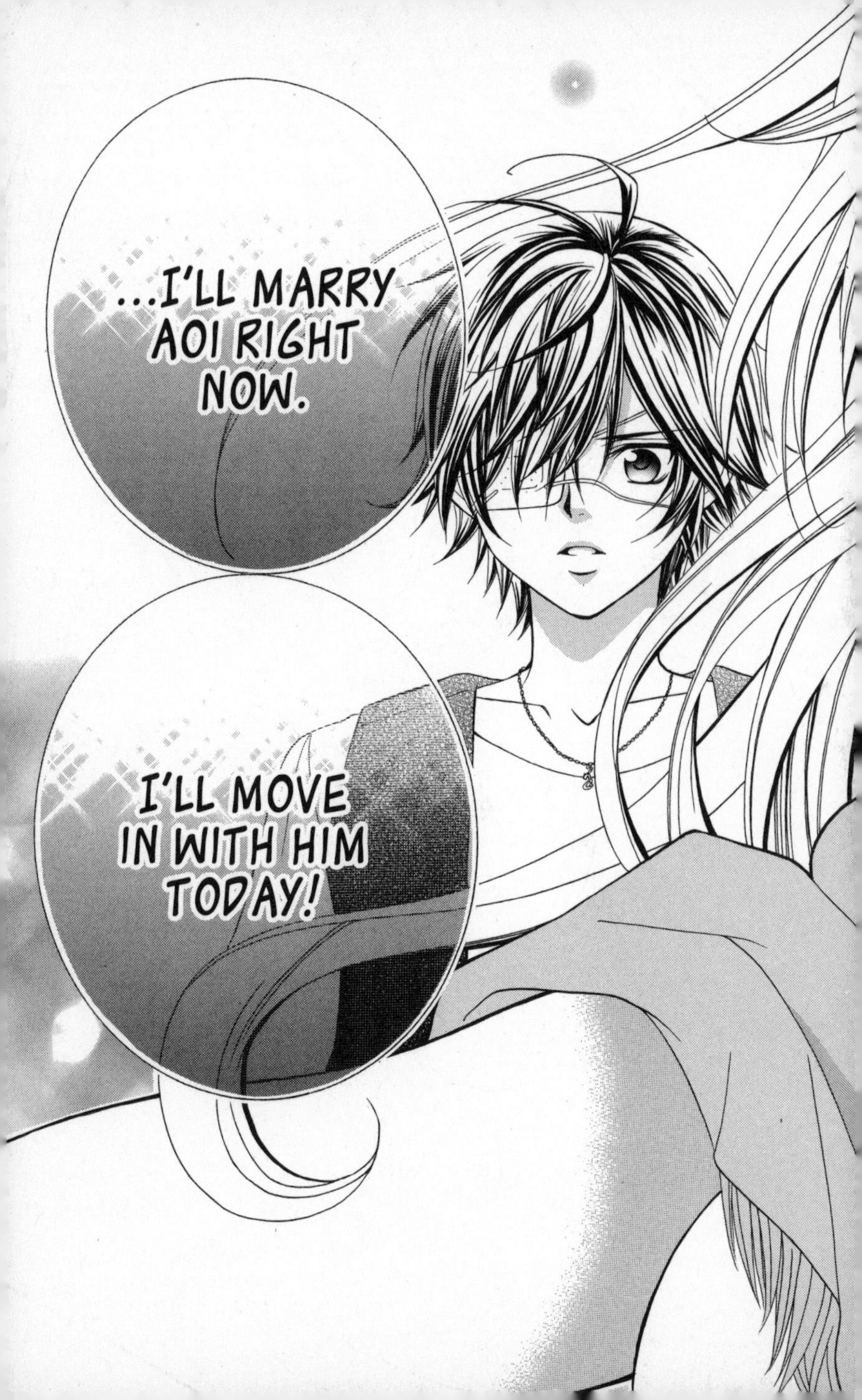
...I'LL MARRY AOI RIGHT NOW.
I'LL MOVE IN WITH HIM TODAY!

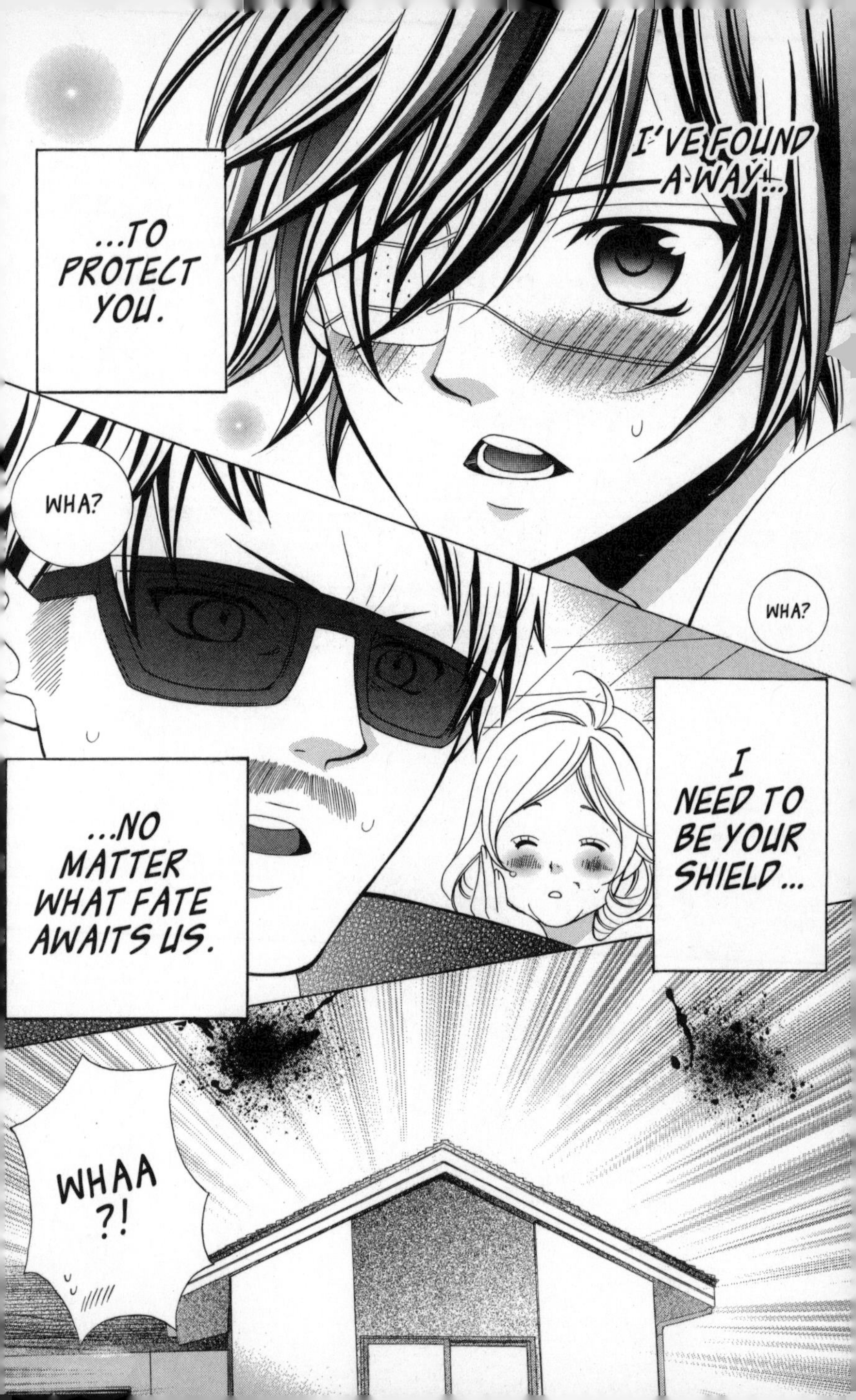
I'VE FOUND A WAY...
...TO PROTECT YOU.
WHA?
WHA?
I NEED TO BE YOUR SHIELD...
...NO MATTER WHAT FATE AWAITS US.
WHAA ?!

IN
SICKNESS...

...AND
IN
HEALTH.

I'D RISK
MY LIFE TO
PROTECT
YOU.

So Cute! Fan Art Feature ♥

EVERYONE'S DRAWINGS ARE SO CUTE, THEY HURT!!

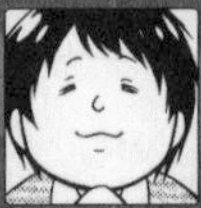

Utaro

Editor Utaro has commented on each one this time!!♪

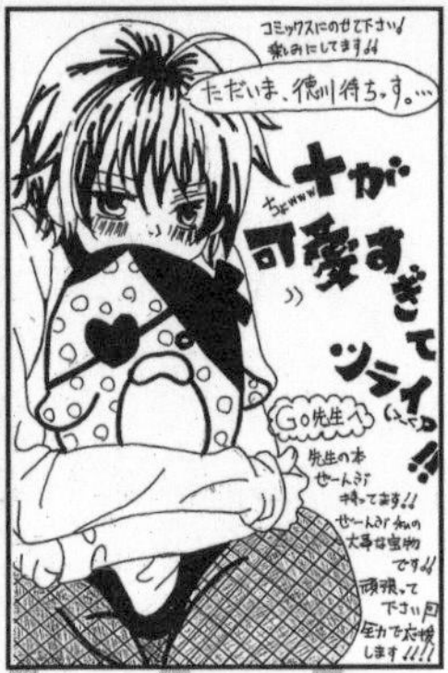

N.Y (Chiba)
←
Ed.: Blushing Mitsuru is super cute. ♥

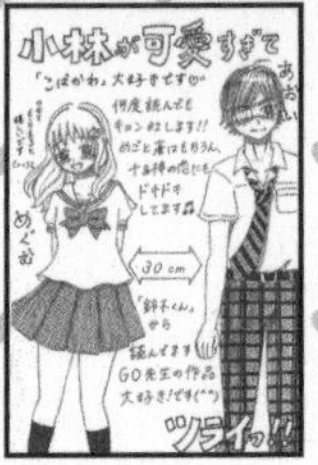

Misakichi (Mie)
→
Ed.: These two are pure!

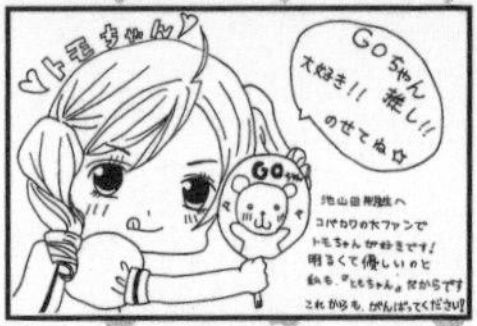

Tomo-chan (Aichi) ↑
Ed.: The GO-chan fan is cute!

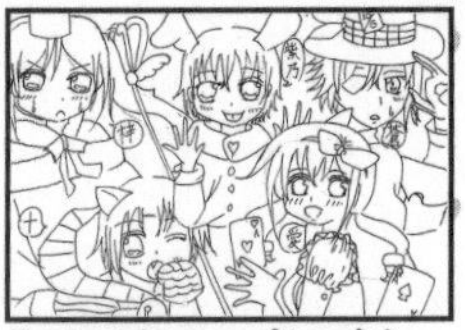

Medeki Bagoma (Nara) ↑
Ed.: Ooh! The five of them in cosplay!!

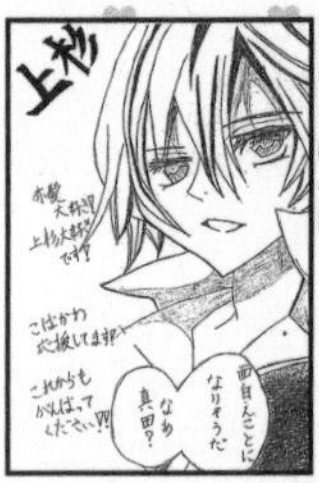

Wakka-san (Tokyo)
←
Ed.: People still love Uesugi!!

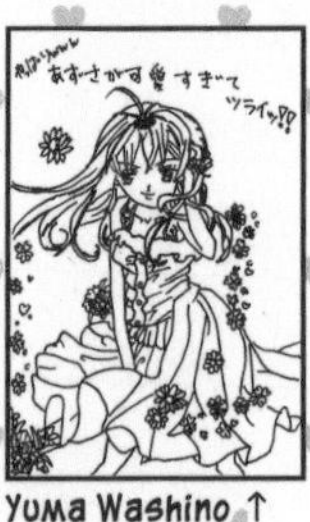

Yuma Washino ↑ (Ehime)
Ed.: This Azusa's beautiful. ♥

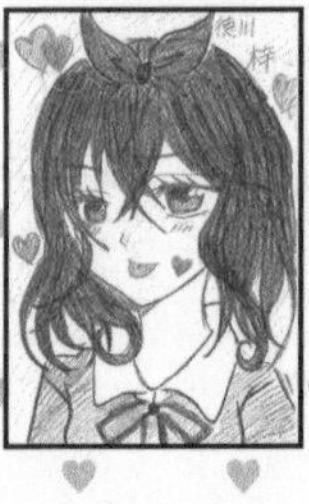

Moe (Yamagata)
←
Ed.: Super-cute Azusa makes me squee! ♥

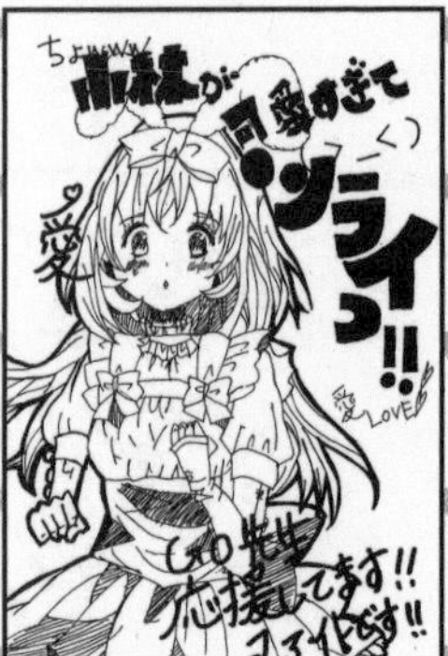

Jitsuko Mikito (Fukuoka) ↑
Ed.: Rabbit ears are the best!

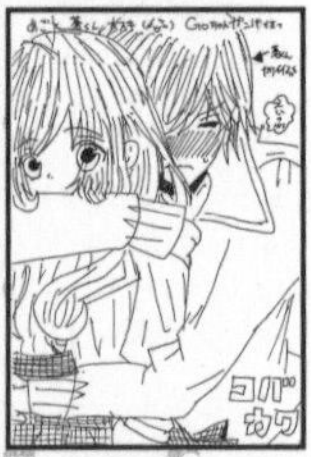

Niko-chan ↑ (Kumamoto)
Ed.: Their cuteness is priceless!

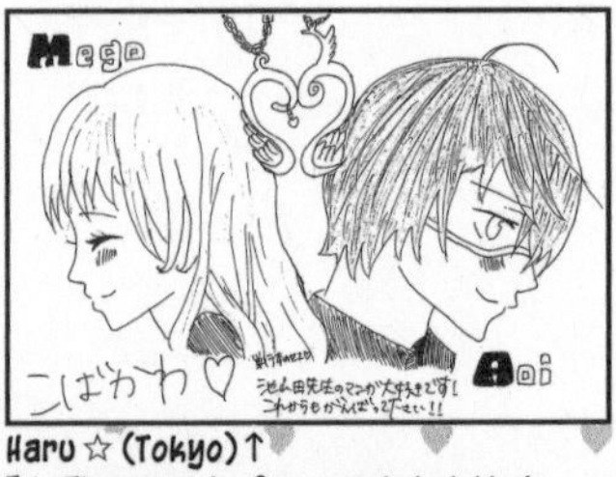

Haru ☆ (Tokyo) ↑
Ed.: They may be far apart, but their hearts are... ♥

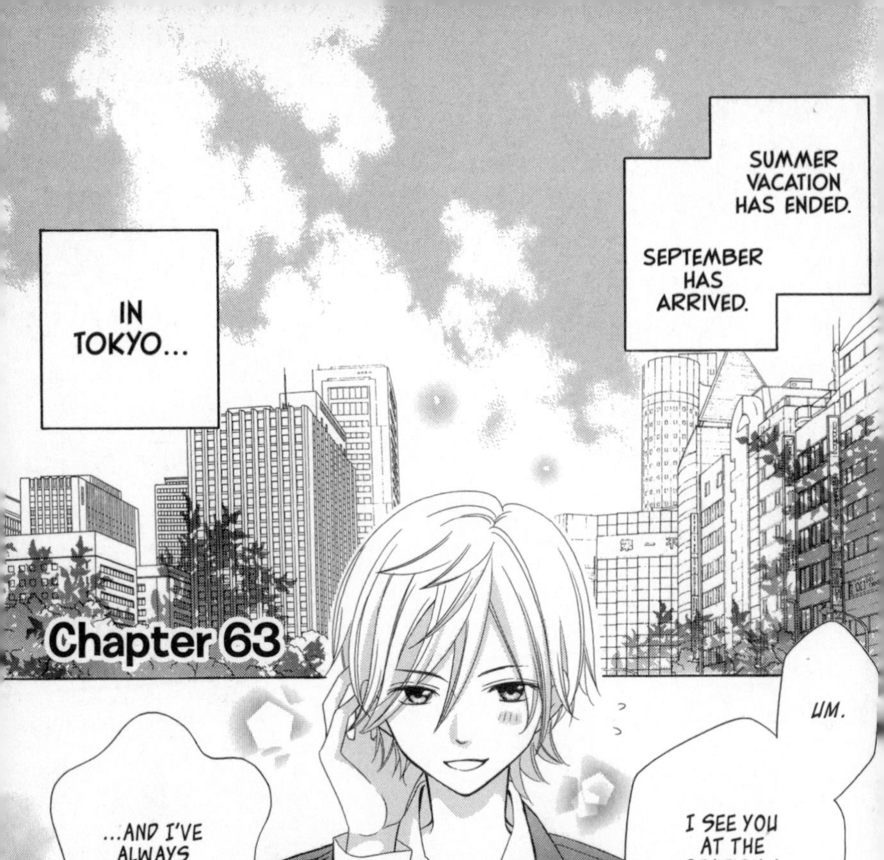
SUMMER VACATION HAS ENDED.
SEPTEMBER HAS ARRIVED.
IN TOKYO...
Chapter 63
UM.
I SEE YOU AT THE STATION A LOT...
...AND I'VE ALWAYS THOUGHT YOU WERE CUTE...

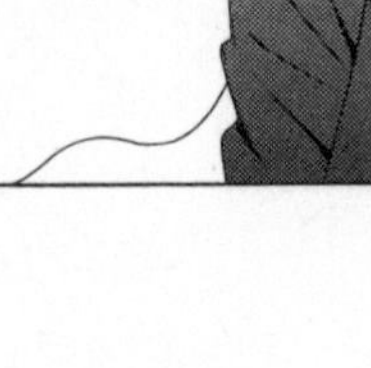

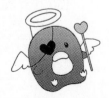

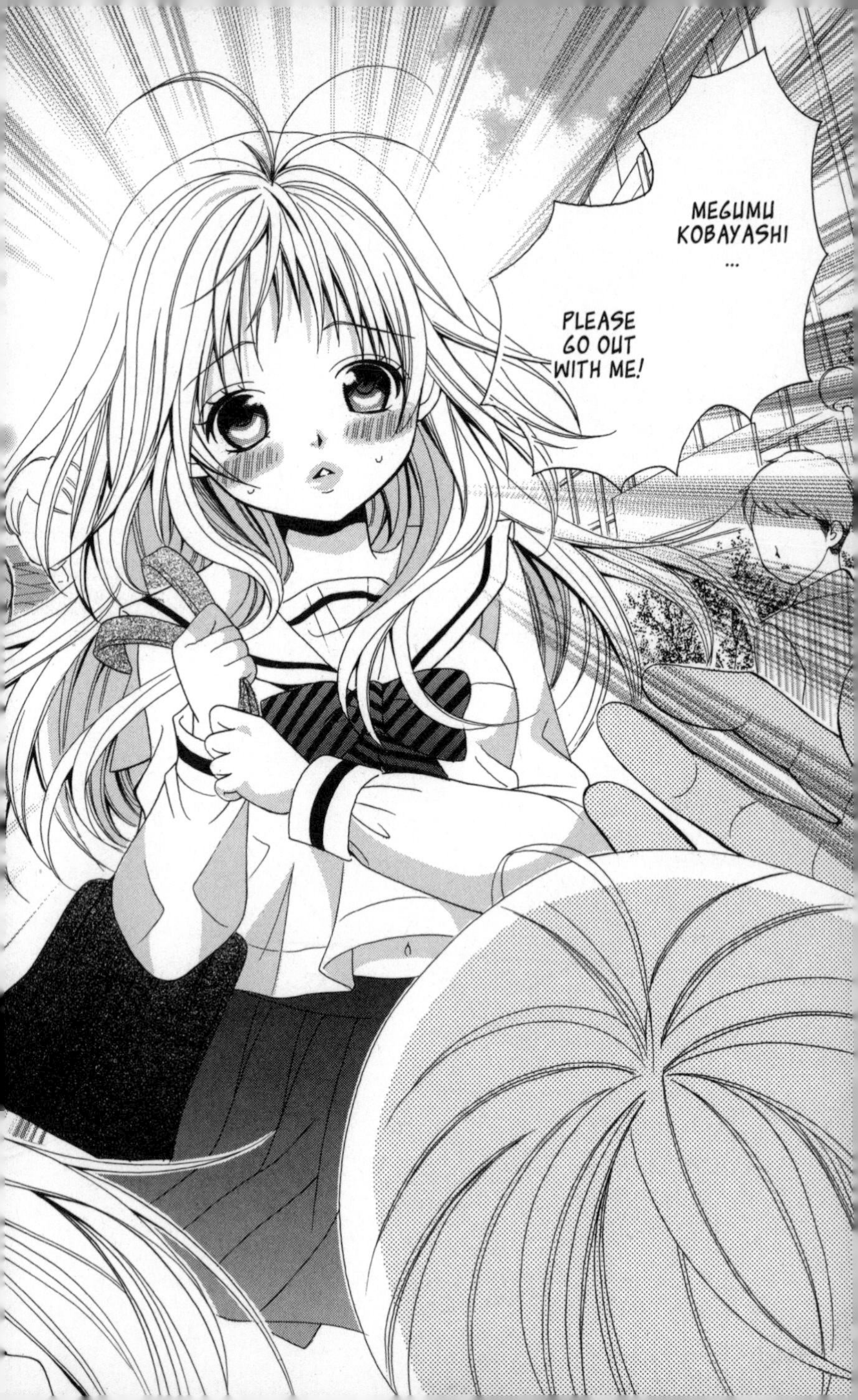
MEGUMU KOBAYASHI ...
PLEASE GO OUT WITH ME!

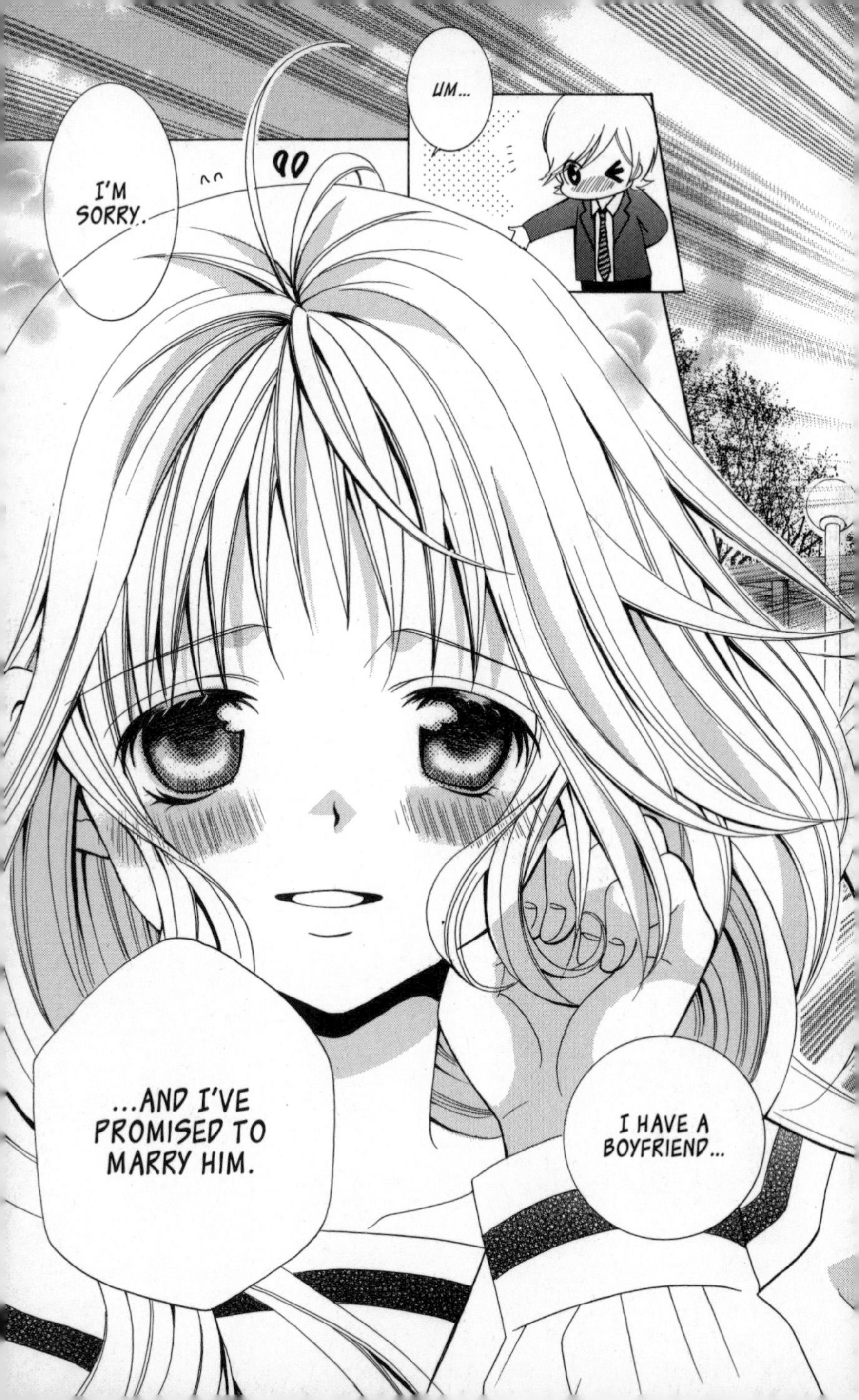
UM...
I'M SORRY..
I HAVE A BOYFRIEND...
...AND I'VE PROMISED TO MARRY HIM.

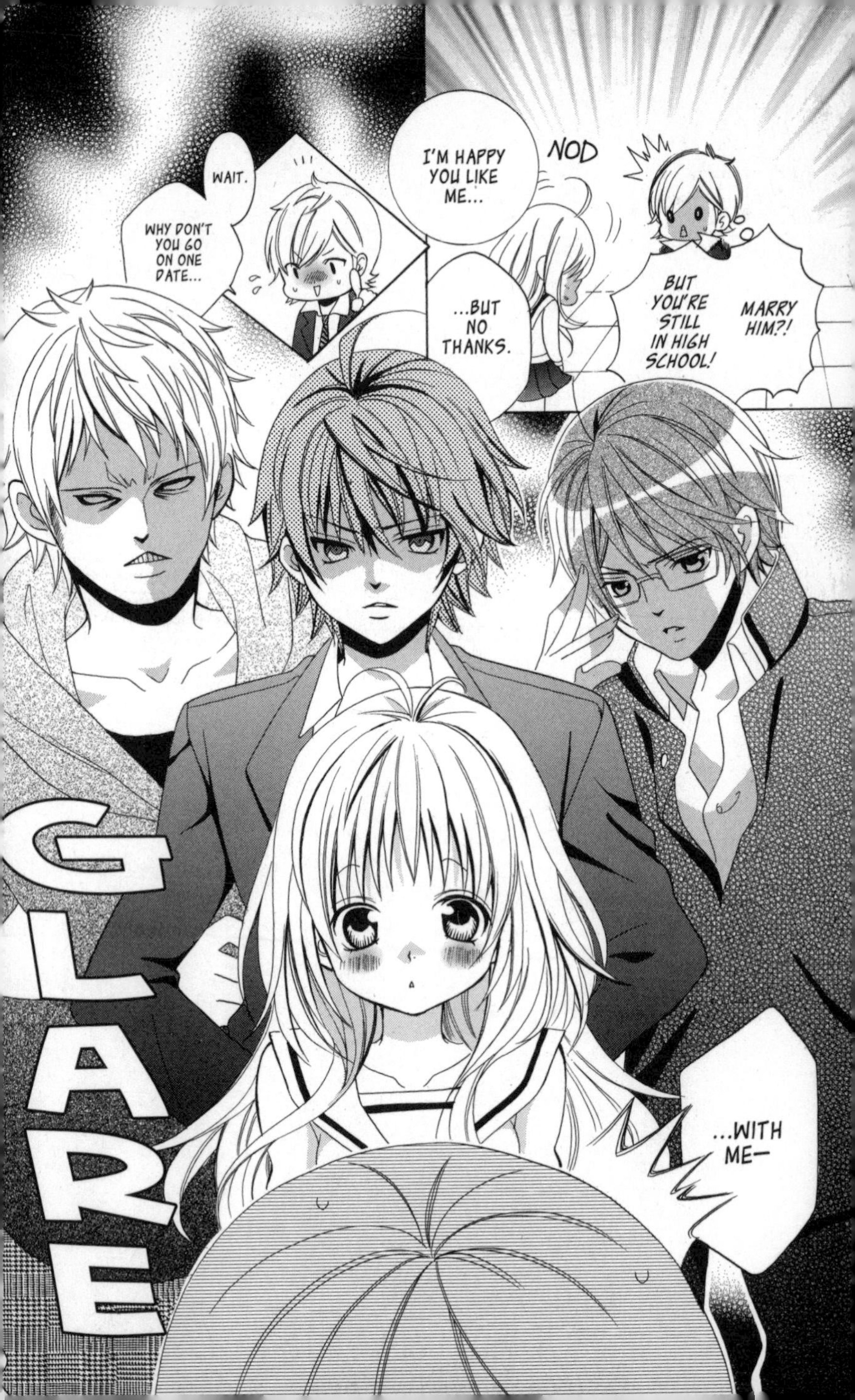
MARRY HIM?!
BUT YOU'RE STILL IN HIGH SCHOOL!
I'M HAPPY YOU LIKE ME...
NOD
...BUT NO THANKS.
WAIT.
WHY DON'T YOU GO ON ONE DATE...
...WITH ME—
GLARE

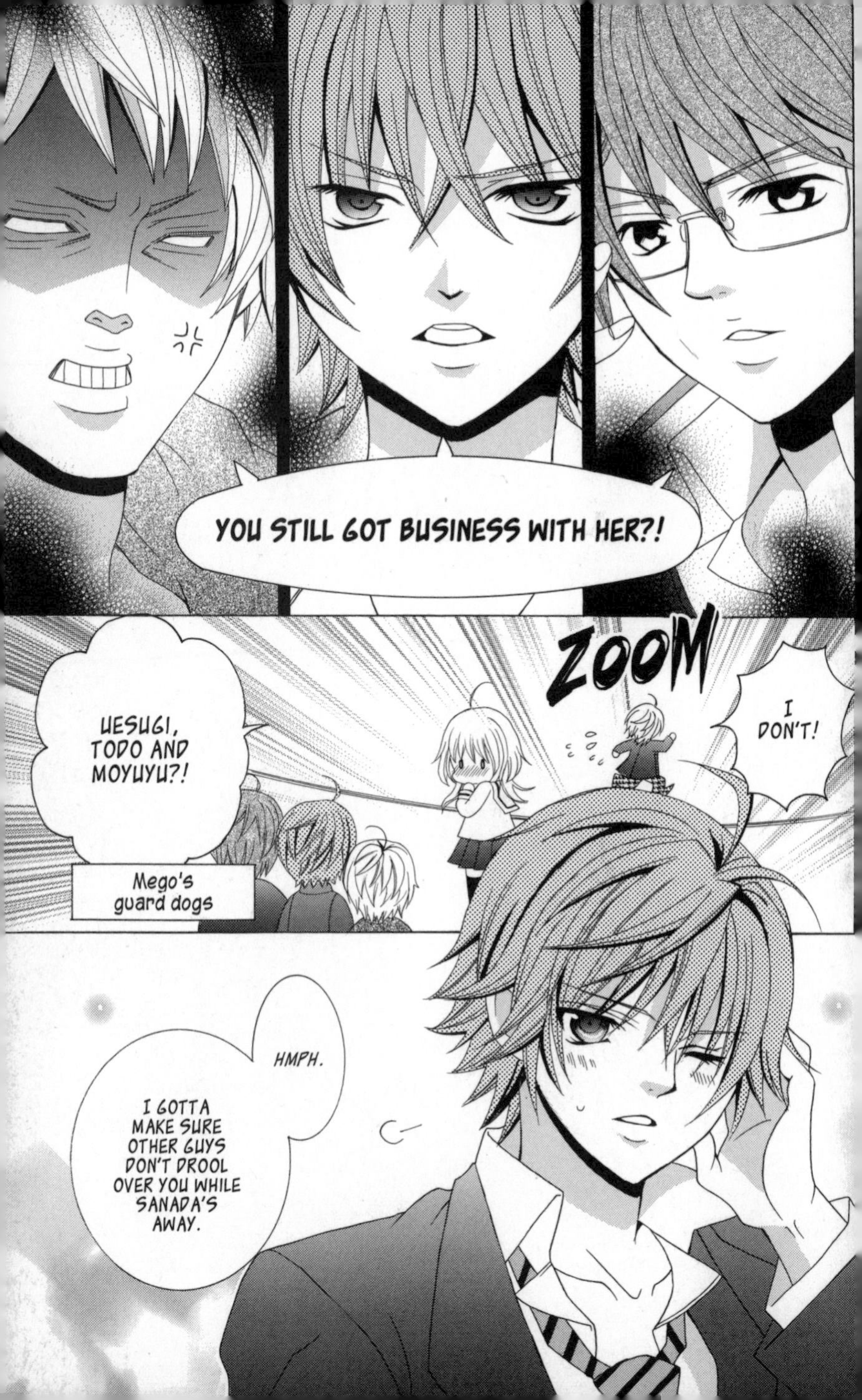
YOU STILL GOT BUSINESS WITH HER?!
I DON'T!
ZOOM
UESUGI, TODO AND MOYUYU?!
Mego's guard dogs
HMPH.
I GOTTA MAKE SURE OTHER GUYS DON'T DROOL OVER YOU WHILE SANADA'S AWAY.

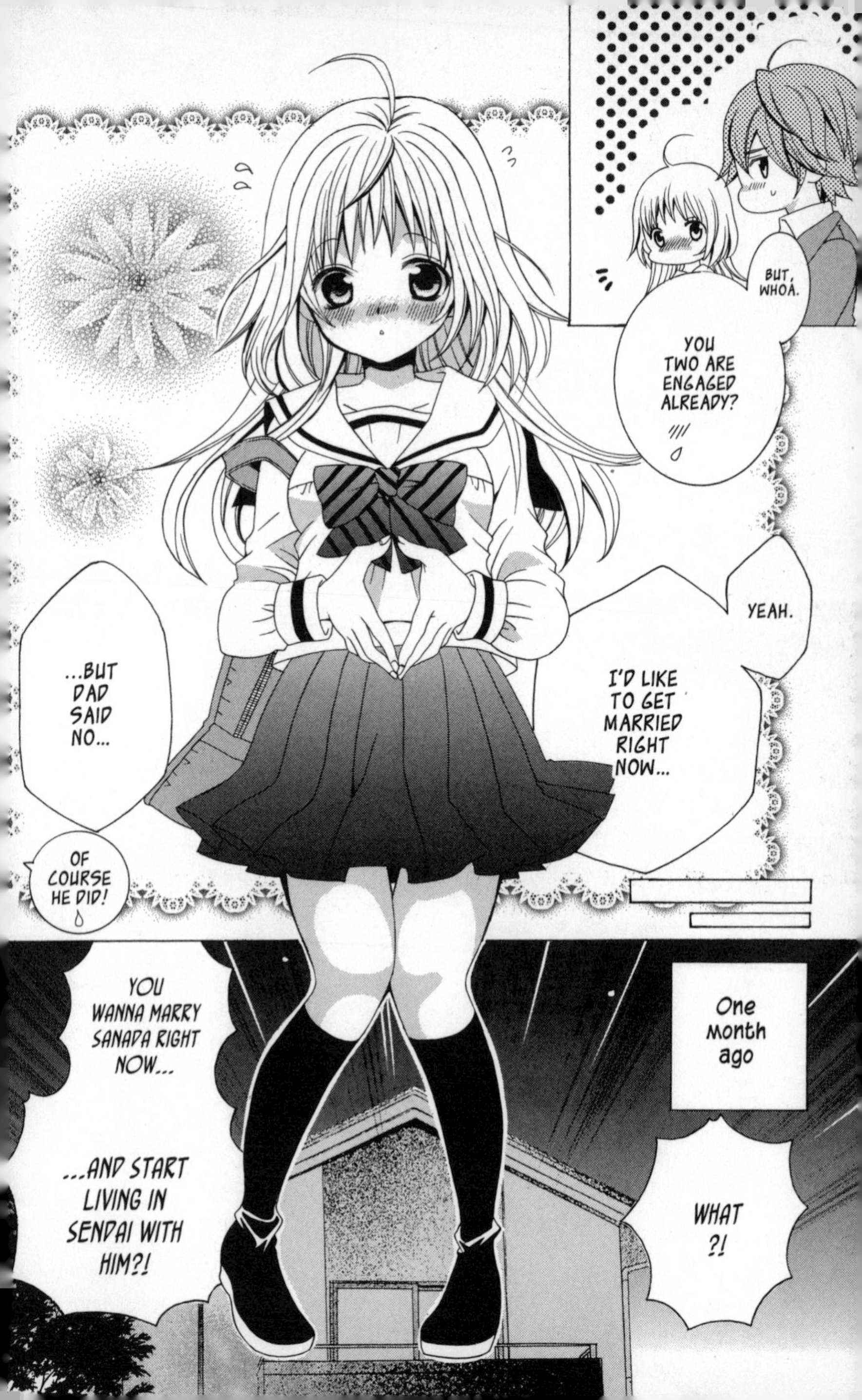
BUT, WHOA.
YOU TWO ARE ENGAGED ALREADY?
YEAH.
I'D LIKE TO GET MARRIED RIGHT NOW...
...BUT DAD SAID NO...
OF COURSE HE DID!
One Month ago
YOU WANNA MARRY SANADA RIGHT NOW...
...AND START LIVING IN SENDAI WITH HIM?!
WHAT?!

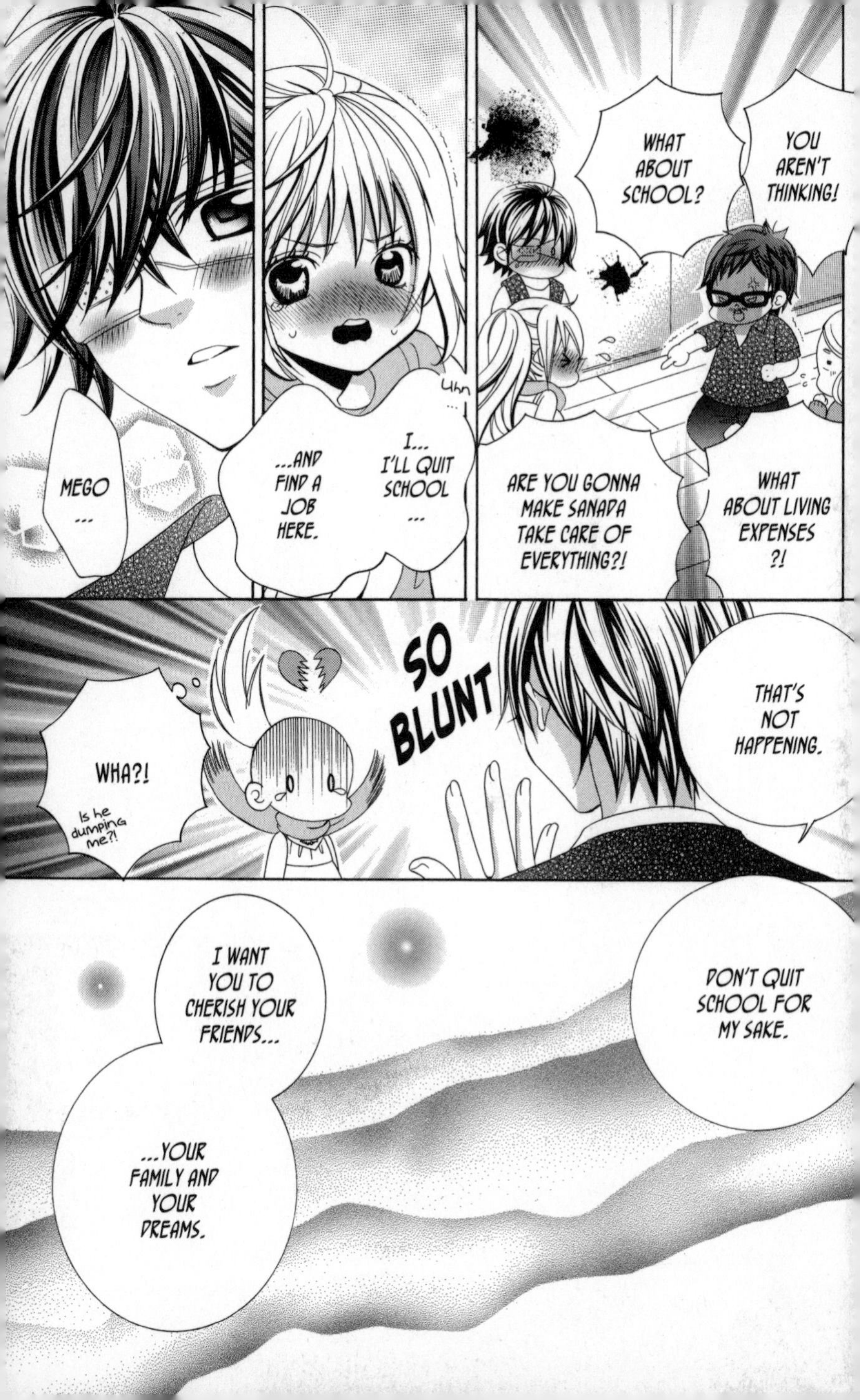
YOU AREN'T THINKING!
WHAT ABOUT SCHOOL?
WHAT ABOUT LIVING EXPENSES ?!
ARE YOU GONNA MAKE SANADA TAKE CARE OF EVERYTHING?!
Uhn ...
I... I'LL QUIT SCHOOL ...
...AND FIND A JOB HERE.
MEGO ...
THAT'S NOT HAPPENING.
SO BLUNT
WHA?!
Is he dumping me?!
DON'T QUIT SCHOOL FOR MY SAKE.
I WANT YOU TO CHERISH YOUR FRIENDS...
...YOUR FAMILY AND YOUR DREAMS.

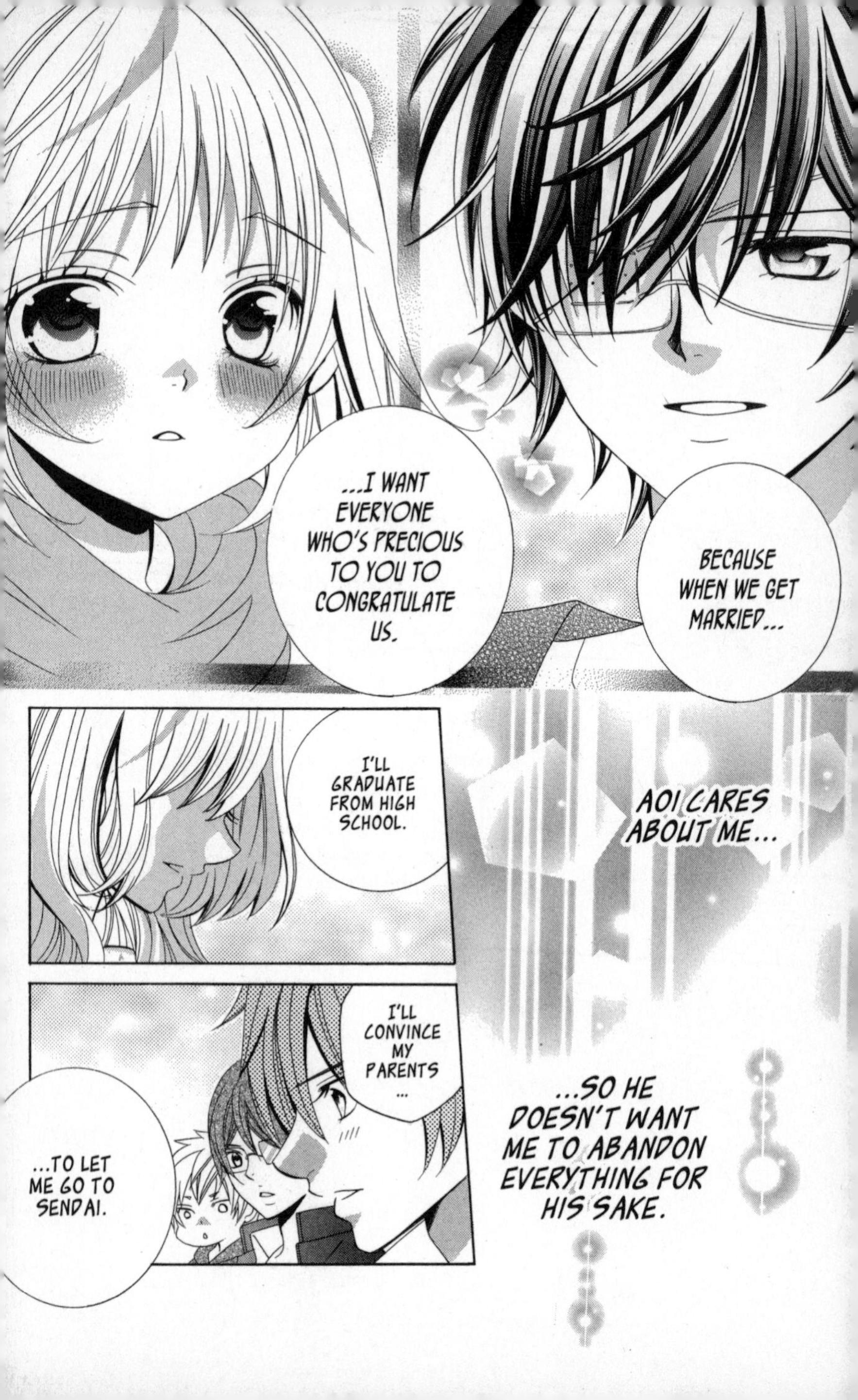
BECAUSE WHEN WE GET MARRIED...
...I WANT EVERYONE WHO'S PRECIOUS TO YOU TO CONGRATULATE US.
AOI CARES ABOUT ME...
...SO HE DOESN'T WANT ME TO ABANDON EVERYTHING FOR HIS SAKE.
I'LL GRADUATE FROM HIGH SCHOOL.
I'LL CONVINCE MY PARENTS...
...TO LET ME GO TO SENDAI.

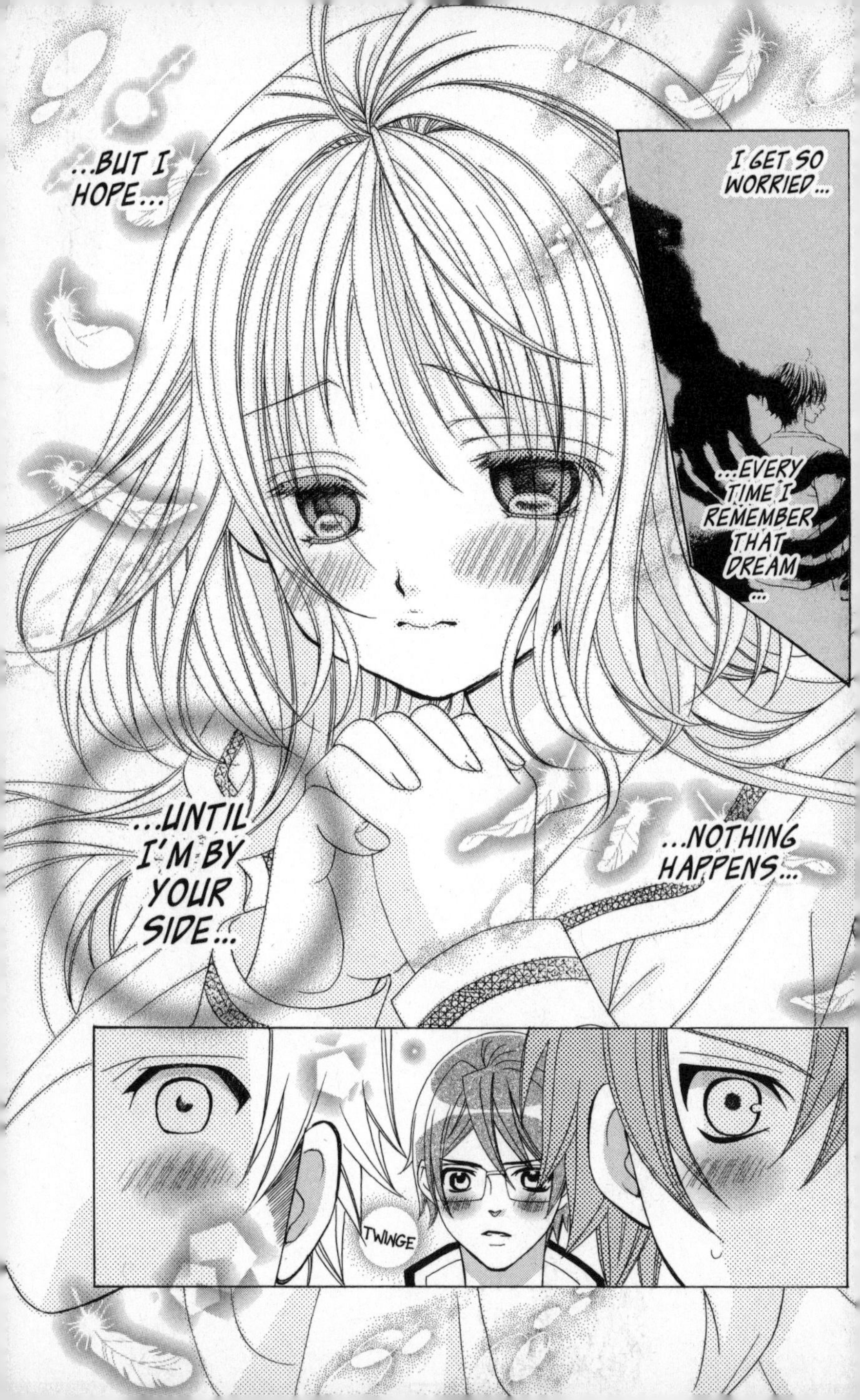
I GET SO WORRIED...
...EVERY TIME I REMEMBER THAT DREAM...
...BUT I HOPE...
...NOTHING HAPPENS...
...UNTIL I'M BY YOUR SIDE...
TWINGE

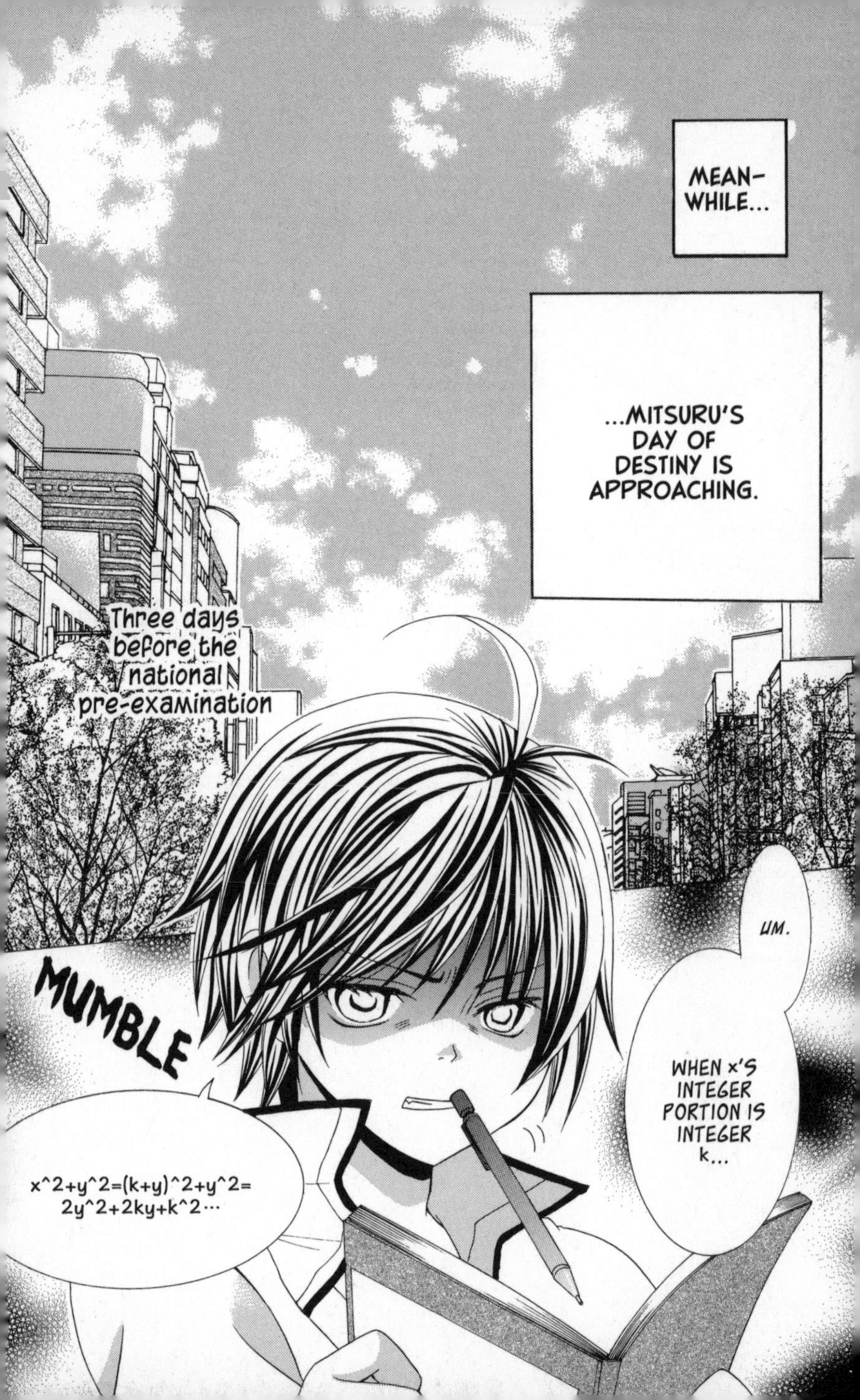
MEAN-WHILE...
...MITSURU'S DAY OF DESTINY IS APPROACHING.
Three days before the national pre-examination
UM.
WHEN x'S INTEGER PORTION IS INTEGER k...
MUMBLE
x^2+y^2=(k+y)^2+y^2=
2y^2+2ky+k^2···

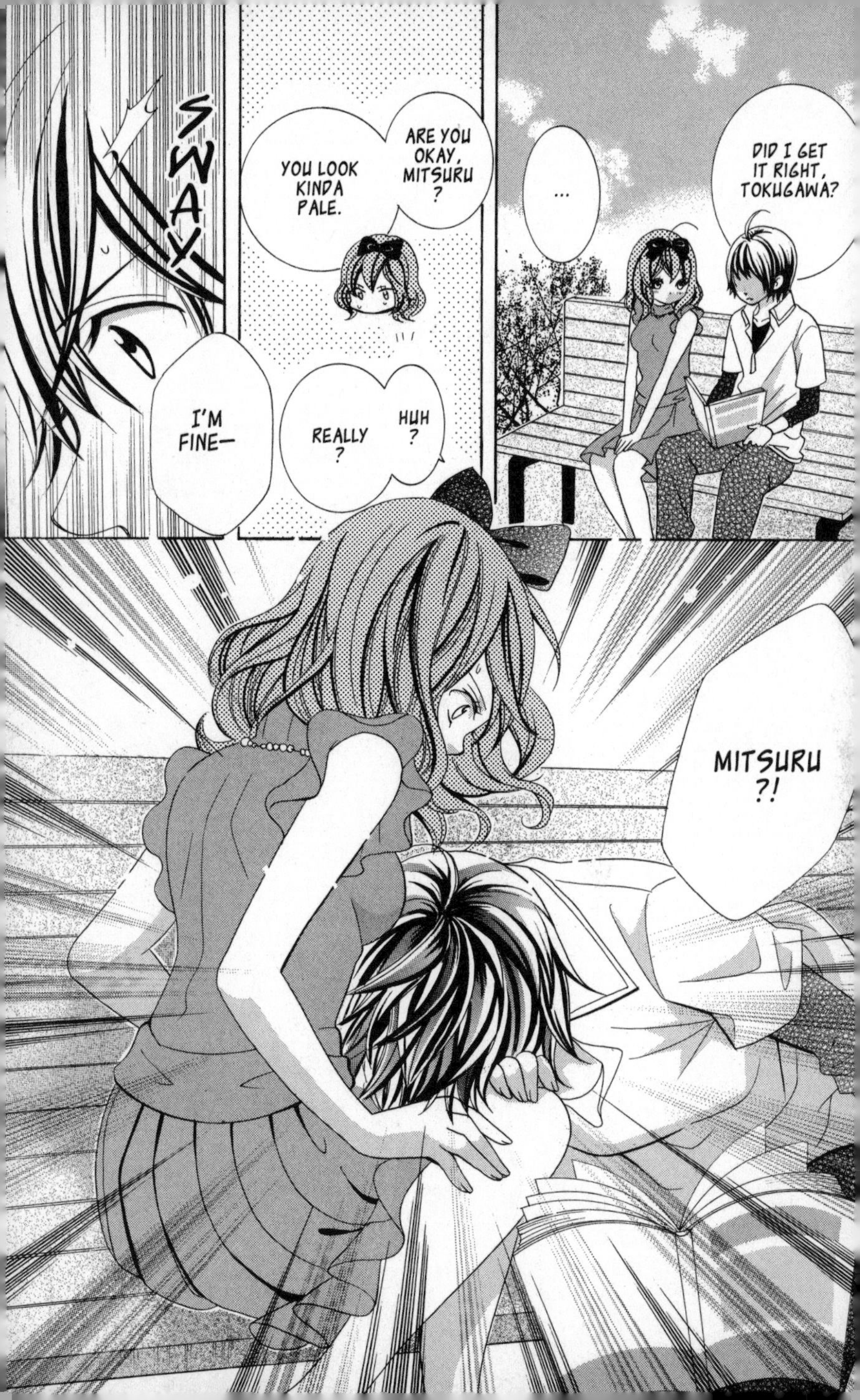
DID I GET IT RIGHT, TOKUGAWA?
...
ARE YOU OKAY, MITSURU?
YOU LOOK KINDA PALE.
HUH?
REALLY?
SWAY
I'M FINE—
MITSURU?!

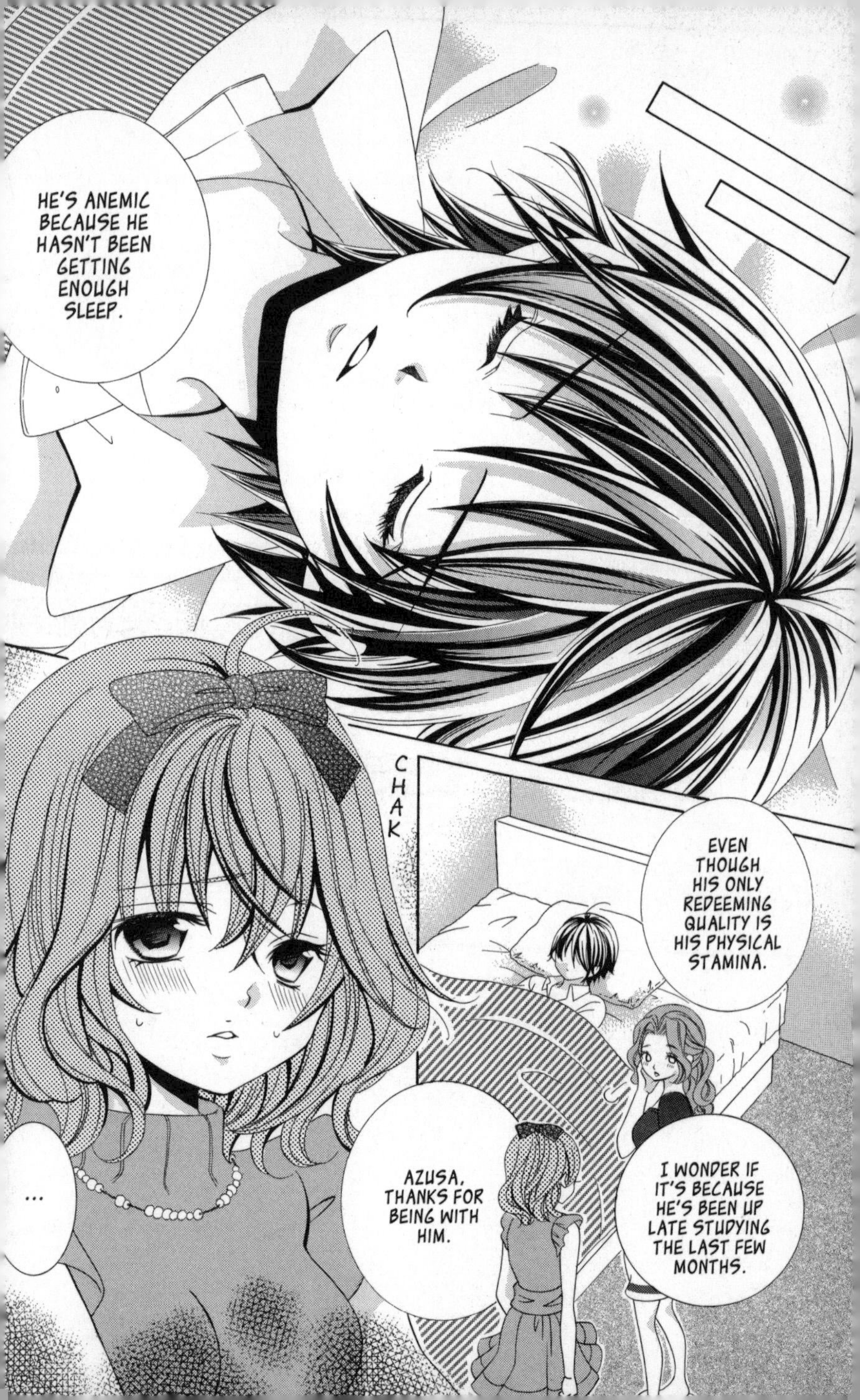
HE'S ANEMIC BECAUSE HE HASN'T BEEN GETTING ENOUGH SLEEP.
CHAK
EVEN THOUGH HIS ONLY REDEEMING QUALITY IS HIS PHYSICAL STAMINA.
I WONDER IF IT'S BECAUSE HE'S BEEN UP LATE STUDYING THE LAST FEW MONTHS.
AZUSA, THANKS FOR BEING WITH HIM.
...

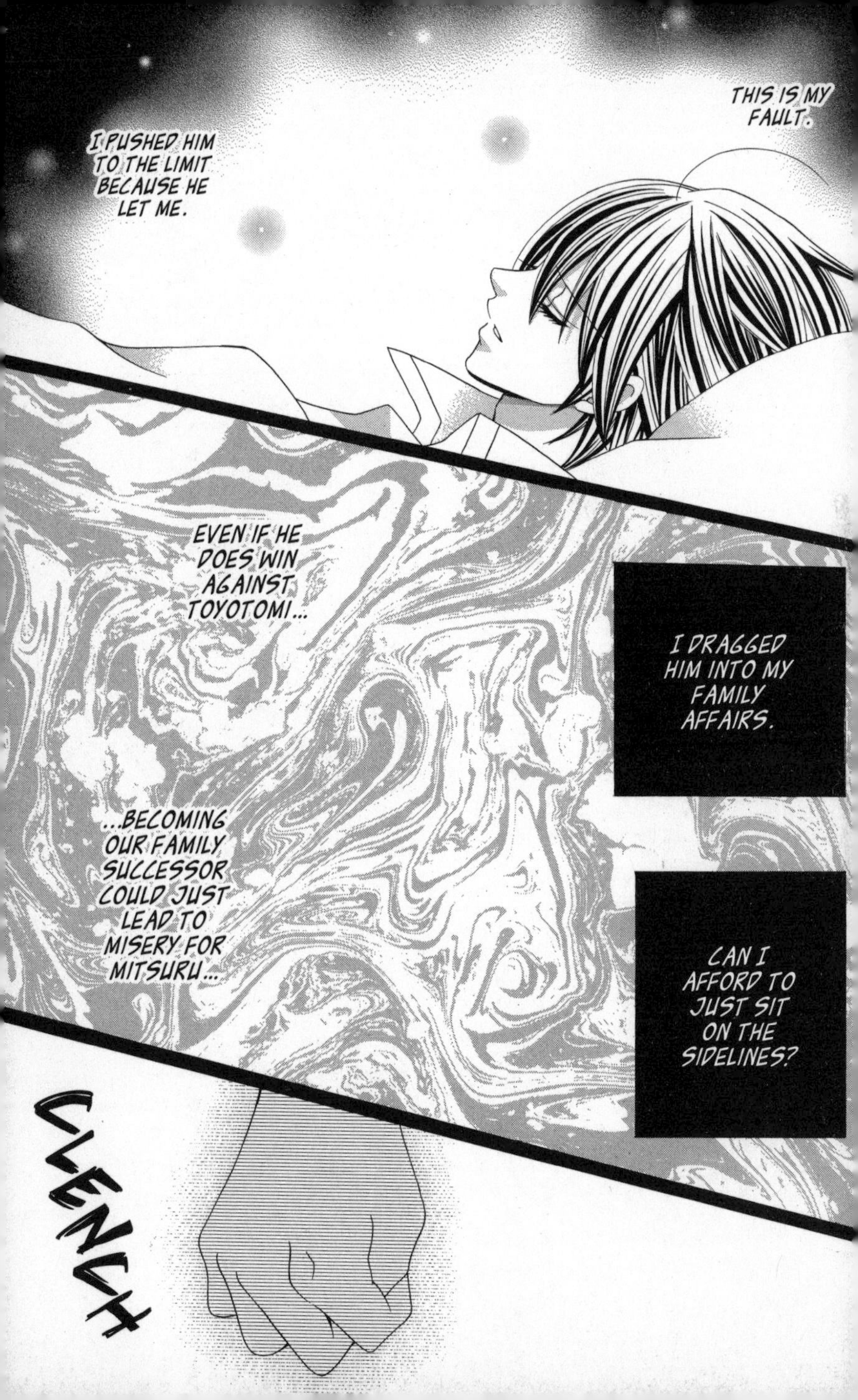
THIS IS MY FAULT.
I PUSHED HIM TO THE LIMIT BECAUSE HE LET ME.
I DRAGGED HIM INTO MY FAMILY AFFAIRS.
EVEN IF HE DOES WIN AGAINST TOYOTOMI...
...BECOMING OUR FAMILY SUCCESSOR COULD JUST LEAD TO MISERY FOR MITSURU...
CAN I AFFORD TO JUST SIT ON THE SIDELINES?
CLENCH

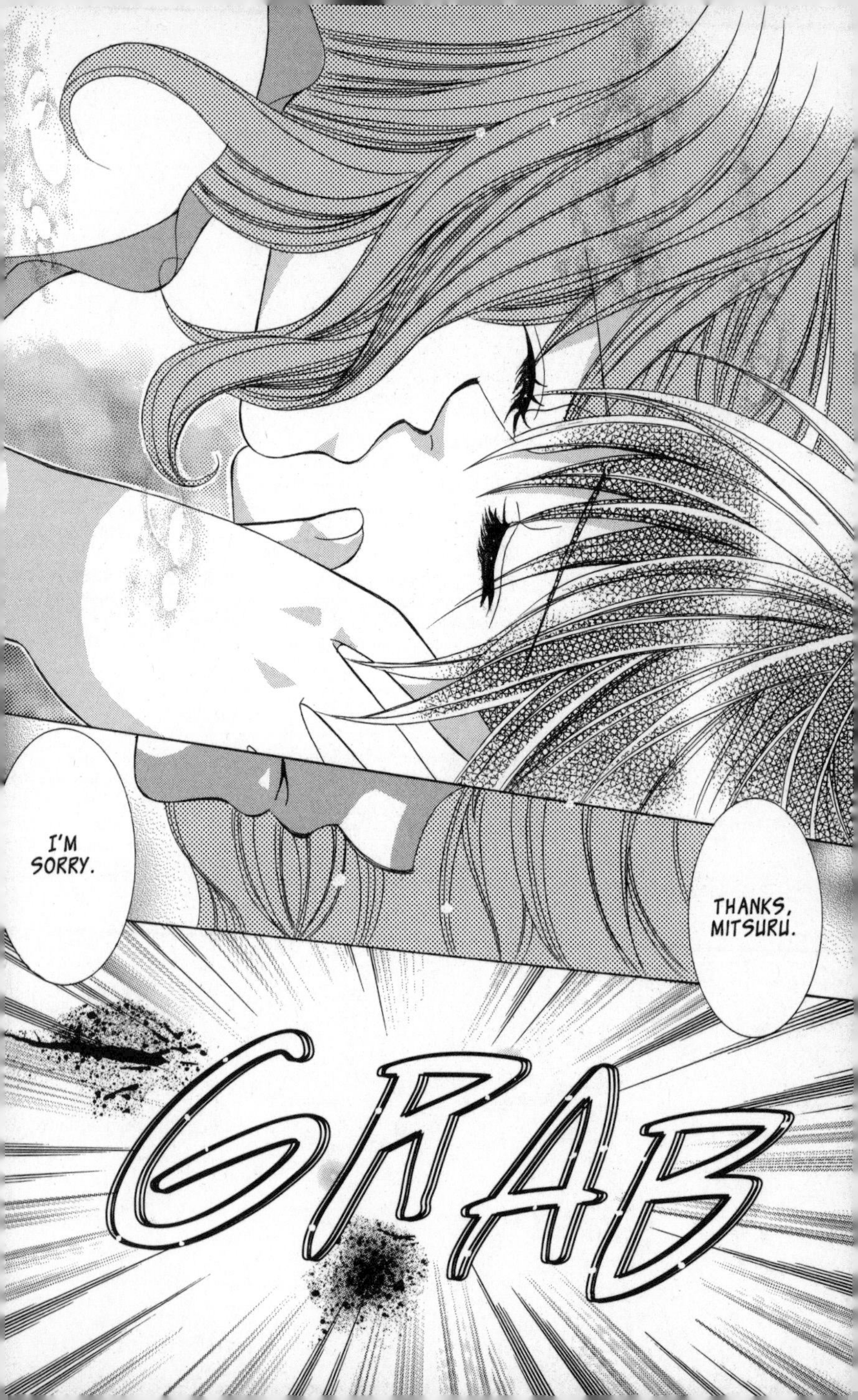
THANKS, MITSURU.
I'M SORRY.
GRAB

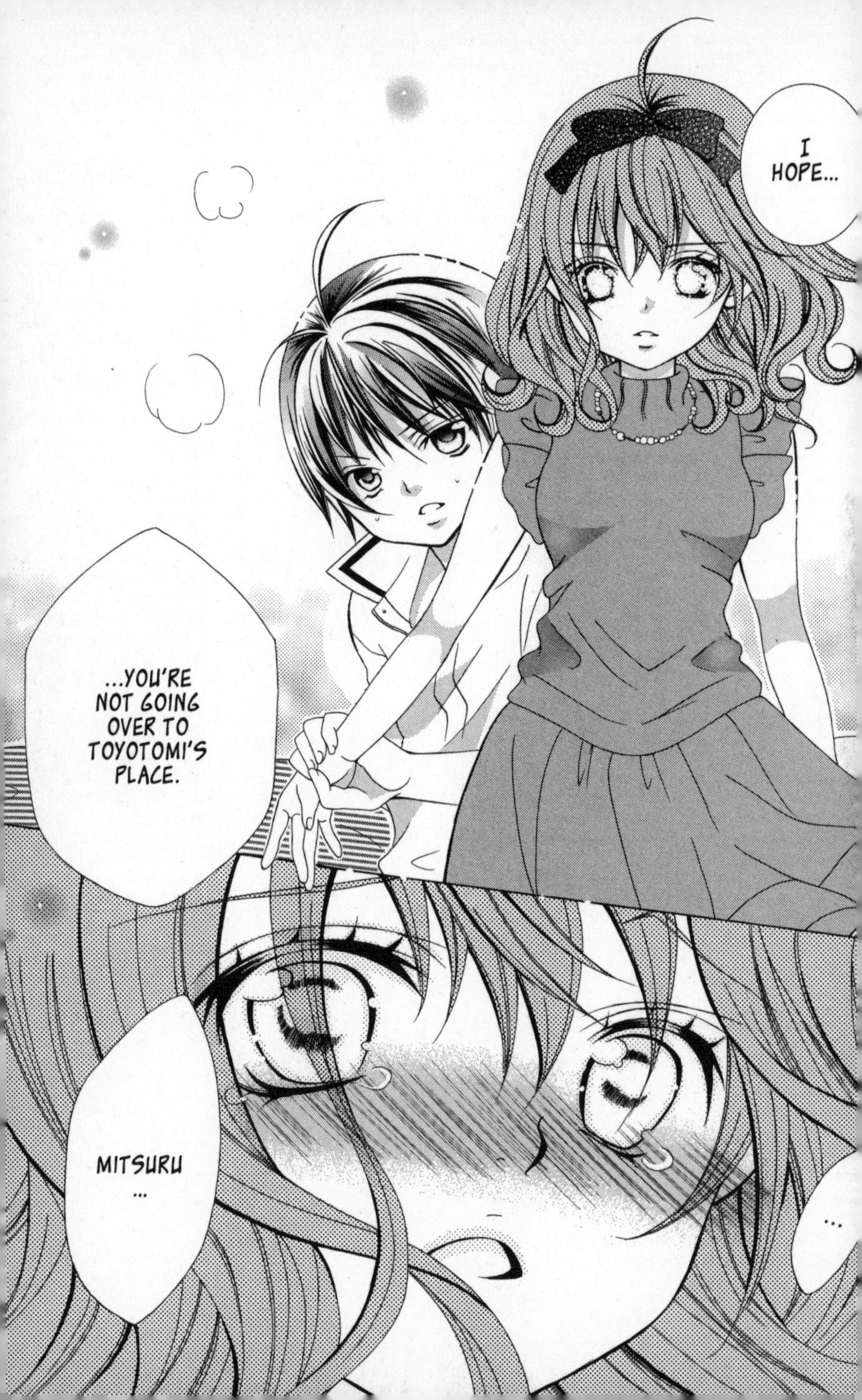
I HOPE...
...YOU'RE NOT GOING OVER TO TOYOTOMI'S PLACE.
...
MITSURU ...

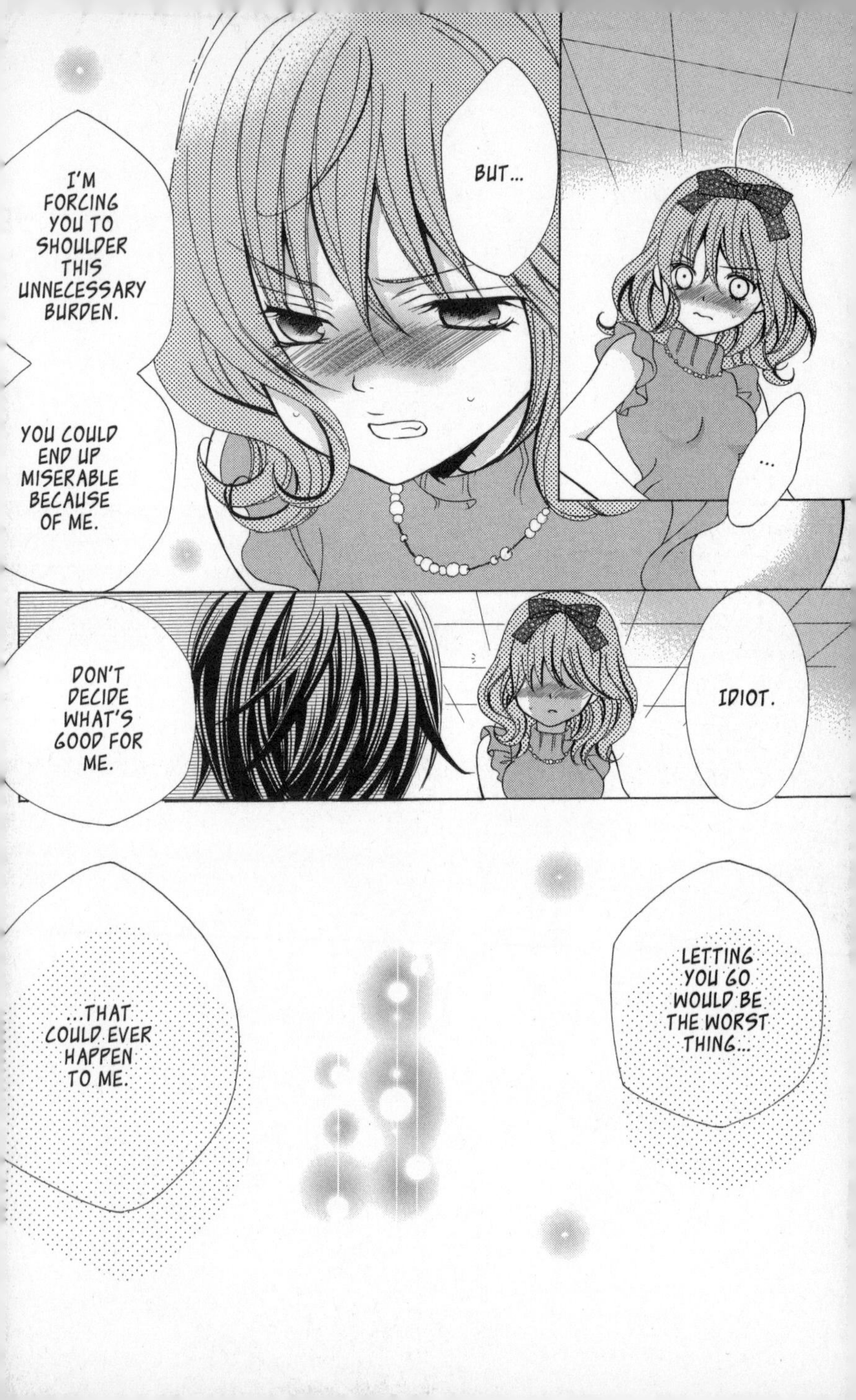
...
BUT...
I'M FORCING YOU TO SHOULDER THIS UNNECESSARY BURDEN.
YOU COULD END UP MISERABLE BECAUSE OF ME.
IDIOT.
DON'T DECIDE WHAT'S GOOD FOR ME.
LETTING YOU GO WOULD BE THE WORST THING...
...THAT COULD EVER HAPPEN TO ME.

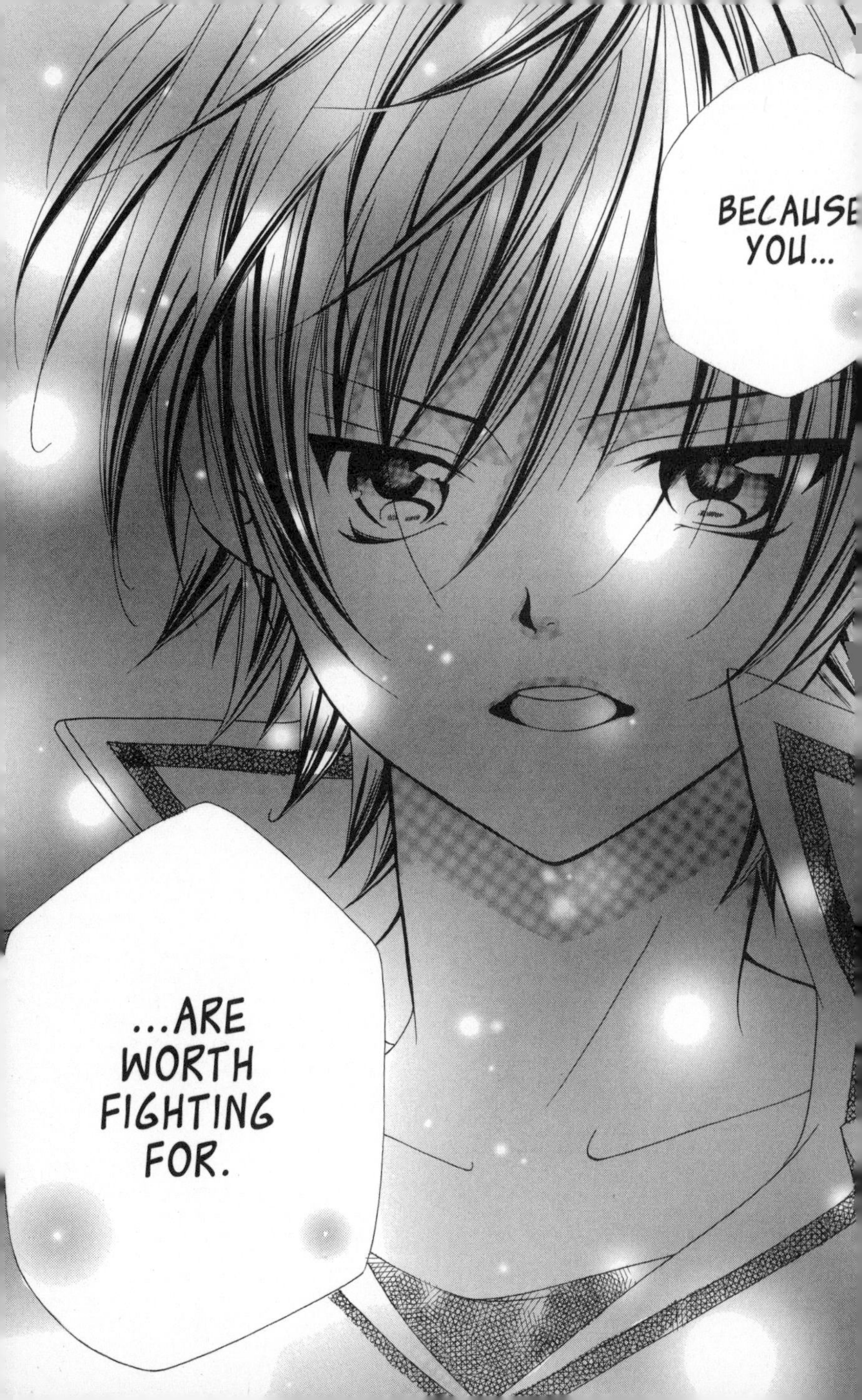
BECAUSE YOU...
...ARE WORTH FIGHTING FOR.

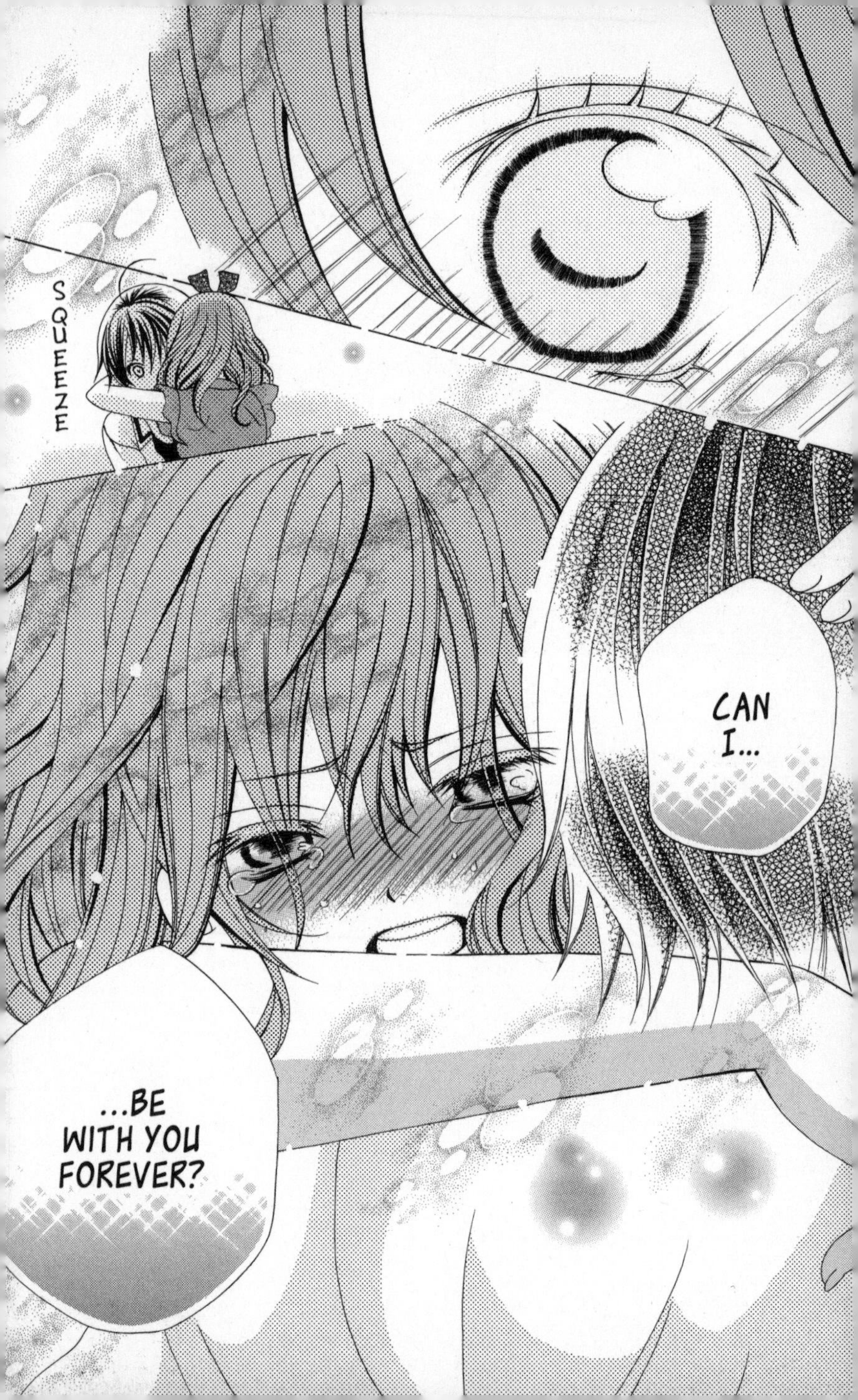
SQUEEZE
CAN I...
...BE WITH YOU FOREVER?

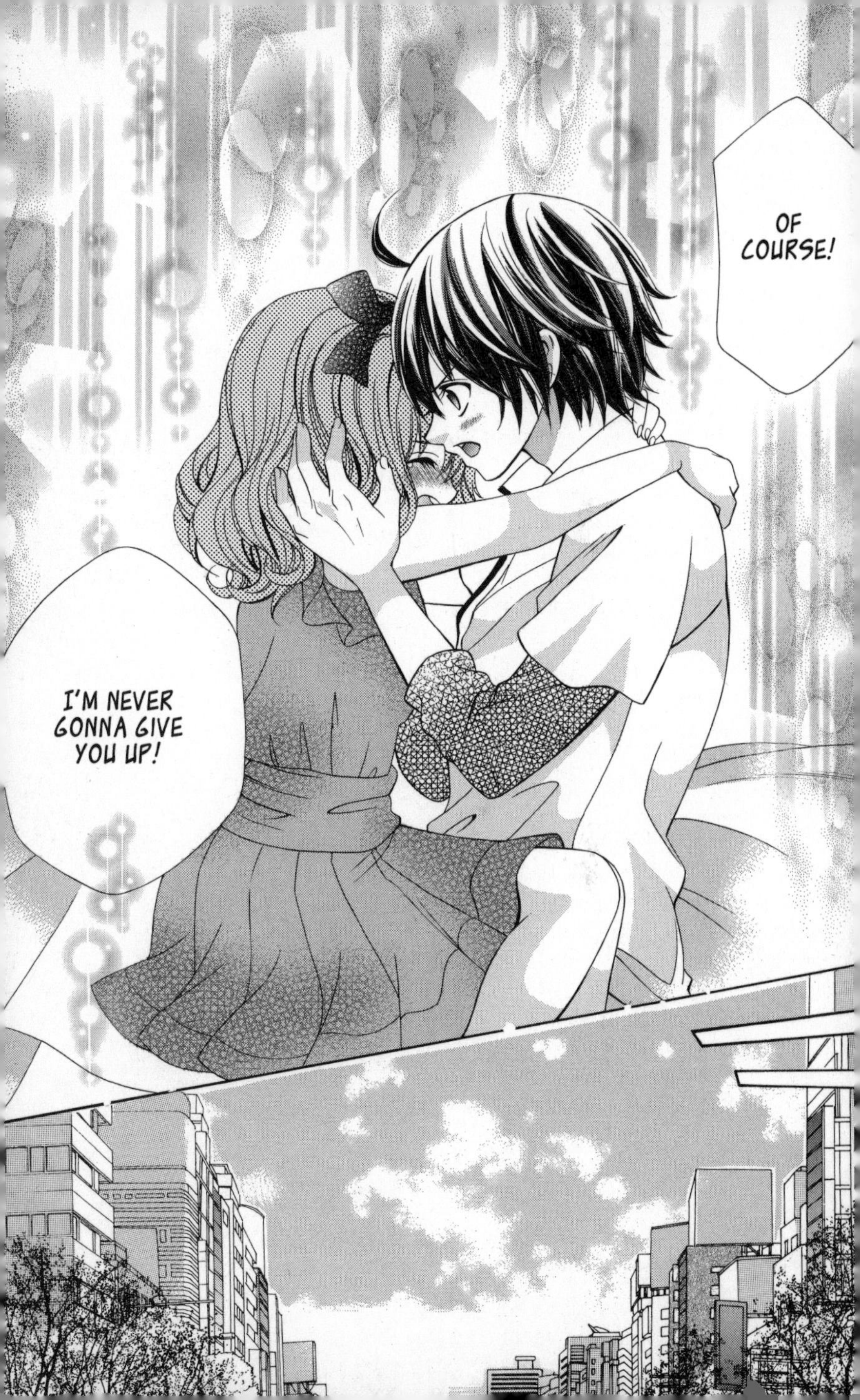
OF COURSE!
I'M NEVER GONNA GIVE YOU UP!

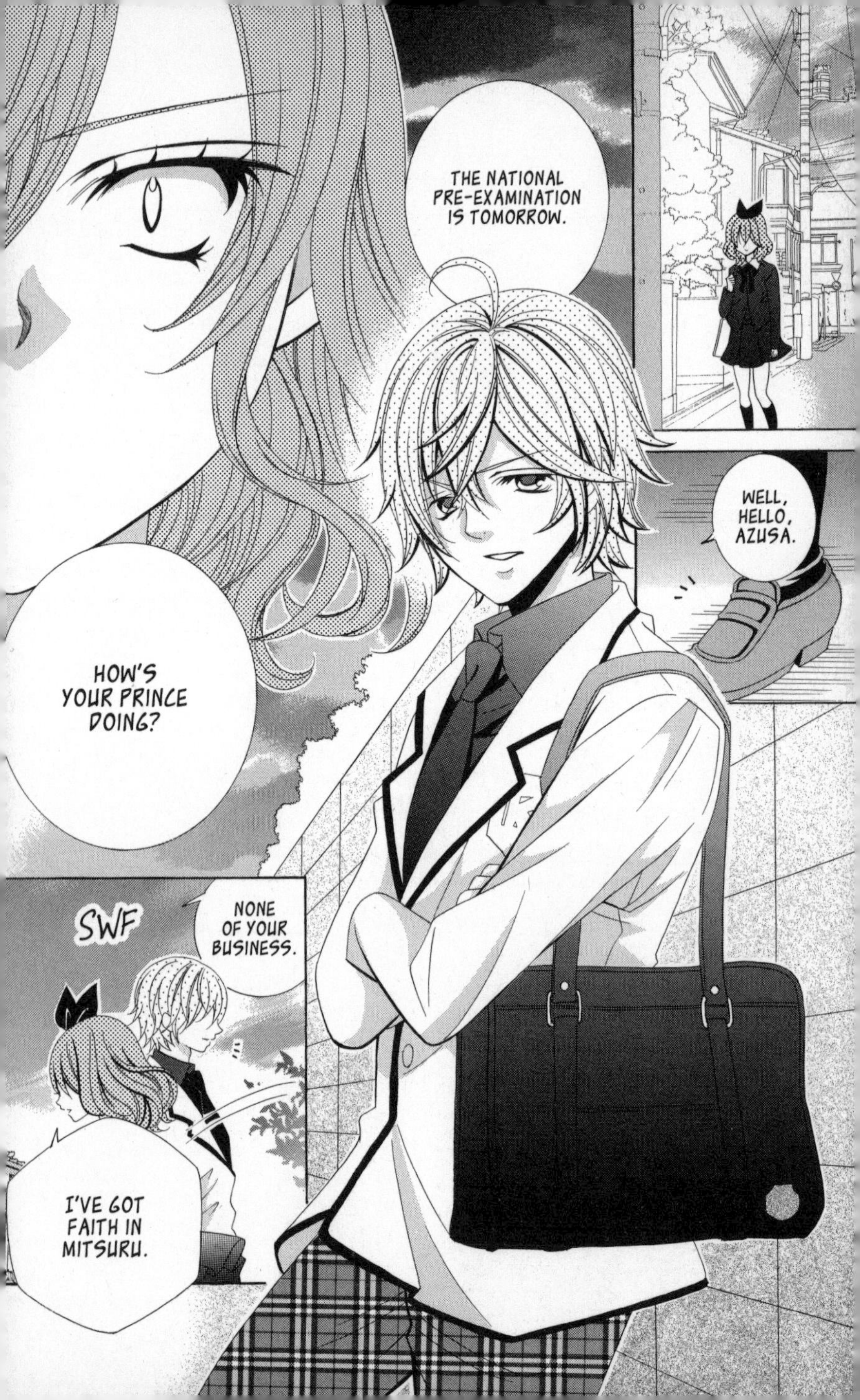
THE NATIONAL PRE-EXAMINATION IS TOMORROW.
WELL, HELLO, AZUSA.
HOW'S YOUR PRINCE DOING?
SWF
NONE OF YOUR BUSINESS.
I'VE GOT FAITH IN MITSURU.

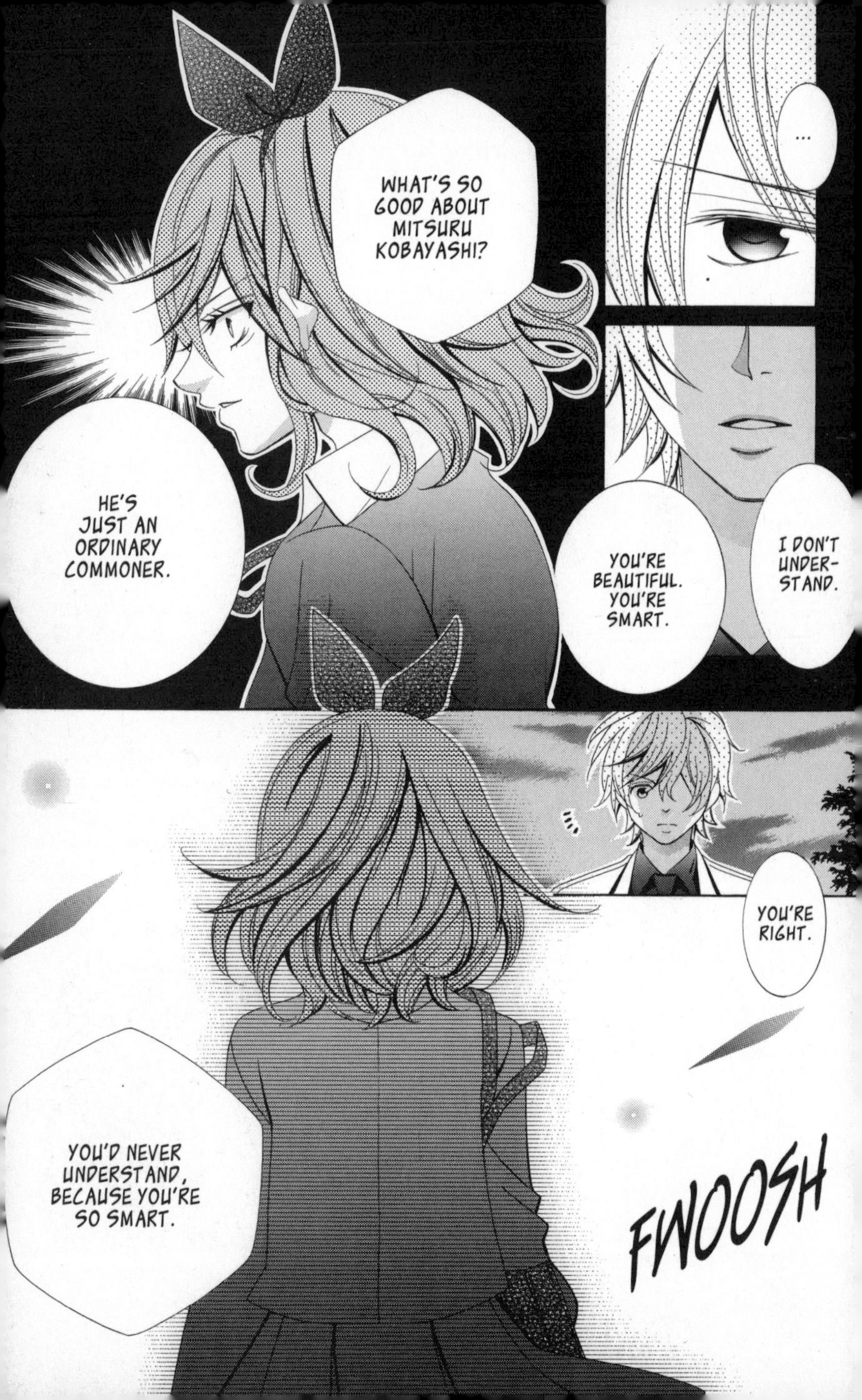
...
I DON'T UNDER-STAND.
YOU'RE BEAUTIFUL. YOU'RE SMART.
WHAT'S SO GOOD ABOUT MITSURU KOBAYASHI?
HE'S JUST AN ORDINARY COMMONER.
YOU'RE RIGHT.
YOU'D NEVER UNDERSTAND, BECAUSE YOU'RE SO SMART.
FWOOSH

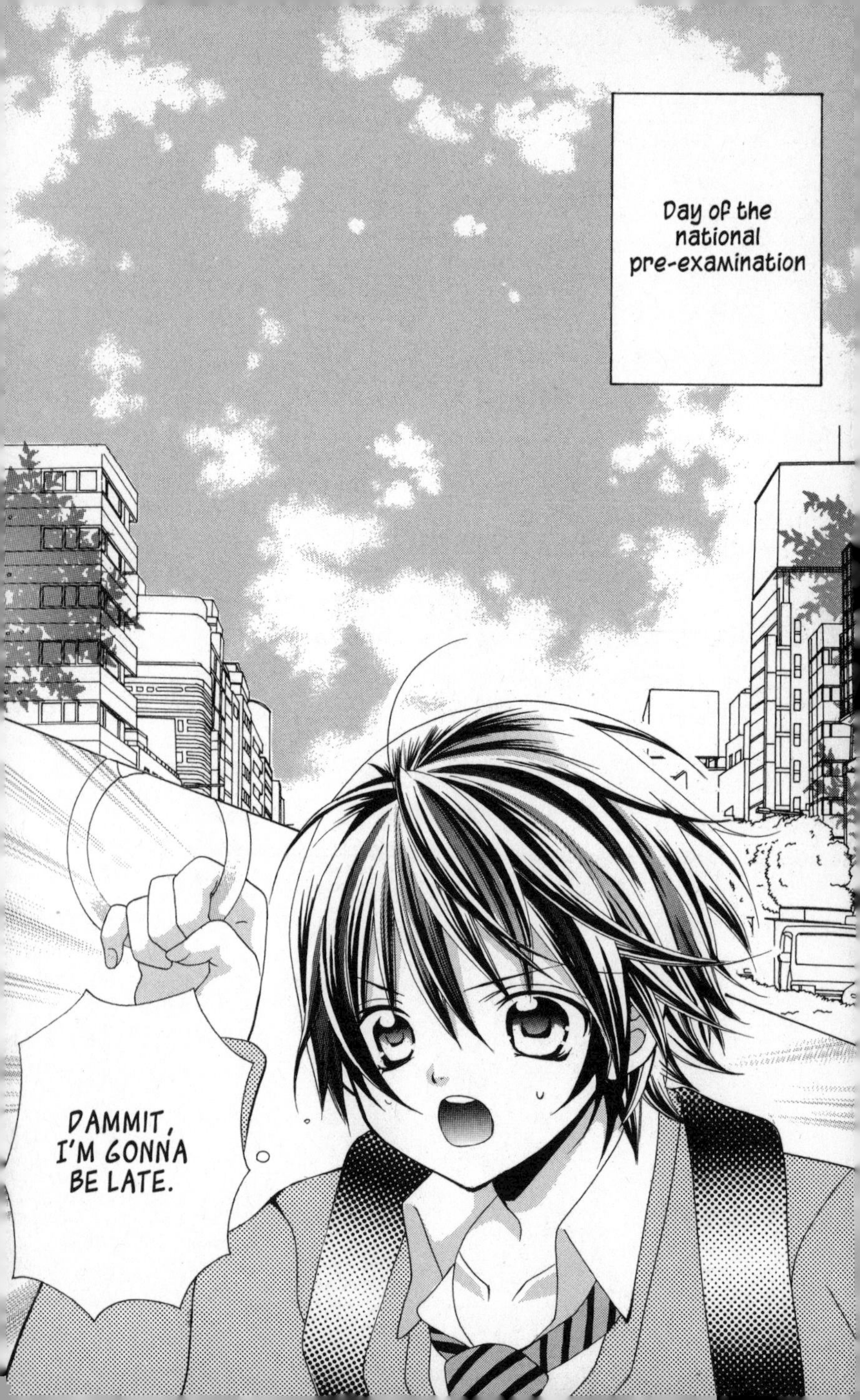
Day of the national pre-examination
DAMMIT, I'M GONNA BE LATE.

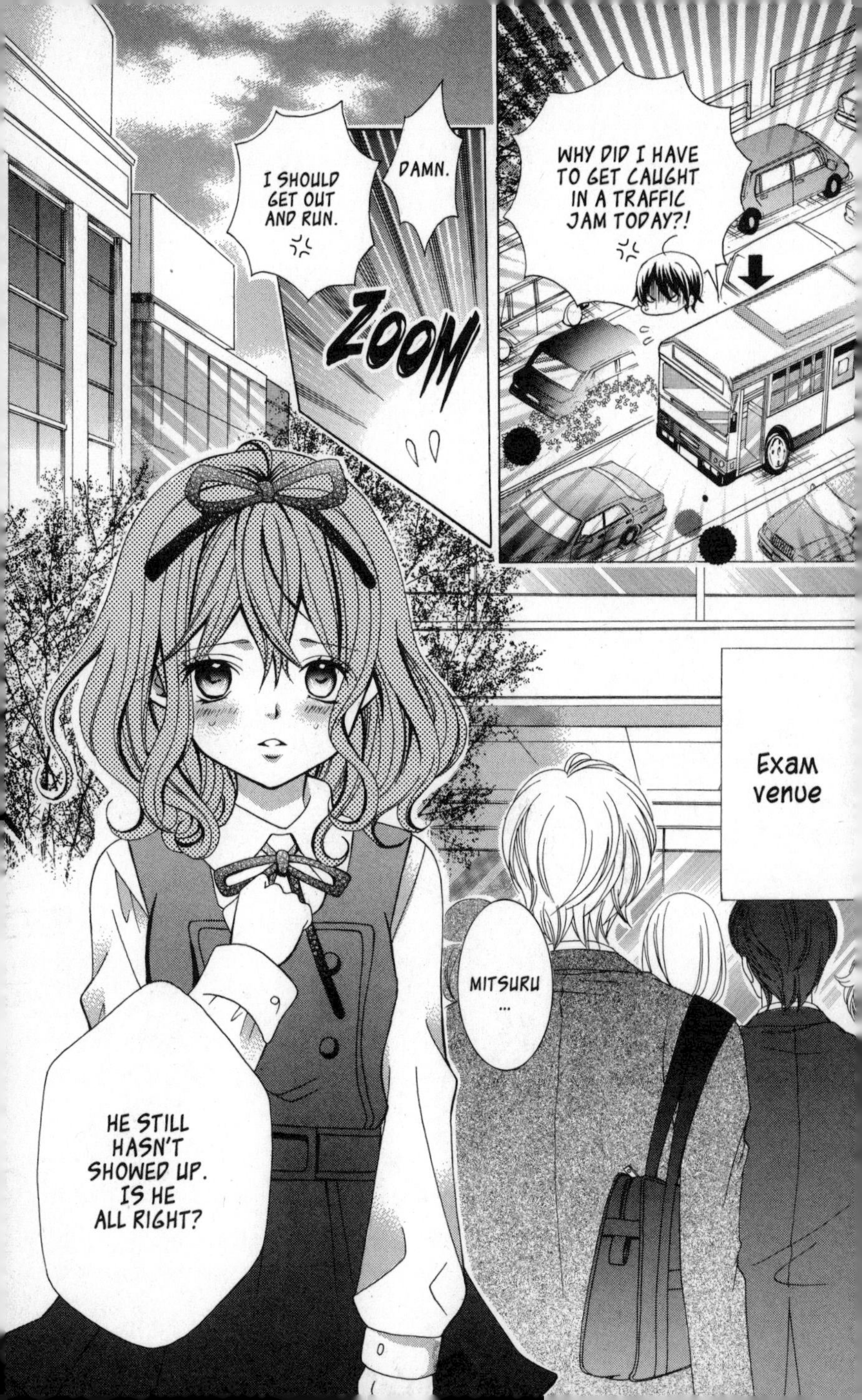
WHY DID I HAVE TO GET CAUGHT IN A TRAFFIC JAM TODAY?!
DAMN.
I SHOULD GET OUT AND RUN.
ZOOM
Exam venue
MITSURU...
HE STILL HASN'T SHOWED UP. IS HE ALL RIGHT?

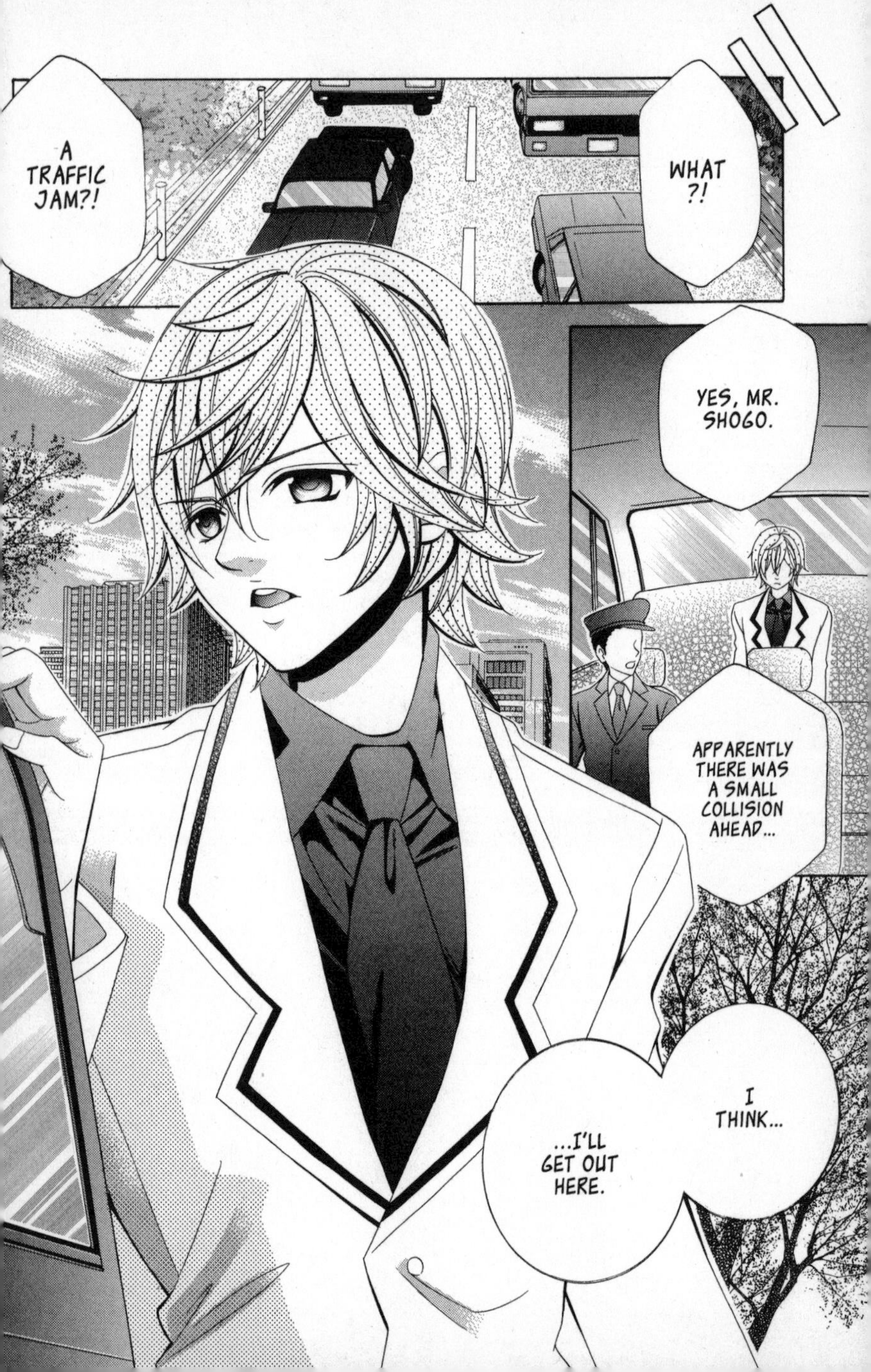
WHAT?!
A TRAFFIC JAM?!
YES, MR. SHOGO.
APPARENTLY THERE WAS A SMALL COLLISION AHEAD...
I THINK...
...I'LL GET OUT HERE.

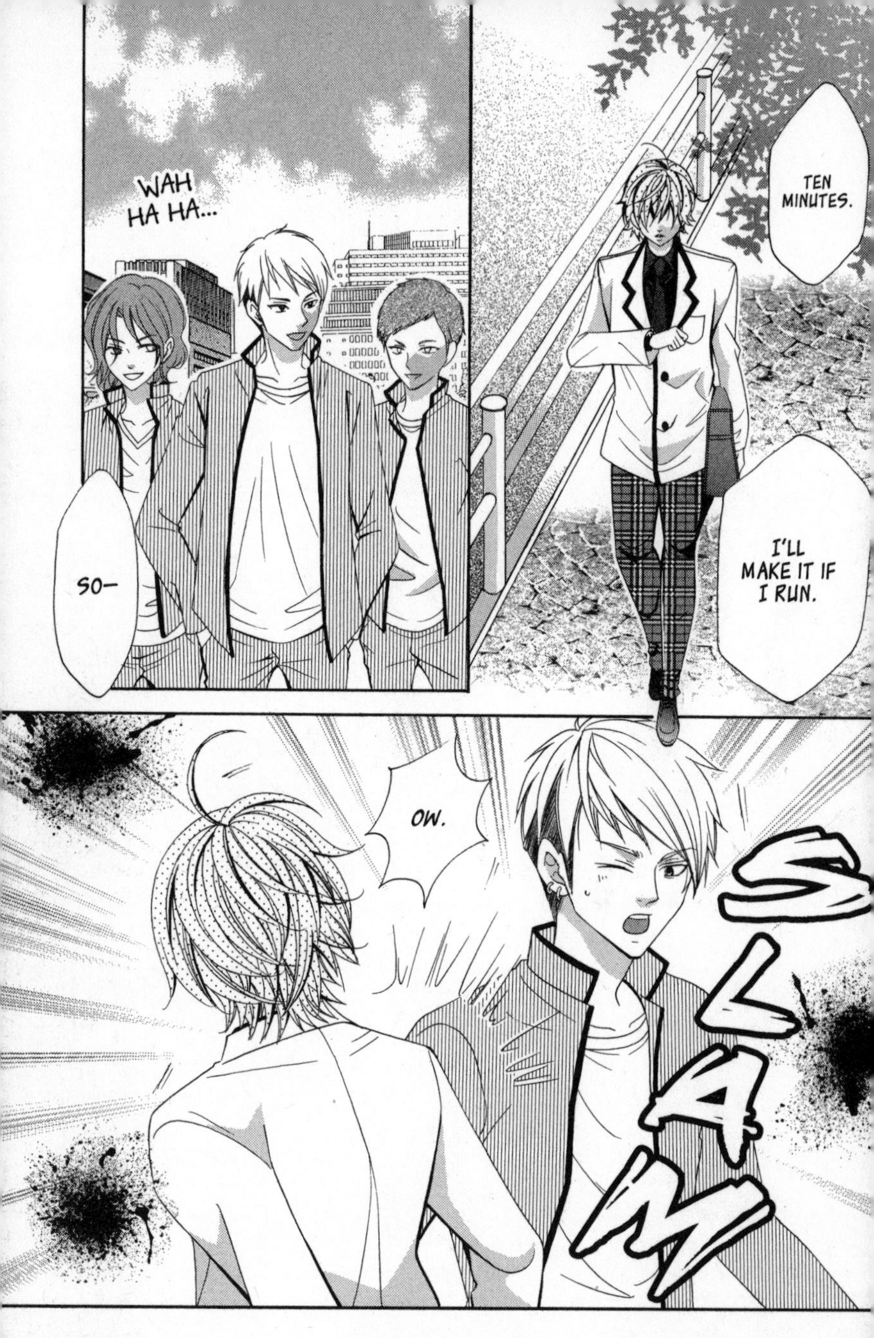
TEN MINUTES.
I'LL MAKE IT IF I RUN.
WAH HA HA...
SO—
SLAM
OW.

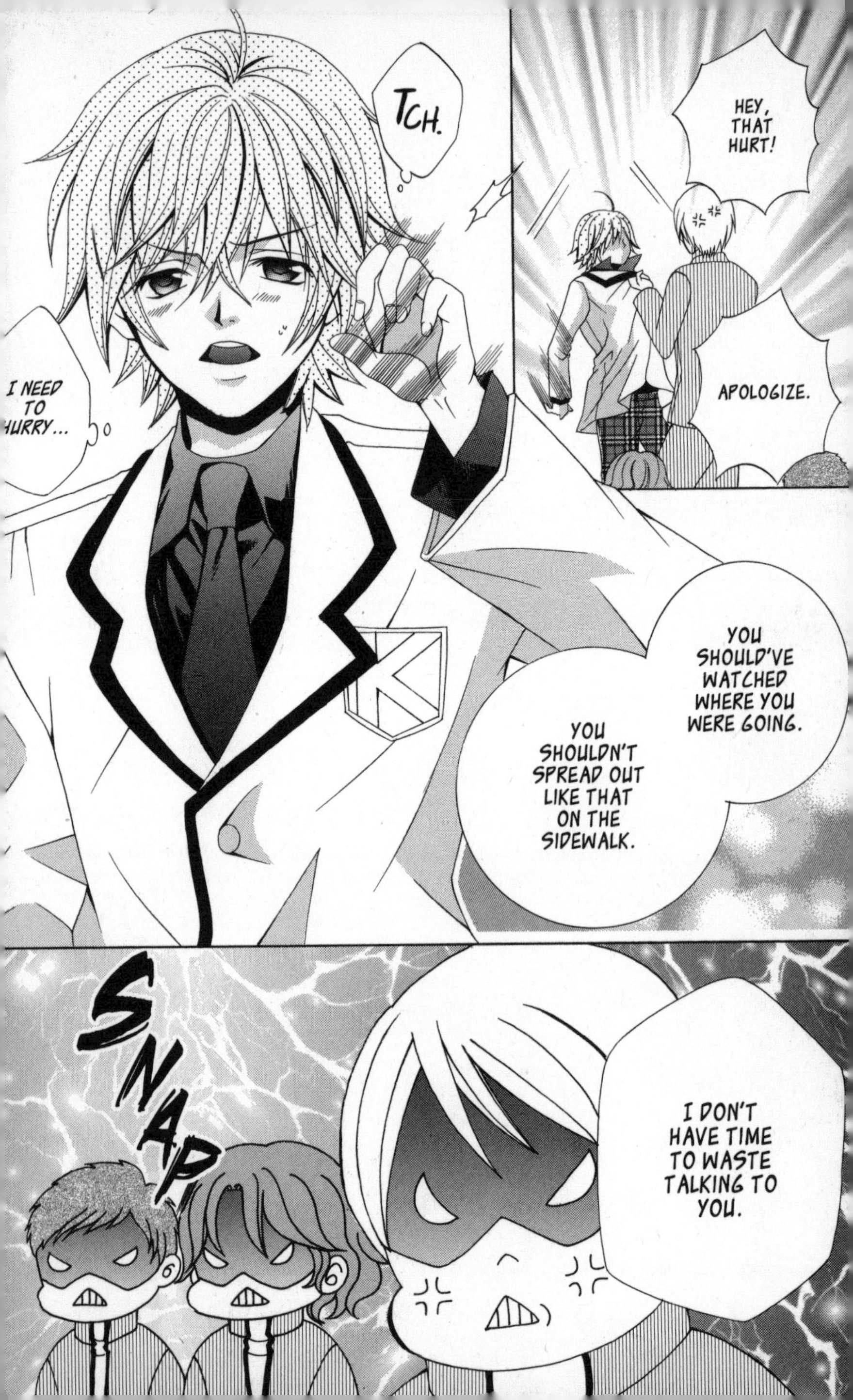
HEY, THAT HURT!
APOLOGIZE.
TCH.
I NEED TO HURRY...
YOU SHOULD'VE WATCHED WHERE YOU WERE GOING.
YOU SHOULDN'T SPREAD OUT LIKE THAT ON THE SIDEWALK.
I DON'T HAVE TIME TO WASTE TALKING TO YOU.
SNAP

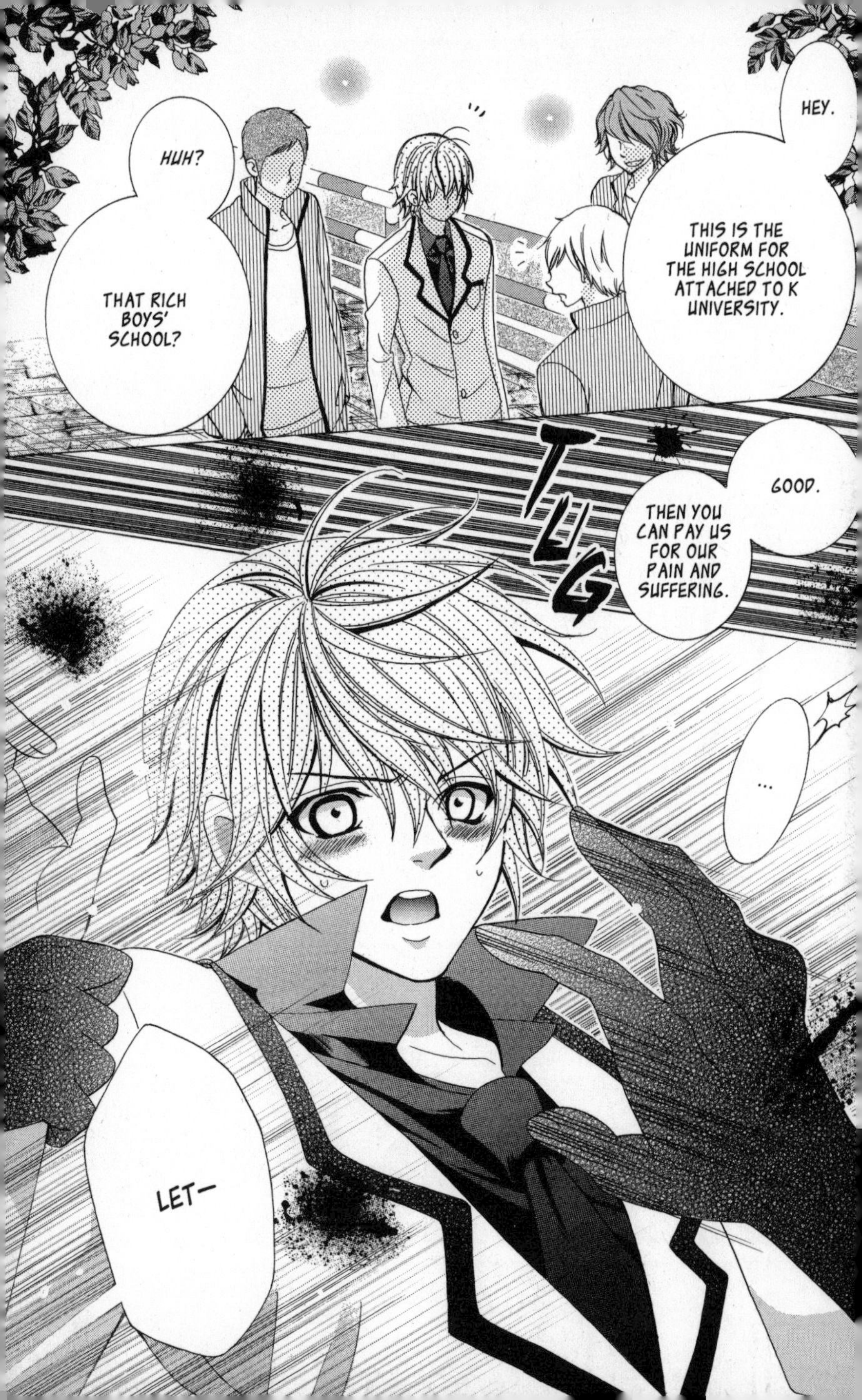
HEY.
THIS IS THE UNIFORM FOR THE HIGH SCHOOL ATTACHED TO K UNIVERSITY.
HUH?
THAT RICH BOYS' SCHOOL?
GOOD.
THEN YOU CAN PAY US FOR OUR PAIN AND SUFFERING.
TUG
...
LET—

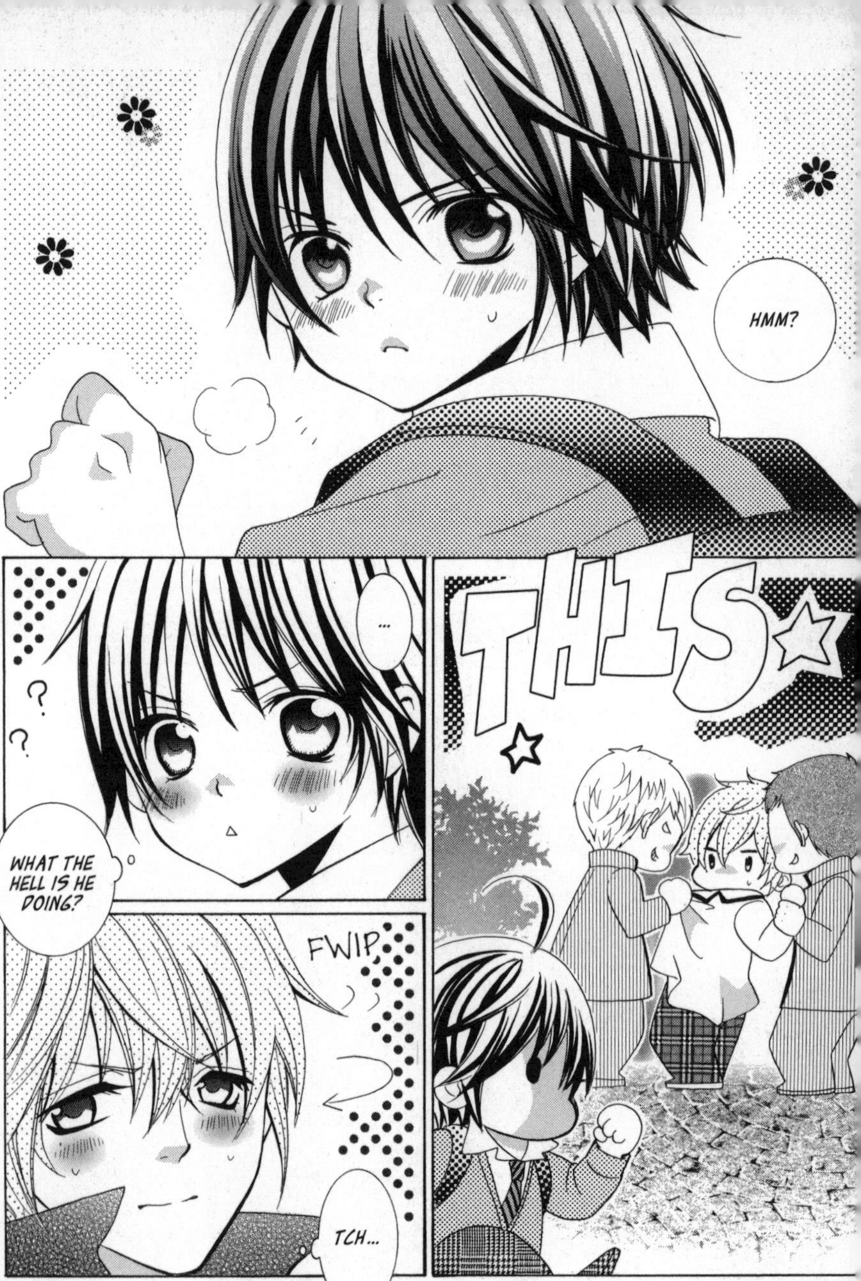
HMM?
THIS☆
...
? ?
WHAT THE HELL IS HE DOING?
FWIP
TCH...

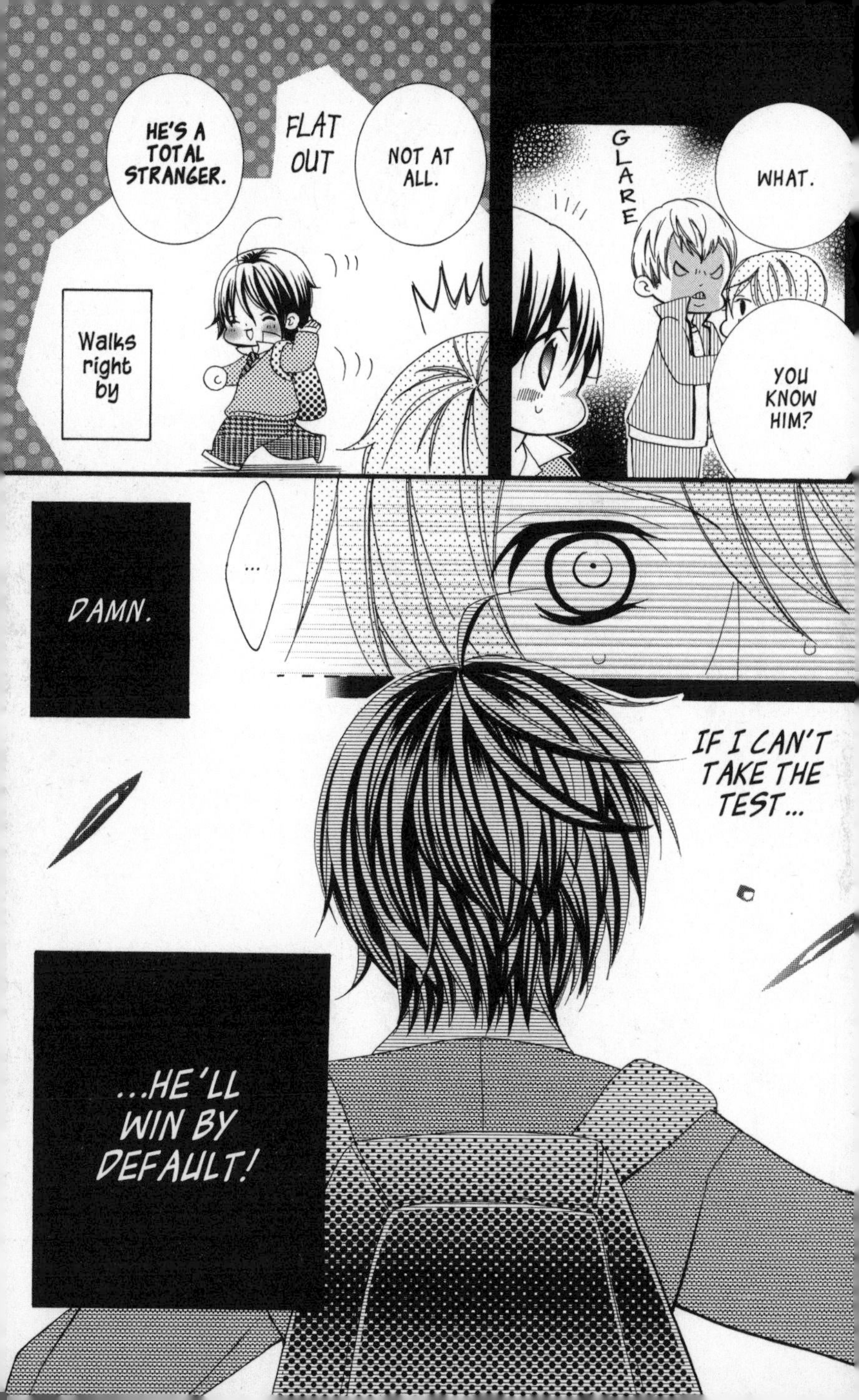
WHAT.
GLARE
YOU KNOW HIM?
NOT AT ALL.
FLAT OUT
HE'S A TOTAL STRANGER.
Walks right by
...
DAMN.
IF I CAN'T TAKE THE TEST...
...HE'LL WIN BY DEFAULT!

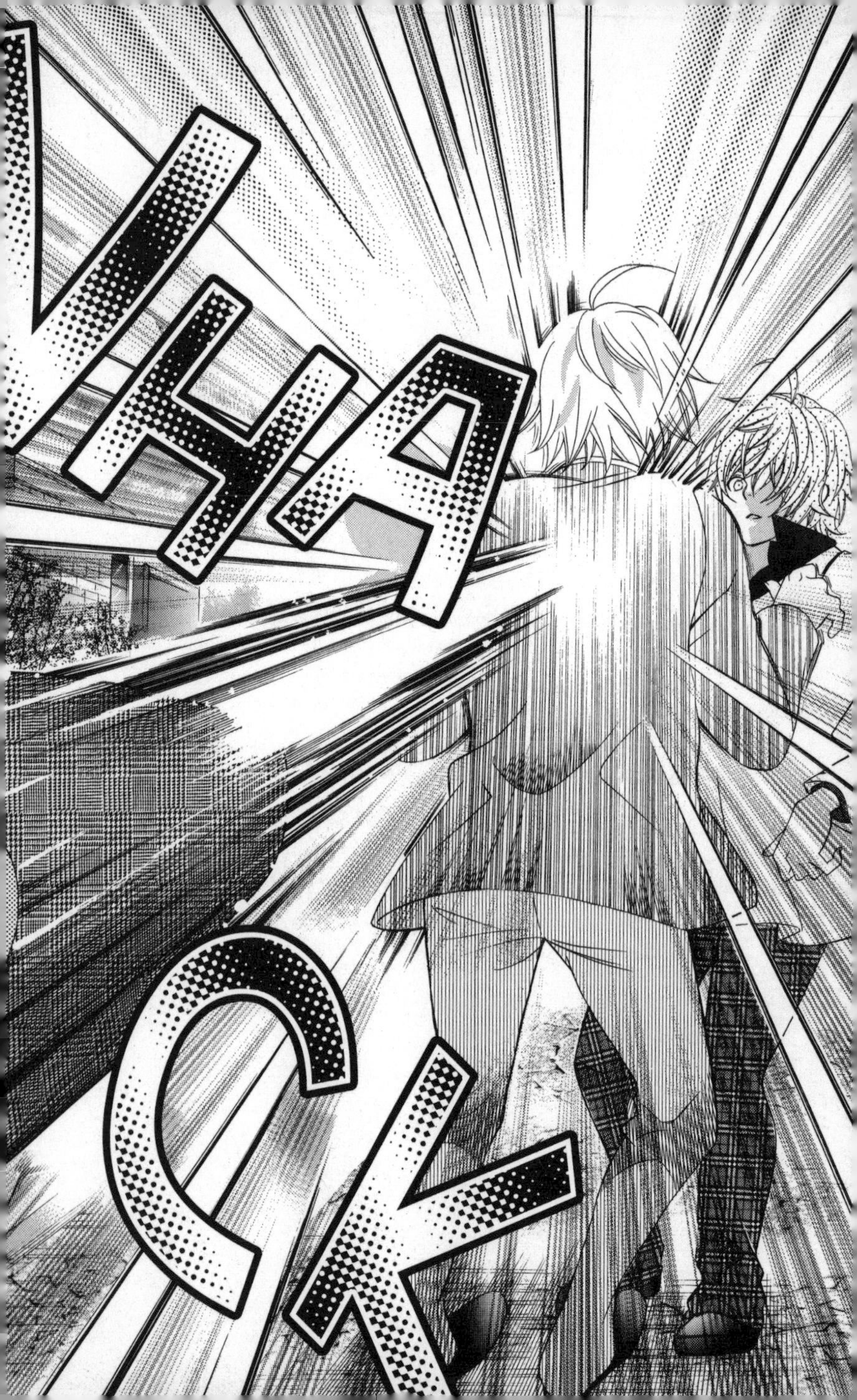
WHACK

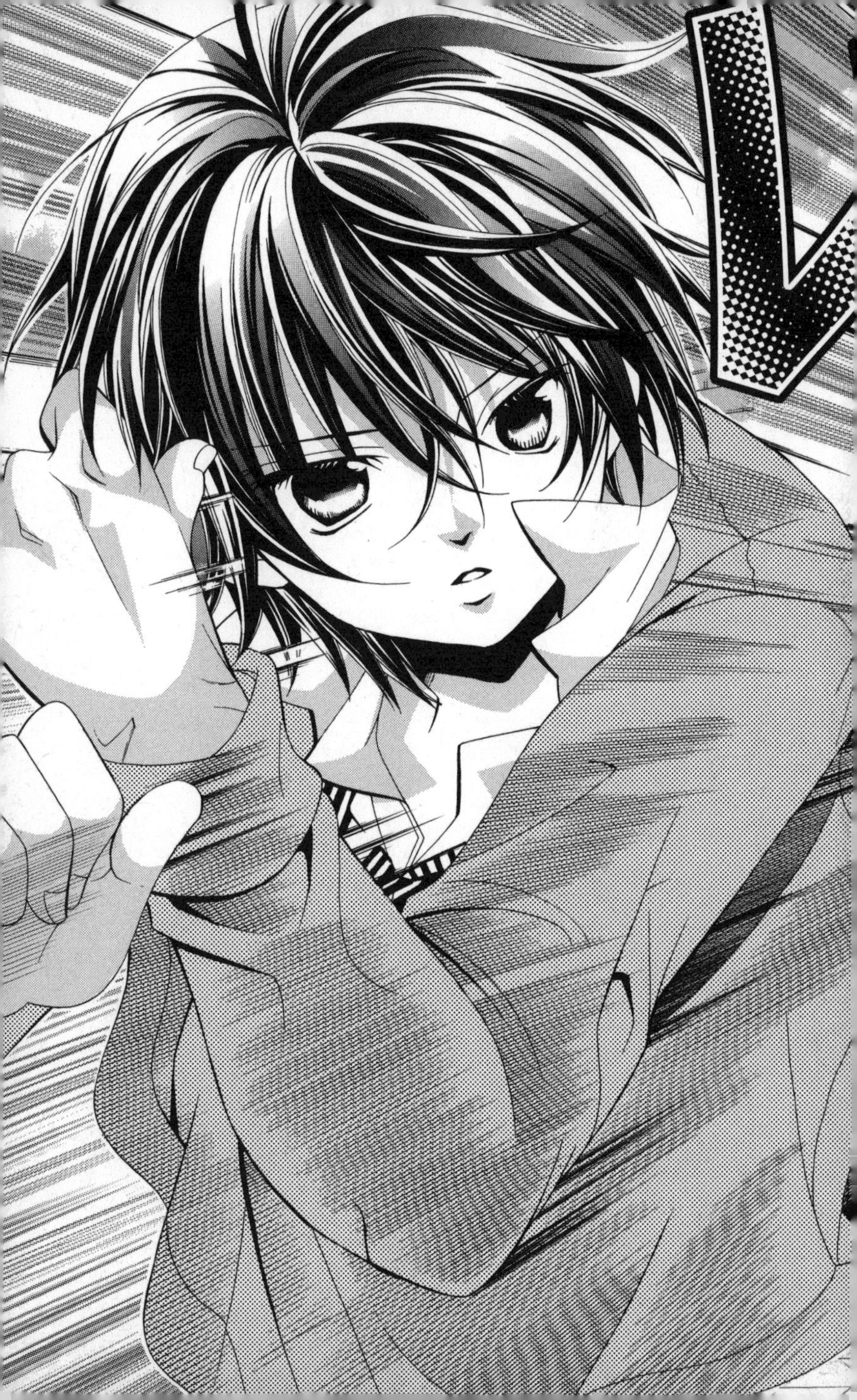

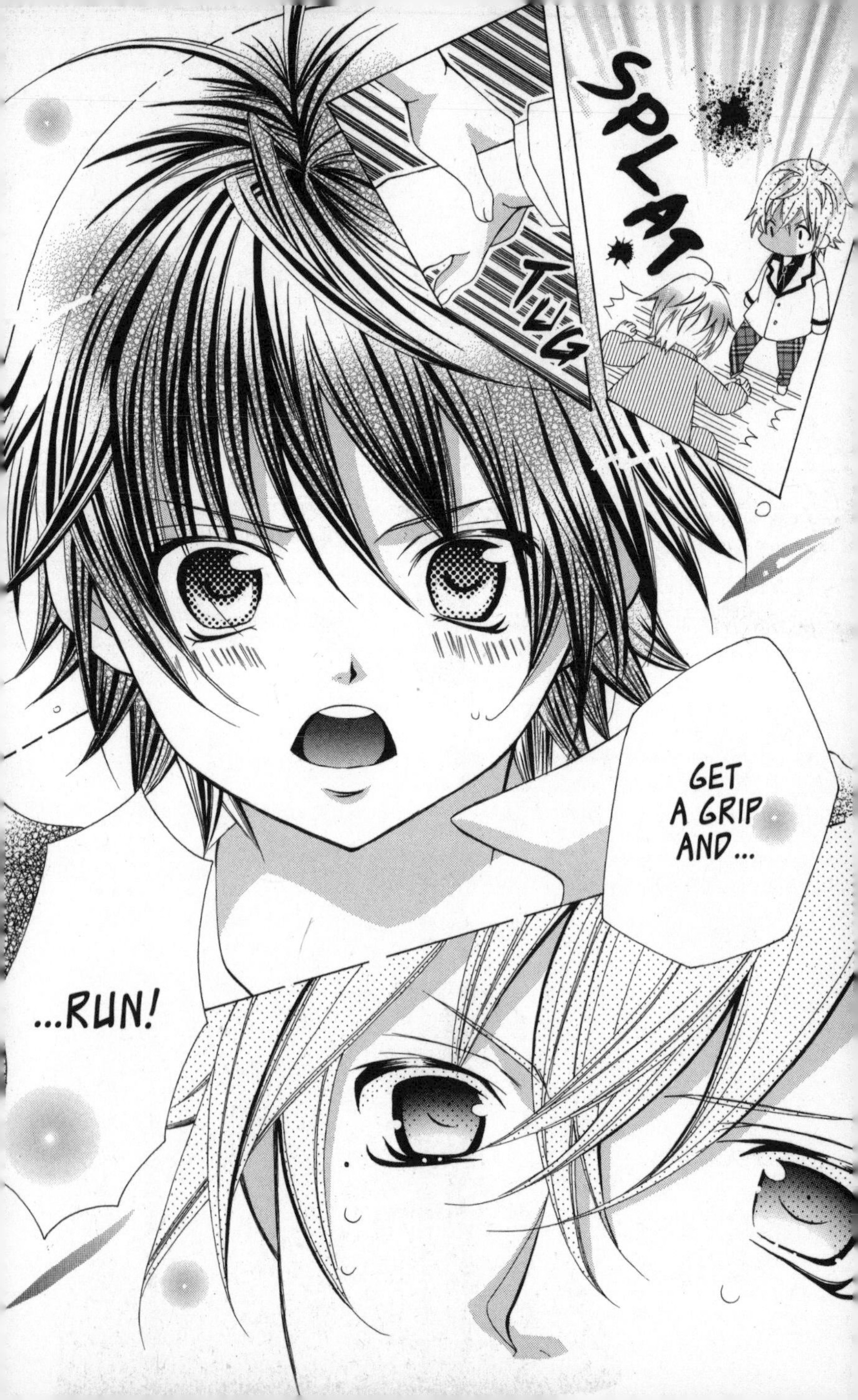
SPLAT
TUG
GET A GRIP AND...
...RUN!

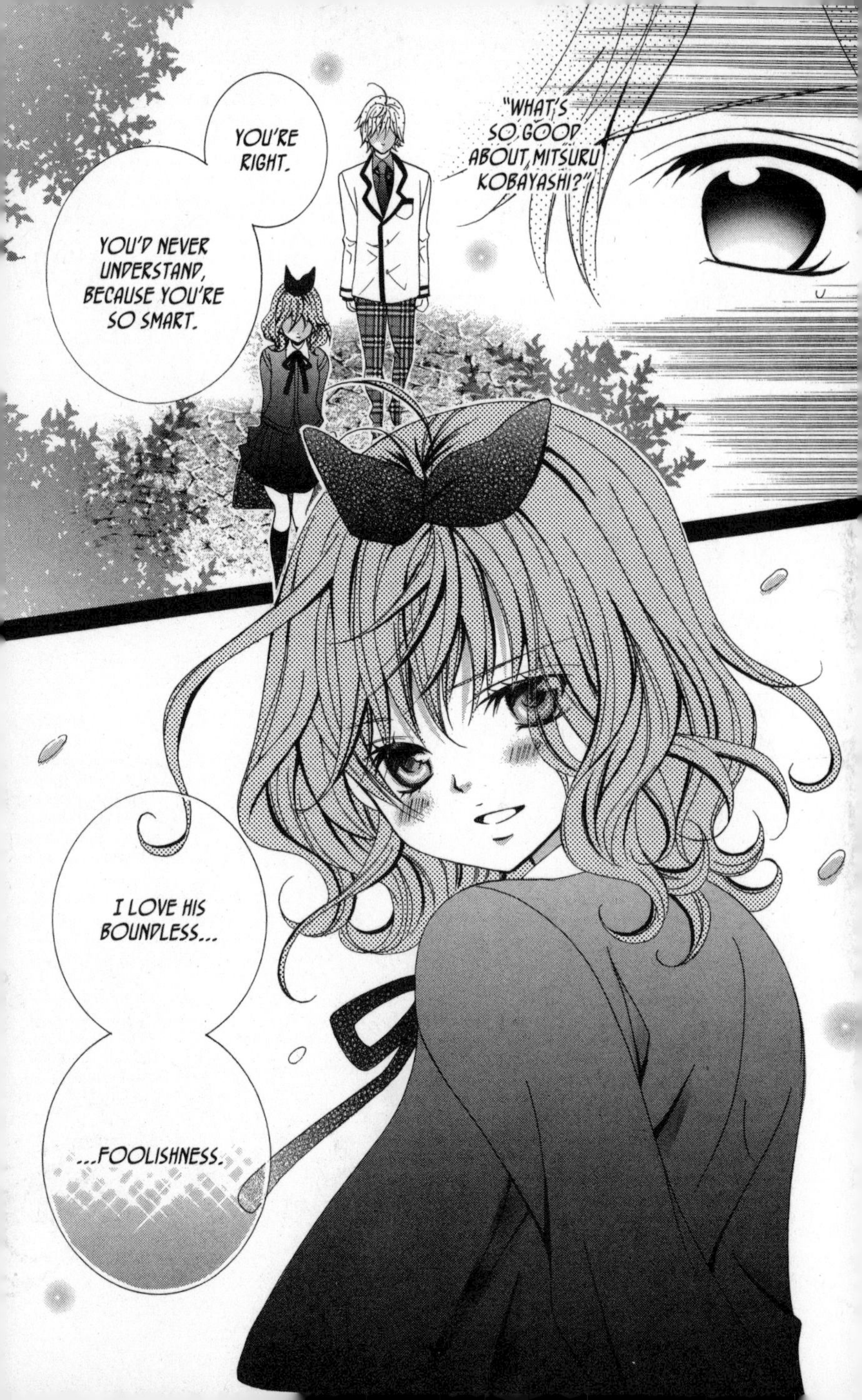
"WHAT'S SO GOOD ABOUT MITSURU KOBAYASHI?"
YOU'RE RIGHT.
YOU'D NEVER UNDERSTAND, BECAUSE YOU'RE SO SMART.
I LOVE HIS BOUNDLESS...
...FOOLISHNESS.

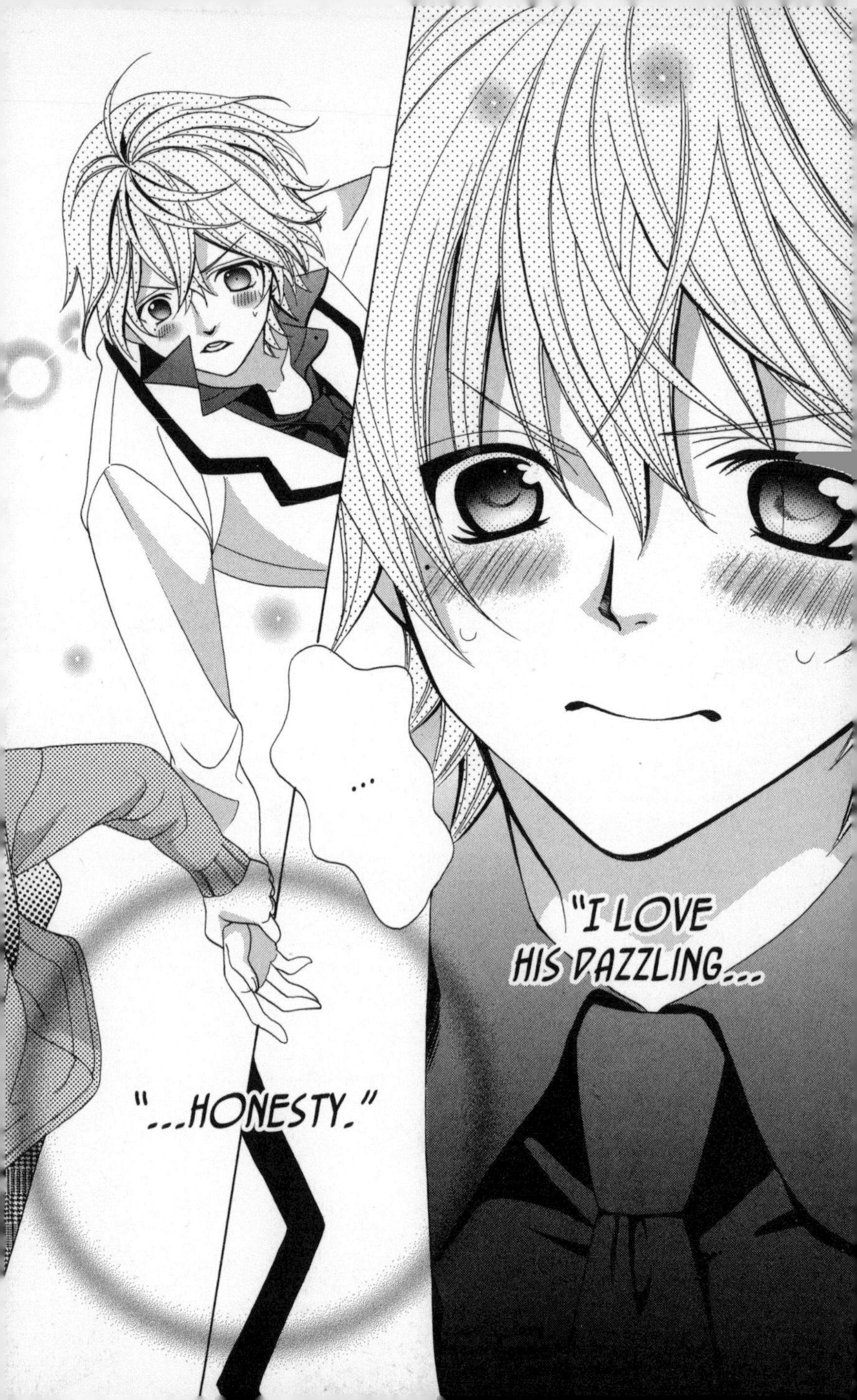
"I LOVE HIS DAZZLING...
...
"...HONESTY."

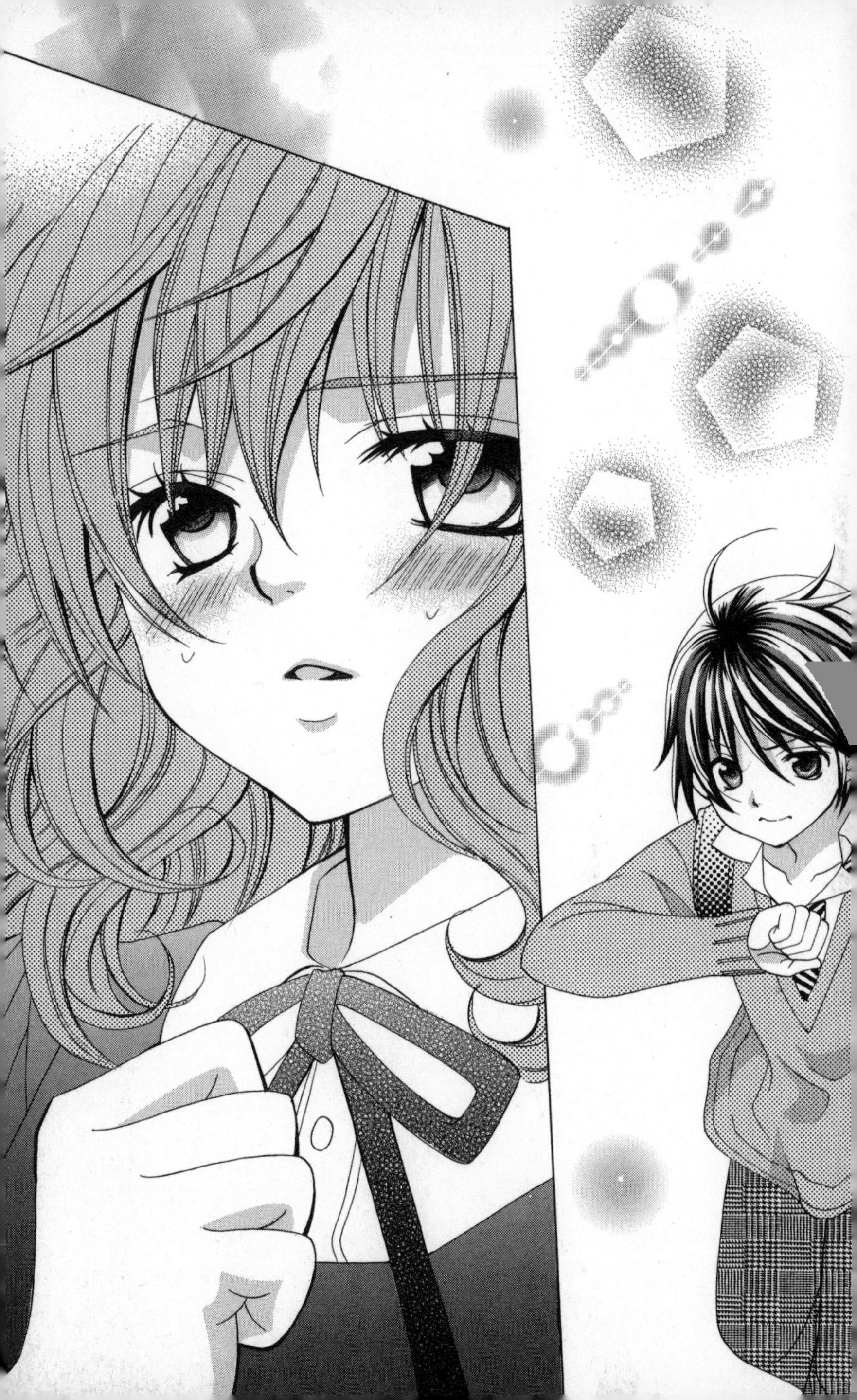

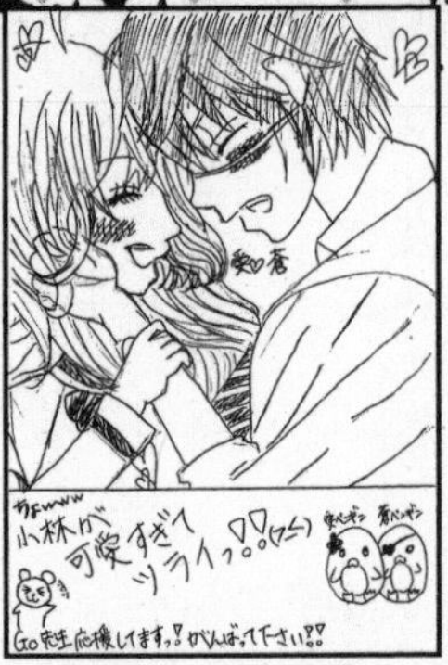
ちょwww
小林が可愛すぎてツライっ!!
GO先生応援してます!! がんばって下さい!!
Yumemi Shimada (Aichi)
Ed.: What a lovey-dovey pair. ♥ The penguins too. ♥

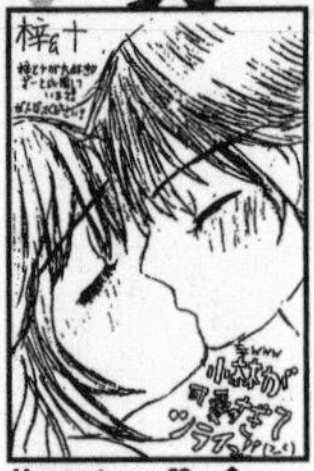
梓&十
小林が可愛すぎてツライ
Masshuu ♡ ↑
(Ibaraki)
Ed.: Azusa and Mitsuru are so in love. ♥

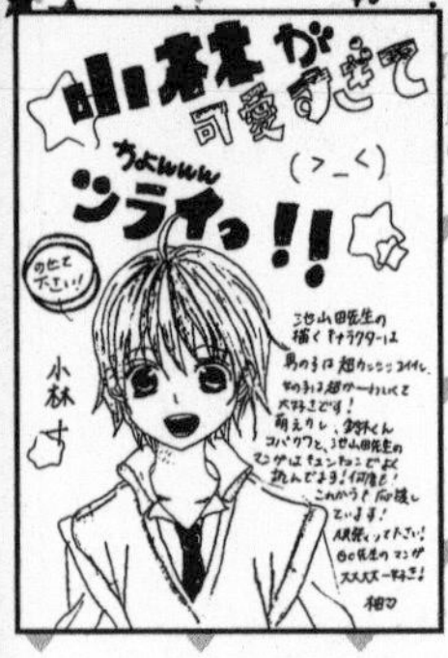
小林が可愛すぎて
ちょwww
ツライっ!!
小林
Yuzu
(Kanagawa)
Ed.: Mitsuru's so cute it hurts!!
←

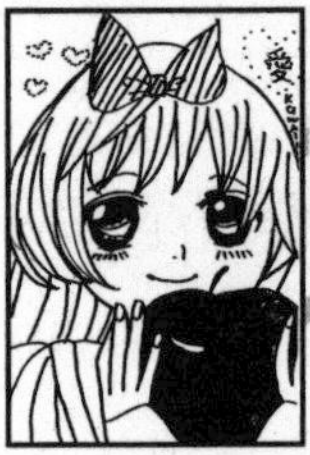
愛
Shion Kai
(Aichi)
Ed.: Megumu is becoming more and more beautiful...
←

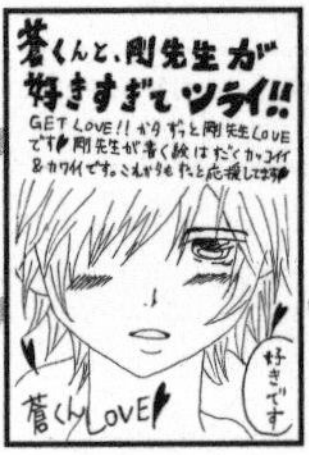
蒼くんと、剛先生が好きすぎてツライ!!
好きです
蒼くんLOVE
Manaka Yokoi
(Osaka)
Ed.: Aoi told me he likes me. ♥
←

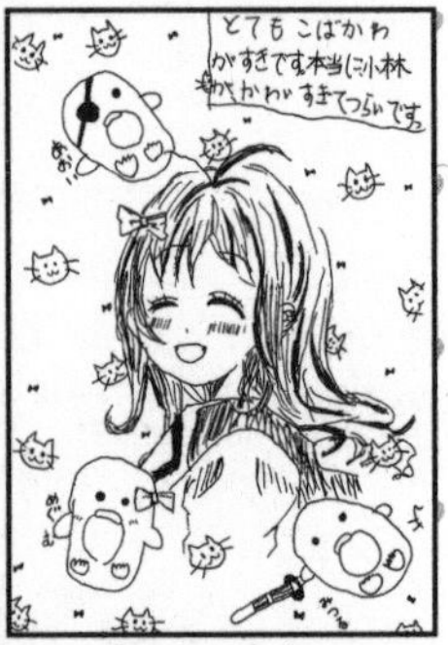
とてもこばかわがすきです本当に小林がかわいすぎてつらいです
Kaeru (Kagawa) ↑
Ed.: Mego and penguins and cats are smiling jewels in a jewel box!!

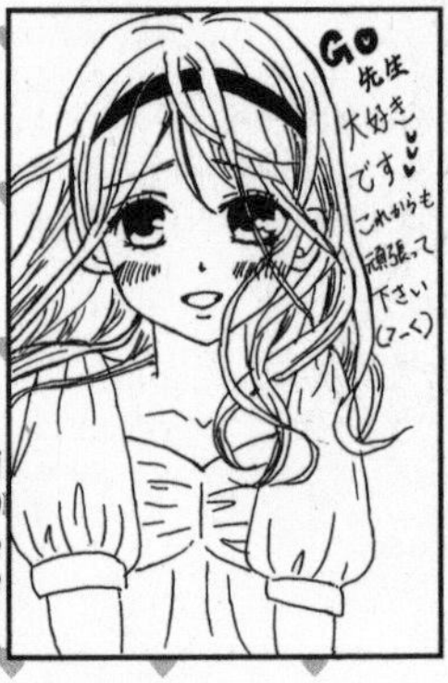
GO先生大好きです
これからも頑張って下さい
Rika Koyanagi
(Saitama)
Ed.: I love the mature Mego too. ♥
→

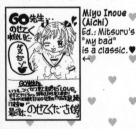

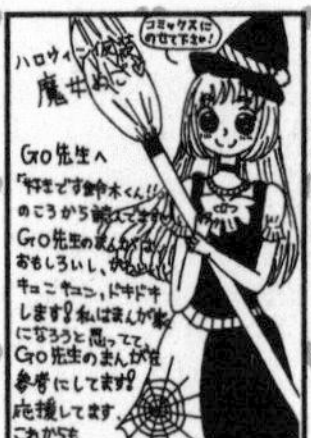
コミックスにのせて下さい!
魔女めぐ
Go先生へ
Hoka Naito
(Mie)
Ed.: No tricks cuz I don't have any treats!!
←

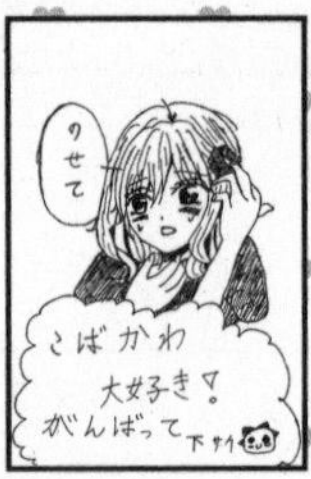
のせて
こばかわ
大好き!
がんばって下サイ
Hoshi ©!
(Miyagi)
Ed.: Yes! We'll publish it!
←

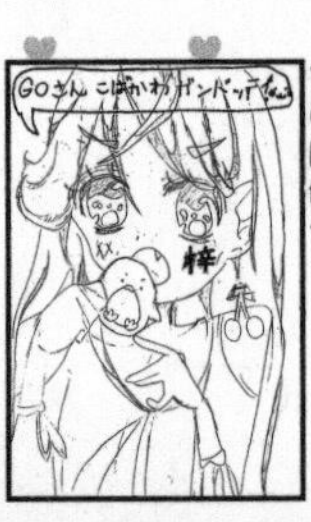
梓
Yui Tanaka
(Aichi)
Ed.: Don't eat the penguin!!
←

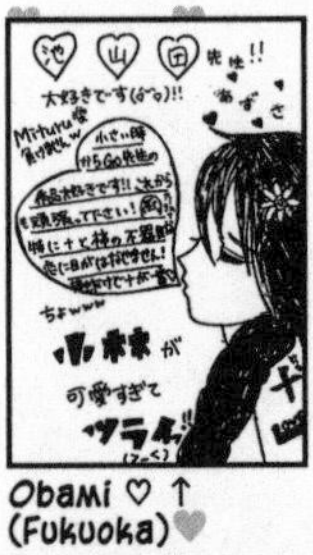
池山田先生!!
大好きです
ちょwww
小林が可愛すぎてツライ!!
Obami ♡ ↑
(Fukuoka)
Ed.: Azusa's not losing!!

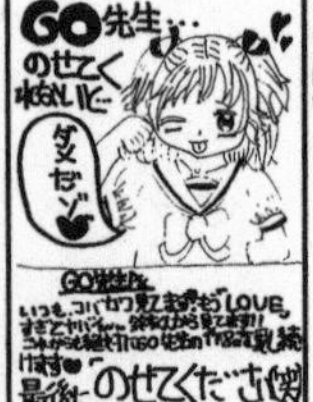
GO先生
Miyu Inoue
(Aichi)
Ed.: Mitsuru's "My bad" is a classic. ♥
←

Chapter 64

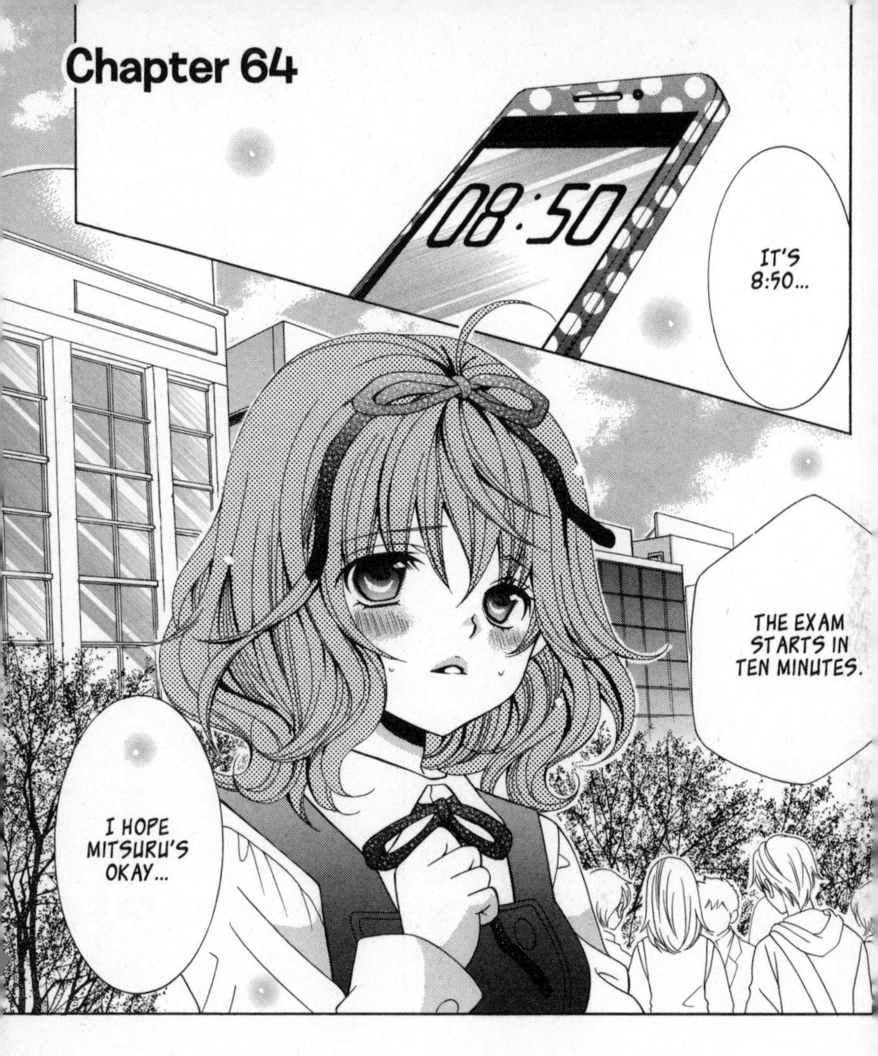
08:50
IT'S 8:50...
THE EXAM STARTS IN TEN MINUTES.
I HOPE MITSURU'S OKAY...

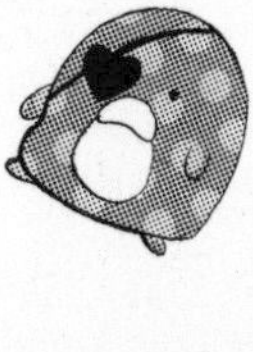

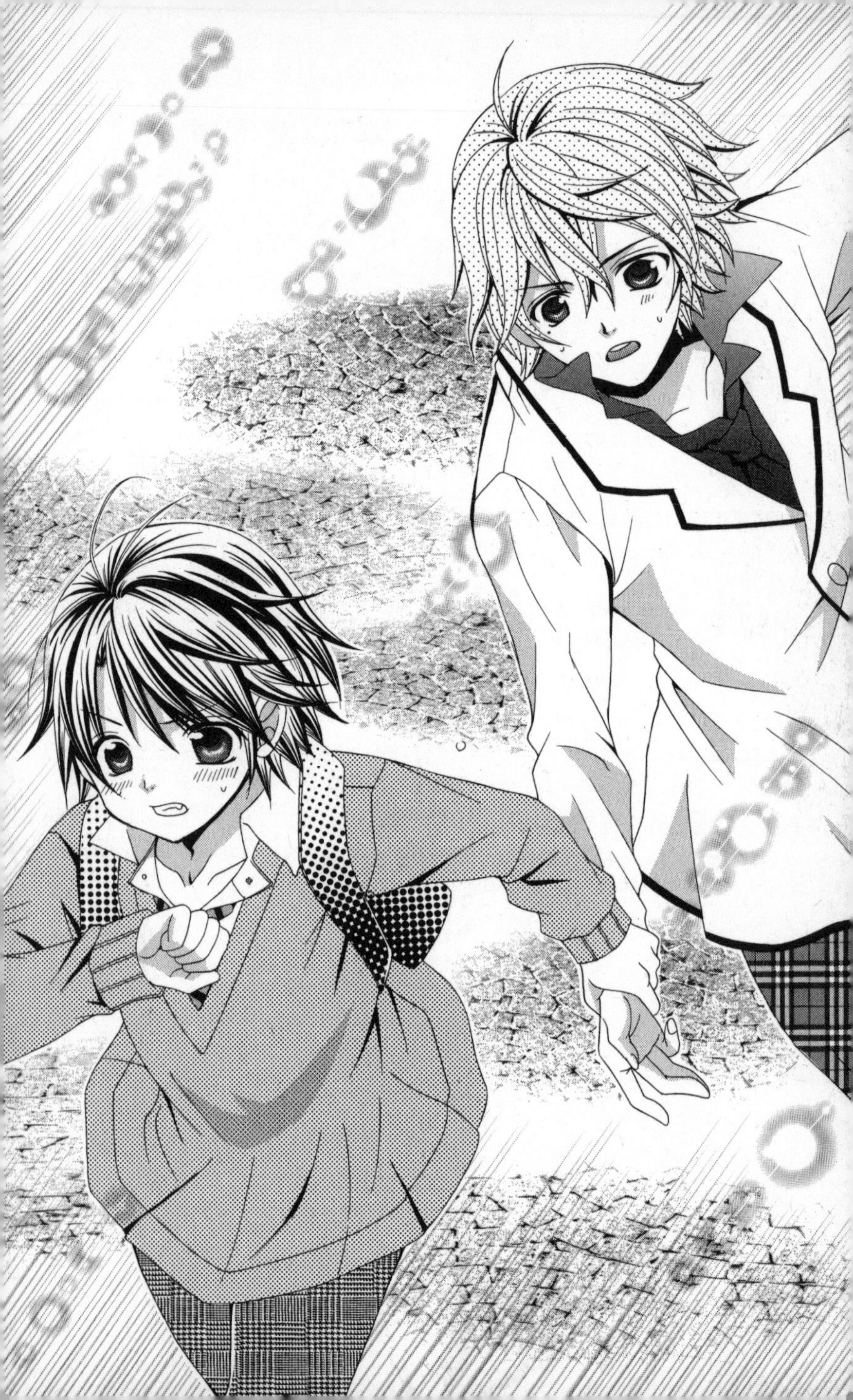

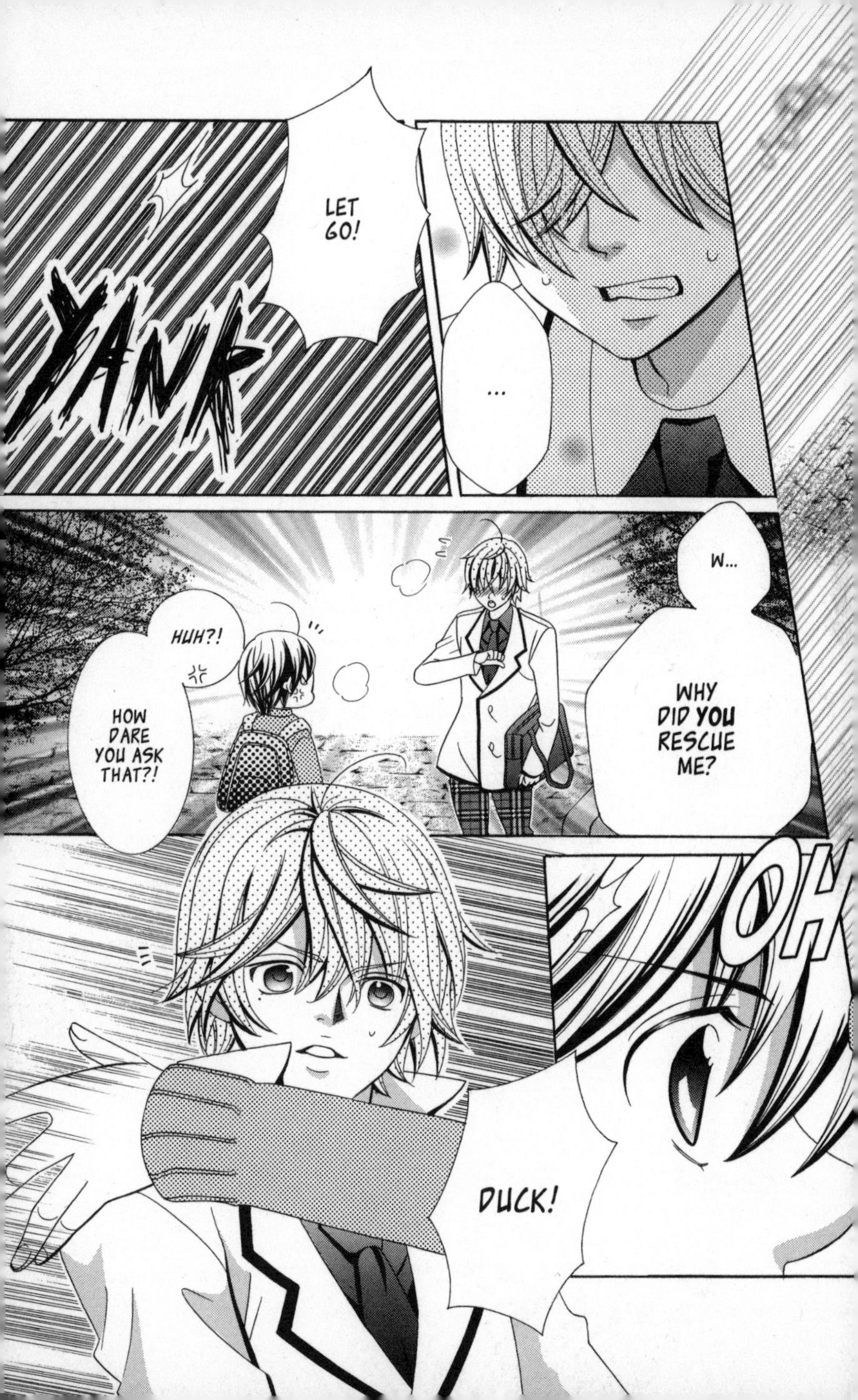

LET GO!
YANK
...
W...
WHY DID YOU RESCUE ME?
HUH?!
HOW DARE YOU ASK THAT?!
OH
DUCK!

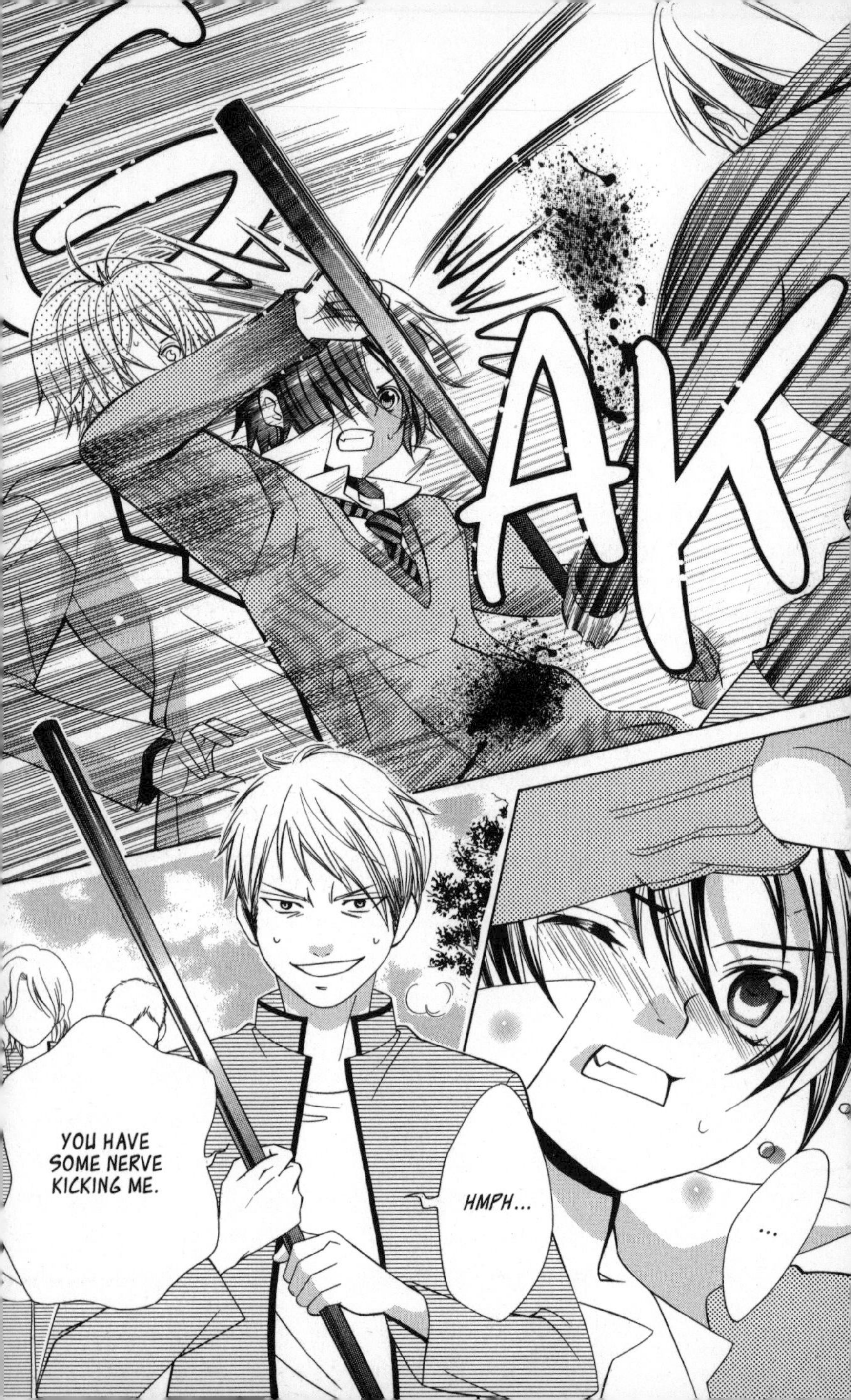
AK
...
HMPH...
YOU HAVE SOME NERVE KICKING ME.

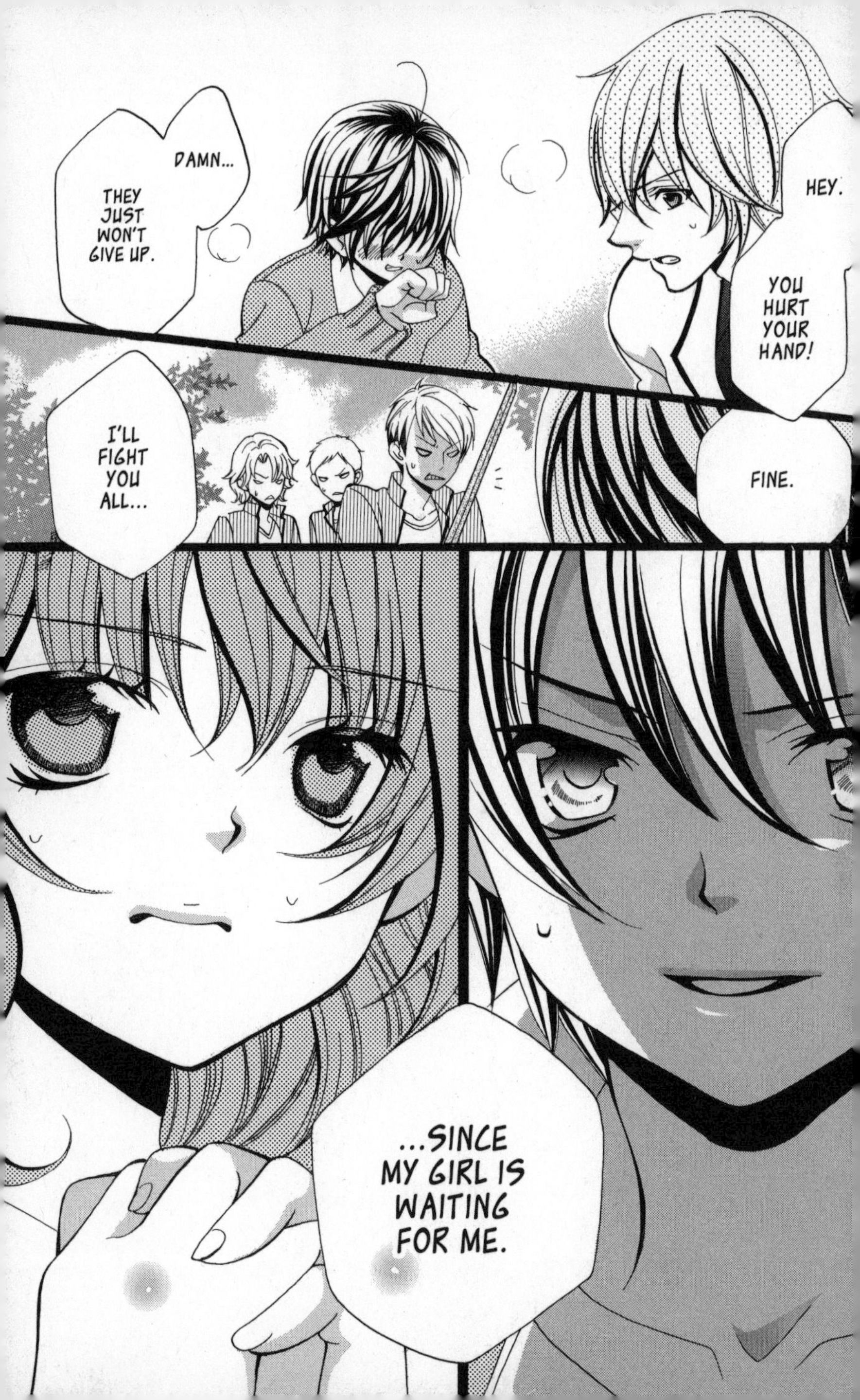
HEY.
YOU HURT YOUR HAND!
DAMN...
THEY JUST WON'T GIVE UP.
FINE.
I'LL FIGHT YOU ALL...
...SINCE MY GIRL IS WAITING FOR ME.

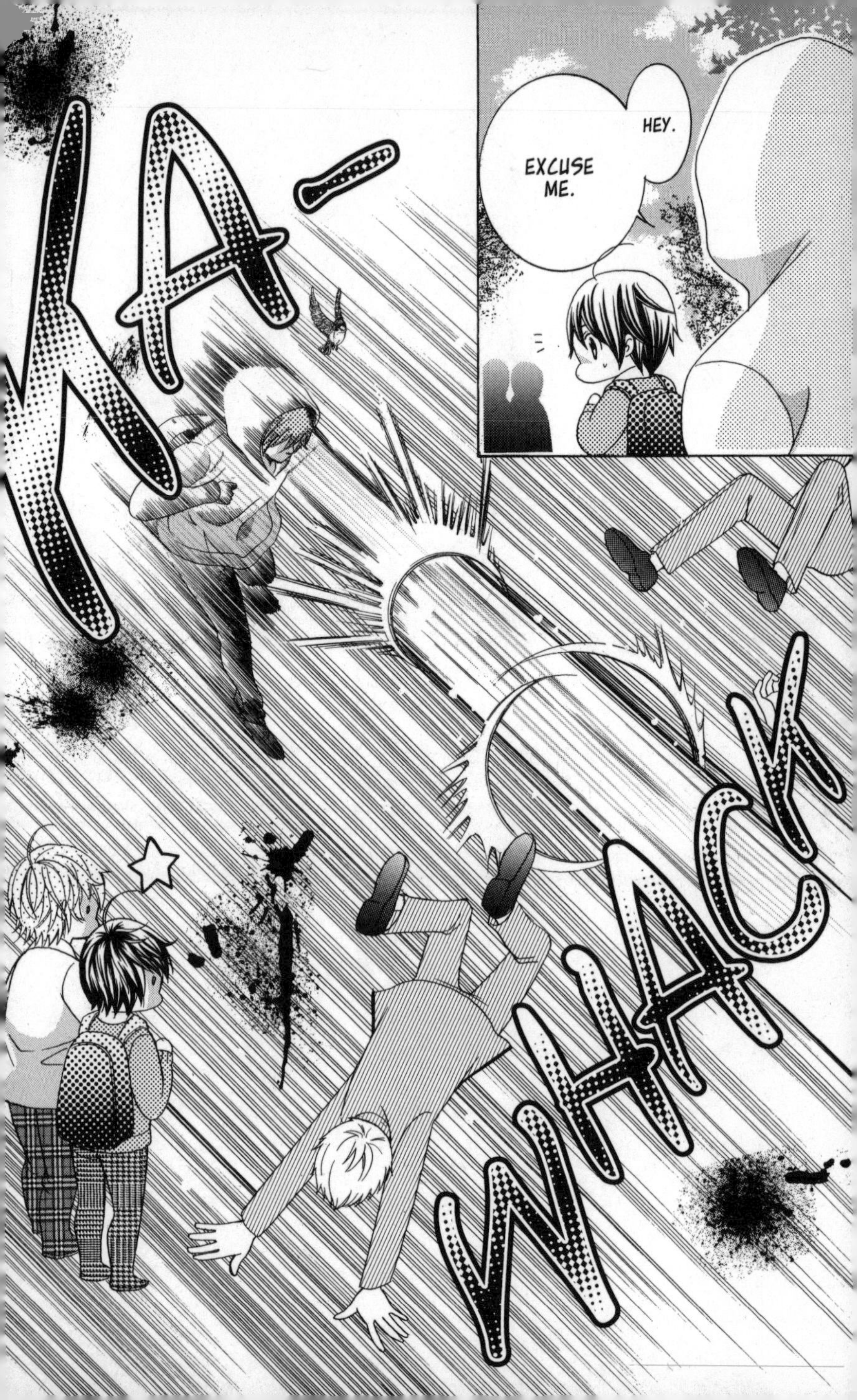
HEY.
EXCUSE ME.
KA-
WHACK

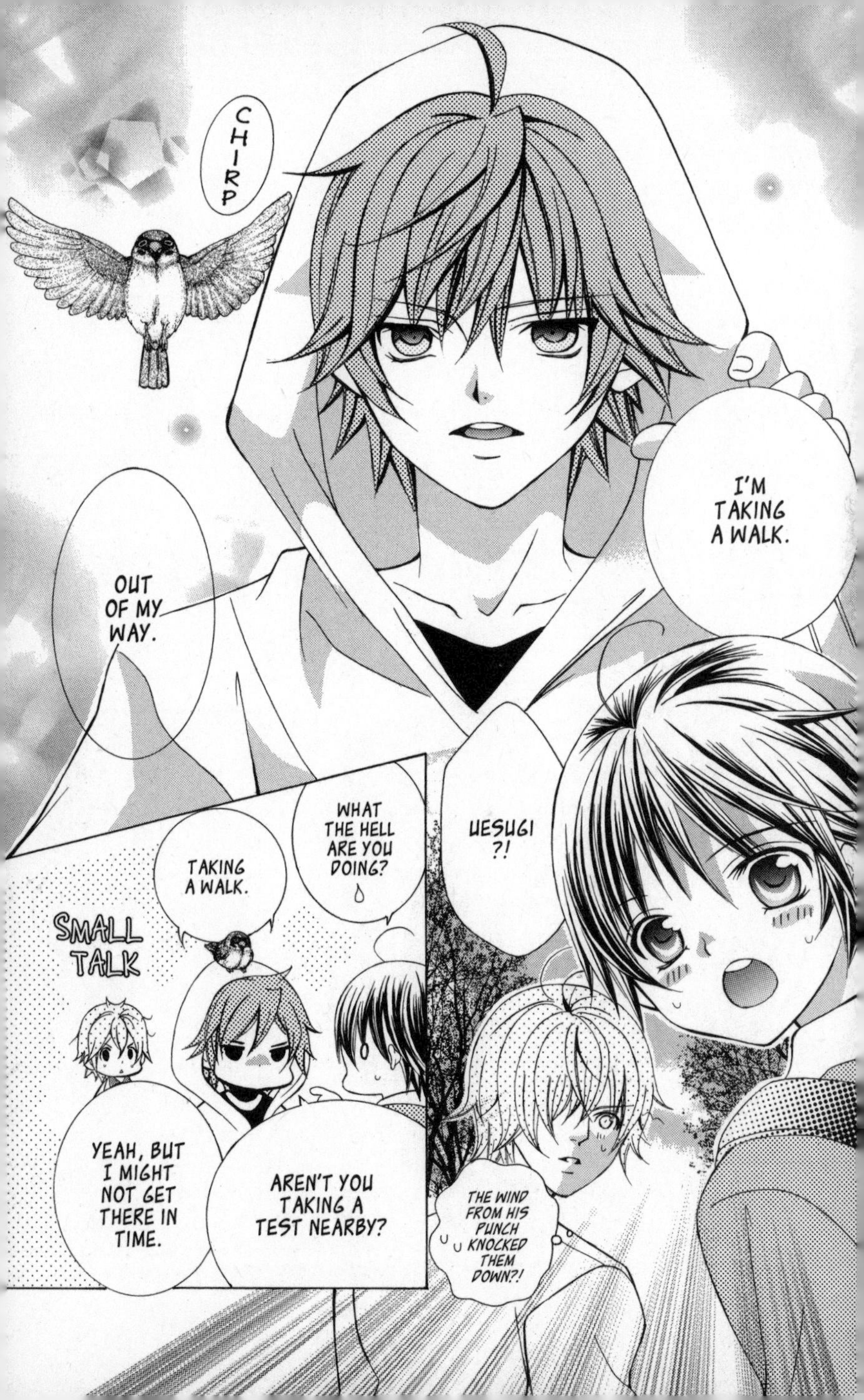
CHIRP
I'M TAKING A WALK.
OUT OF MY WAY.
UESUGI?!
THE WIND FROM HIS PUNCH KNOCKED THEM DOWN?!
WHAT THE HELL ARE YOU DOING?
TAKING A WALK.
SMALL TALK
AREN'T YOU TAKING A TEST NEARBY?
YEAH, BUT I MIGHT NOT GET THERE IN TIME.

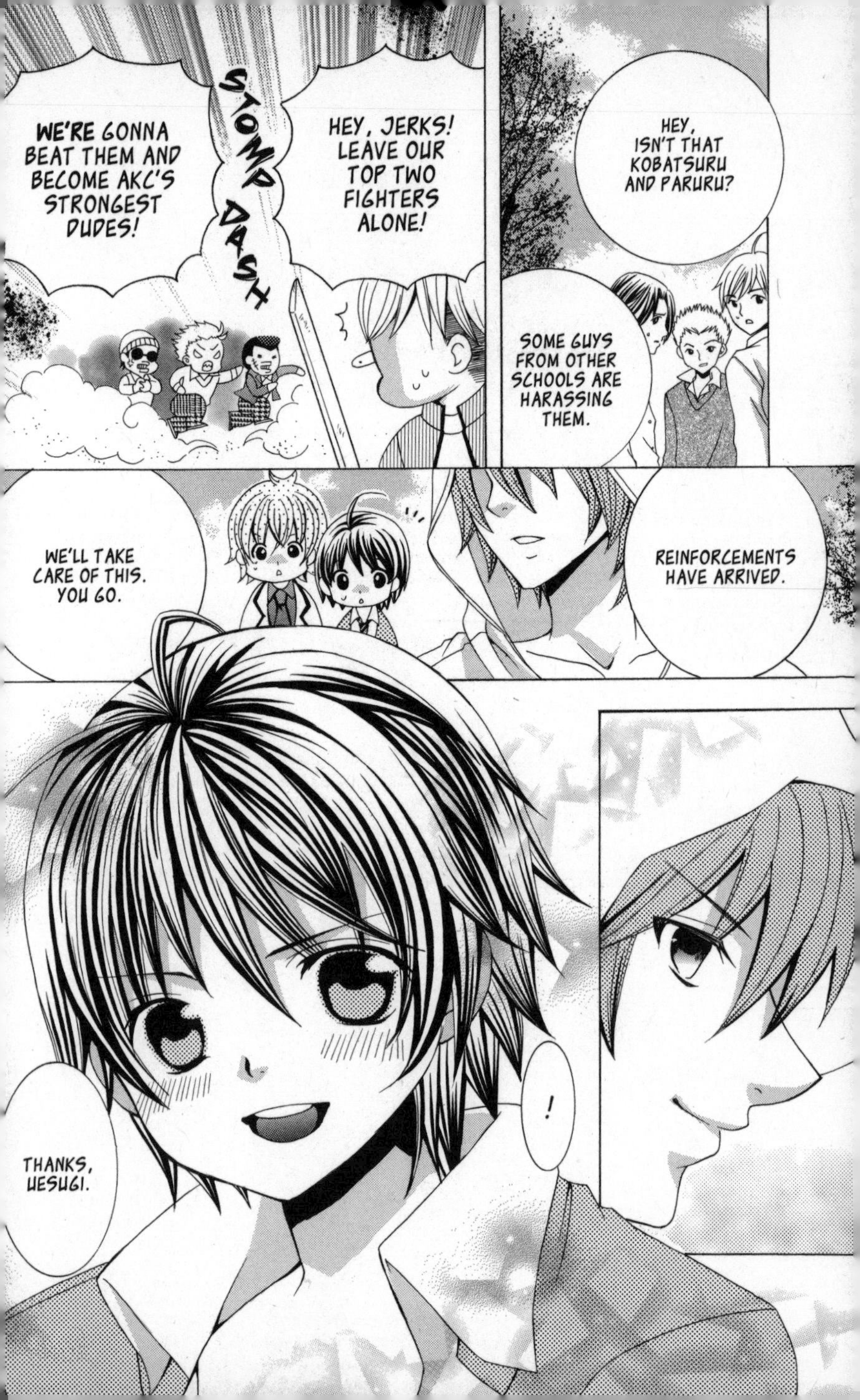
HEY, ISN'T THAT KOBATSURU AND PARURU?
SOME GUYS FROM OTHER SCHOOLS ARE HARASSING THEM.
HEY, JERKS! LEAVE OUR TOP TWO FIGHTERS ALONE!
STOMP DASH
WE'RE GONNA BEAT THEM AND BECOME AKC'S STRONGEST DUDES!
REINFORCEMENTS HAVE ARRIVED.
WE'LL TAKE CARE OF THIS. YOU GO.
!
THANKS, UESUGI.

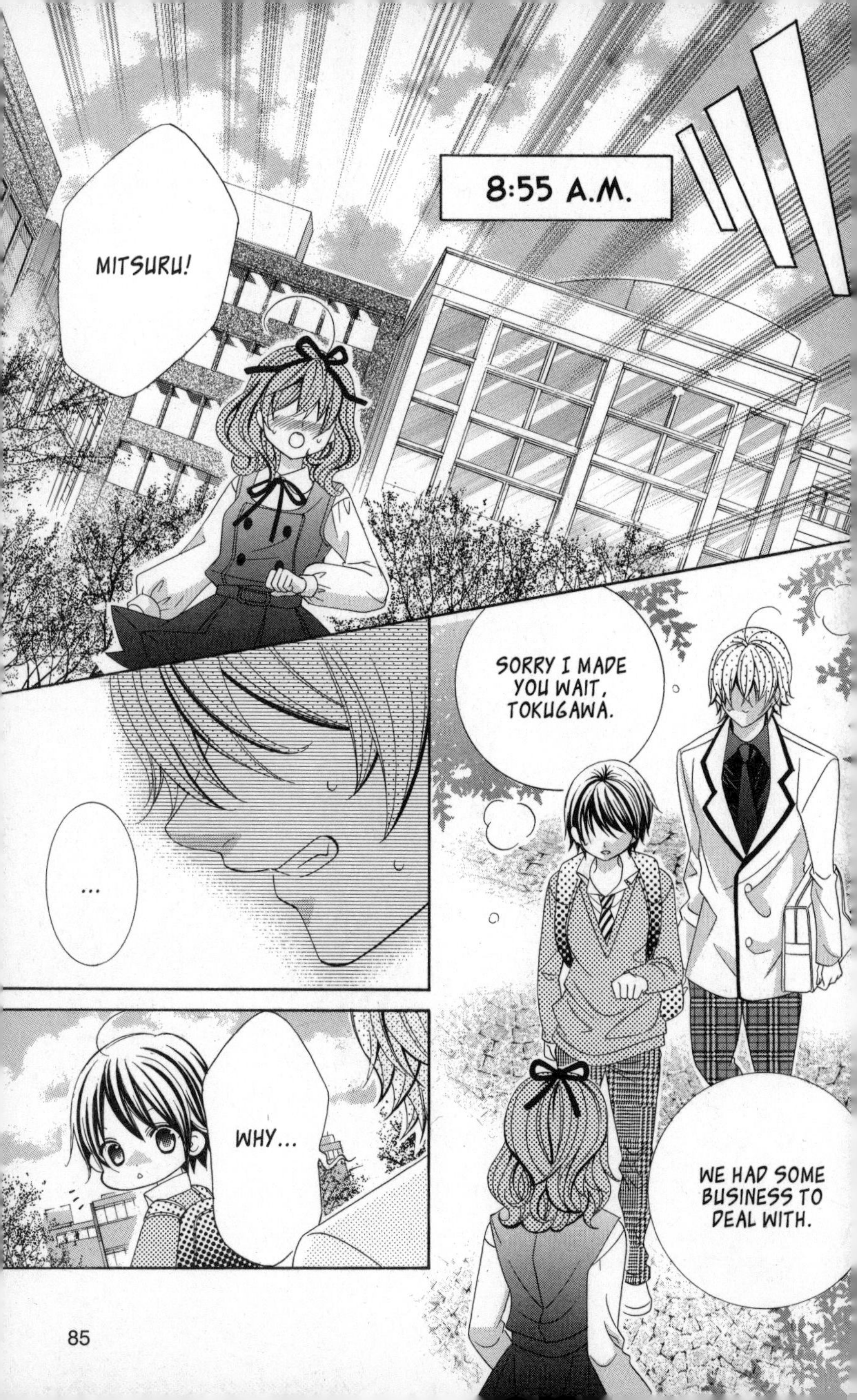
8:55 A.M.
MITSURU!
SORRY I MADE YOU WAIT, TOKUGAWA.
WE HAD SOME BUSINESS TO DEAL WITH.
...
WHY...

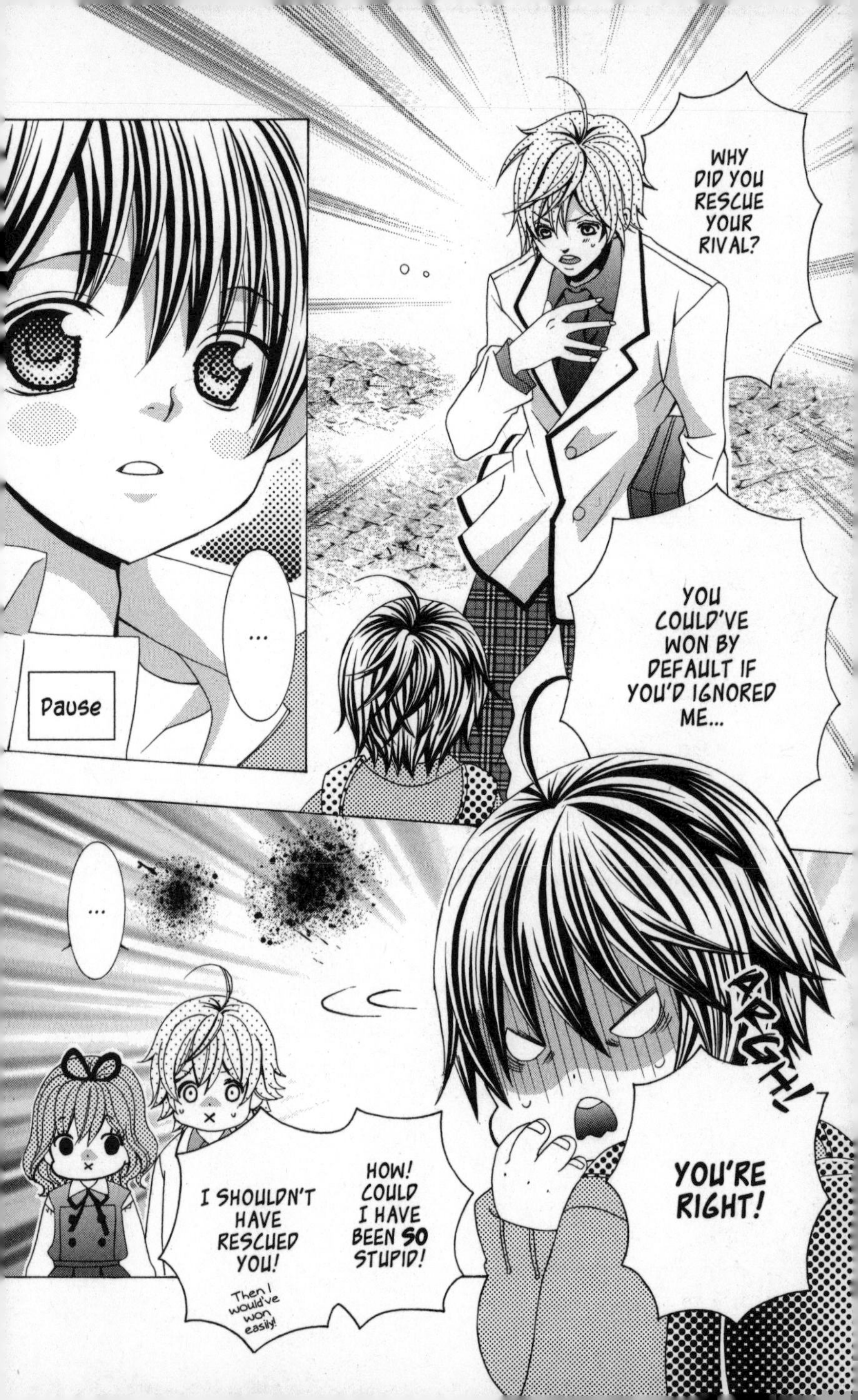
WHY DID YOU RESCUE YOUR RIVAL?
YOU COULD'VE WON BY DEFAULT IF YOU'D IGNORED ME...
...
Pause
ARGH!
YOU'RE RIGHT!
HOW! COULD I HAVE BEEN **SO** STUPID!
I SHOULDN'T HAVE RESCUED YOU!
Then I would've won easily!
...

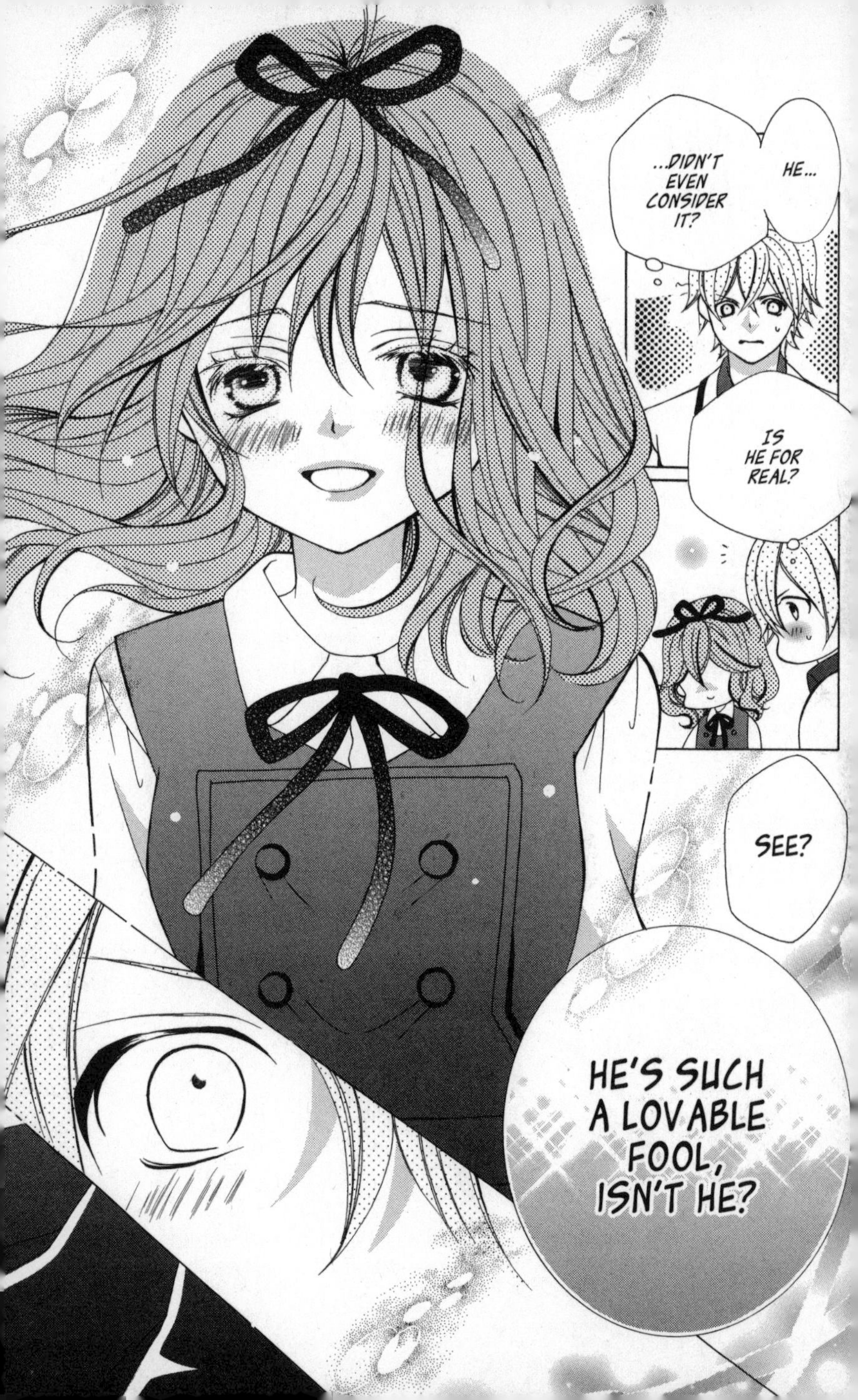
HE...
...DIDN'T EVEN CONSIDER IT?
IS HE FOR REAL?
SEE?
HE'S SUCH A LOVABLE FOOL, ISN'T HE?

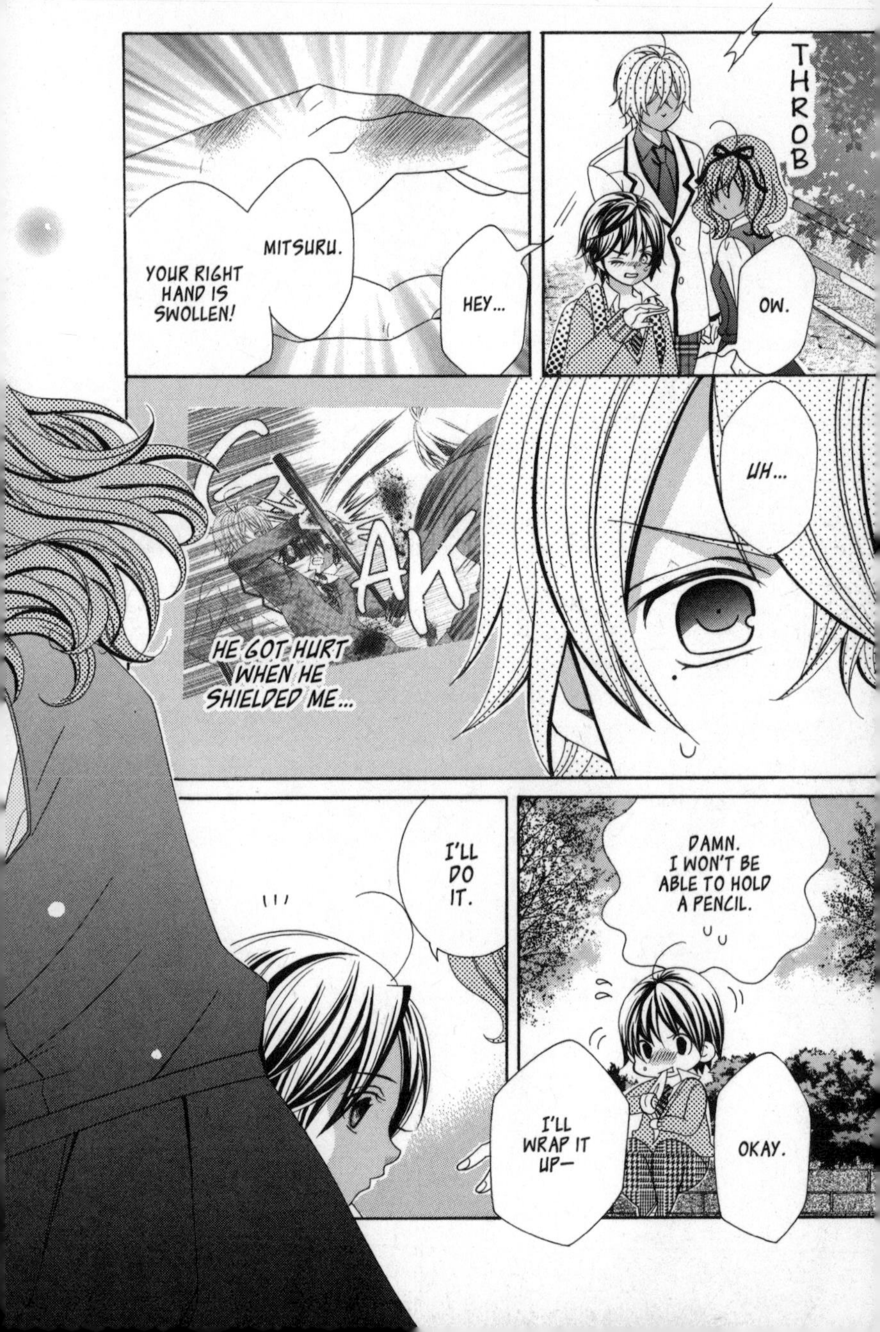
THROB
OW.
HEY...
MITSURU.
YOUR RIGHT HAND IS SWOLLEN!
UH...
AK
HE GOT HURT WHEN HE SHIELDED ME...
DAMN. I WON'T BE ABLE TO HOLD A PENCIL.
OKAY.
I'LL WRAP IT UP—
I'LL DO IT.

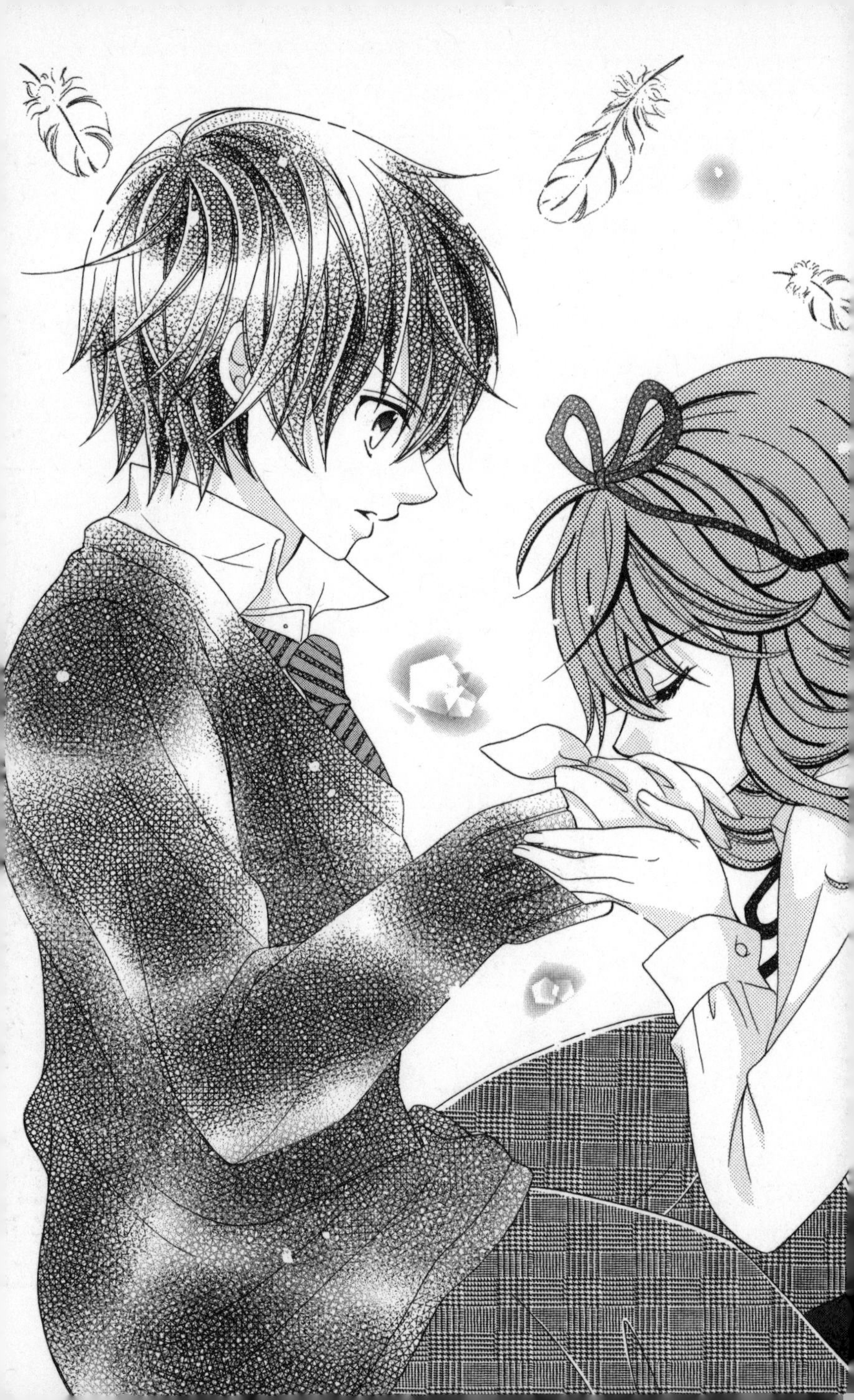

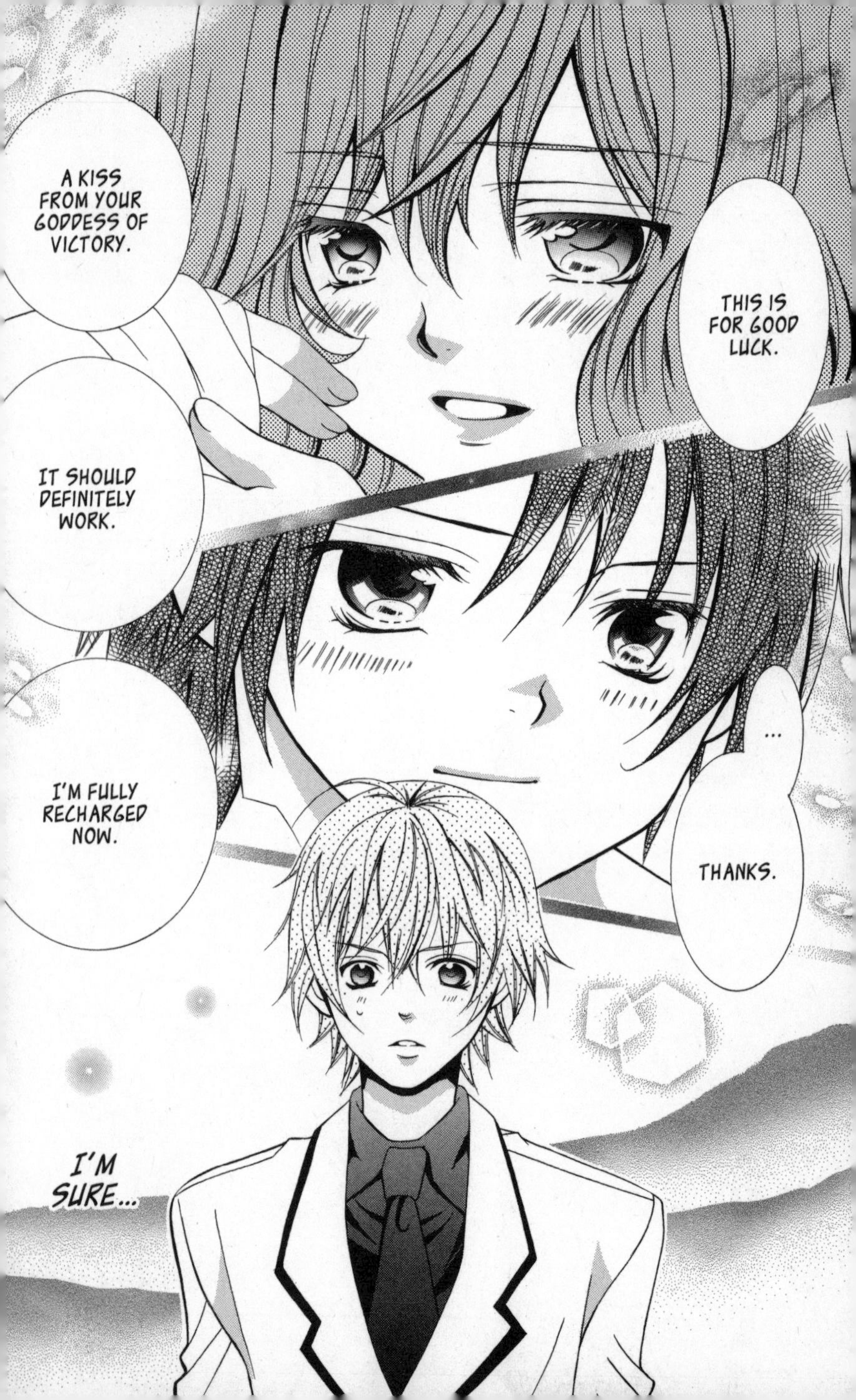
THIS IS FOR GOOD LUCK.
A KISS FROM YOUR GODDESS OF VICTORY.
IT SHOULD DEFINITELY WORK.
...
THANKS.
I'M FULLY RECHARGED NOW.
I'M SURE...

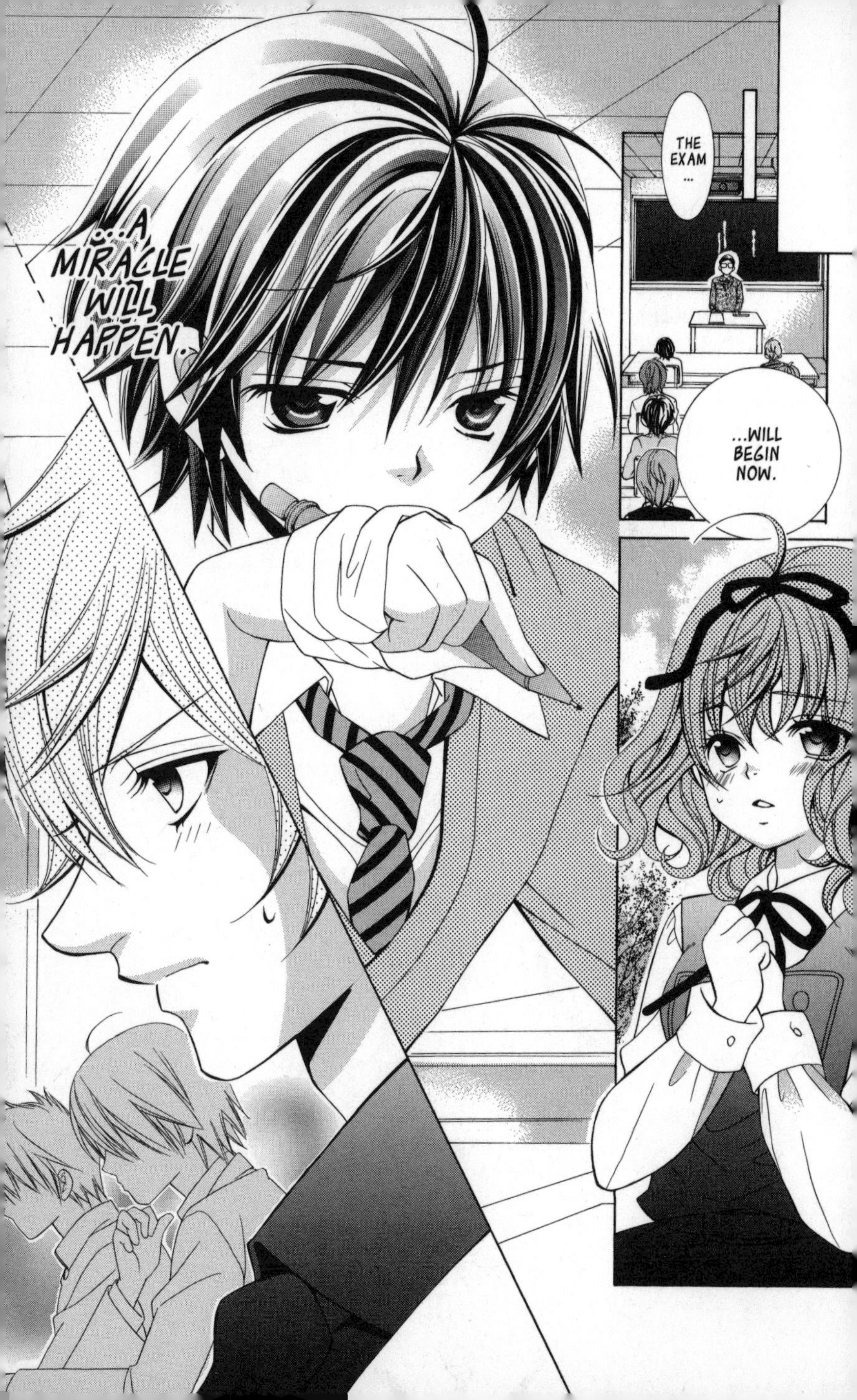
THE EXAM...
...WILL BEGIN NOW.
...A MIRACLE WILL HAPPEN.

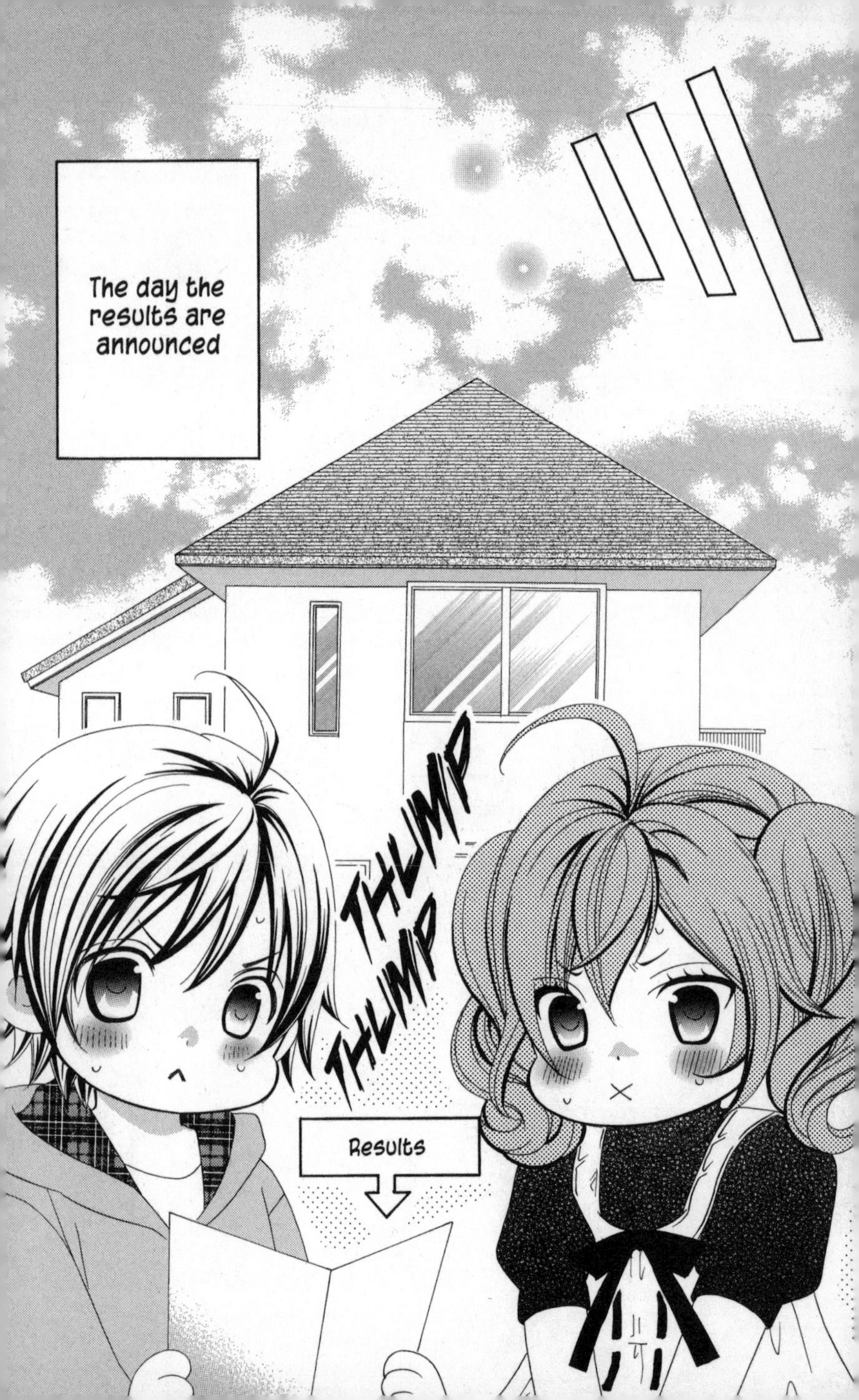
The day the results are announced
THUMP THUMP
Results

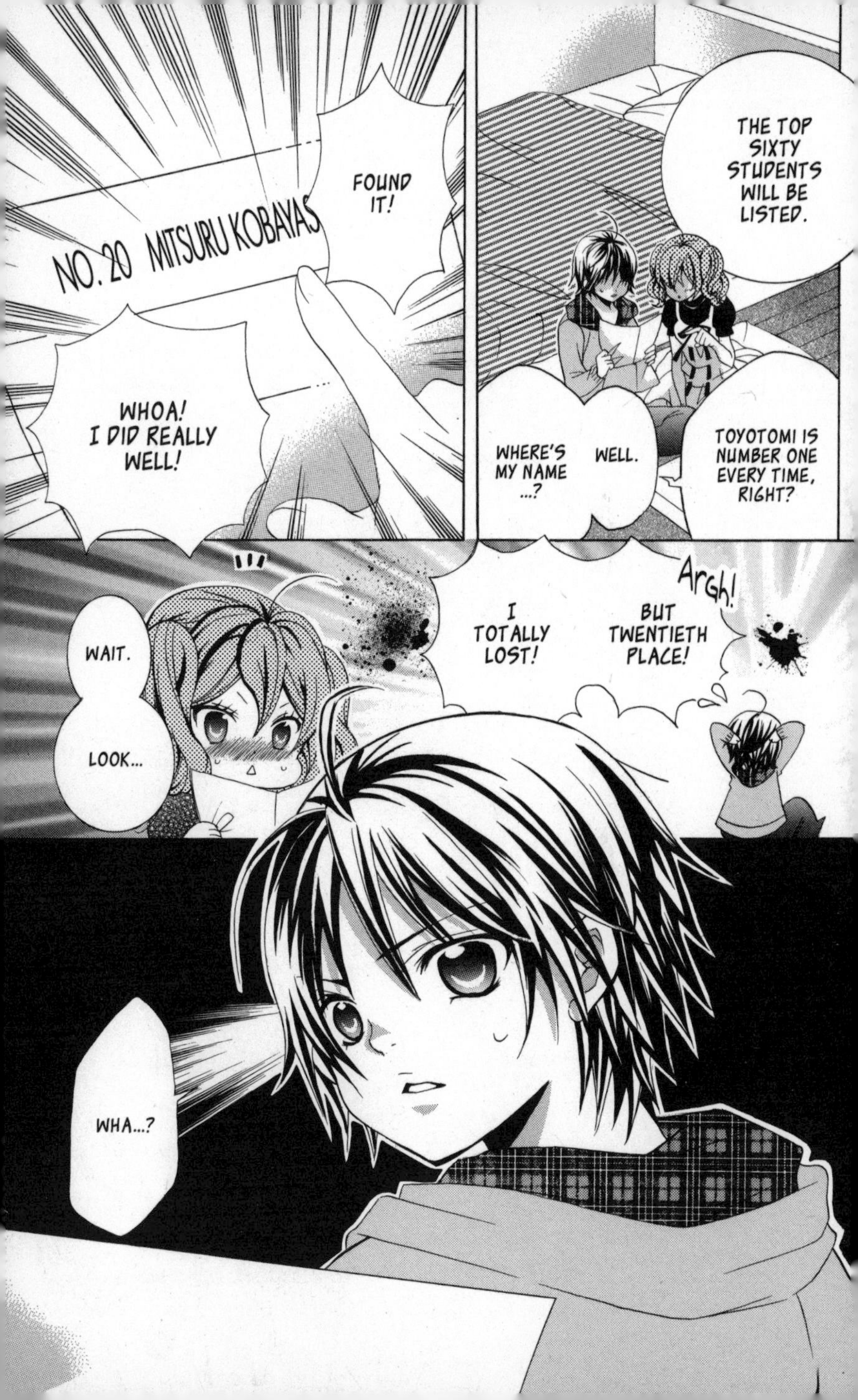
THE TOP SIXTY STUDENTS WILL BE LISTED.
TOYOTOMI IS NUMBER ONE EVERY TIME, RIGHT?
WELL.
WHERE'S MY NAME ...?
FOUND IT!
NO. 20 MITSURU KOBAYAS
WHOA! I DID REALLY WELL!
Argh!
BUT TWENTIETH PLACE!
I TOTALLY LOST!
WAIT.
LOOK...
WHA...?

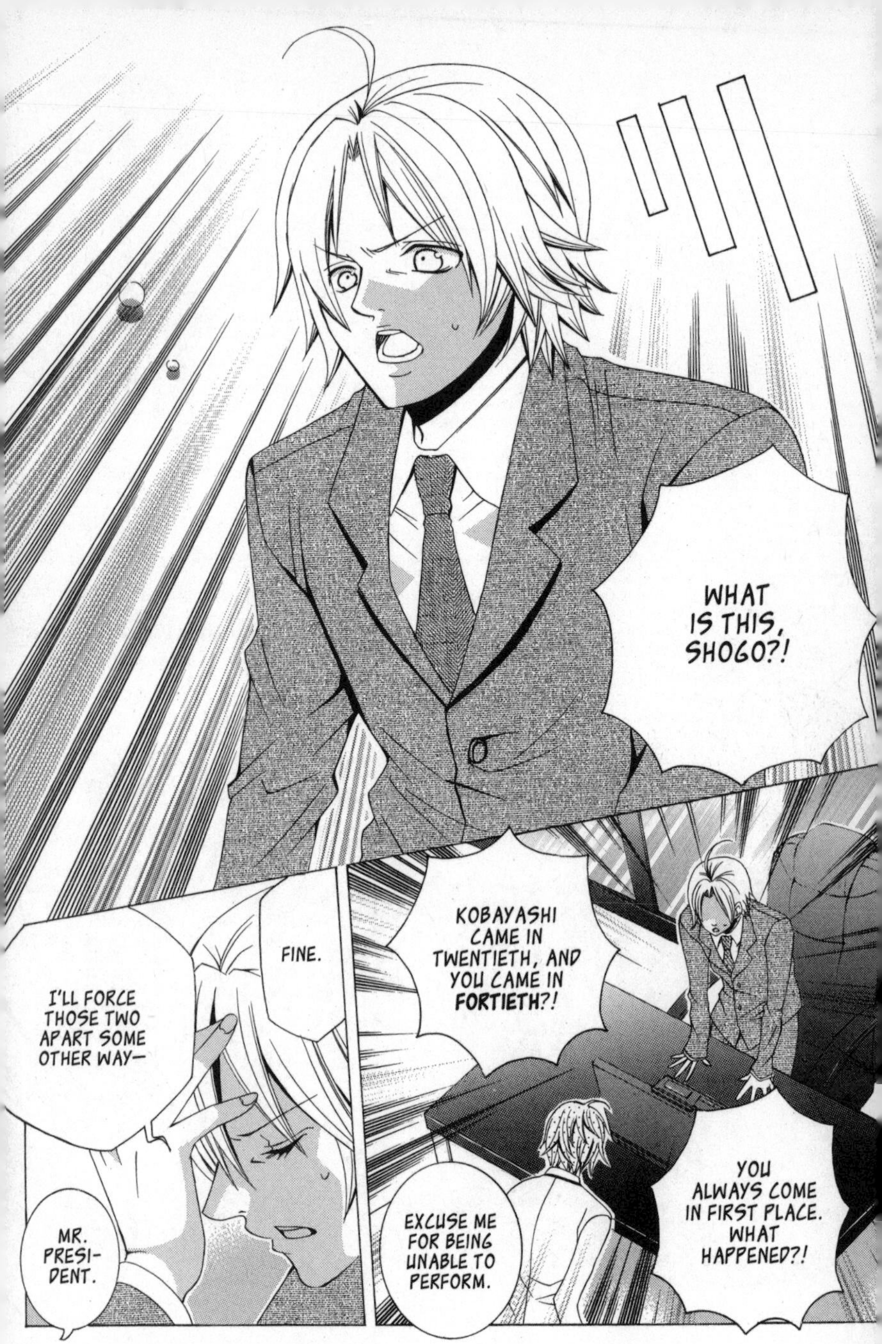
WHAT IS THIS, SHOGO?!
KOBAYASHI CAME IN TWENTIETH, AND YOU CAME IN **FORTIETH**?!
YOU ALWAYS COME IN FIRST PLACE. WHAT HAPPENED?!
EXCUSE ME FOR BEING UNABLE TO PERFORM.
FINE.
I'LL FORCE THOSE TWO APART SOME OTHER WAY—
MR. PRESIDENT.

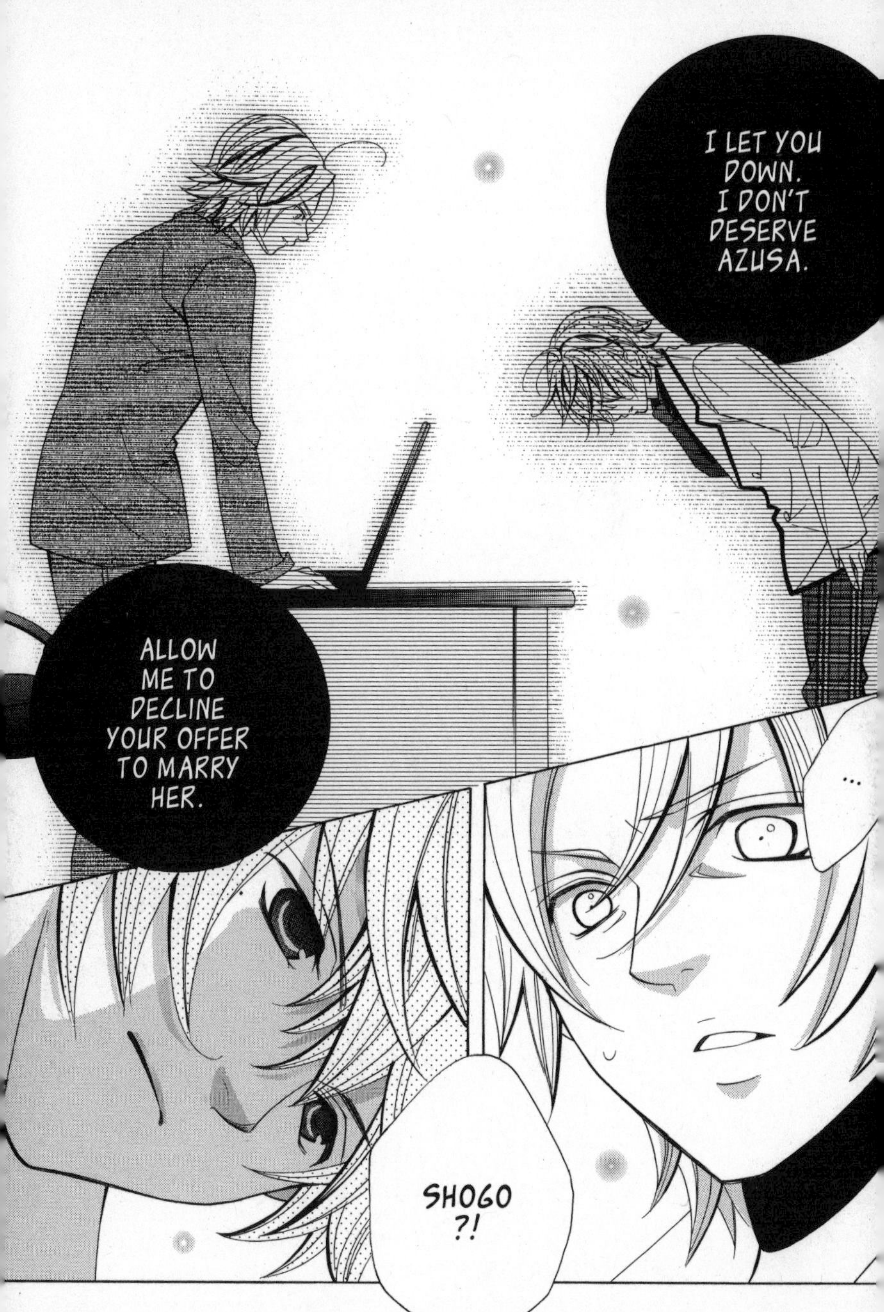
I LET YOU DOWN. I DON'T DESERVE AZUSA.
ALLOW ME TO DECLINE YOUR OFFER TO MARRY HER.
...
SHOGO ?!

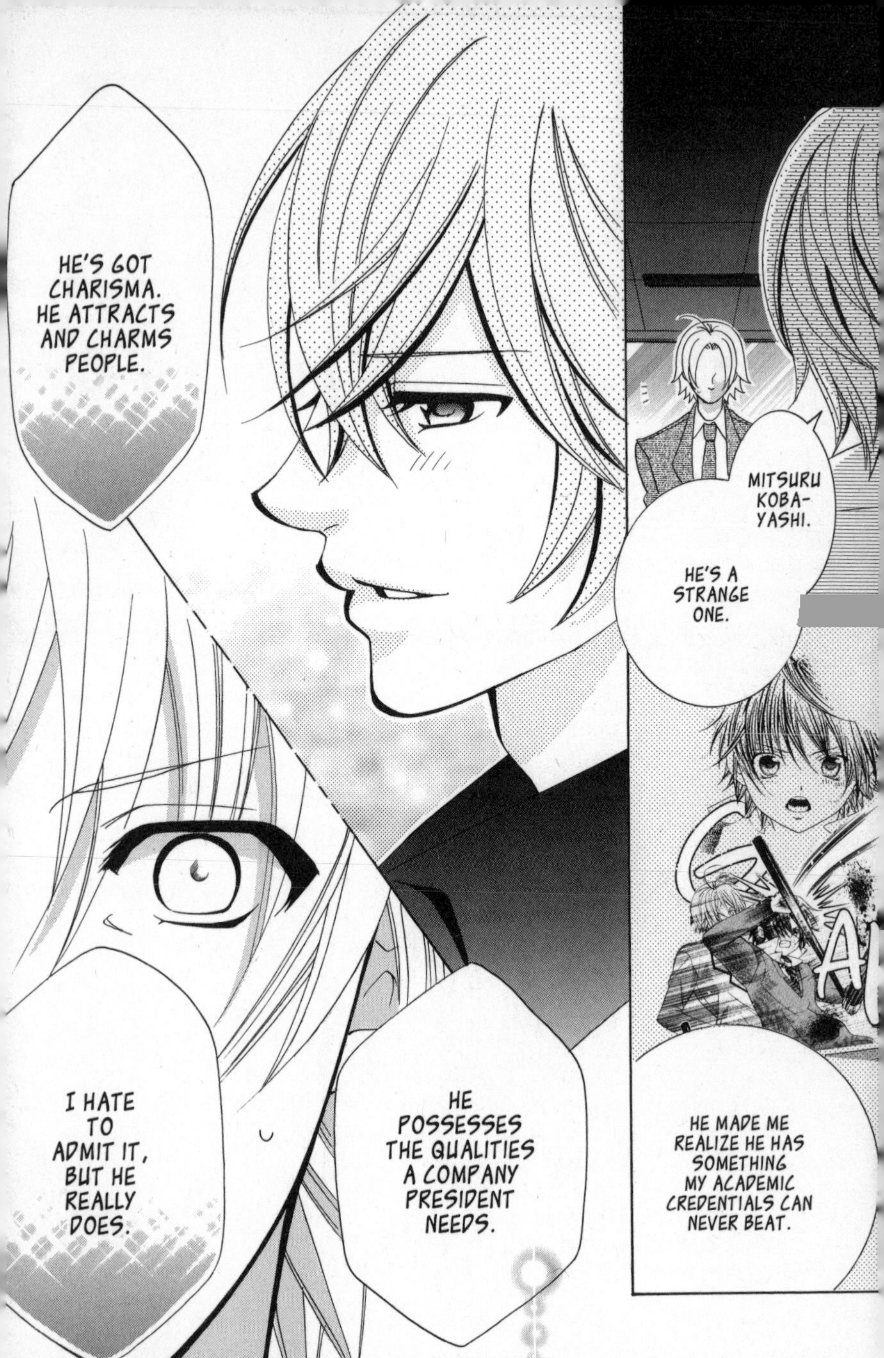
MITSURU KOBA-YASHI.
HE'S A STRANGE ONE.
HE MADE ME REALIZE HE HAS SOMETHING MY ACADEMIC CREDENTIALS CAN NEVER BEAT.
HE'S GOT CHARISMA. HE ATTRACTS AND CHARMS PEOPLE.
HE POSSESSES THE QUALITIES A COMPANY PRESIDENT NEEDS.
I HATE TO ADMIT IT, BUT HE REALLY DOES.

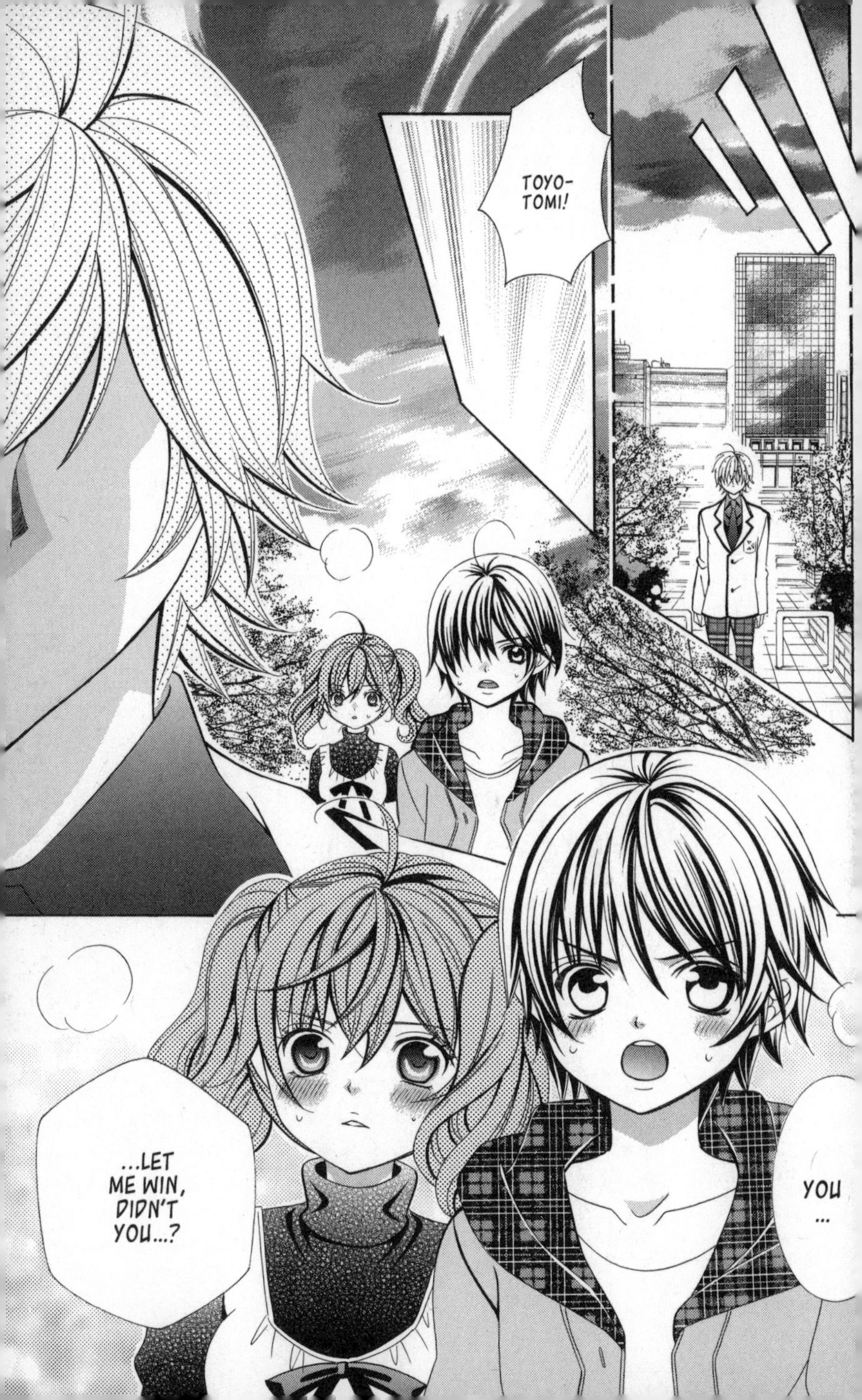
TOYO-TOMI!
YOU ...
...LET ME WIN, DIDN'T YOU...?

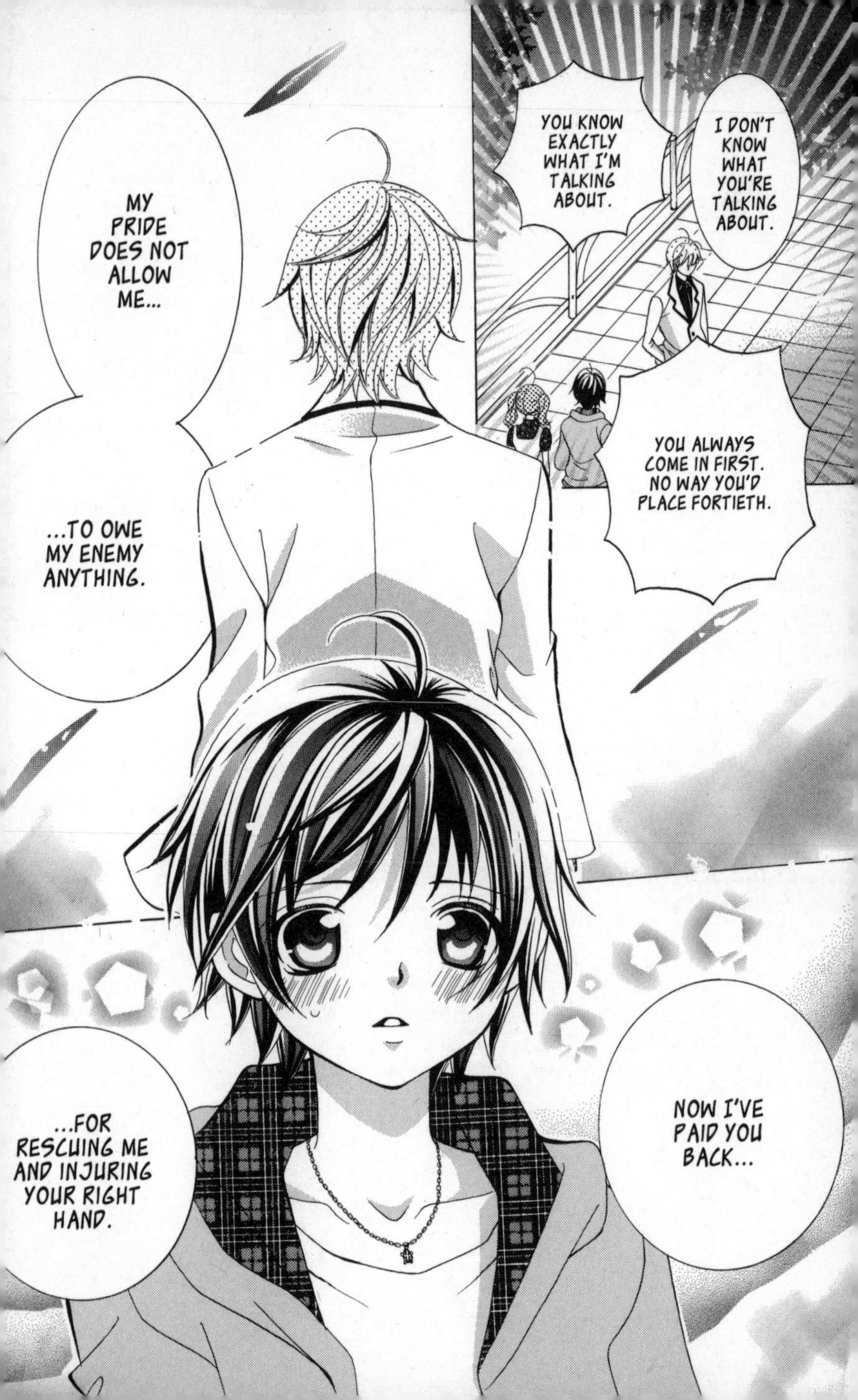
I DON'T KNOW WHAT YOU'RE TALKING ABOUT.
YOU KNOW EXACTLY WHAT I'M TALKING ABOUT.
YOU ALWAYS COME IN FIRST. NO WAY YOU'D PLACE FORTIETH.
MY PRIDE DOES NOT ALLOW ME...
...TO OWE MY ENEMY ANYTHING.
NOW I'VE PAID YOU BACK...
...FOR RESCUING ME AND INJURING YOUR RIGHT HAND.

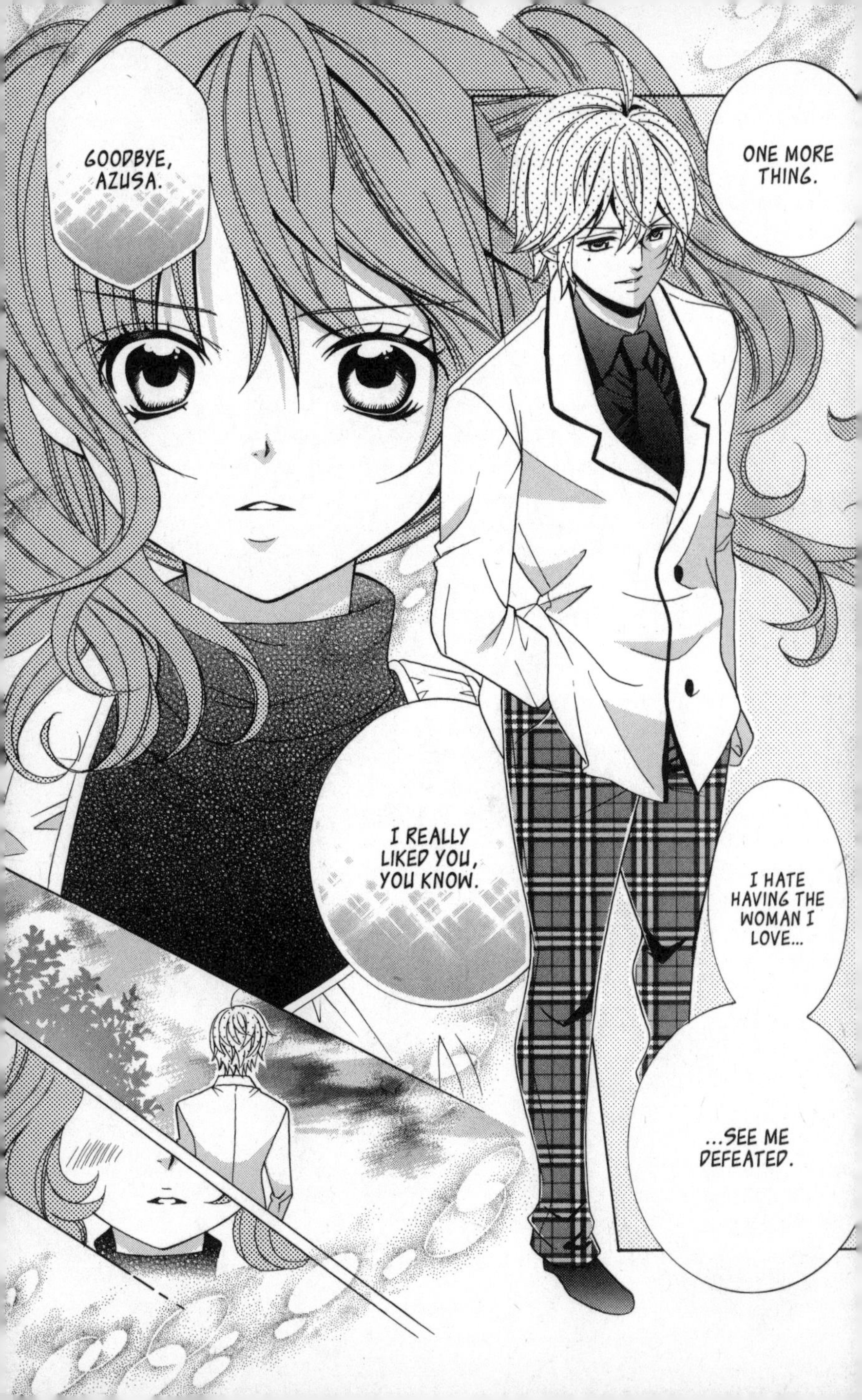
ONE MORE THING.
I HATE HAVING THE WOMAN I LOVE...
...SEE ME DEFEATED.
GOODBYE, AZUSA.
I REALLY LIKED YOU, YOU KNOW.

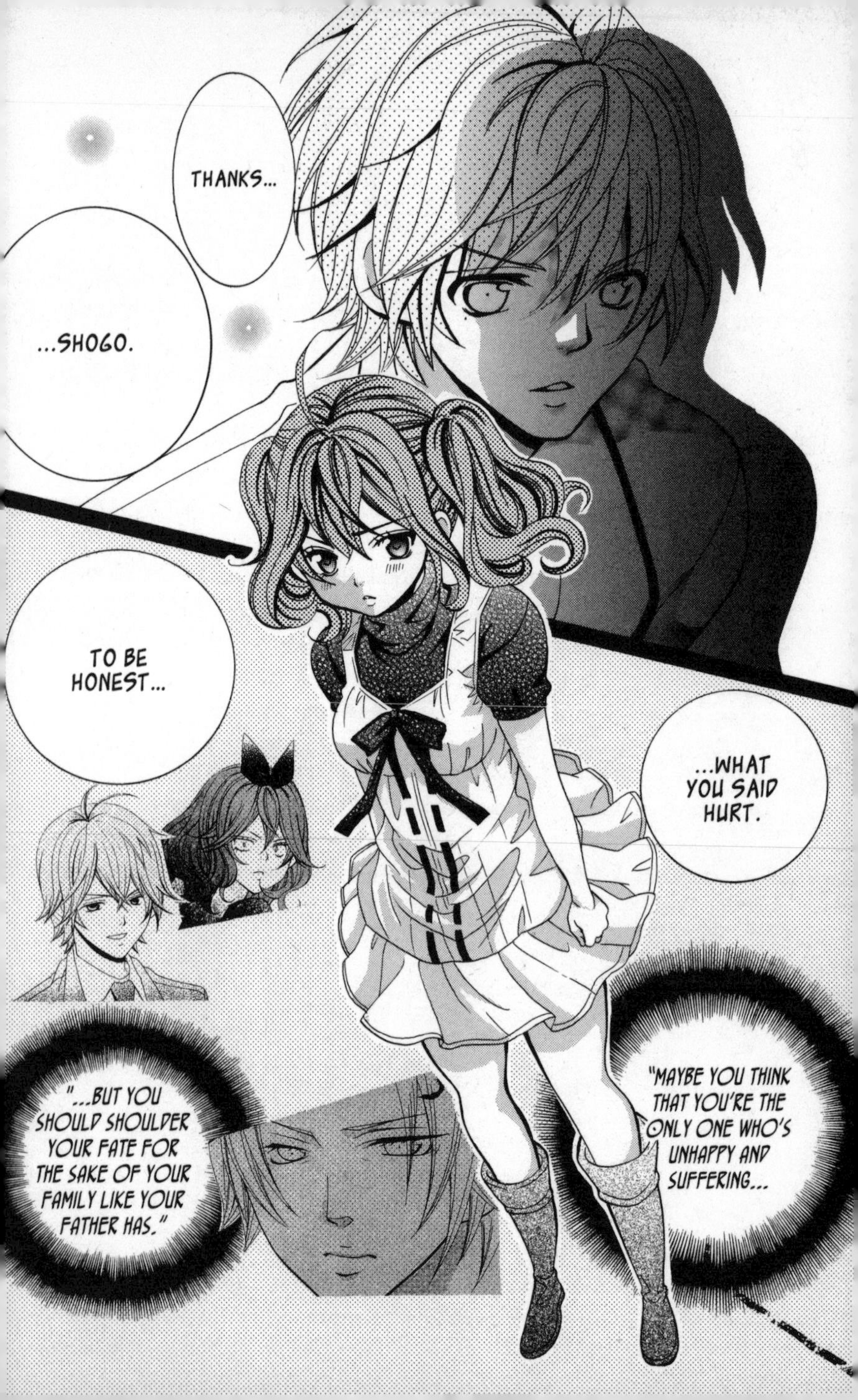
THANKS...
...SHOGO.
TO BE HONEST...
...WHAT YOU SAID HURT.
"MAYBE YOU THINK THAT YOU'RE THE ONLY ONE WHO'S UNHAPPY AND SUFFERING...
"...BUT YOU SHOULD SHOULDER YOUR FATE FOR THE SAKE OF YOUR FAMILY LIKE YOUR FATHER HAS."

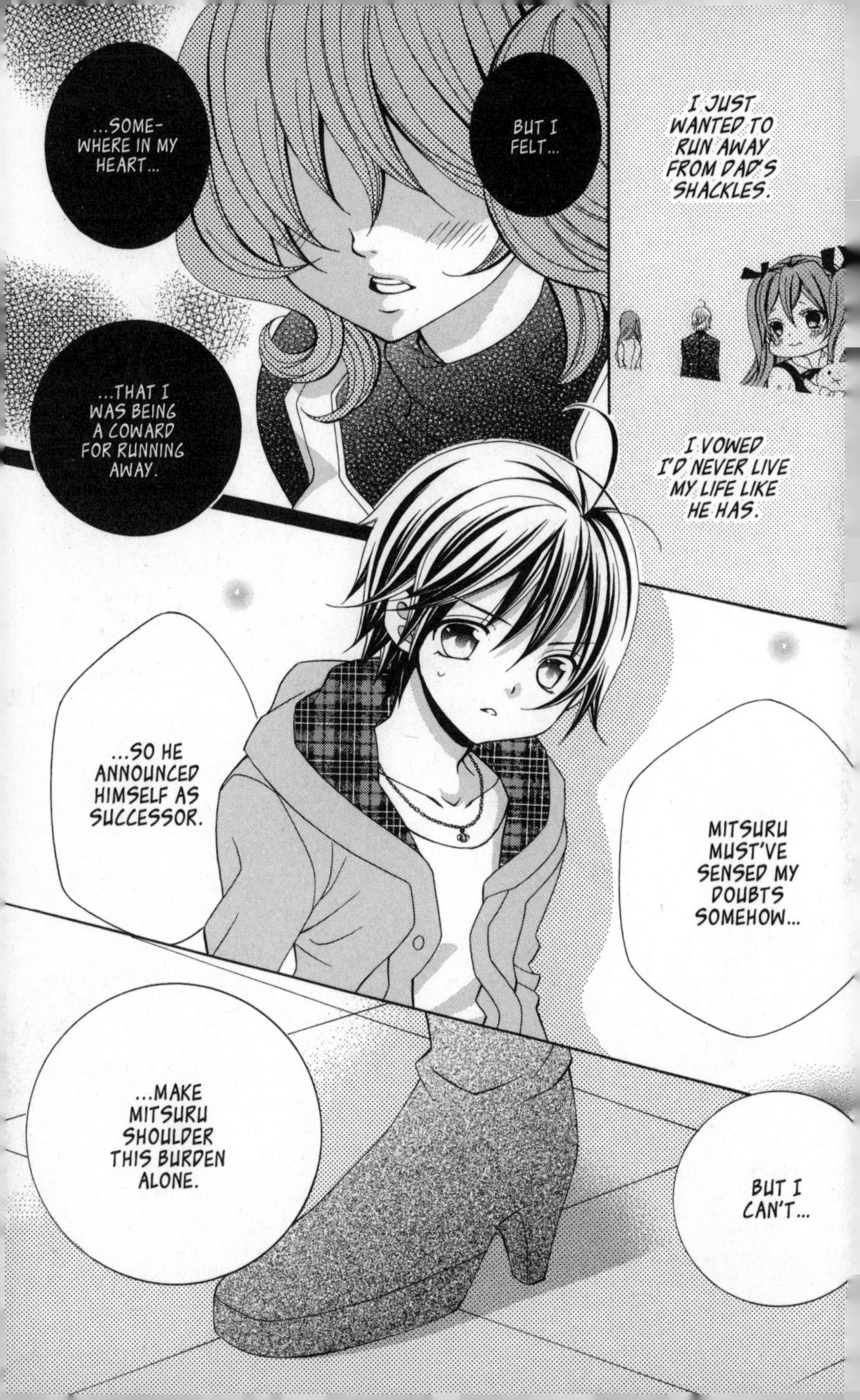
I JUST WANTED TO RUN AWAY FROM DAD'S SHACKLES.
I VOWED I'D NEVER LIVE MY LIFE LIKE HE HAS.
BUT I FELT...
...SOME-WHERE IN MY HEART...
...THAT I WAS BEING A COWARD FOR RUNNING AWAY.
MITSURU MUST'VE SENSED MY DOUBTS SOMEHOW...
...SO HE ANNOUNCED HIMSELF AS SUCCESSOR.
BUT I CAN'T...
...MAKE MITSURU SHOULDER THIS BURDEN ALONE.

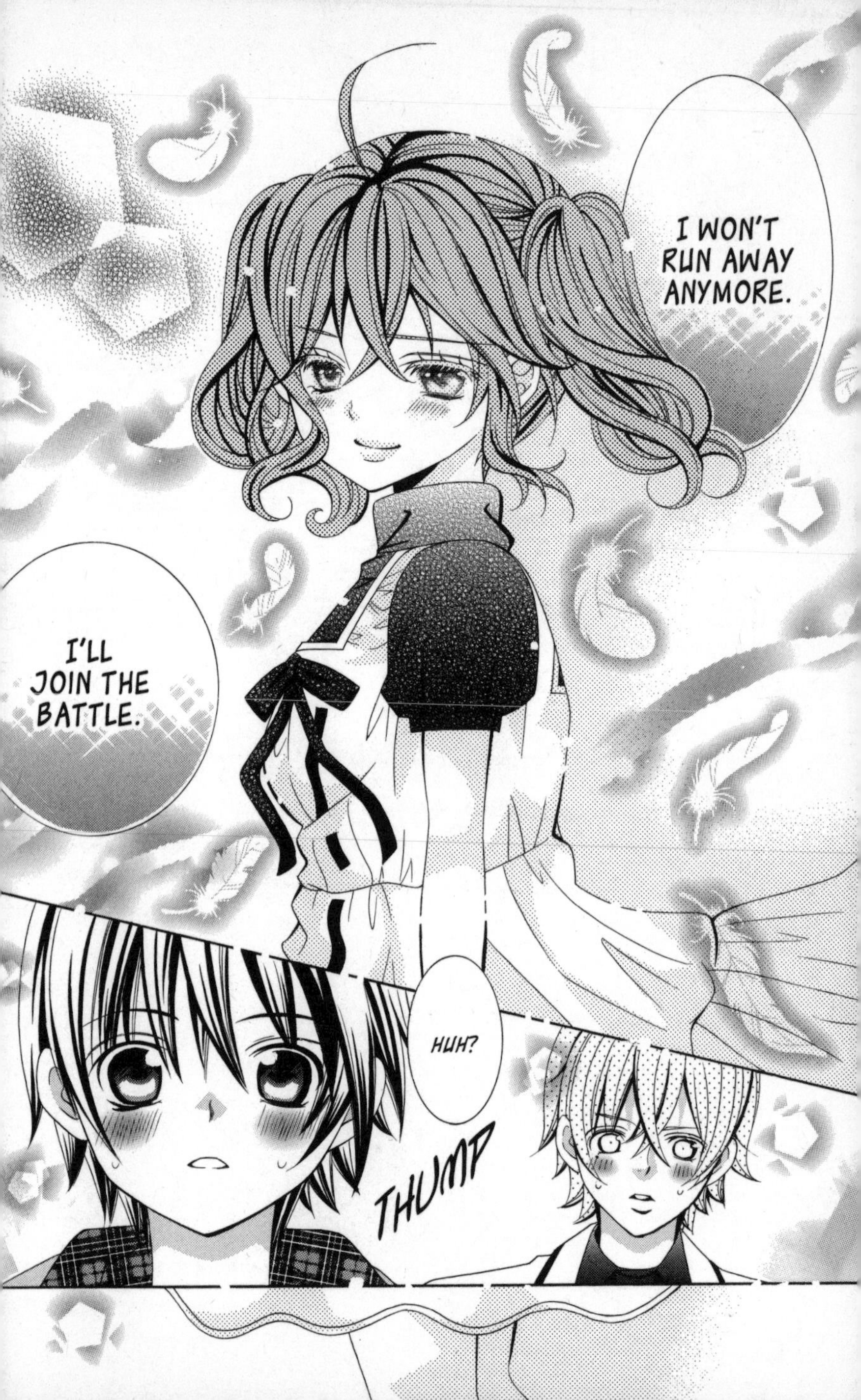
I WON'T RUN AWAY ANYMORE.
I'LL JOIN THE BATTLE.
HUH?
THUMP

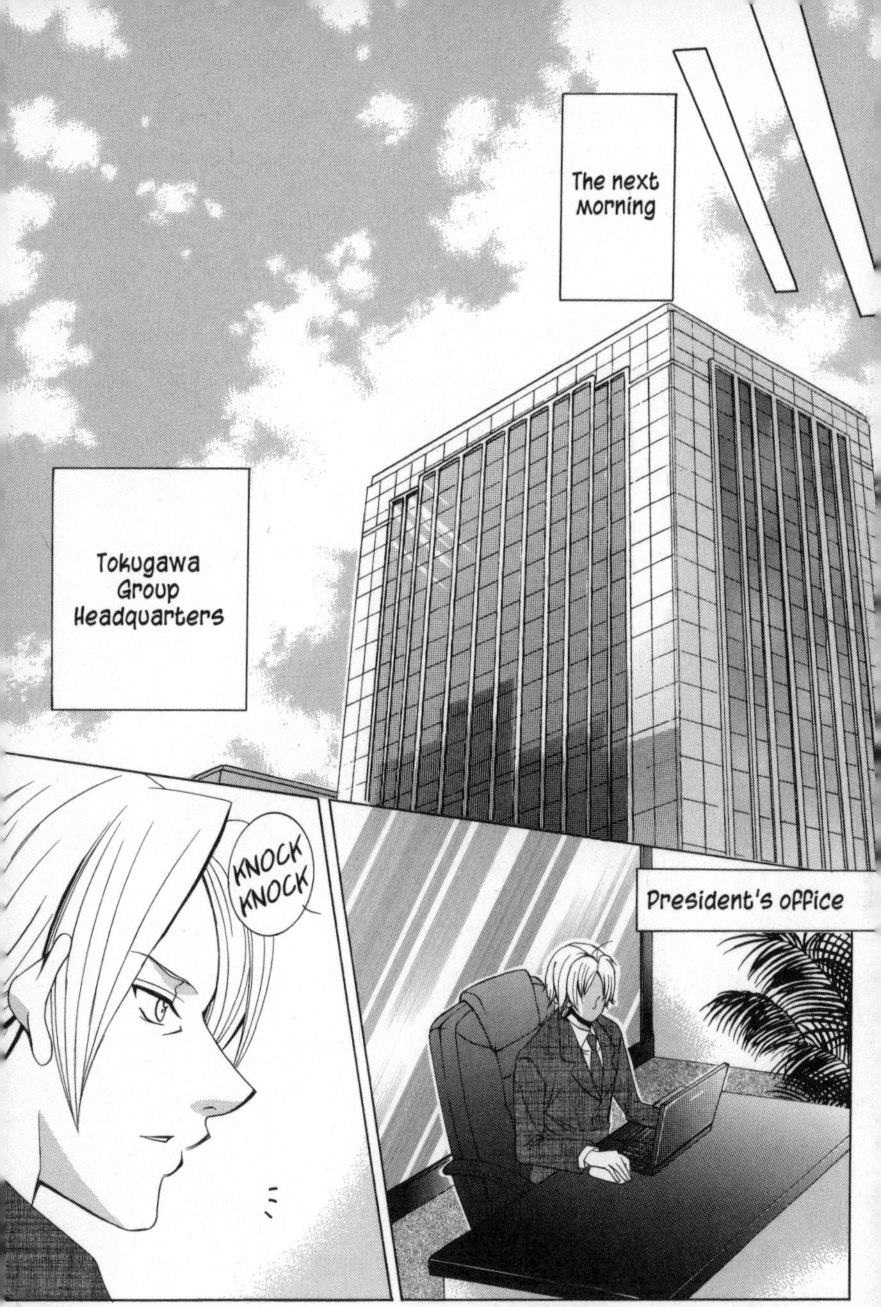
The next Morning
Tokugawa Group Headquarters
President's office
KNOCK KNOCK

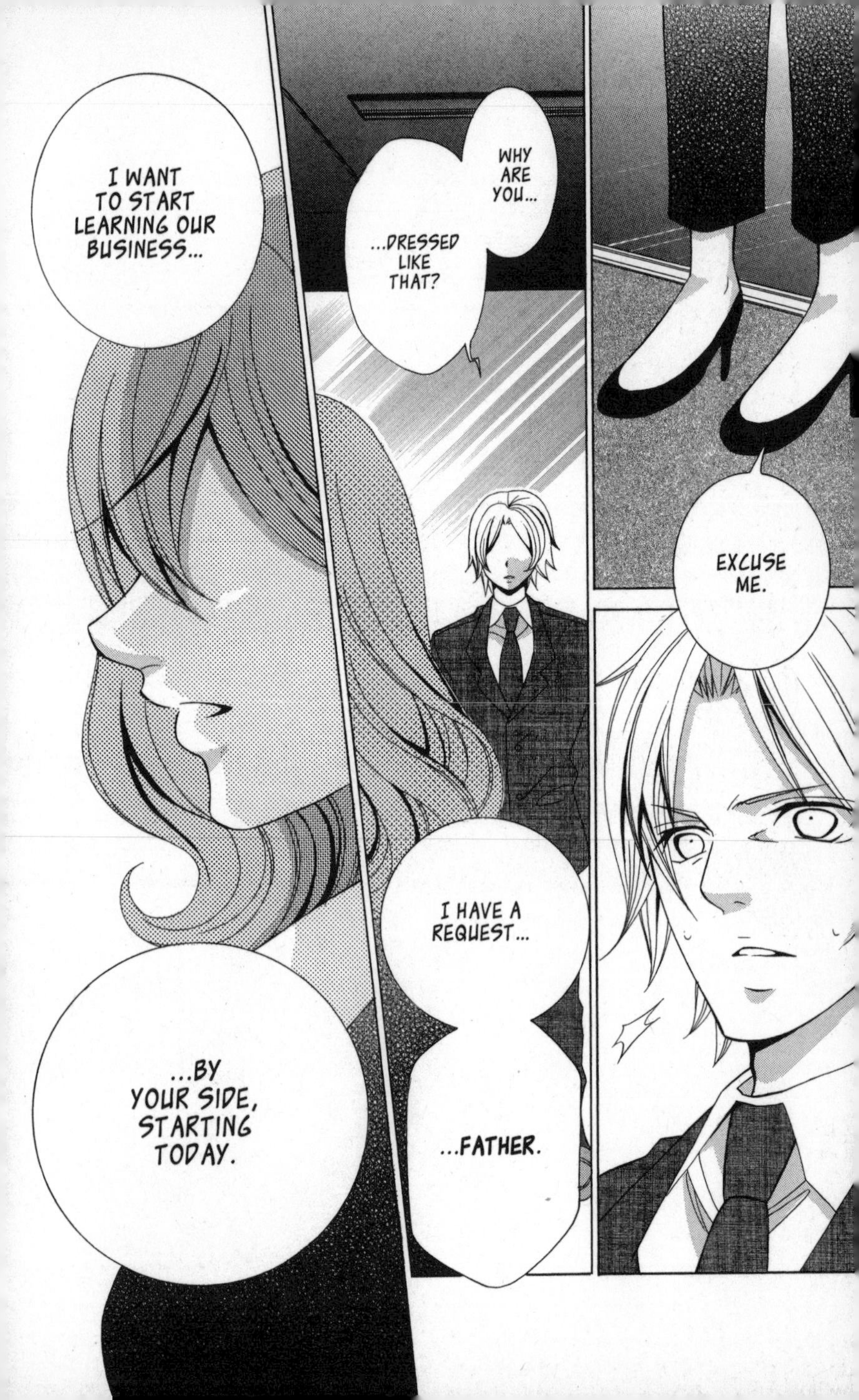

EXCUSE ME.
WHY ARE YOU...
...DRESSED LIKE THAT?
I HAVE A REQUEST...
...FATHER.
I WANT TO START LEARNING OUR BUSINESS...
...BY YOUR SIDE, STARTING TODAY.

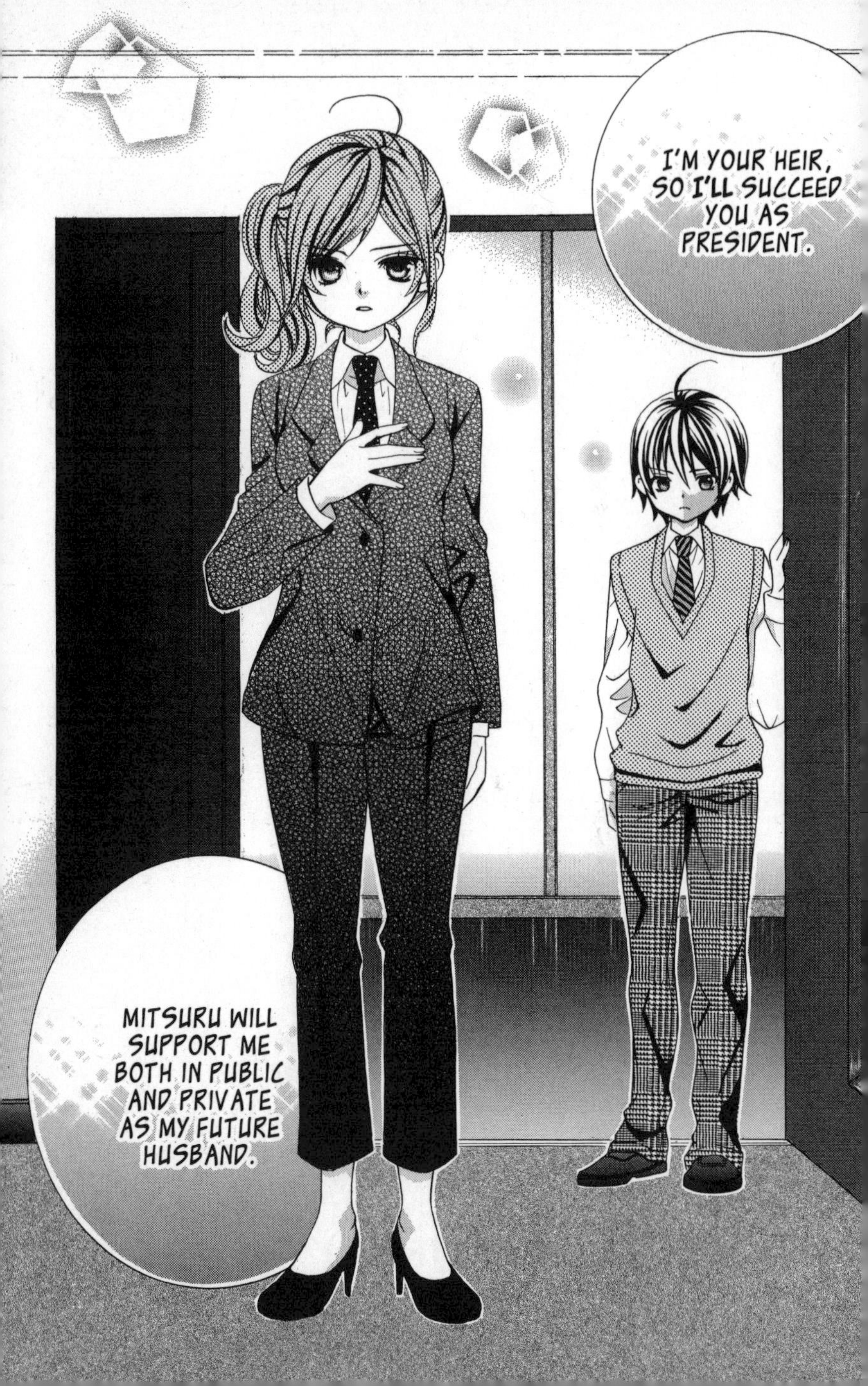
I'M YOUR HEIR, SO I'LL SUCCEED YOU AS PRESIDENT.
MITSURU WILL SUPPORT ME BOTH IN PUBLIC AND PRIVATE AS MY FUTURE HUSBAND.

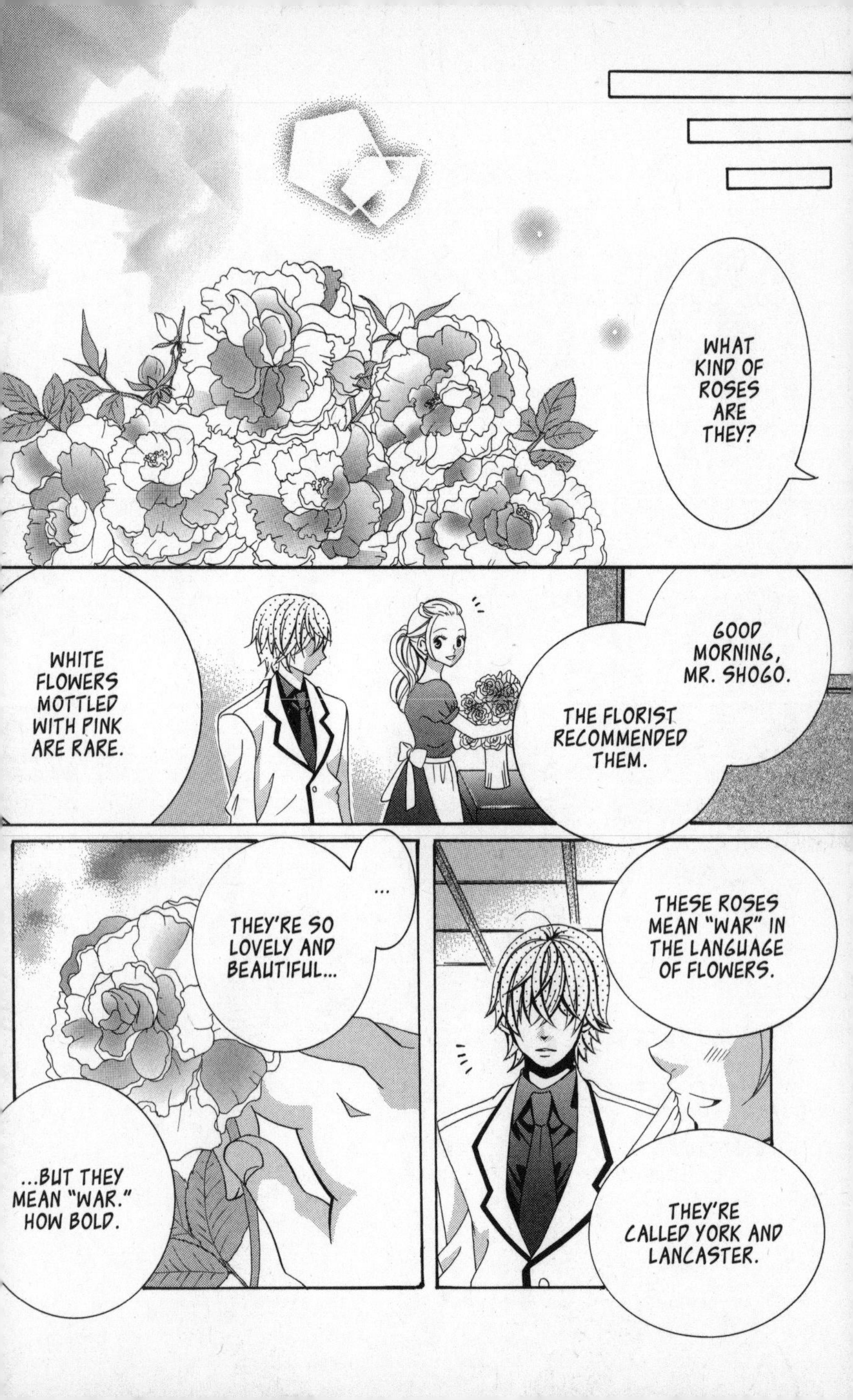
WHAT KIND OF ROSES ARE THEY?
GOOD MORNING, MR. SHOGO.
THE FLORIST RECOMMENDED THEM.
WHITE FLOWERS MOTTLED WITH PINK ARE RARE.
THESE ROSES MEAN "WAR" IN THE LANGUAGE OF FLOWERS.
THEY'RE CALLED YORK AND LANCASTER.
...
THEY'RE SO LOVELY AND BEAUTIFUL...
...BUT THEY MEAN "WAR." HOW BOLD.

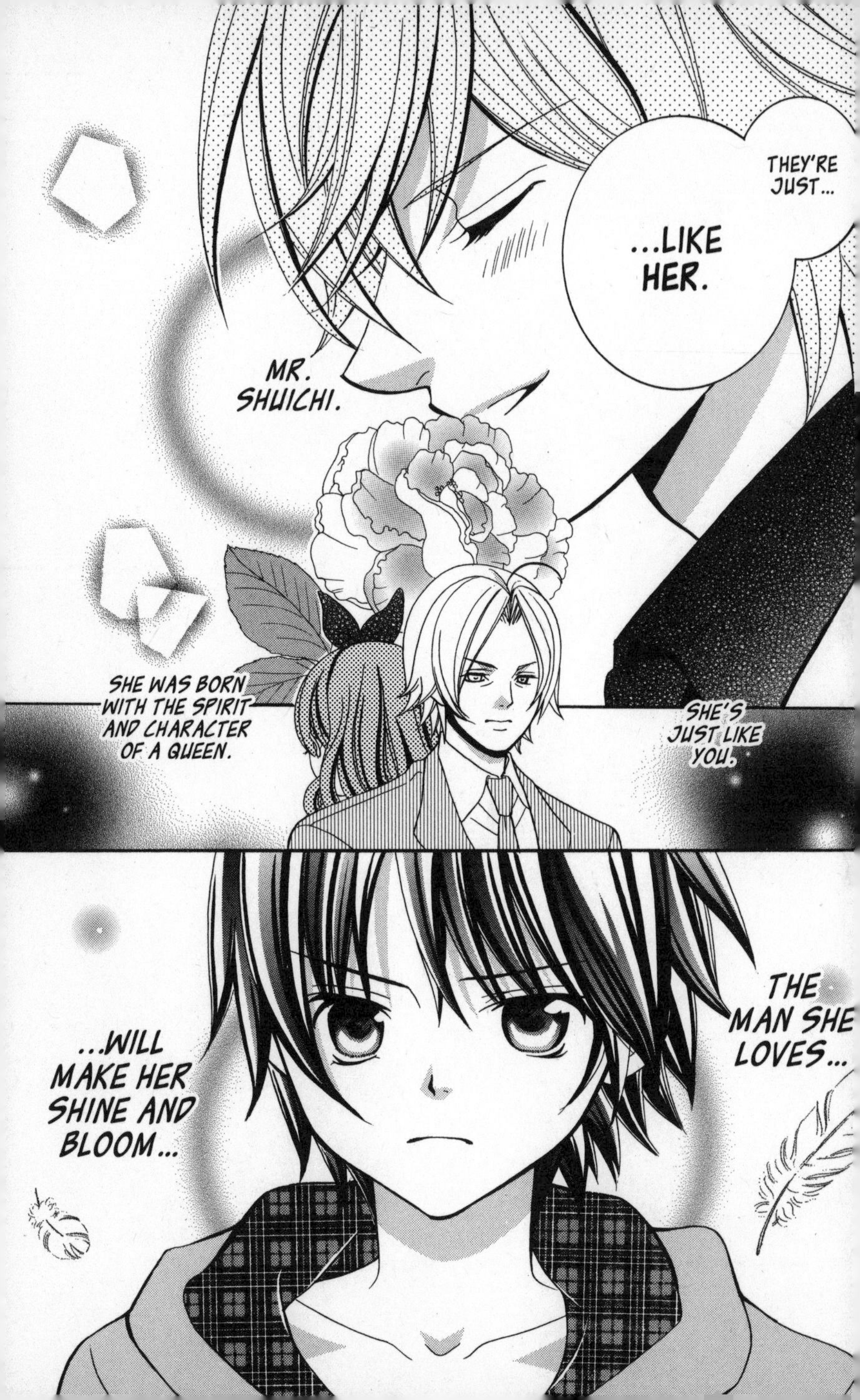
THEY'RE JUST...
...LIKE HER.
MR. SHUICHI.
SHE'S JUST LIKE YOU.
SHE WAS BORN WITH THE SPIRIT AND CHARACTER OF A QUEEN.
THE MAN SHE LOVES...
...WILL MAKE HER SHINE AND BLOOM...

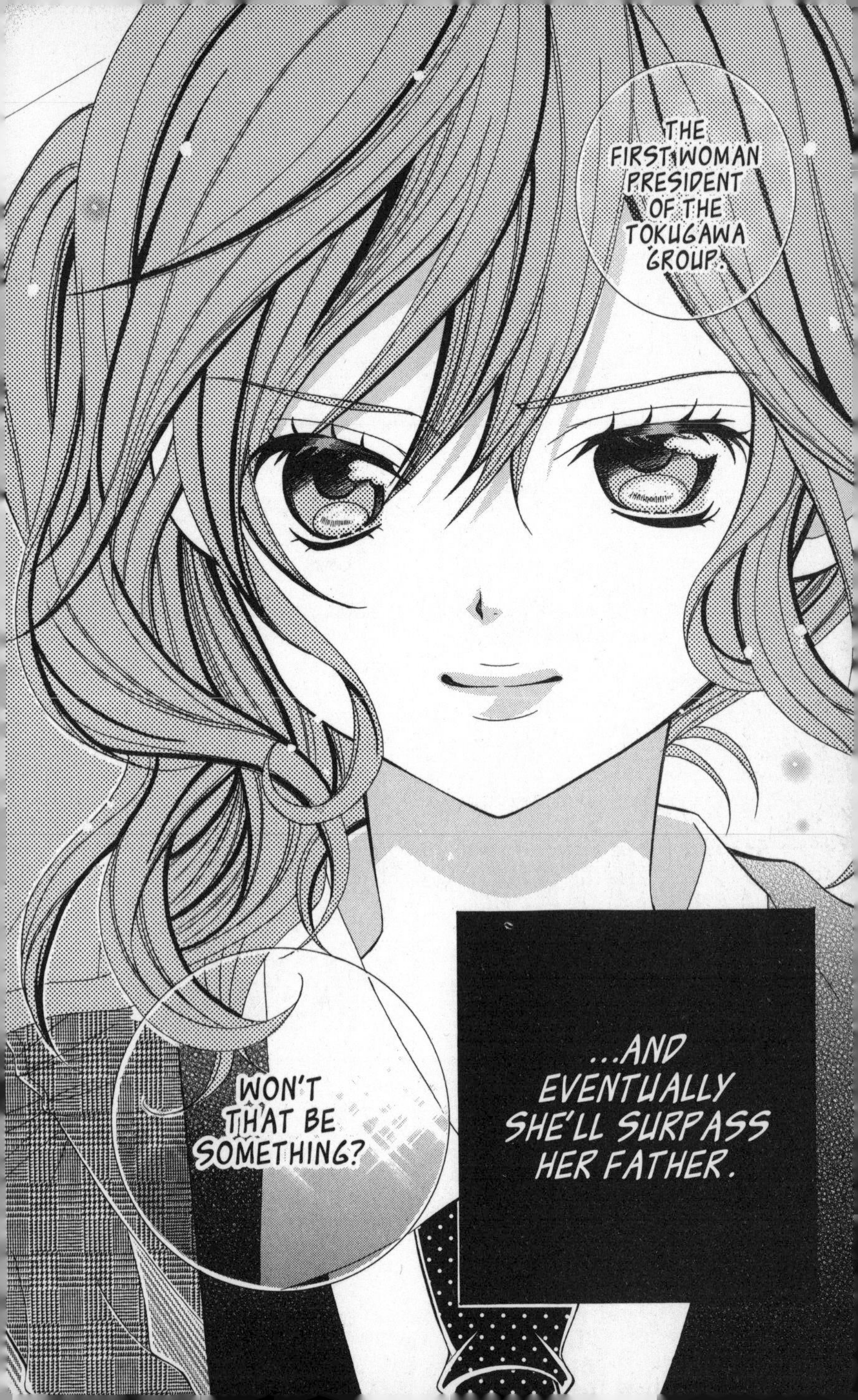
THE FIRST WOMAN PRESIDENT OF THE TOKUGAWA GROUP...
...AND EVENTUALLY SHE'LL SURPASS HER FATHER.
WON'T THAT BE SOMETHING?

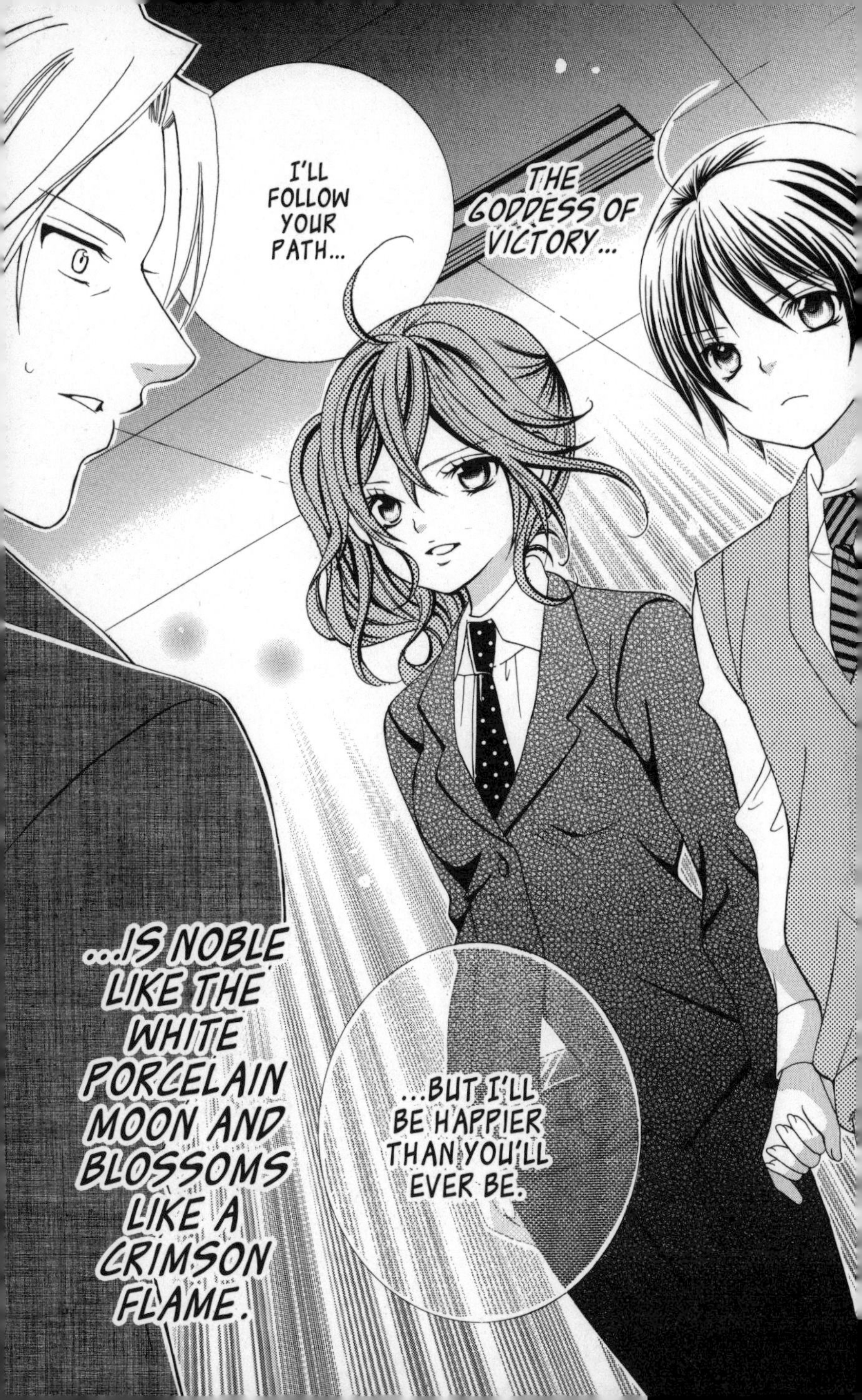
THE GODDESS OF VICTORY...
I'LL FOLLOW YOUR PATH...
...BUT I'LL BE HAPPIER THAN YOU'LL EVER BE.
...IS NOBLE LIKE THE WHITE PORCELAIN MOON AND BLOSSOMS LIKE A CRIMSON FLAME.

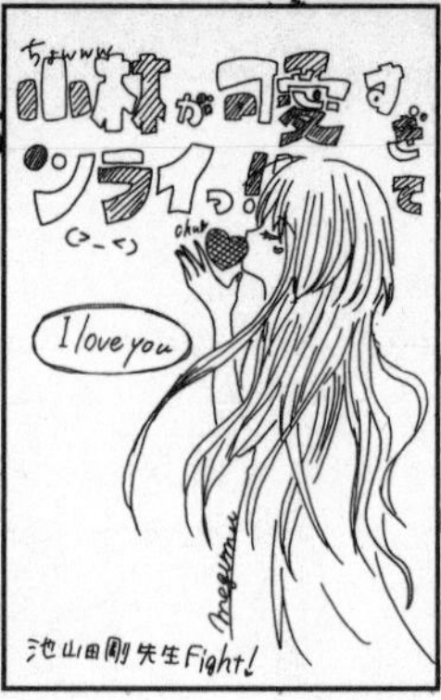
ちょwww
小林が可愛すぎてツライっ!!
(>_<)
I love you
池山田剛先生Fight!

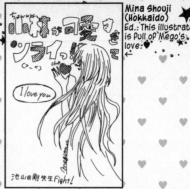

Mina Shouji (Hokkaido)
Ed.: This illustration is full of Mego's love. ♥
←

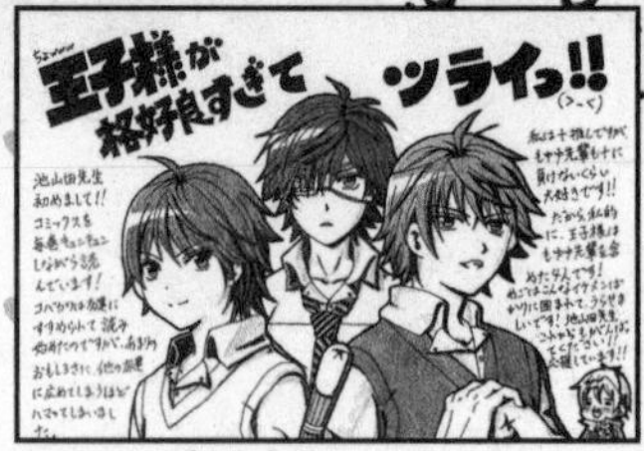
王子様が格好良すぎてツライっ!!
(>_<)

Anime ota (Gifu) ↑
Ed.: Moyuyu's here too!!

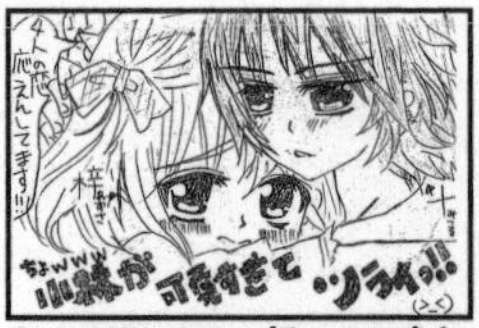
ちょwww 小林が可愛すぎてツライっ!!
(>_<)

Fuumi Kitahara (Fukuoka) ↑
Ed.: You can't help rooting for their love...

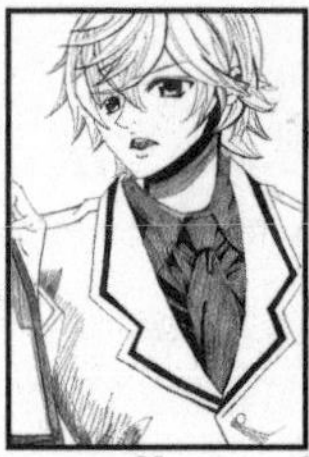

Ryoma (Saitama)
Ed.: Shogo's first appearance!!
←

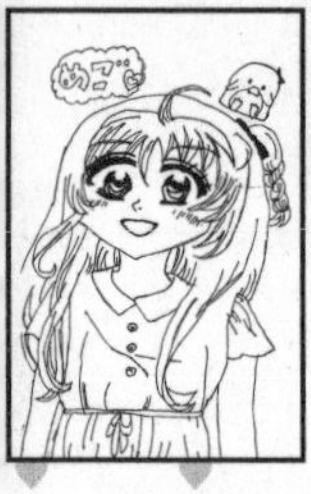

Mei Fujiwara (Iwate)
Ed.: Mego and penguin Mego are super cute!!
←

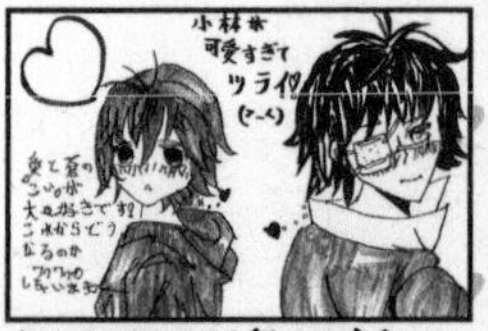
小林 可愛すぎて ツライ!!
(>_<)

Honoka Utsuki (Tokyo) ↑
Ed.: Cross-dressed Mego is cute too!!

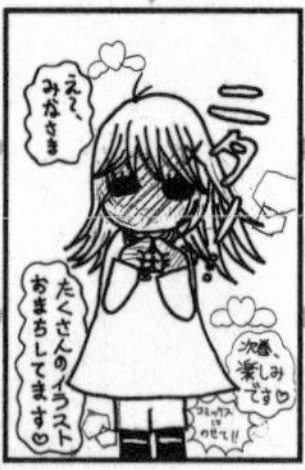

Shii-chan (Shizuoka)
Ed.: Yes, we'll be waiting. ♥
→

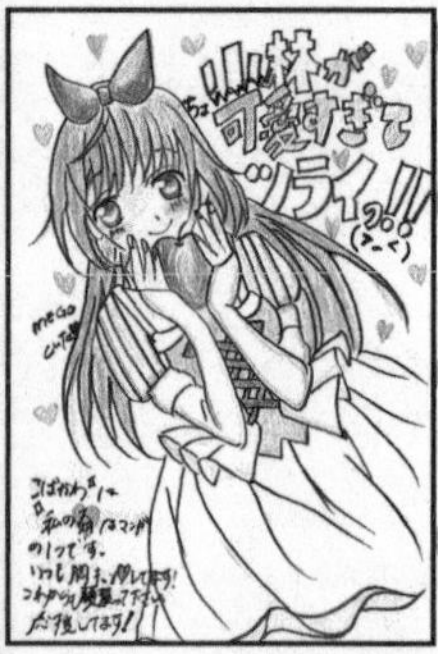
ちょwww 小林が可愛すぎてツライっ!!
(>_<)

Akiko Kurahashi (Shizuoka)
Ed.: Mego's so, so cute. ♥
←

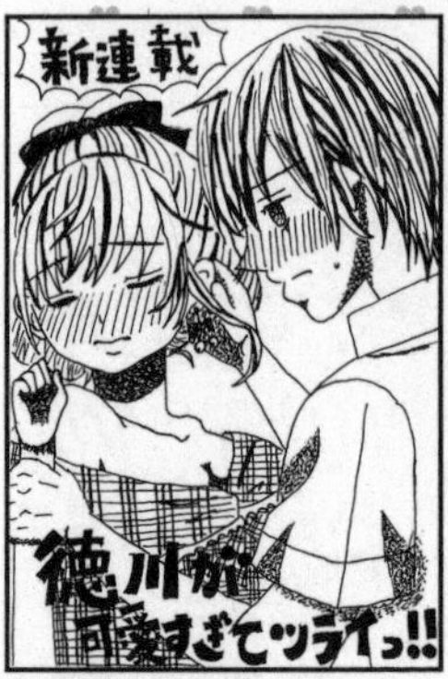
新連載
徳川が可愛すぎてツライっ!!

Ayumi Momose ↑ (Kanagawa)
Ed.: Whaa!! A-a new series?!

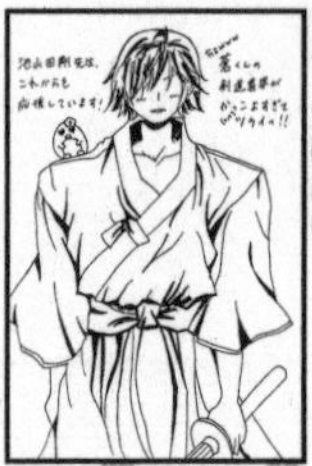

Misa Takagi (Osaka)
Ed.: Looks cool in his kendo uniform!

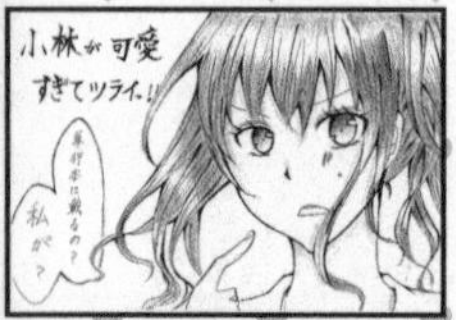
小林が可愛すぎてツライ!!

Takami Kita (Hyogo) ↑
Ed.: Yes, it's been published!

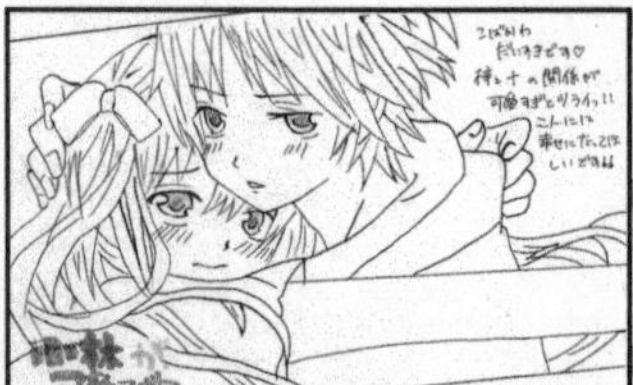

Rena (Kumamoto)
Ed.: I'll make Azusa happy! By Mitsuru.
←

Chapter 65

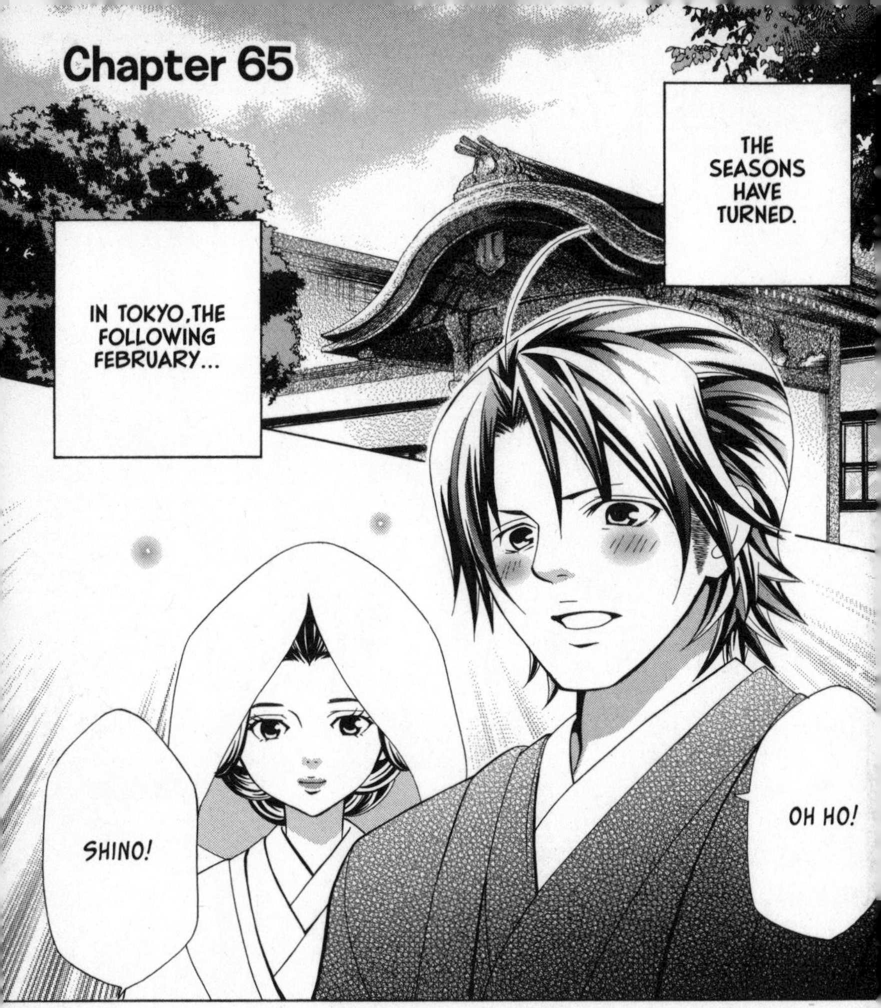
THE SEASONS HAVE TURNED.
IN TOKYO, THE FOLLOWING FEBRUARY...
OH HO!
SHINO!

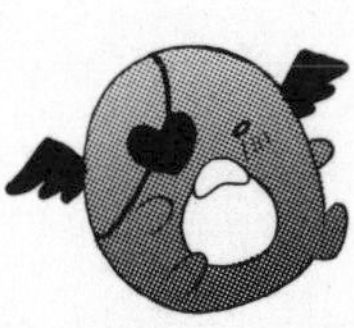

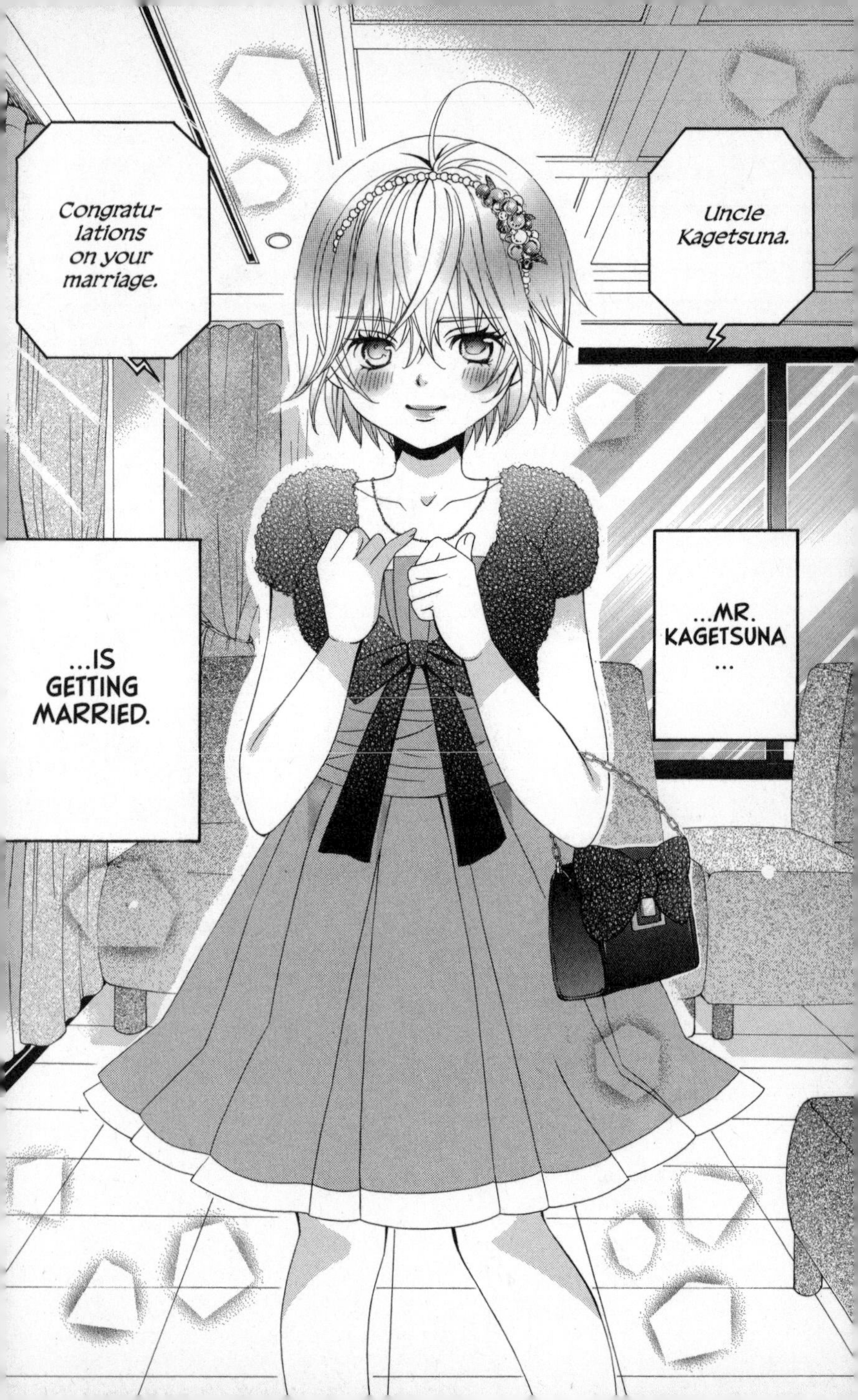
Uncle Kagetsuna.
Congratu-lations on your marriage.
...MR. KAGETSUNA ...
...IS GETTING MARRIED.

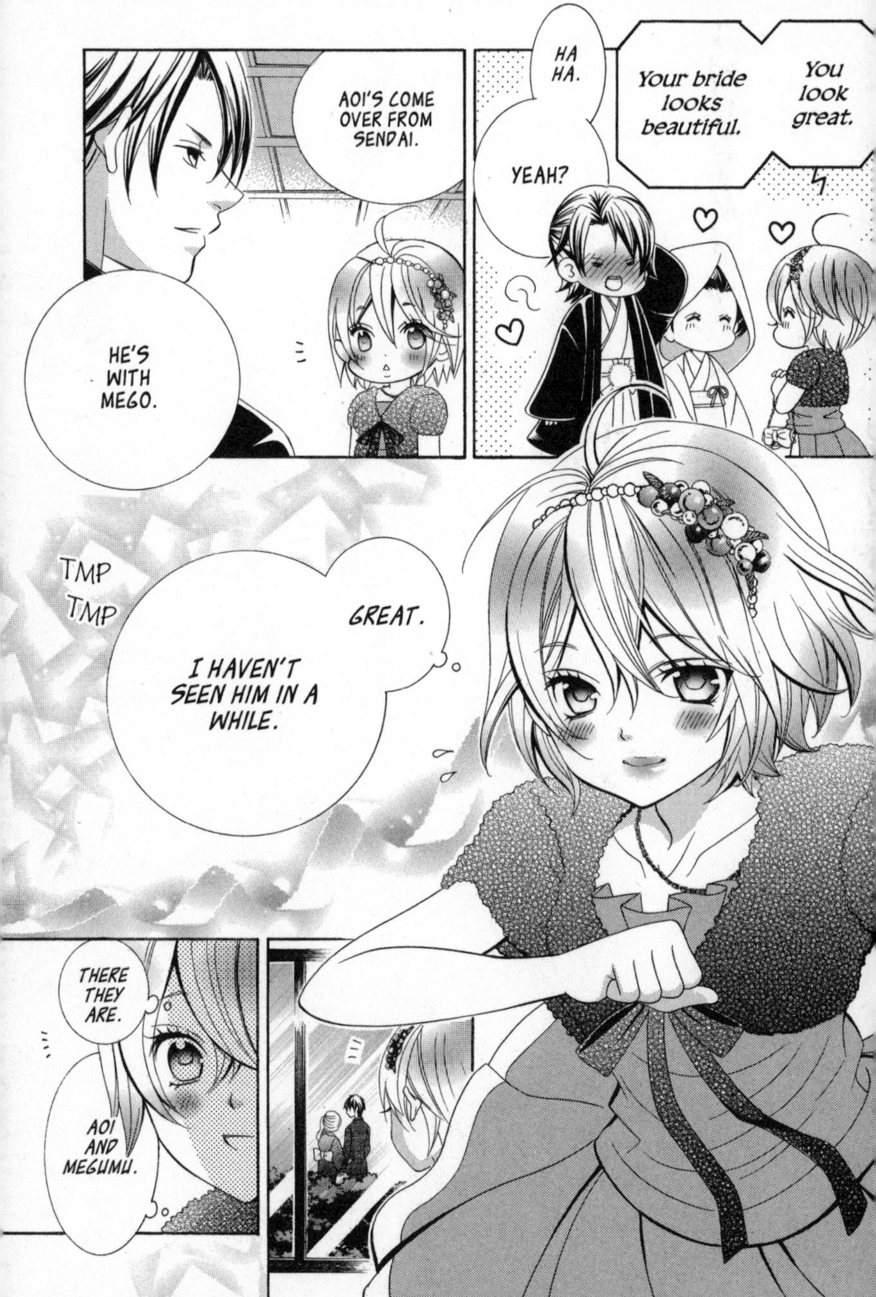
You look great.
Your bride looks beautiful.
HA HA.
YEAH?
AOI'S COME OVER FROM SENDAI.
HE'S WITH MEGO.
GREAT.
I HAVEN'T SEEN HIM IN A WHILE.
TMP TMP
THERE THEY ARE.
AOI AND MEGUMU.

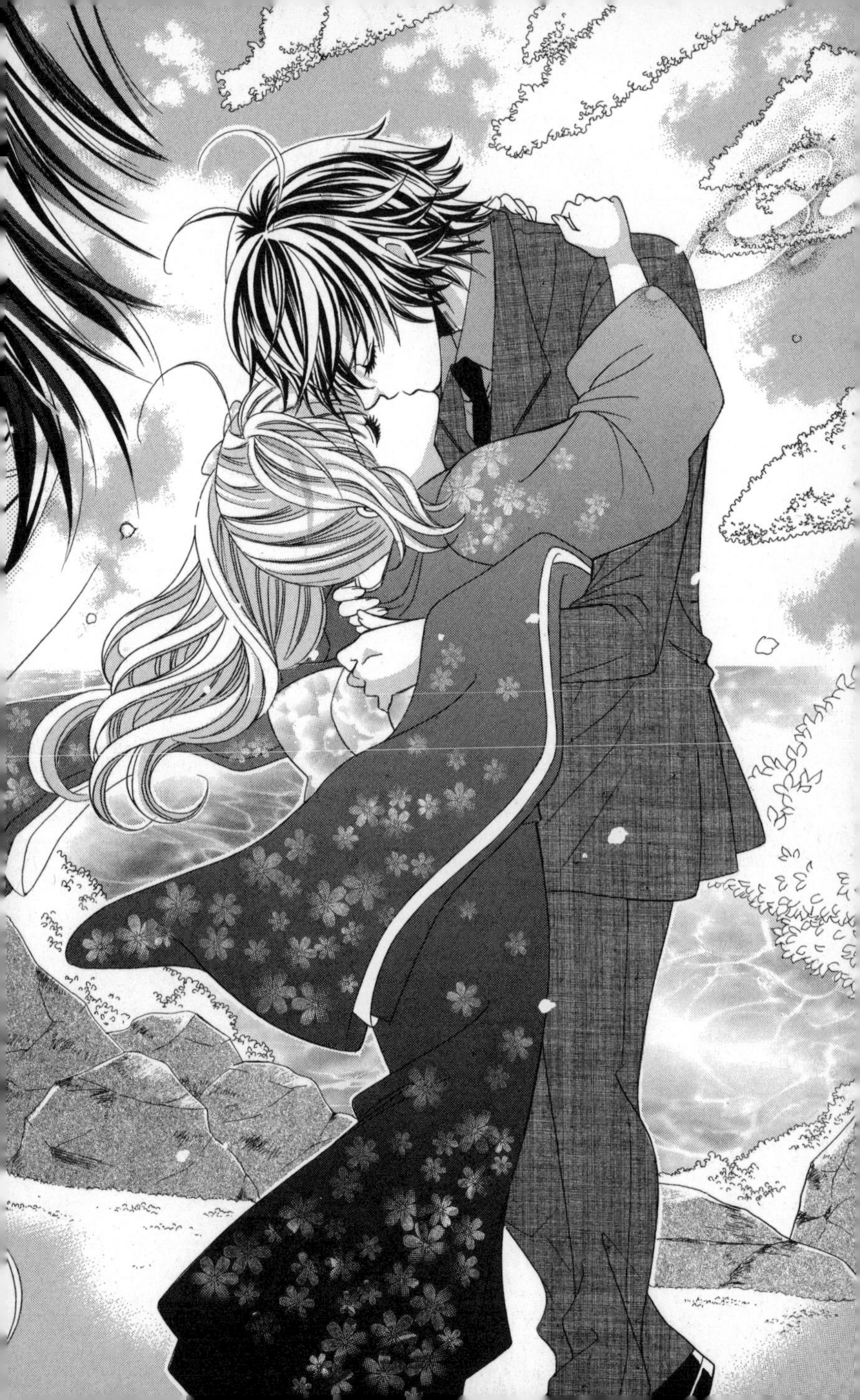

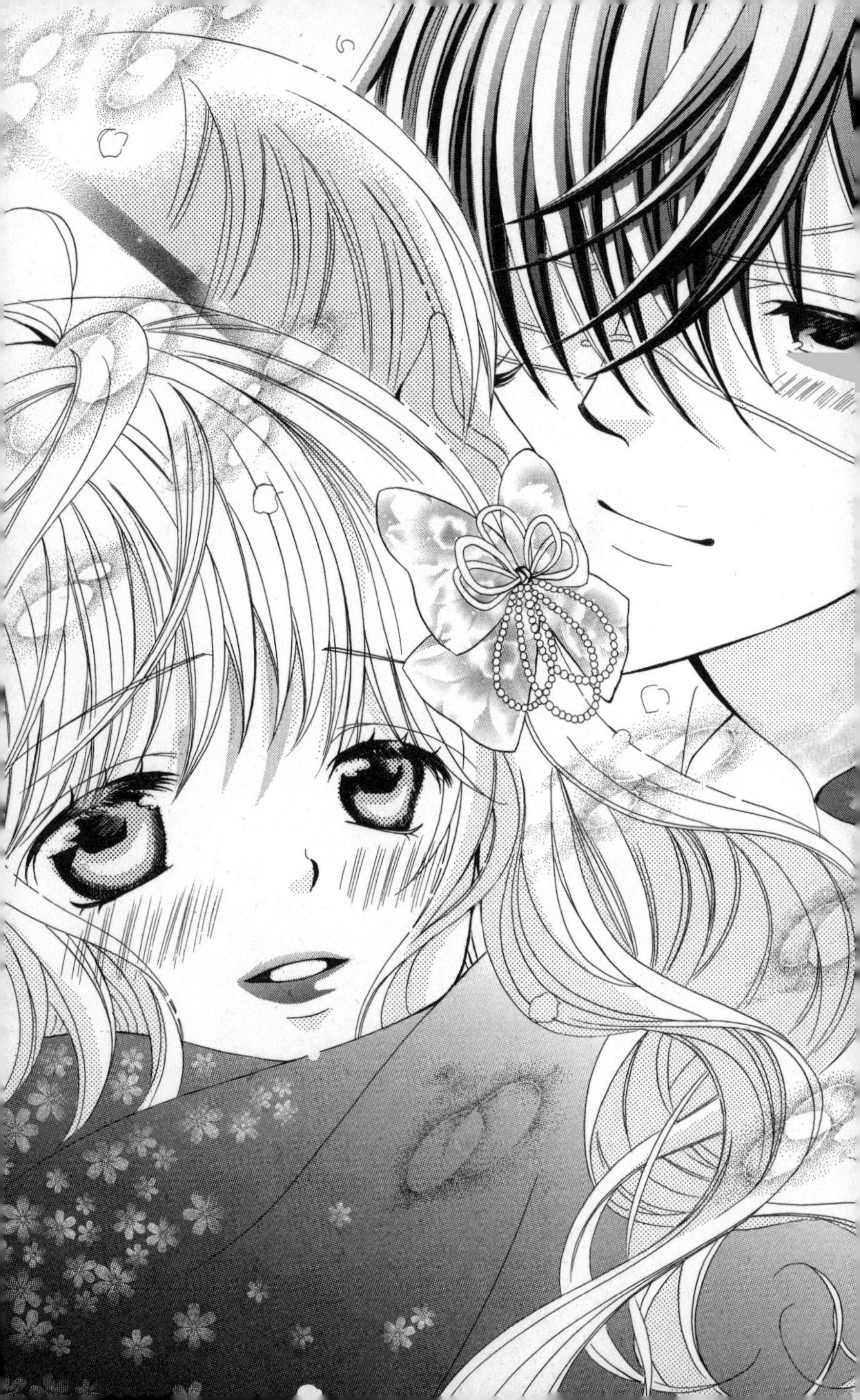

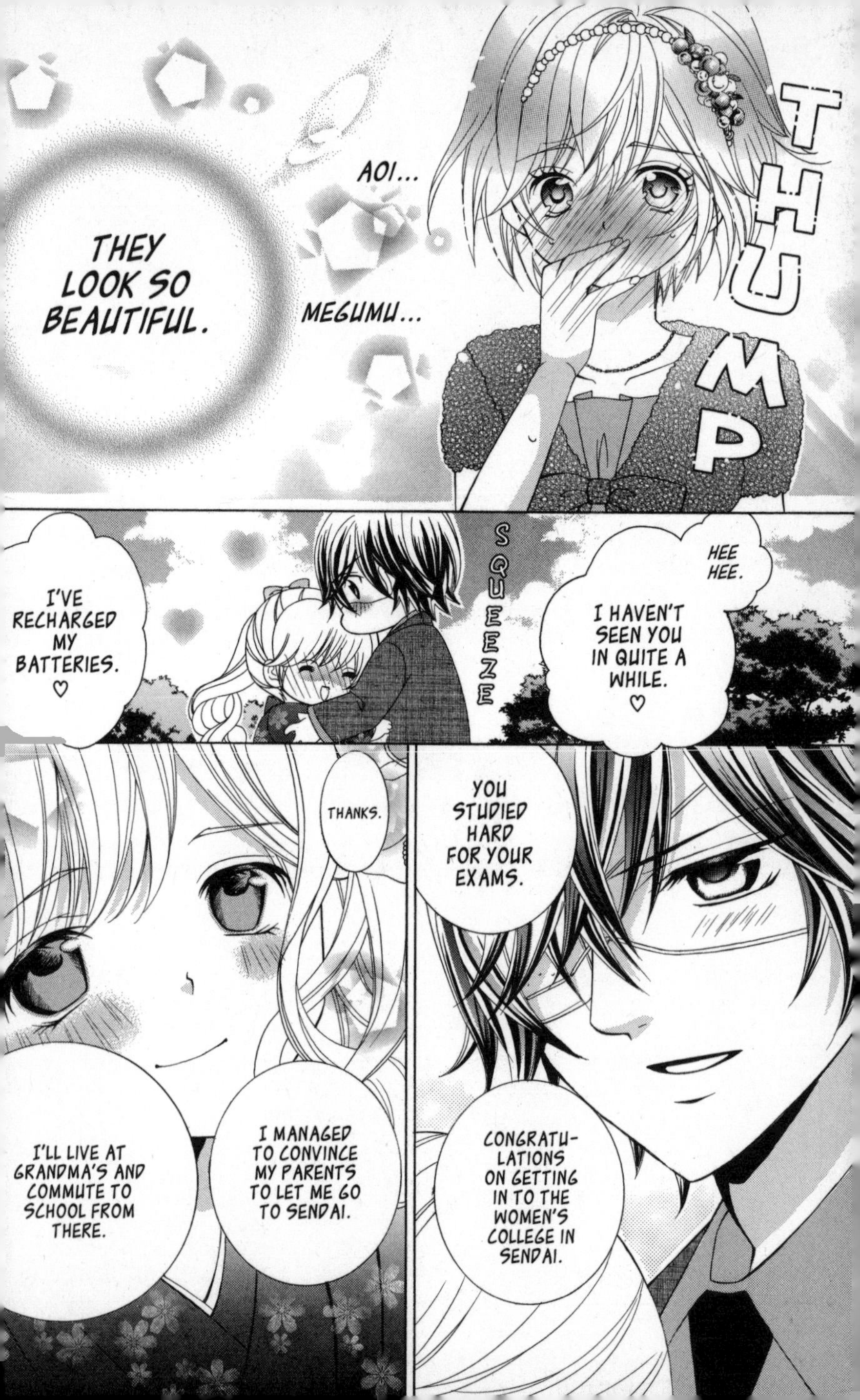
THUMP
AOI...
MEGUMU...
THEY LOOK SO BEAUTIFUL.
HEE HEE.
I HAVEN'T SEEN YOU IN QUITE A WHILE. ♡
SQUEEZE
I'VE RECHARGED MY BATTERIES. ♡
YOU STUDIED HARD FOR YOUR EXAMS.
CONGRATULATIONS ON GETTING IN TO THE WOMEN'S COLLEGE IN SENDAI.
THANKS.
I MANAGED TO CONVINCE MY PARENTS TO LET ME GO TO SENDAI.
I'LL LIVE AT GRANDMA'S AND COMMUTE TO SCHOOL FROM THERE.

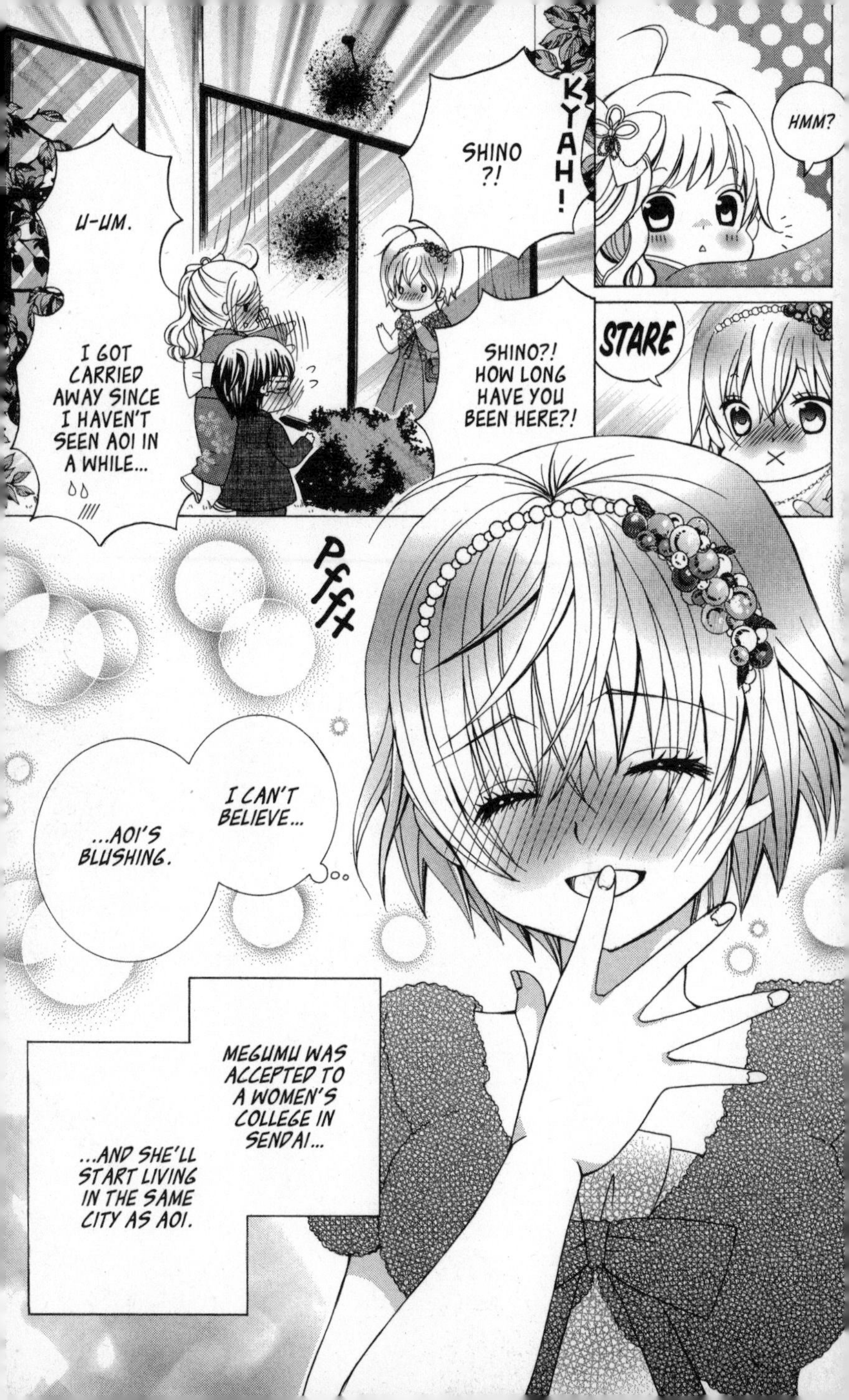
HMM?
STARE
SHINO ?!
KYAH!
SHINO?! HOW LONG HAVE YOU BEEN HERE?!
U-UM.
I GOT CARRIED AWAY SINCE I HAVEN'T SEEN AOI IN A WHILE...
Pfft
I CAN'T BELIEVE...
...AOI'S BLUSHING.
MEGUMU WAS ACCEPTED TO A WOMEN'S COLLEGE IN SENDAI...
...AND SHE'LL START LIVING IN THE SAME CITY AS AOI.

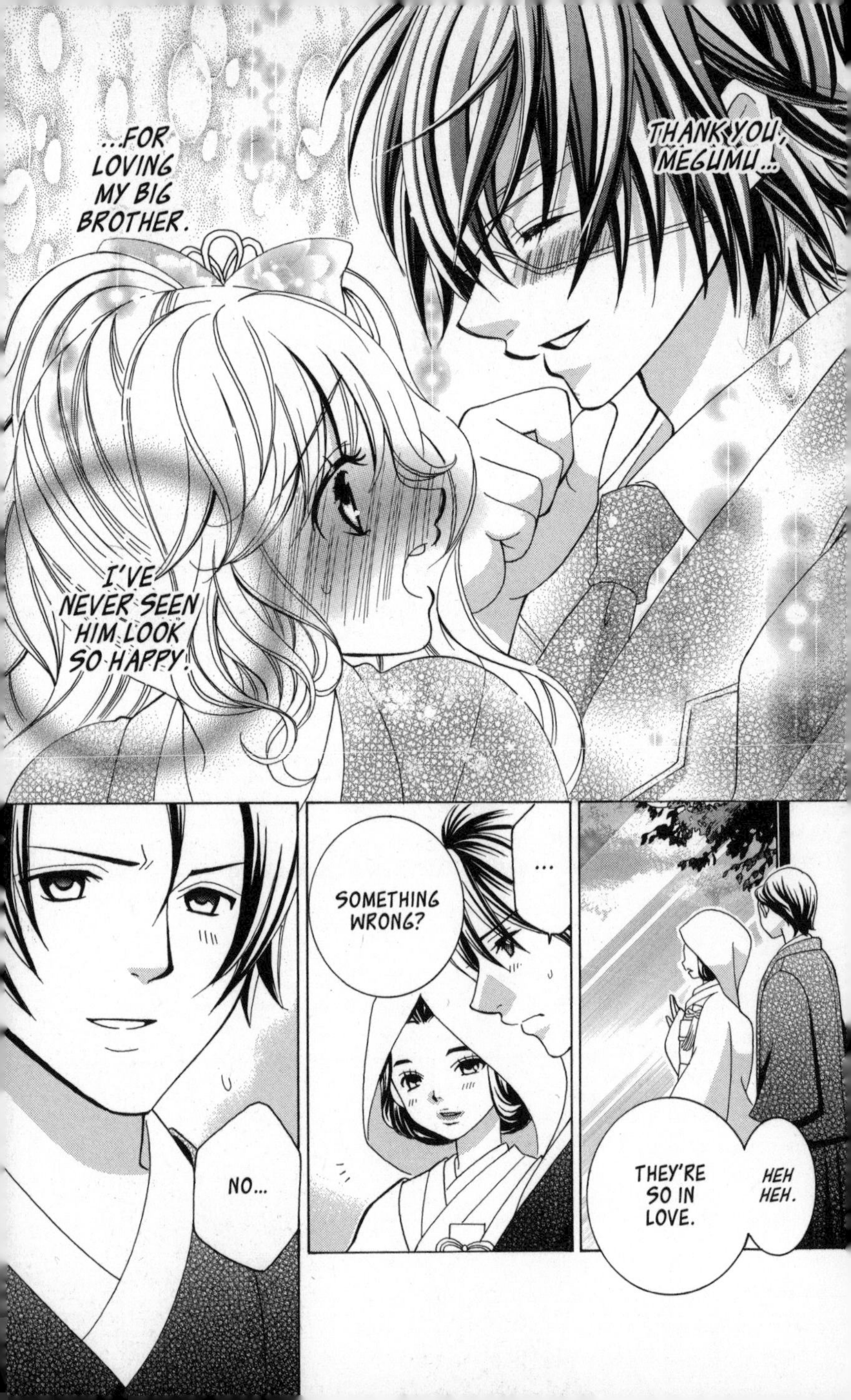
THANK YOU, MEGUMU...
...FOR LOVING MY BIG BROTHER.
I'VE NEVER SEEN HIM LOOK SO HAPPY.
HEH HEH.
THEY'RE SO IN LOVE.
...
SOMETHING WRONG?
NO...

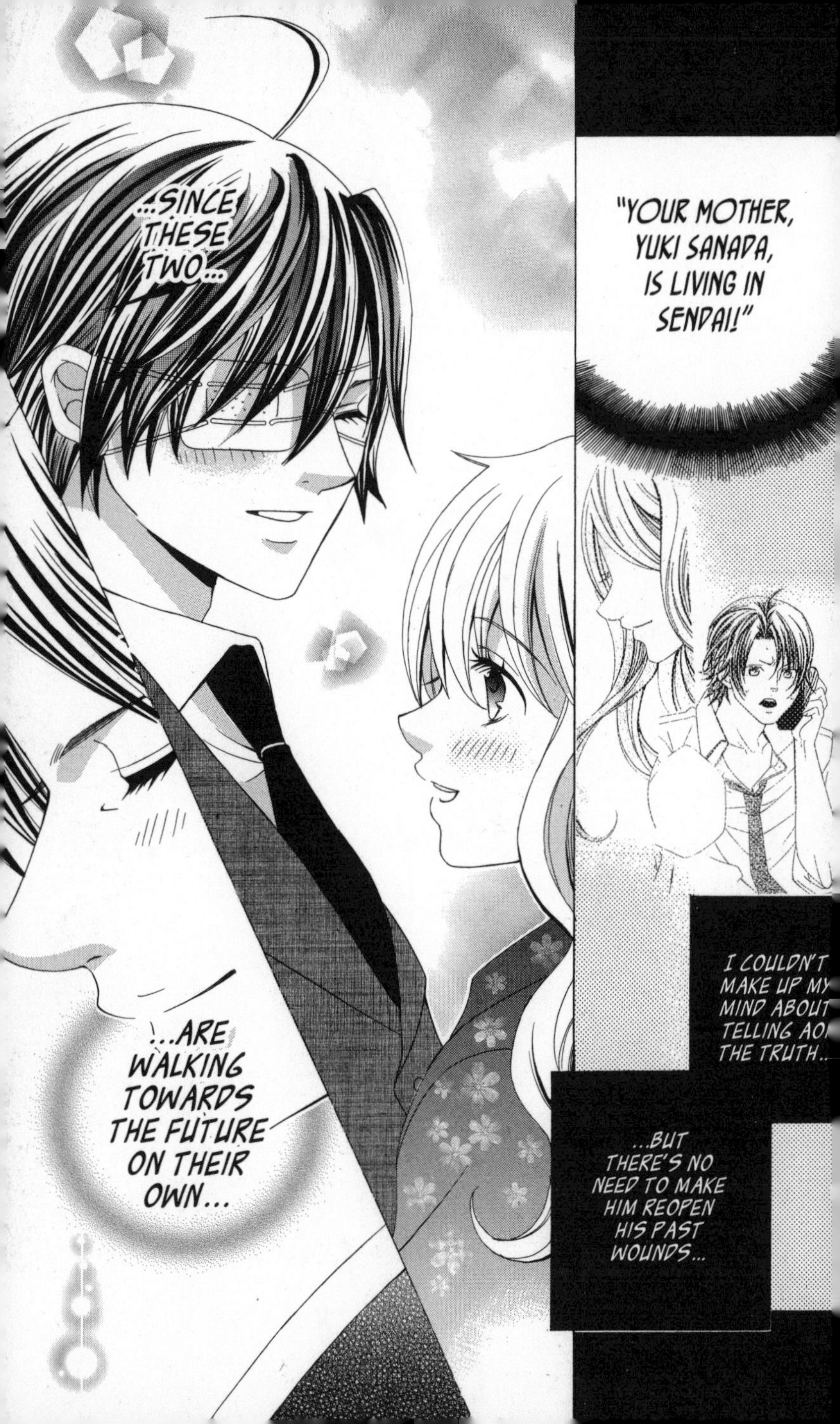
"YOUR MOTHER, YUKI SANADA, IS LIVING IN SENDAI!"
I COULDN'T MAKE UP MY MIND ABOUT TELLING AO THE TRUTH..
...BUT THERE'S NO NEED TO MAKE HIM REOPEN HIS PAST WOUNDS...
...SINCE THESE TWO...
...ARE WALKING TOWARDS THE FUTURE ON THEIR OWN...

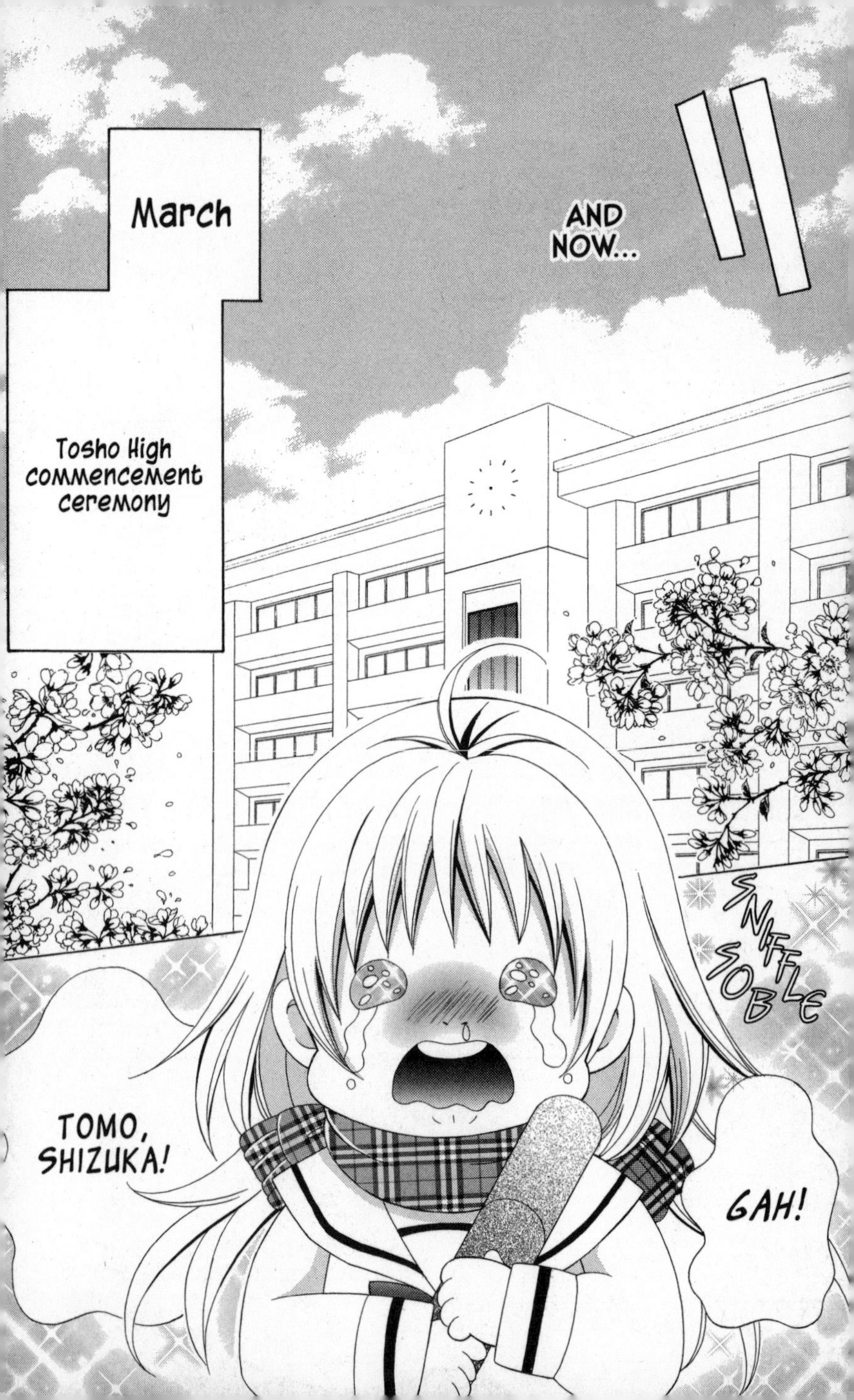
AND NOW...
March
Tosho High commencement ceremony
SNIFFLE
SOB
GAH!
TOMO, SHIZUKA!

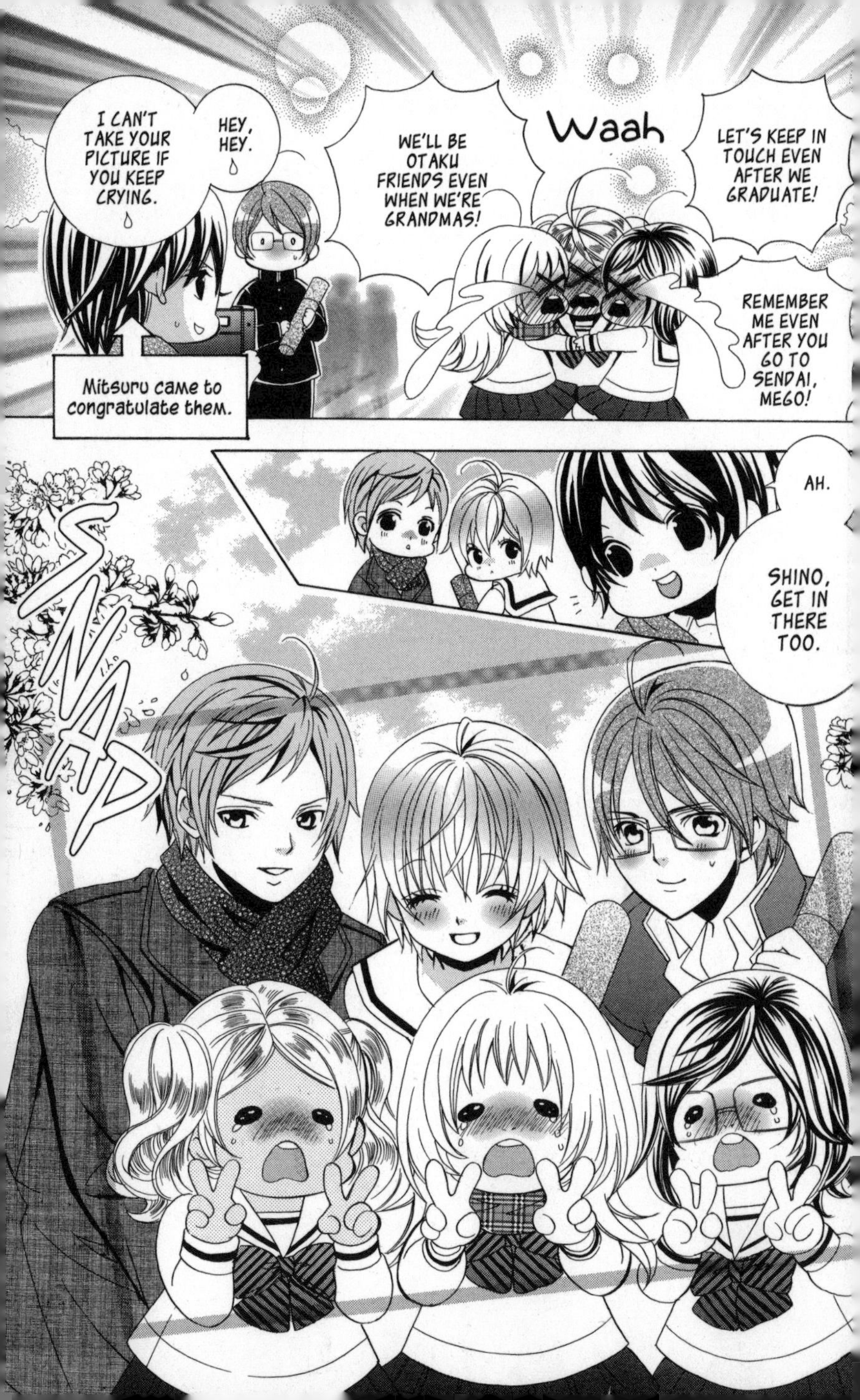
LET'S KEEP IN TOUCH EVEN AFTER WE GRADUATE!
REMEMBER ME EVEN AFTER YOU GO TO SENDAI, MEGO!
Waah
WE'LL BE OTAKU FRIENDS EVEN WHEN WE'RE GRANDMAS!
HEY, HEY.
I CAN'T TAKE YOUR PICTURE IF YOU KEEP CRYING.
Mitsuru came to congratulate them.
AH.
SHINO, GET IN THERE TOO.
SNAP

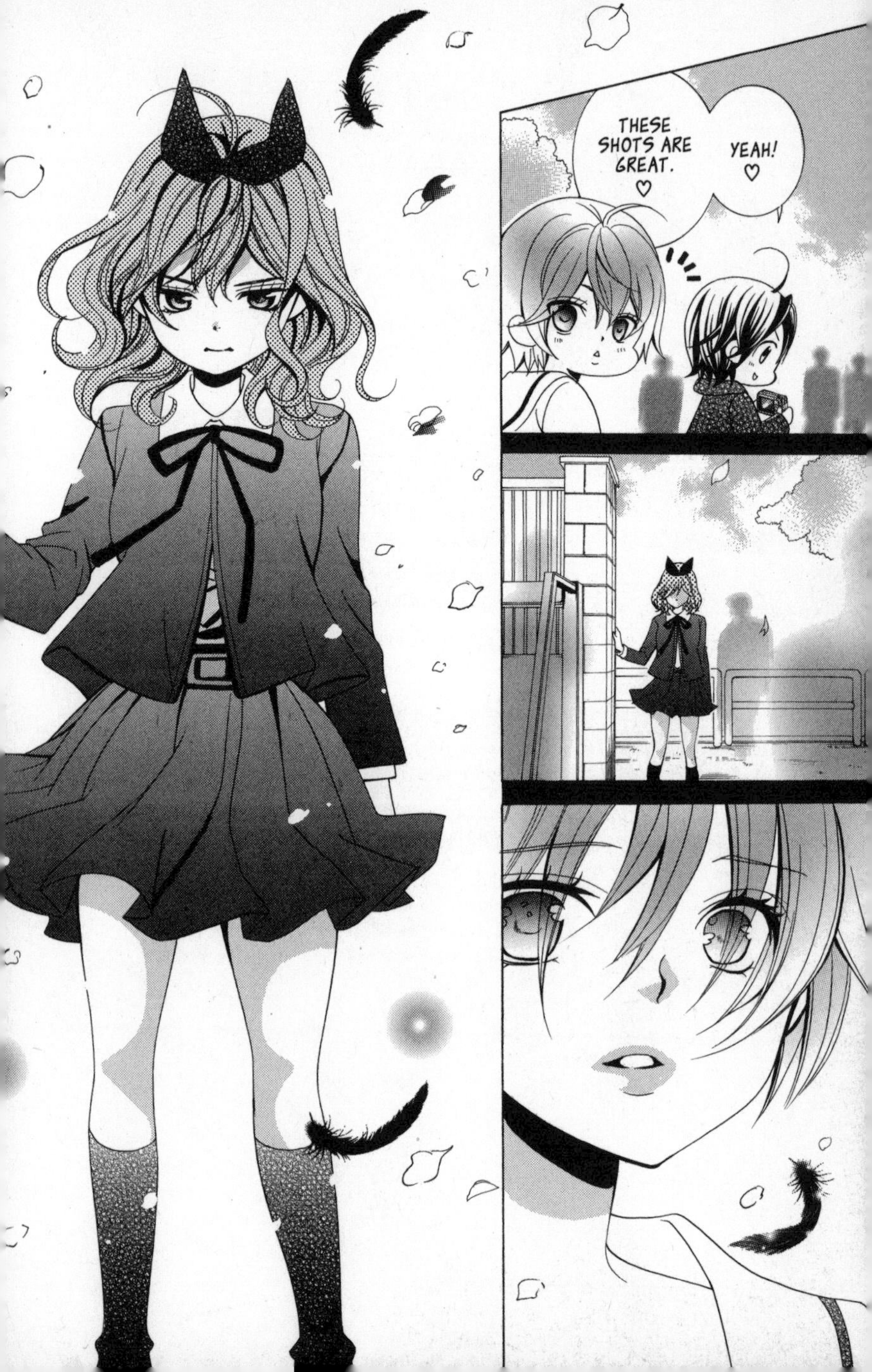
THESE SHOTS ARE GREAT. ♡
YEAH! ♡

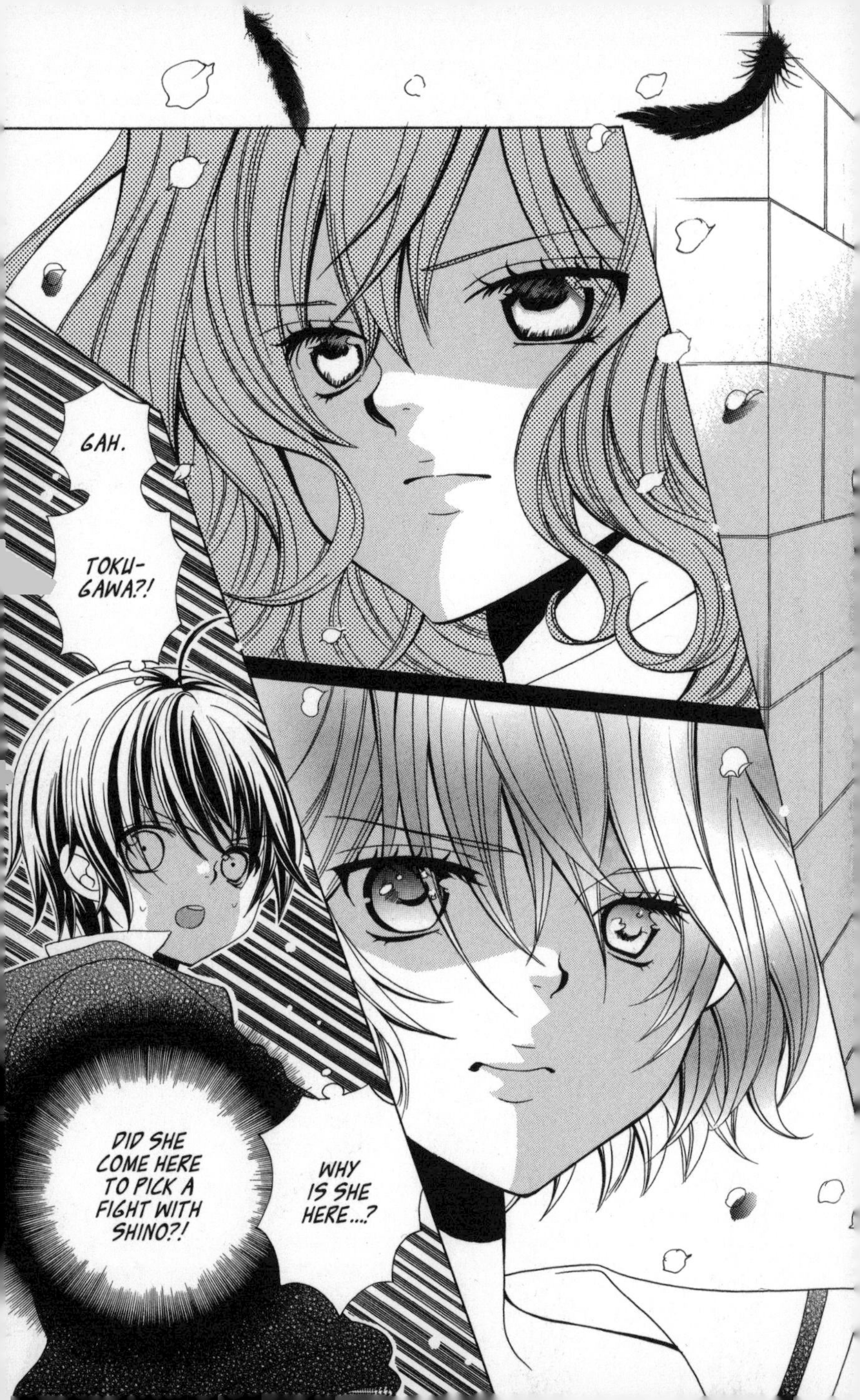
GAH.
TOKU-GAWA?!
WHY IS SHE HERE...?
DID SHE COME HERE TO PICK A FIGHT WITH SHINO?!

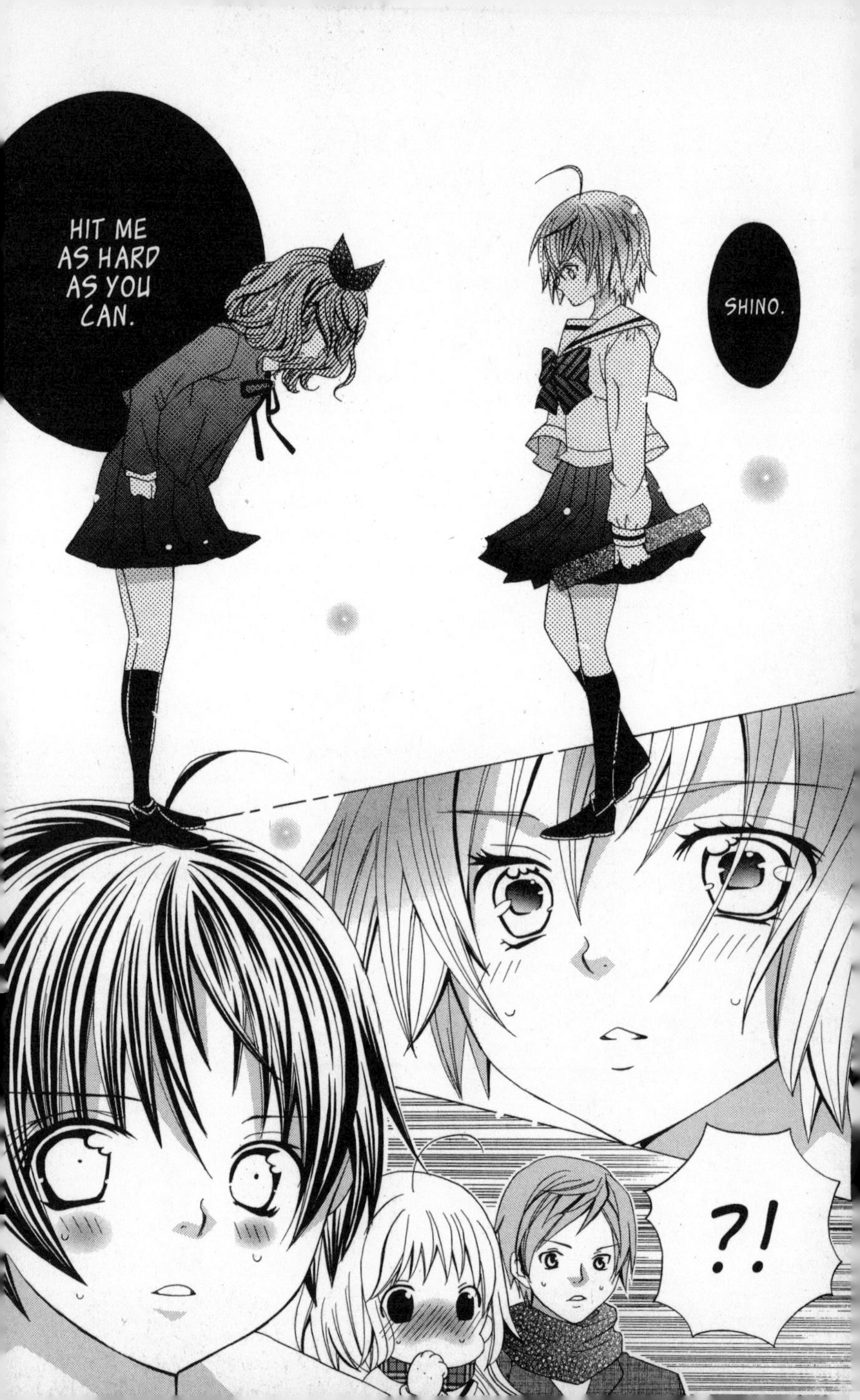
SHINO.
HIT ME AS HARD AS YOU CAN.
?!

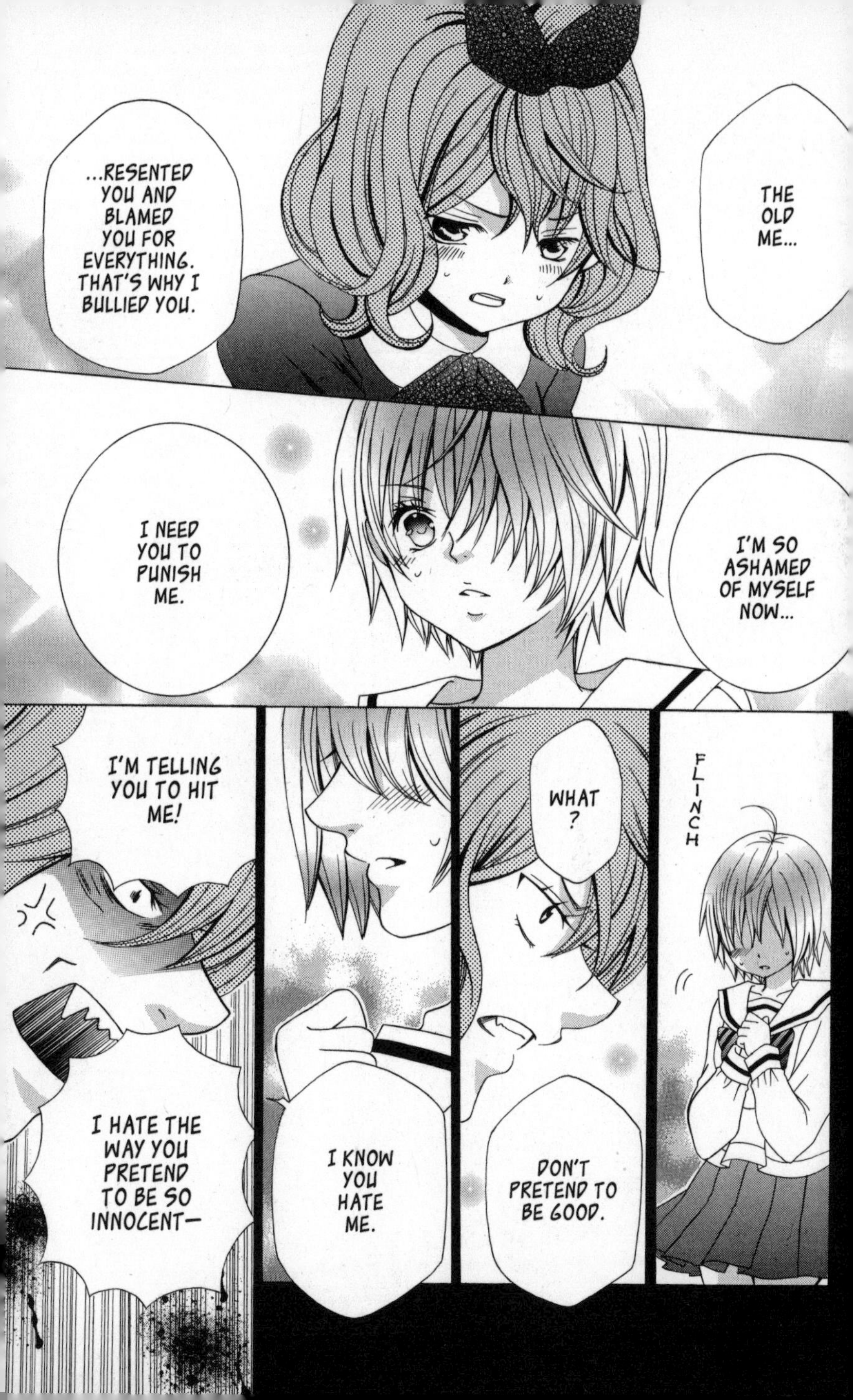
THE OLD ME...
...RESENTED YOU AND BLAMED YOU FOR EVERYTHING. THAT'S WHY I BULLIED YOU.
I'M SO ASHAMED OF MYSELF NOW...
I NEED YOU TO PUNISH ME.
FLINCH
WHAT?
DON'T PRETEND TO BE GOOD.
I KNOW YOU HATE ME.
I'M TELLING YOU TO HIT ME!
I HATE THE WAY YOU PRETEND TO BE SO INNOCENT—

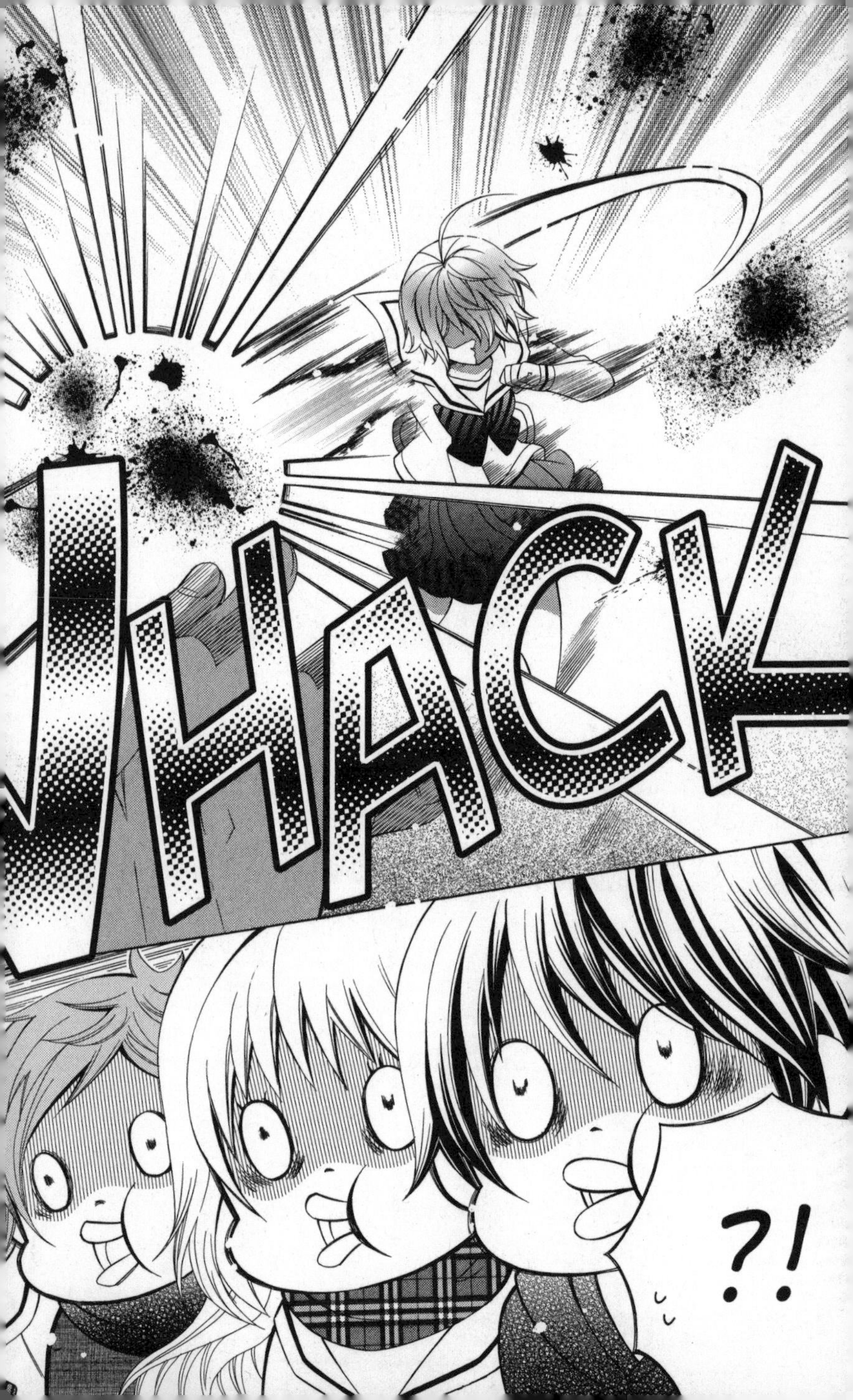
WHACK
?!

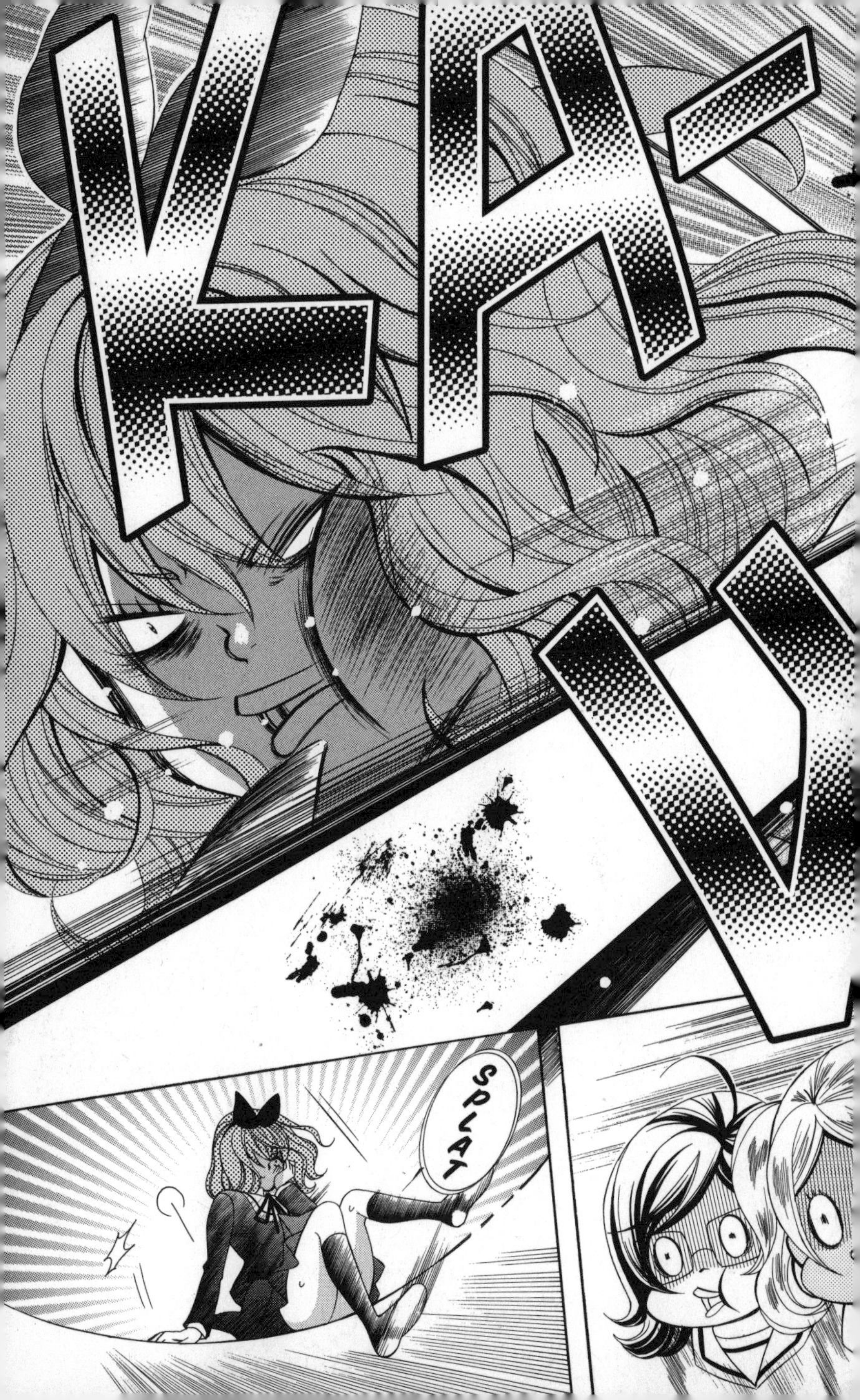
SPLAT

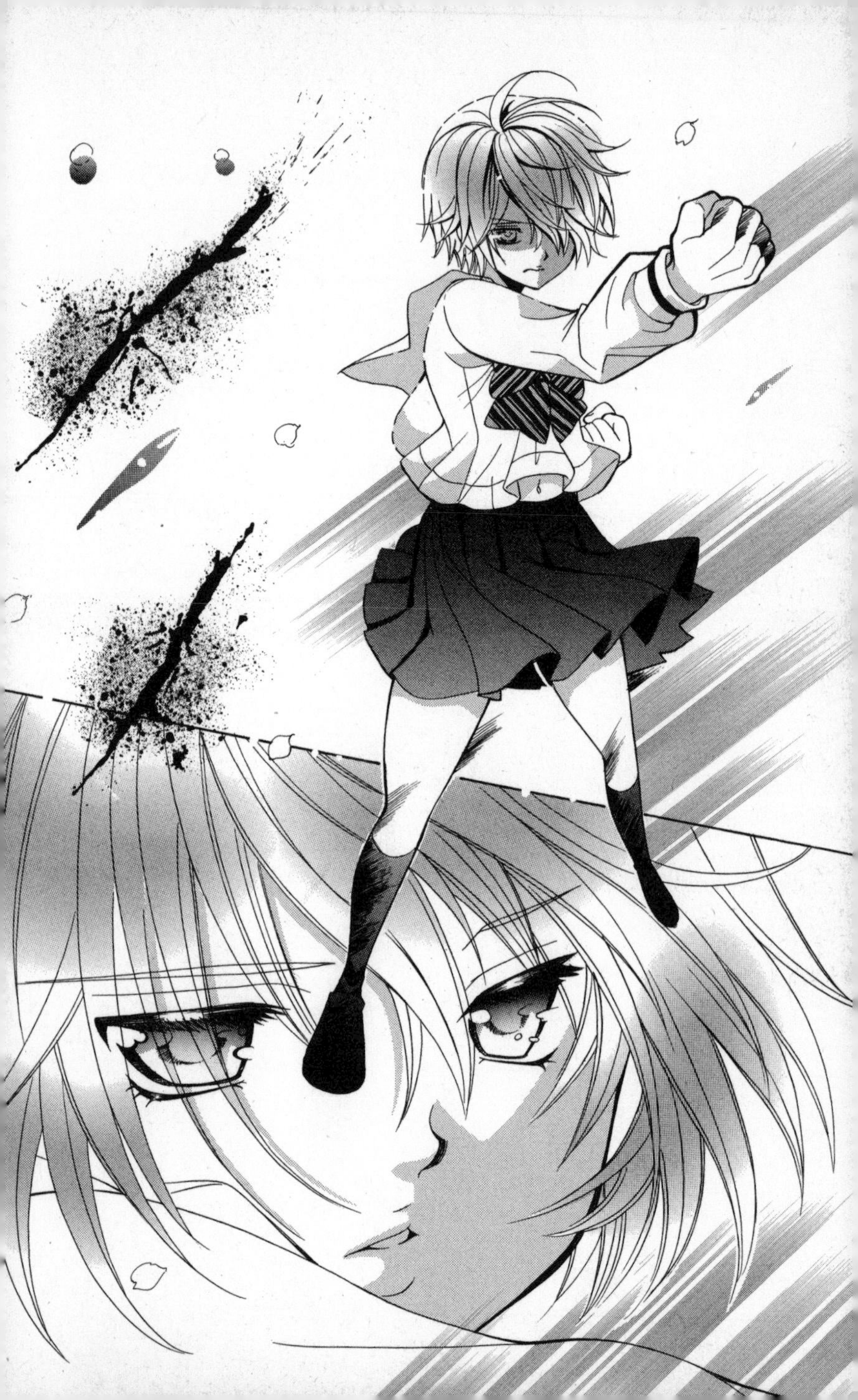

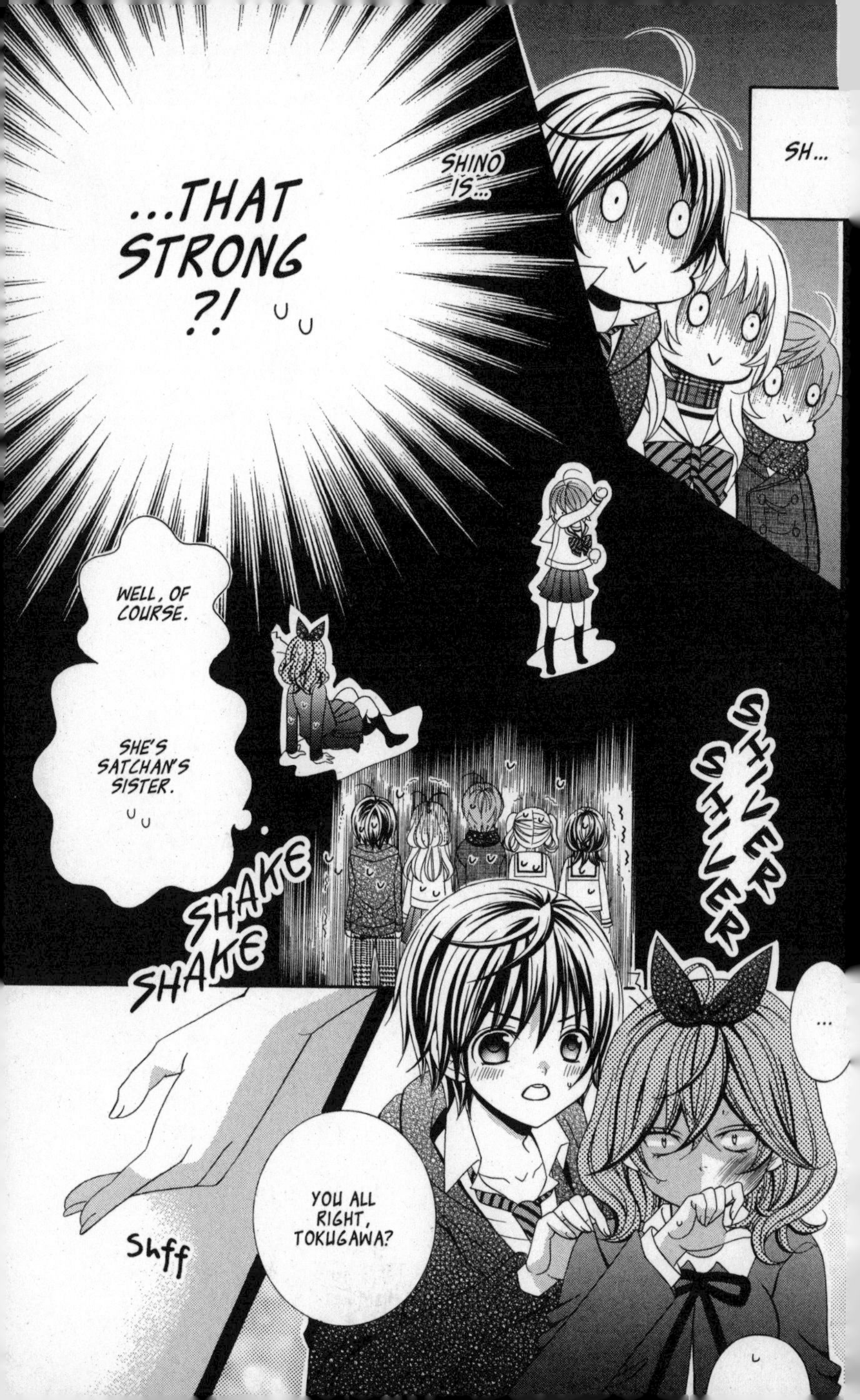
SH...
SHINO IS...
...THAT STRONG ?!
SHIVER SHIVER
WELL, OF COURSE.
SHE'S SATCHAN'S SISTER.
SHAKE SHAKE
...
YOU ALL RIGHT, TOKUGAWA?
Shff

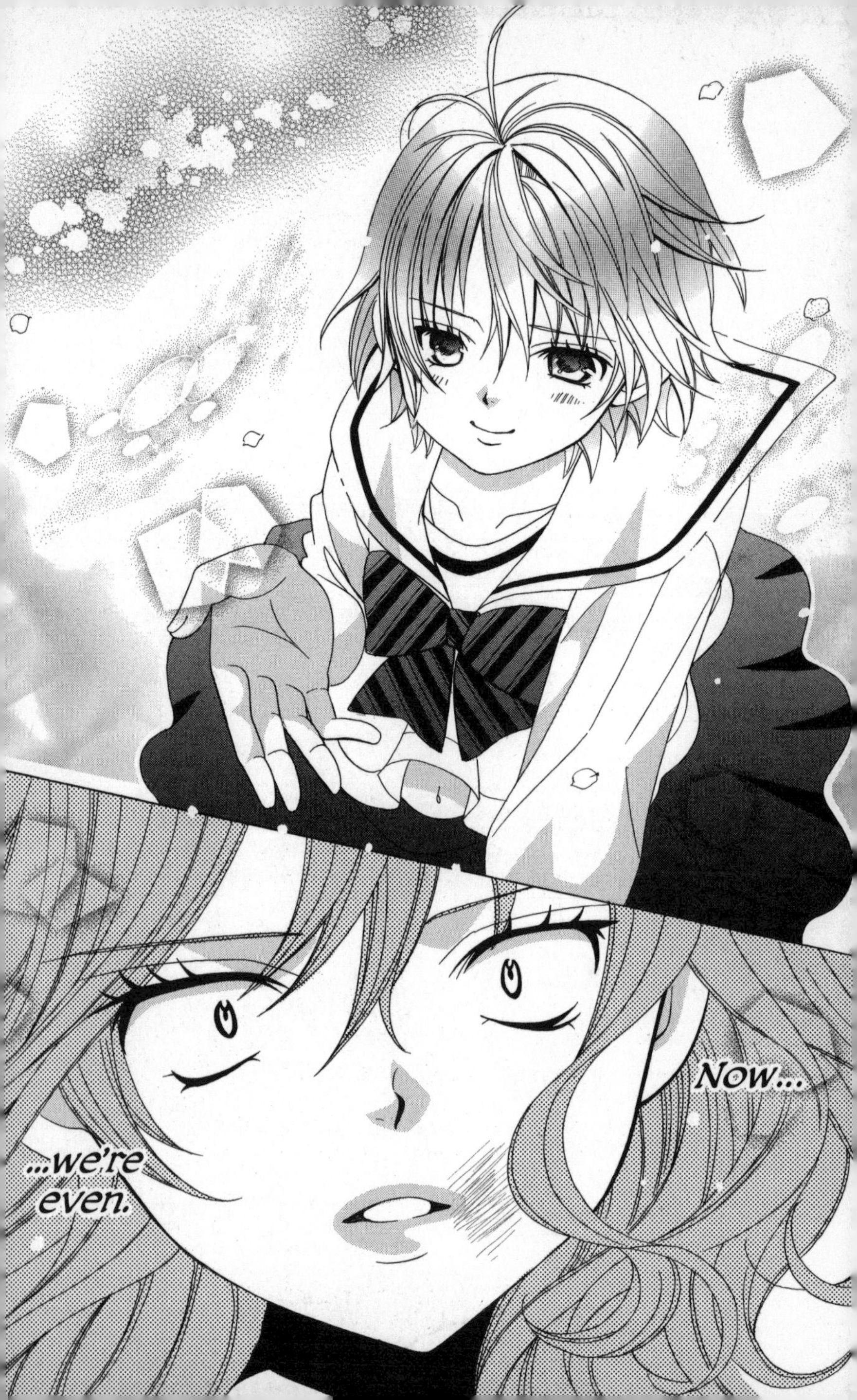
Now...
...we're even.

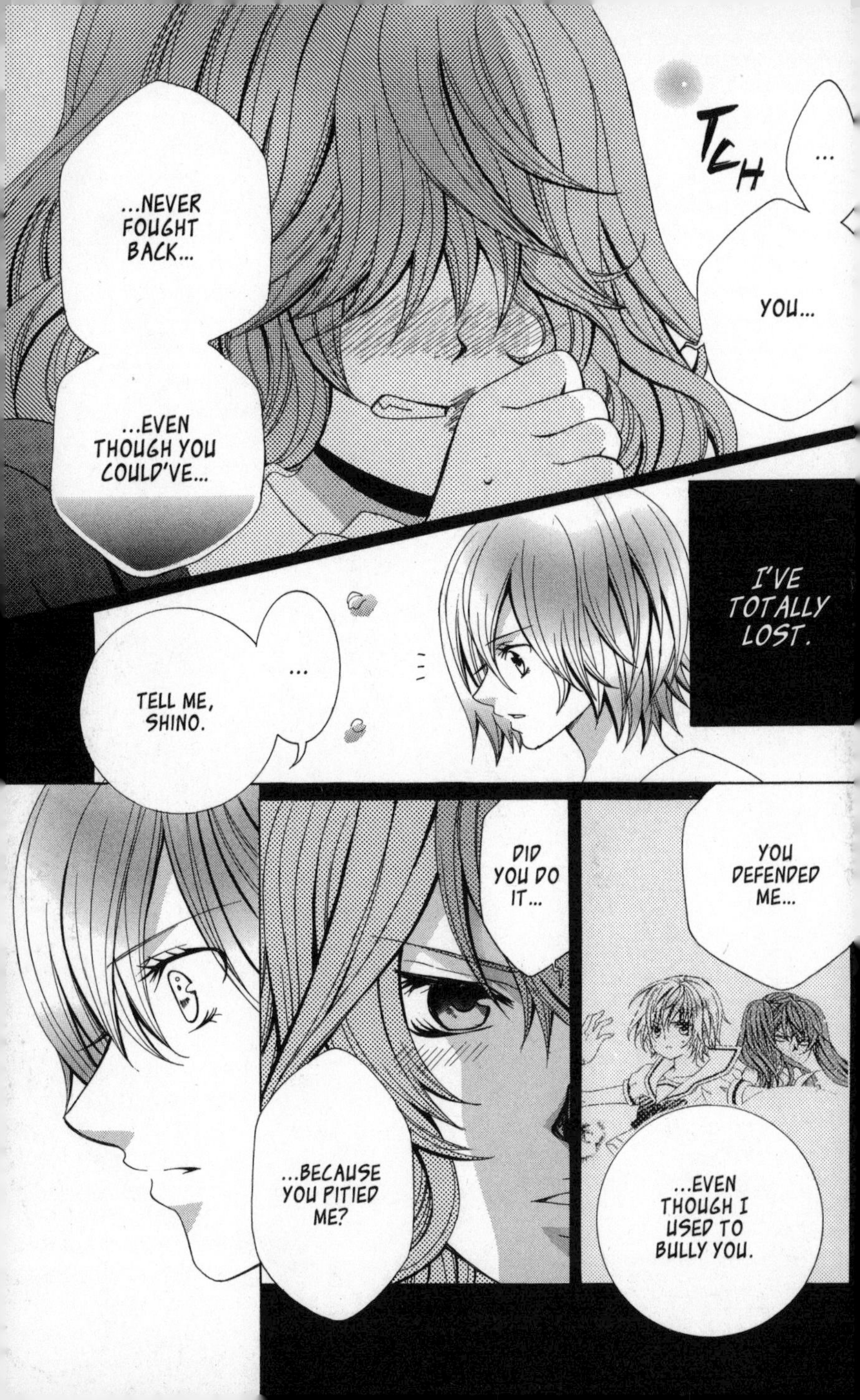
TCH
...
YOU...
...NEVER FOUGHT BACK...
...EVEN THOUGH YOU COULD'VE...
I'VE TOTALLY LOST.
... TELL ME, SHINO.
YOU DEFENDED ME...
...EVEN THOUGH I USED TO BULLY YOU.
DID YOU DO IT...
...BECAUSE YOU PITIED ME?

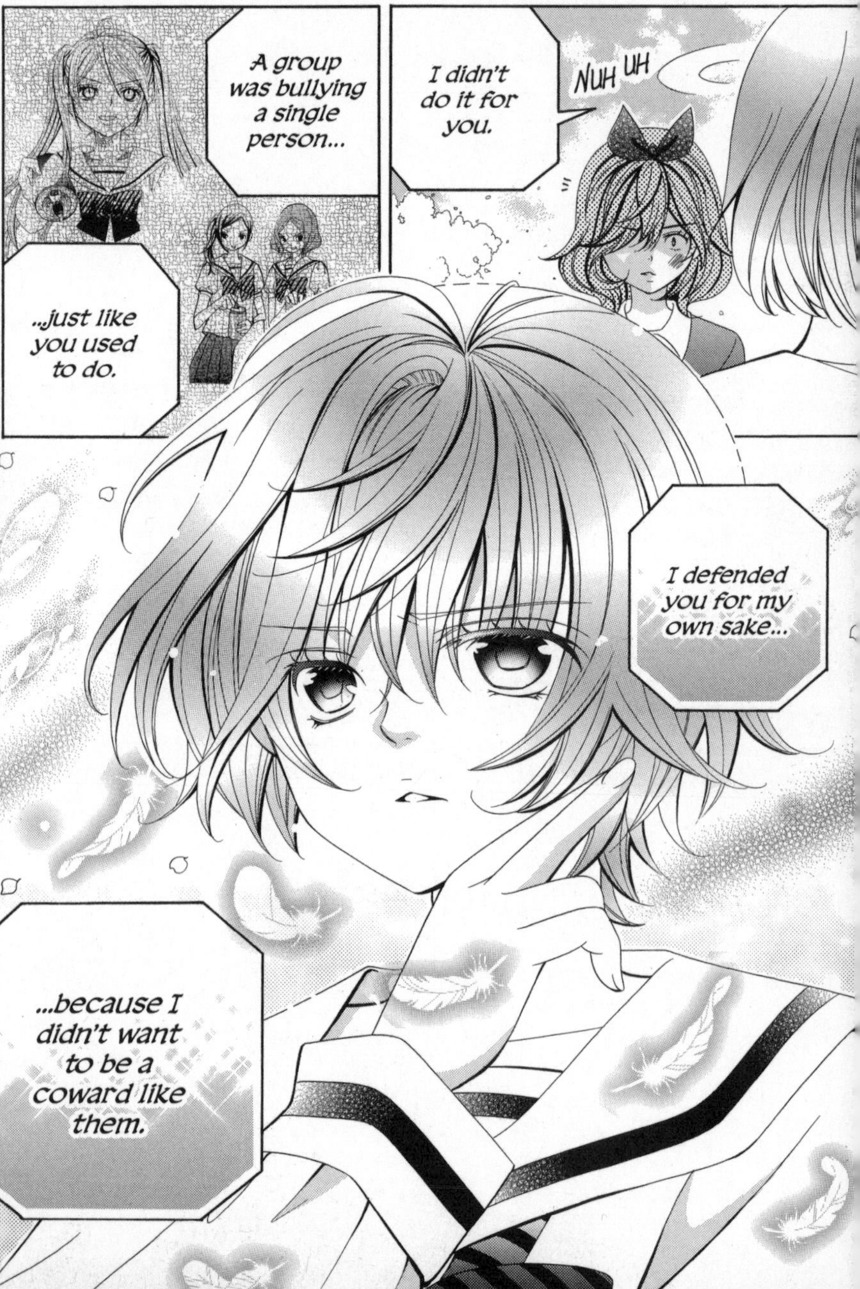
NUH UH
I didn't do it for you.
A group was bullying a single person...
...just like you used to do.
I defended you for my own sake...
...because I didn't want to be a coward like them.

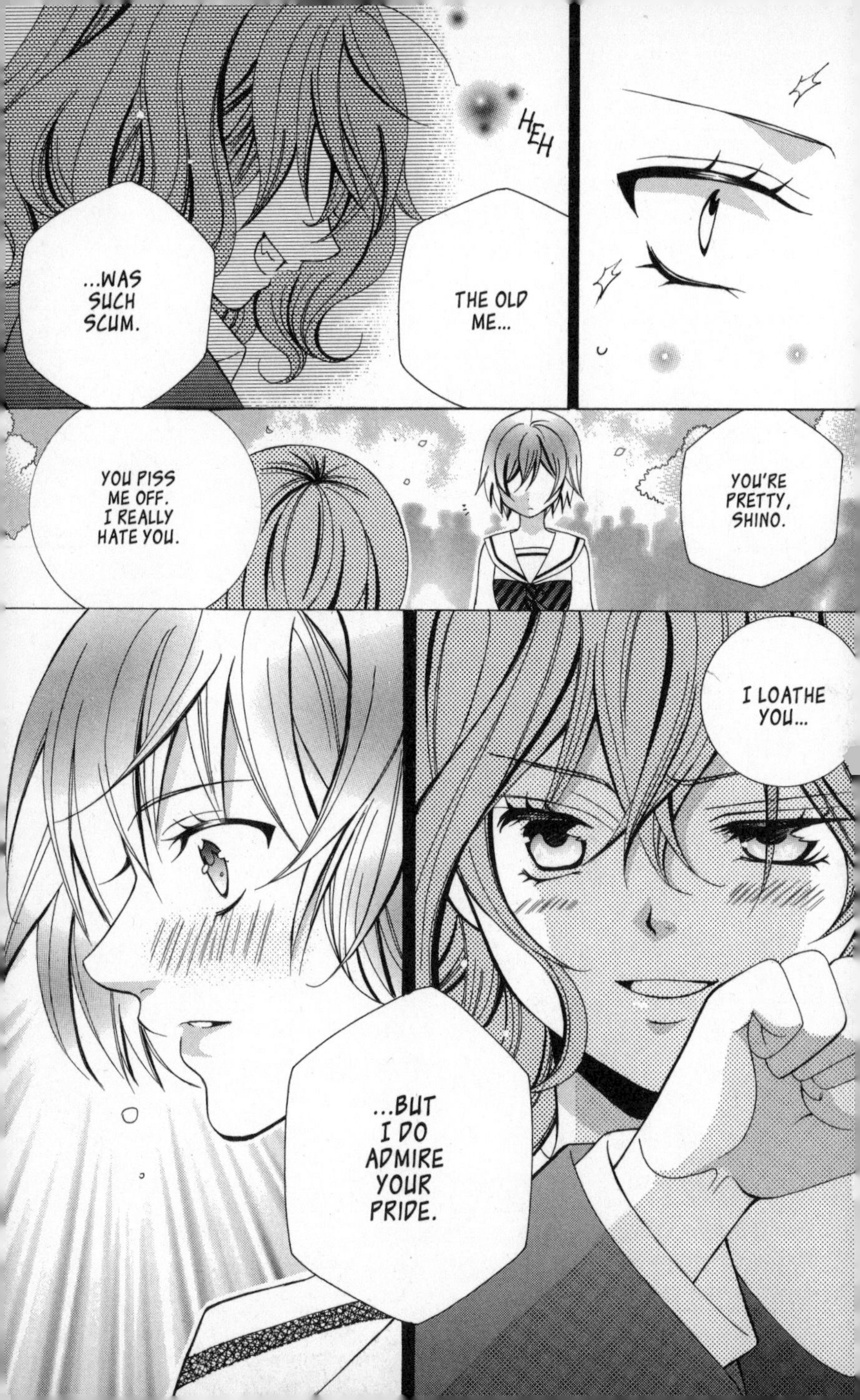
HEH
THE OLD ME...
...WAS SUCH SCUM.
YOU'RE PRETTY, SHINO.
YOU PISS ME OFF. I REALLY HATE YOU.
I LOATHE YOU...
...BUT I DO ADMIRE YOUR PRIDE.

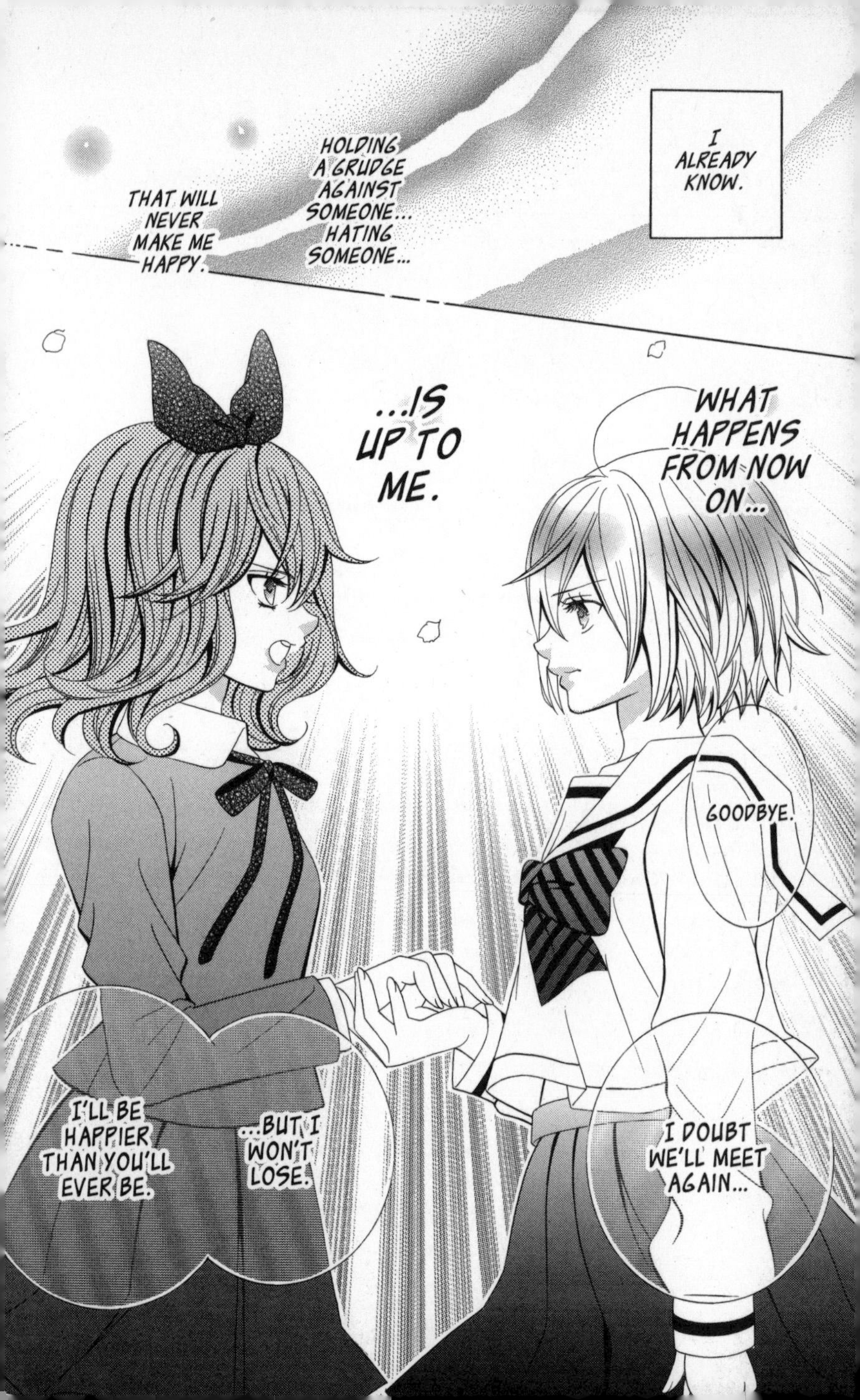
I ALREADY KNOW.
HOLDING A GRUDGE AGAINST SOMEONE... HATING SOMEONE...
THAT WILL NEVER MAKE ME HAPPY.
WHAT HAPPENS FROM NOW ON...
...IS UP TO ME.
GOODBYE.
I DOUBT WE'LL MEET AGAIN...
...BUT I WON'T LOSE.
I'LL BE HAPPIER THAN YOU'LL EVER BE.

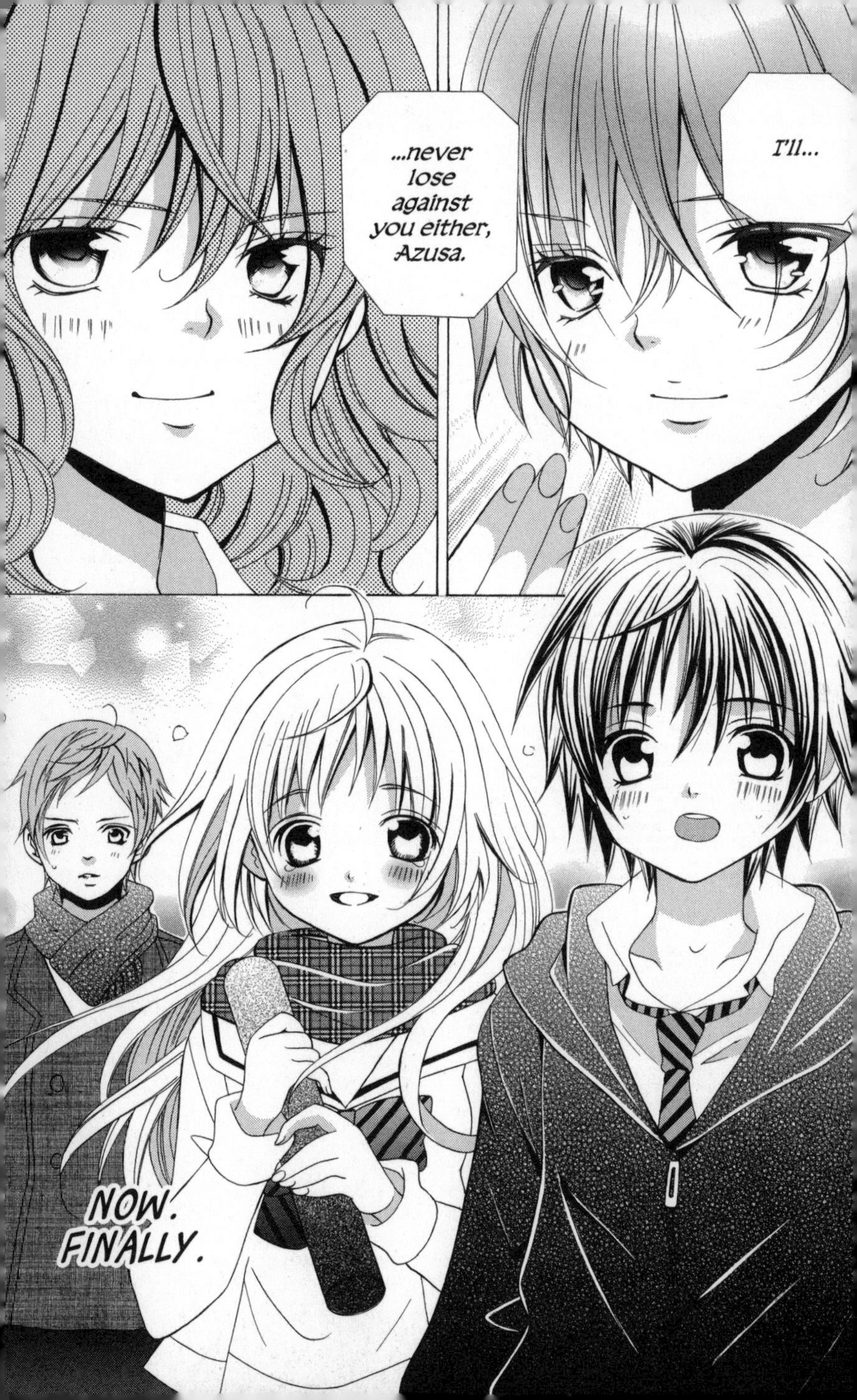
I'll...
...never lose against you either, Azusa.
NOW. FINALLY.

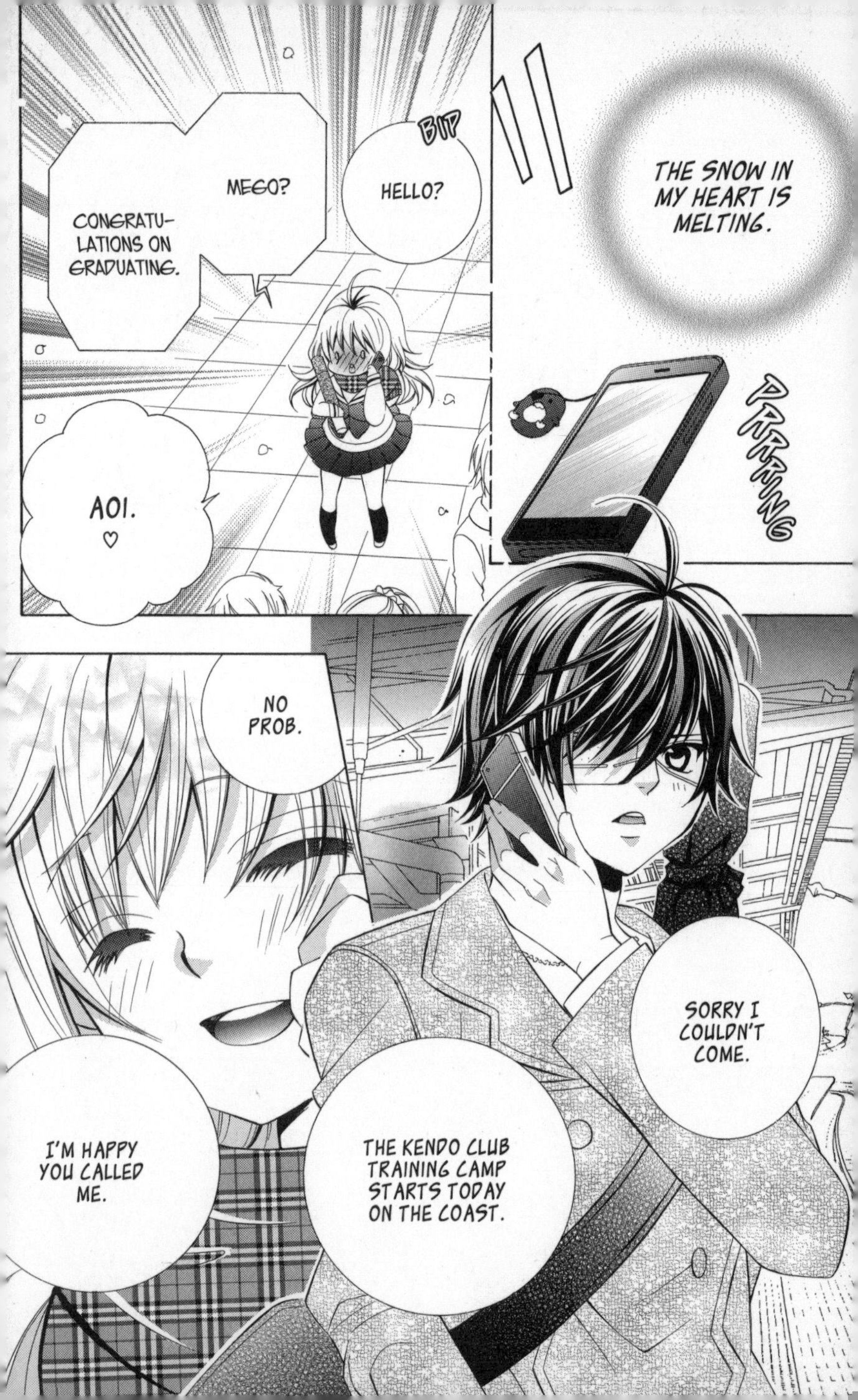
THE SNOW IN MY HEART IS MELTING.
PRRRING
BIP
HELLO?
MEGO?
CONGRATULATIONS ON GRADUATING.
AOI. ♡
SORRY I COULDN'T COME.
THE KENDO CLUB TRAINING CAMP STARTS TODAY ON THE COAST.
NO PROB.
I'M HAPPY YOU CALLED ME.

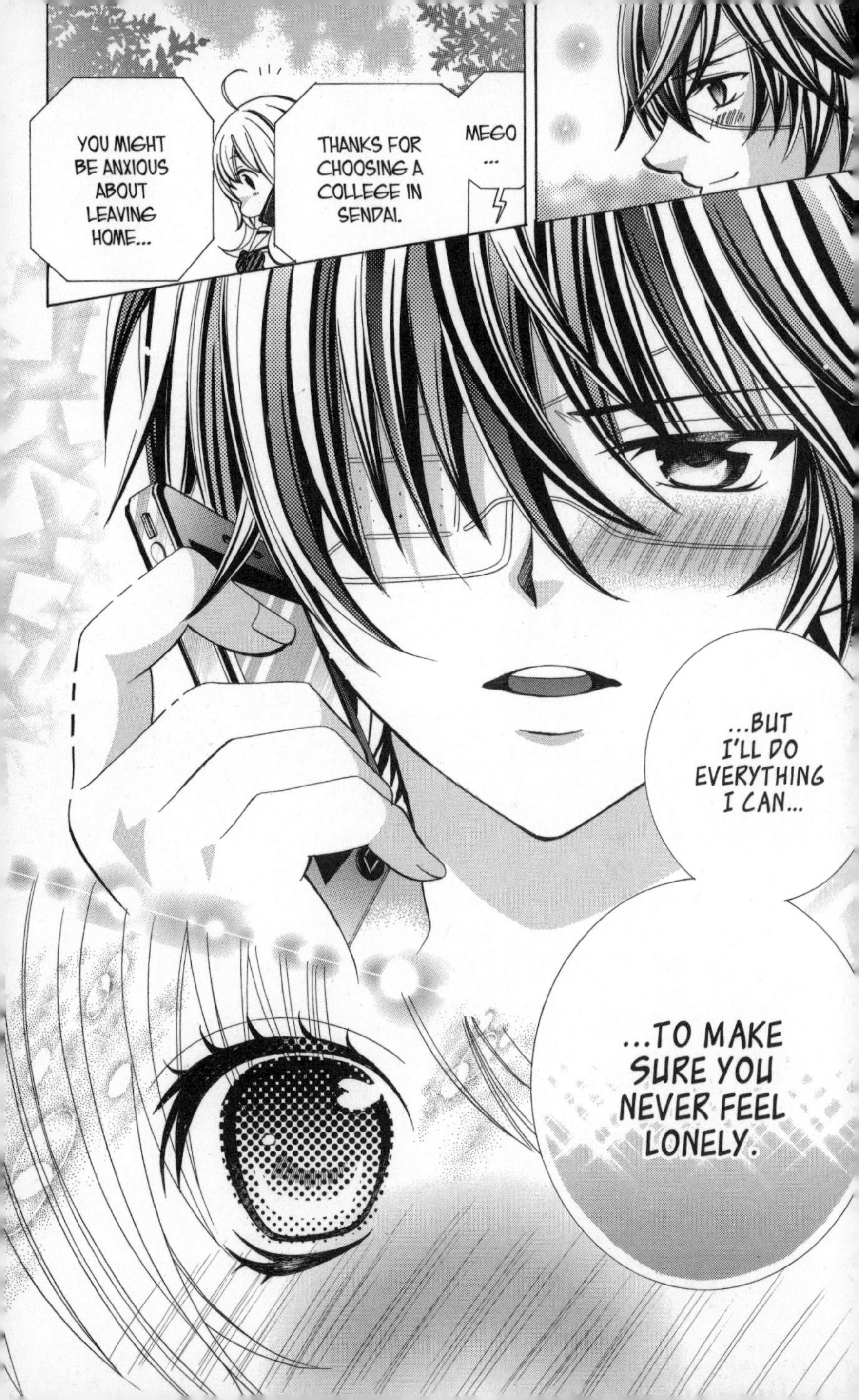
MEGO...
THANKS FOR CHOOSING A COLLEGE IN SENDAI.
YOU MIGHT BE ANXIOUS ABOUT LEAVING HOME...
...BUT I'LL DO EVERYTHING I CAN...
...TO MAKE SURE YOU NEVER FEEL LONELY.

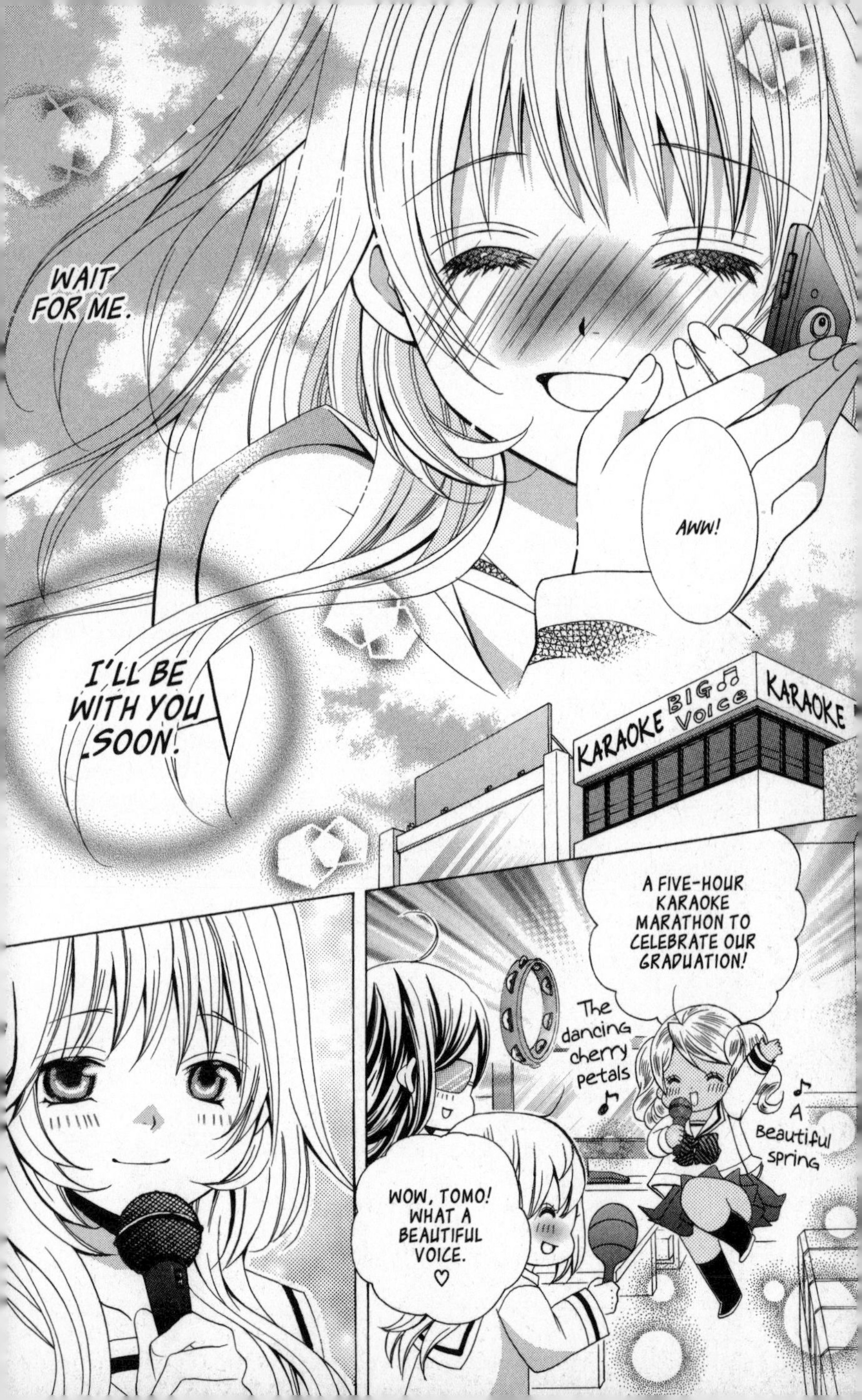
AWW!
WAIT FOR ME.
I'LL BE WITH YOU SOON!
KARAOKE
BIG Voice
KARAOKE
KARAOKE
A FIVE-HOUR KARAOKE MARATHON TO CELEBRATE OUR GRADUATION!
A Beautiful spring
The dancing cherry petals
WOW, TOMO! WHAT A BEAUTIFUL VOICE. ♡

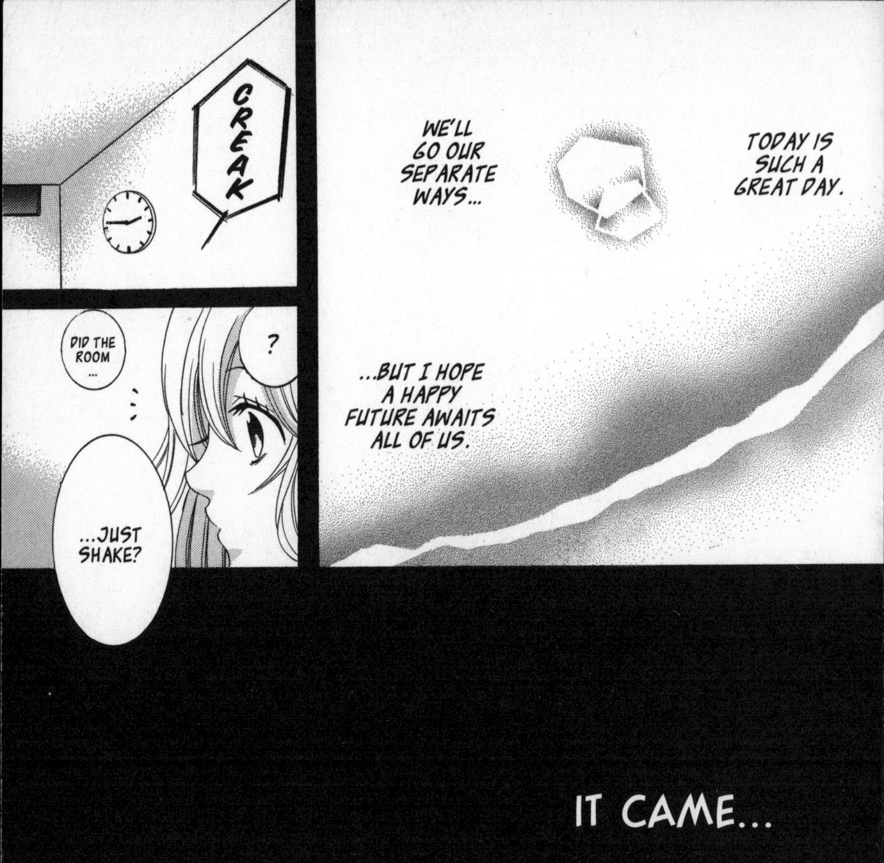
TODAY IS SUCH A GREAT DAY.
WE'LL GO OUR SEPARATE WAYS...
...BUT I HOPE A HAPPY FUTURE AWAITS ALL OF US.
CREAK
?
DID THE ROOM ...
...JUST SHAKE?
IT CAME...

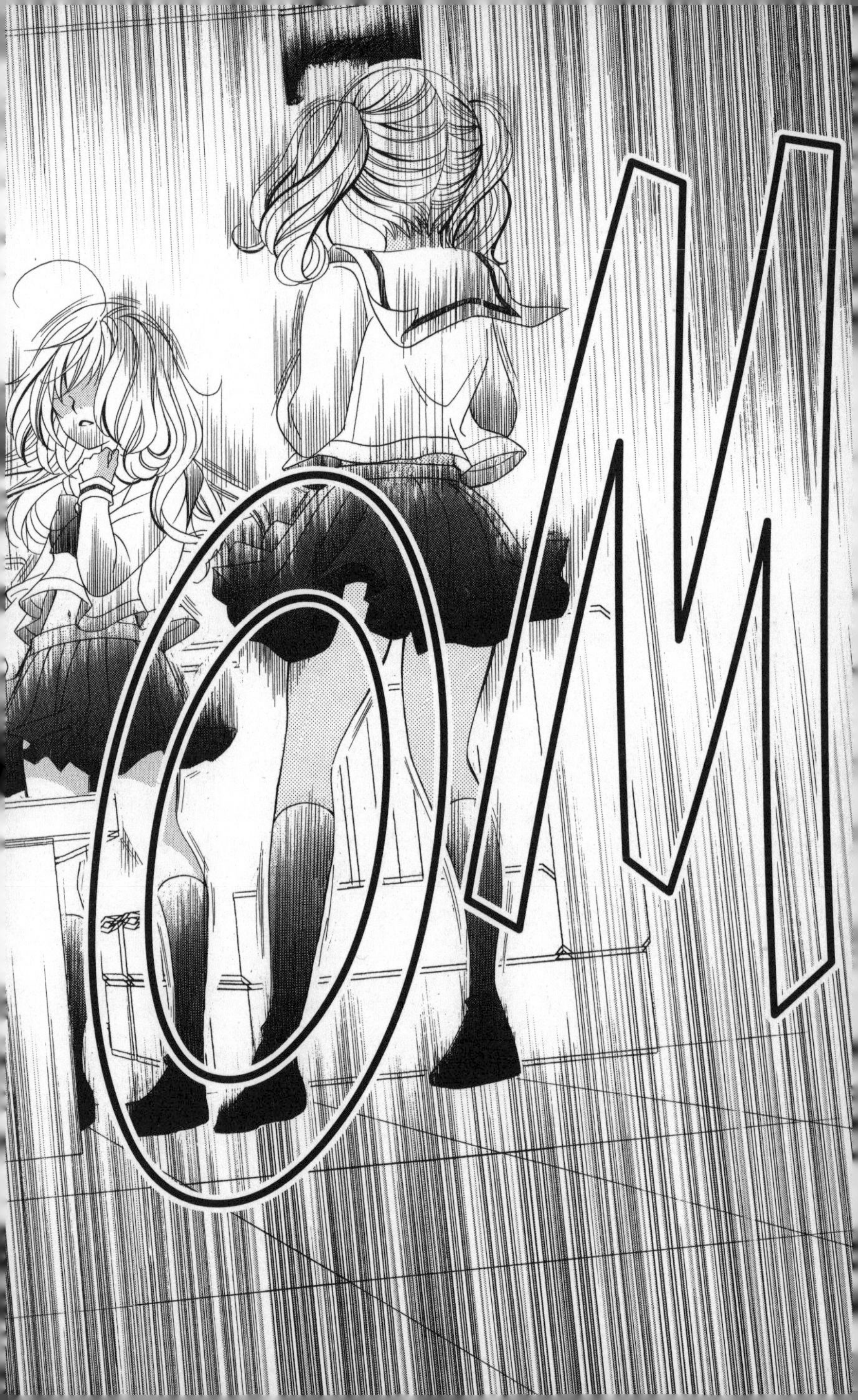

OM

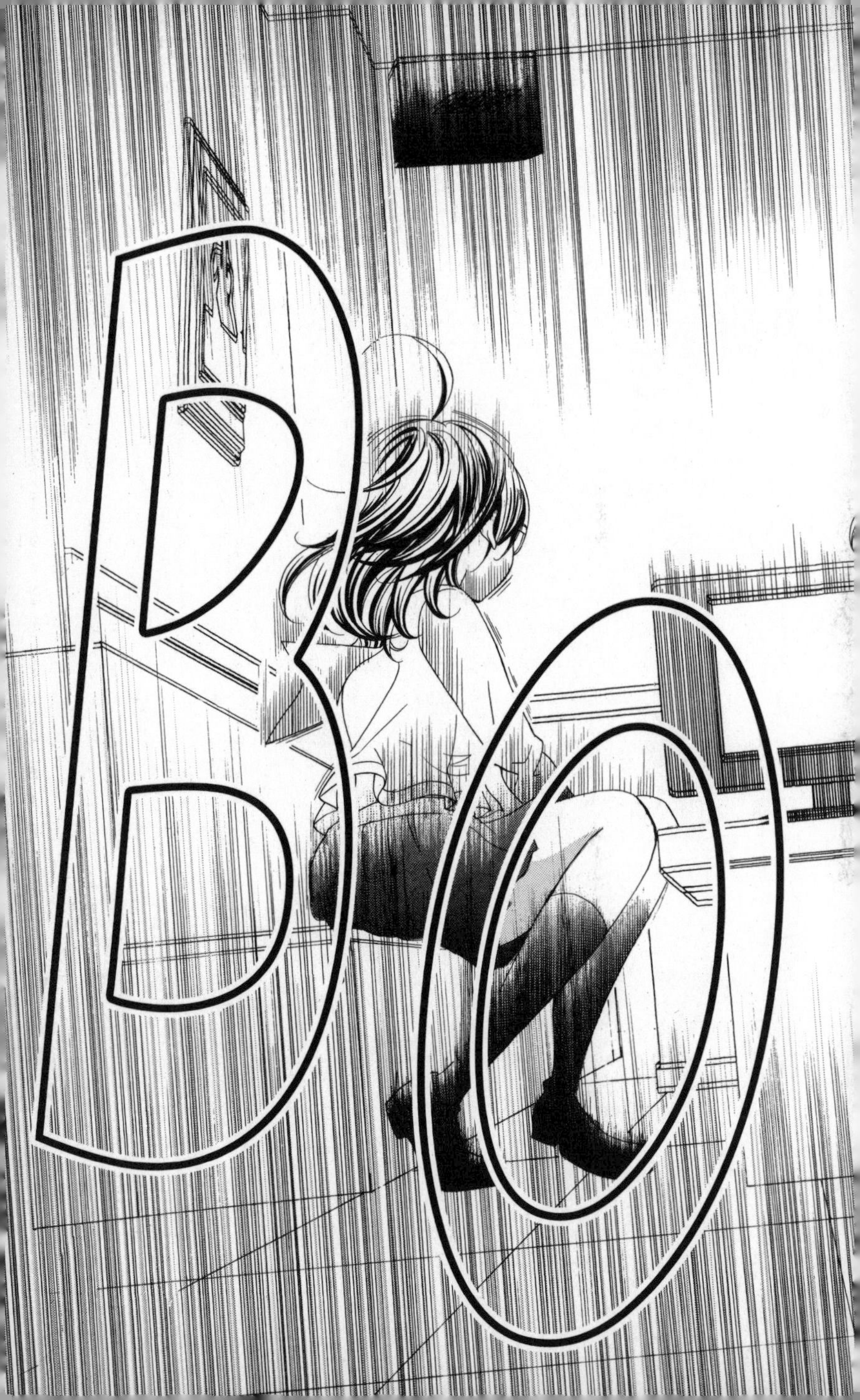
BO

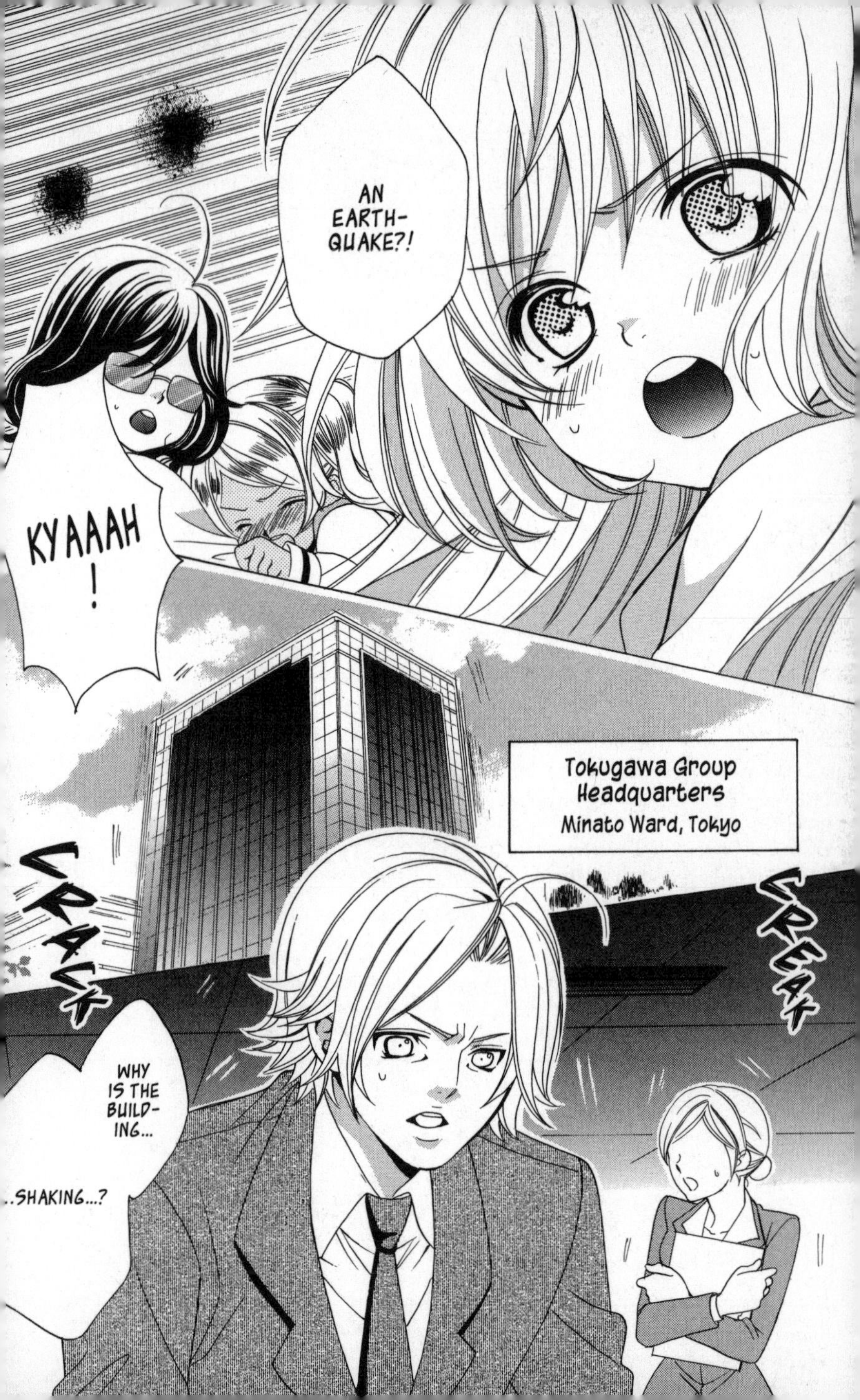
AN EARTH-QUAKE?!
KYAAAH !
Tokugawa Group Headquarters
Minato Ward, Tokyo
CREAK
CRACK
WHY IS THE BUILD-ING...
...SHAKING...?

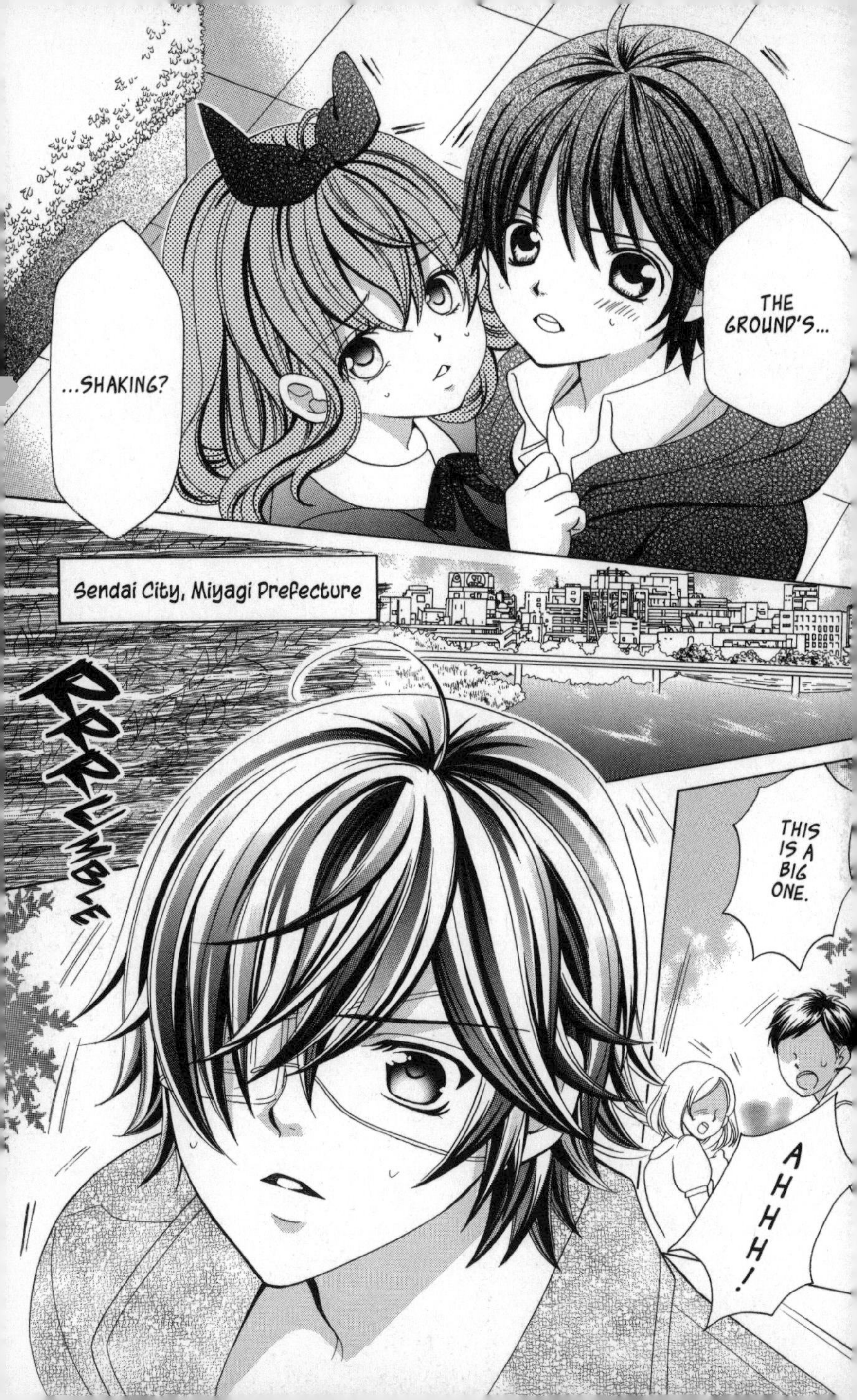
THE GROUND'S...
...SHAKING?
Sendai City, Miyagi Prefecture
THIS IS A BIG ONE.
AHHHH!
RRRUMBLE

MARCH 11, 2011.

2:46 P.M.

THE
TOHOKU
EARTHQUAKE.

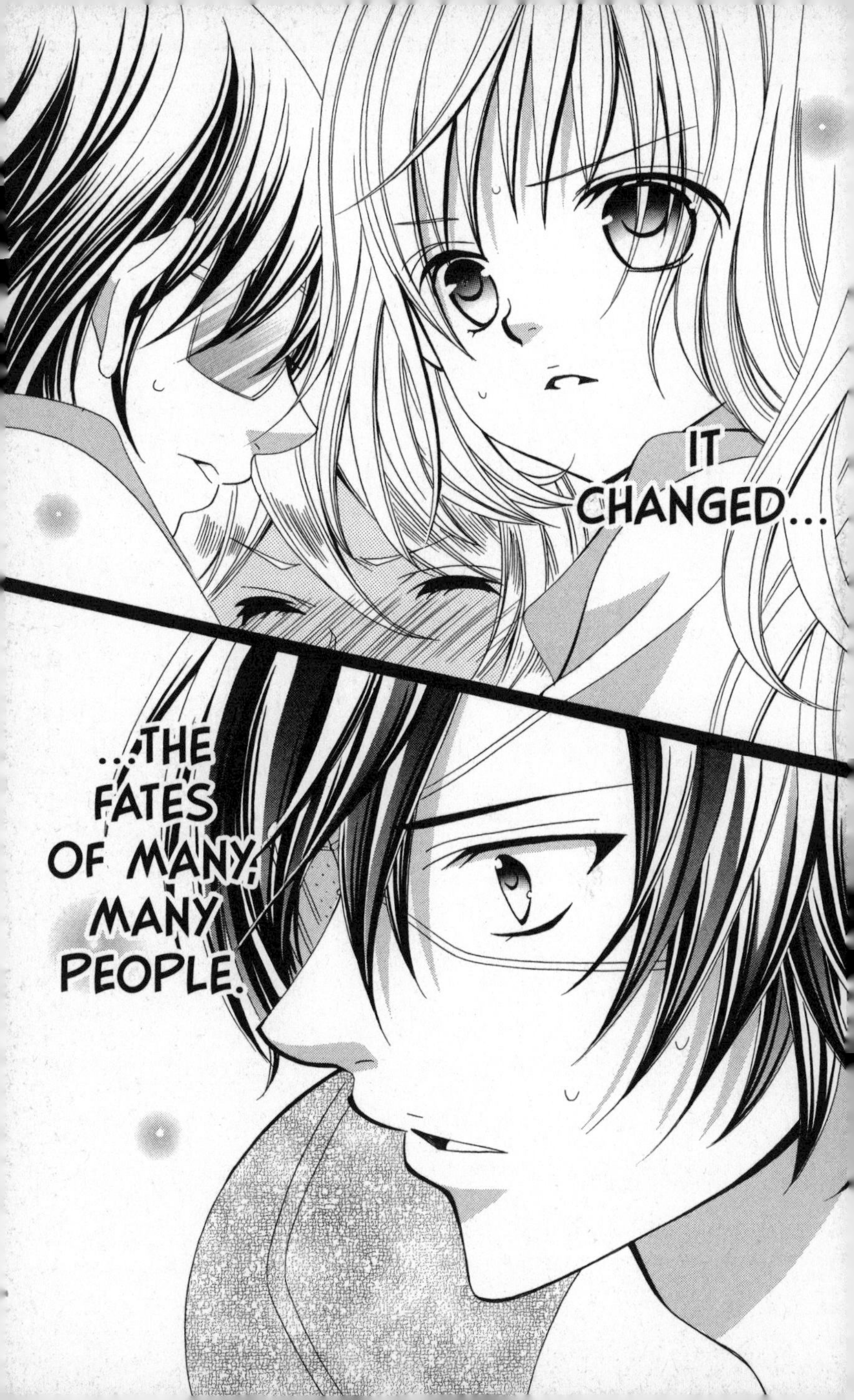
IT CHANGED...
...THE FATES OF MANY, MANY PEOPLE.

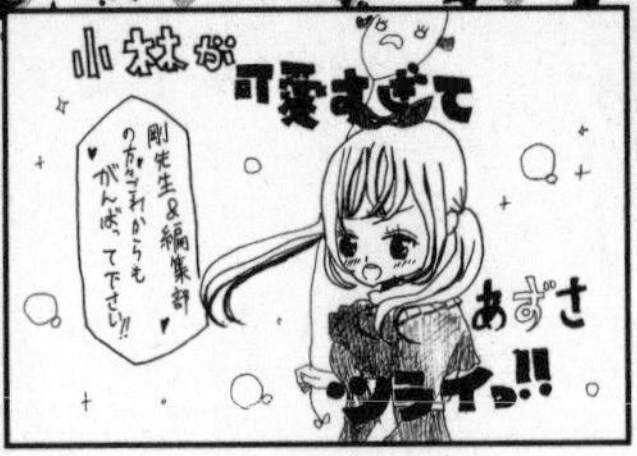
あずさ

Neneka Yoshimoto (Okayama)
Ed.: The balloon is Azusa?!
←

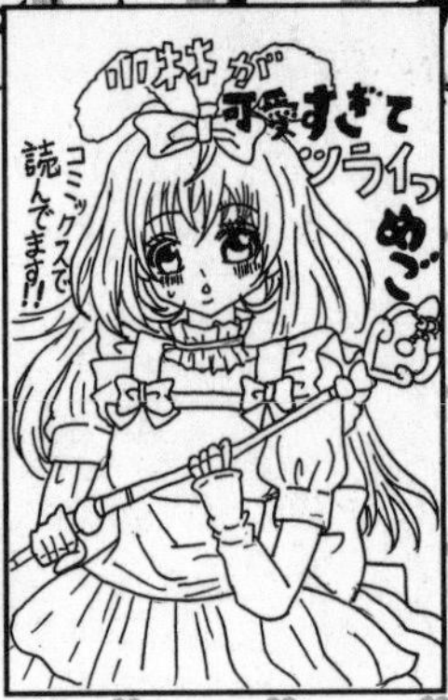

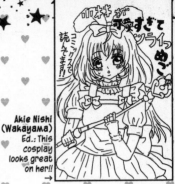

Akie Nishi (Wakayama)
Ed.: This cosplay looks great on her!!
→

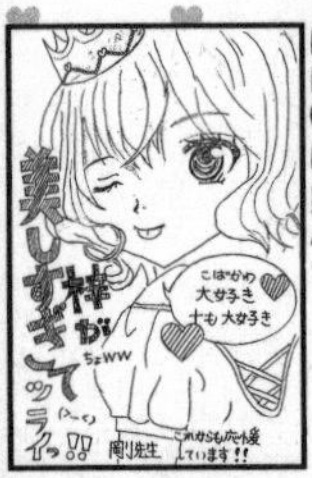

Kotomi Hirono (Nagasaki)
Ed.: I'll be with you forever, Azusa!!
←

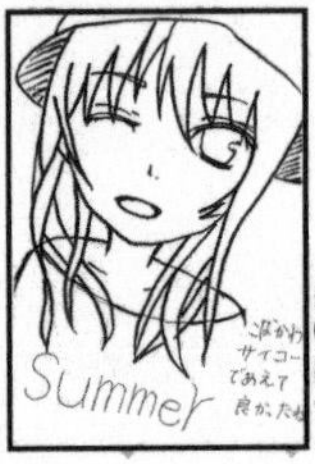
Summer

Honoka (Nagasaki)
Ed.: A cool wink!!
←

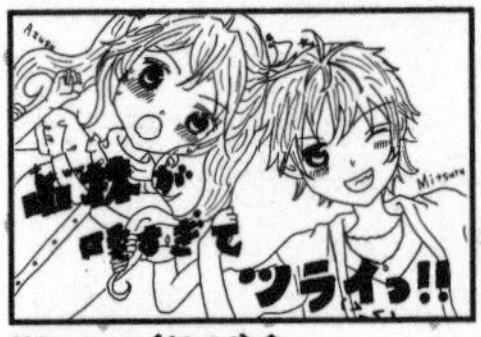

Mitchan (Aichi) ↑
Ed.: I wanna watch over their love...

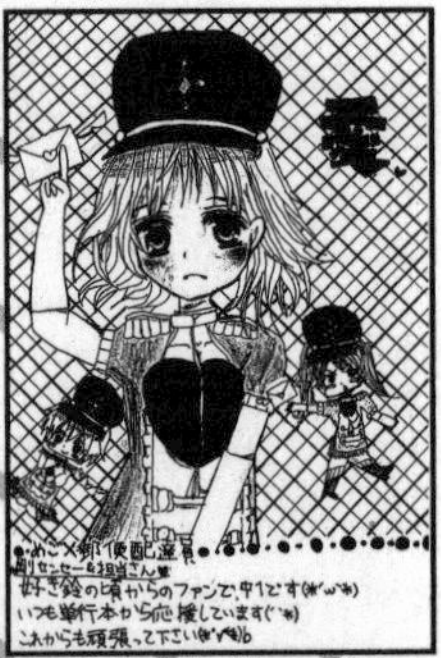

Aoi Takishita (Osaka) ↑
Ed.: You'll really be looking forward to the mail!!

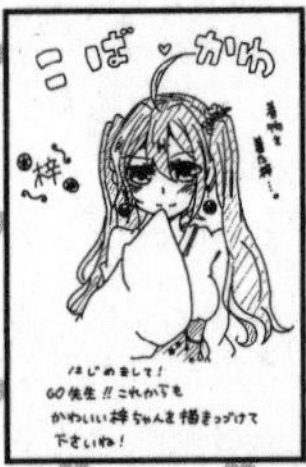

Mayu Yamasaki (Hokkaido)
Ed.: She looks beautiful in her kimono.♥
←

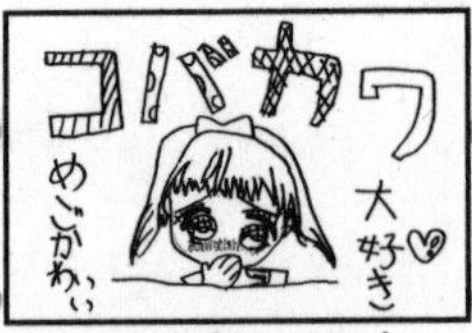
コバカワ
めごかわい
大好き♡

Hinata Ishii (Hiroshima)
Ed.: Mego makes me smile!!

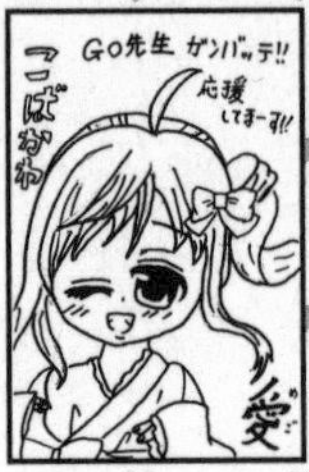

Yuzuki Yamamoto (Gunma)
Ed.: I fell in love with the yukata-clad Mego.♥
←

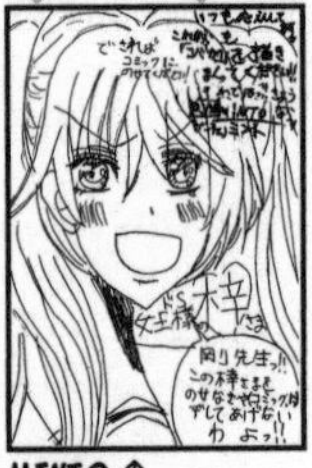

MINTO ↑
(Nagasaki)
Ed.: Queen Azusa's cool too!!

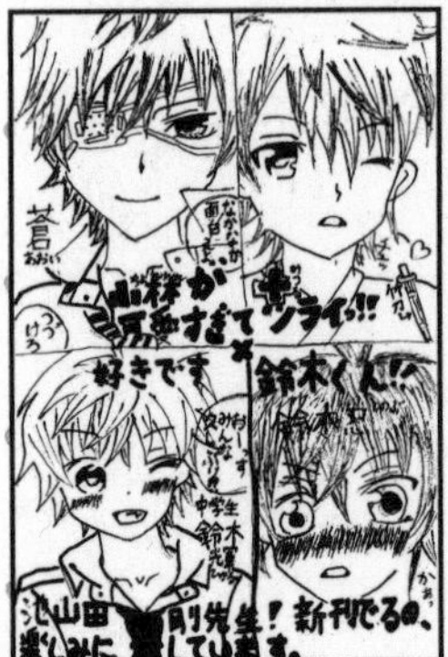

Saori Imai (Nara) ↑
Ed.: A So Cute! and Suzuki-kun collab!!

Send your fan mail to:

Go Ikeyamada
c/o Shojo Beat
VIZ Media, LLC
P.O. Box 77010
San Francisco, CA 94107

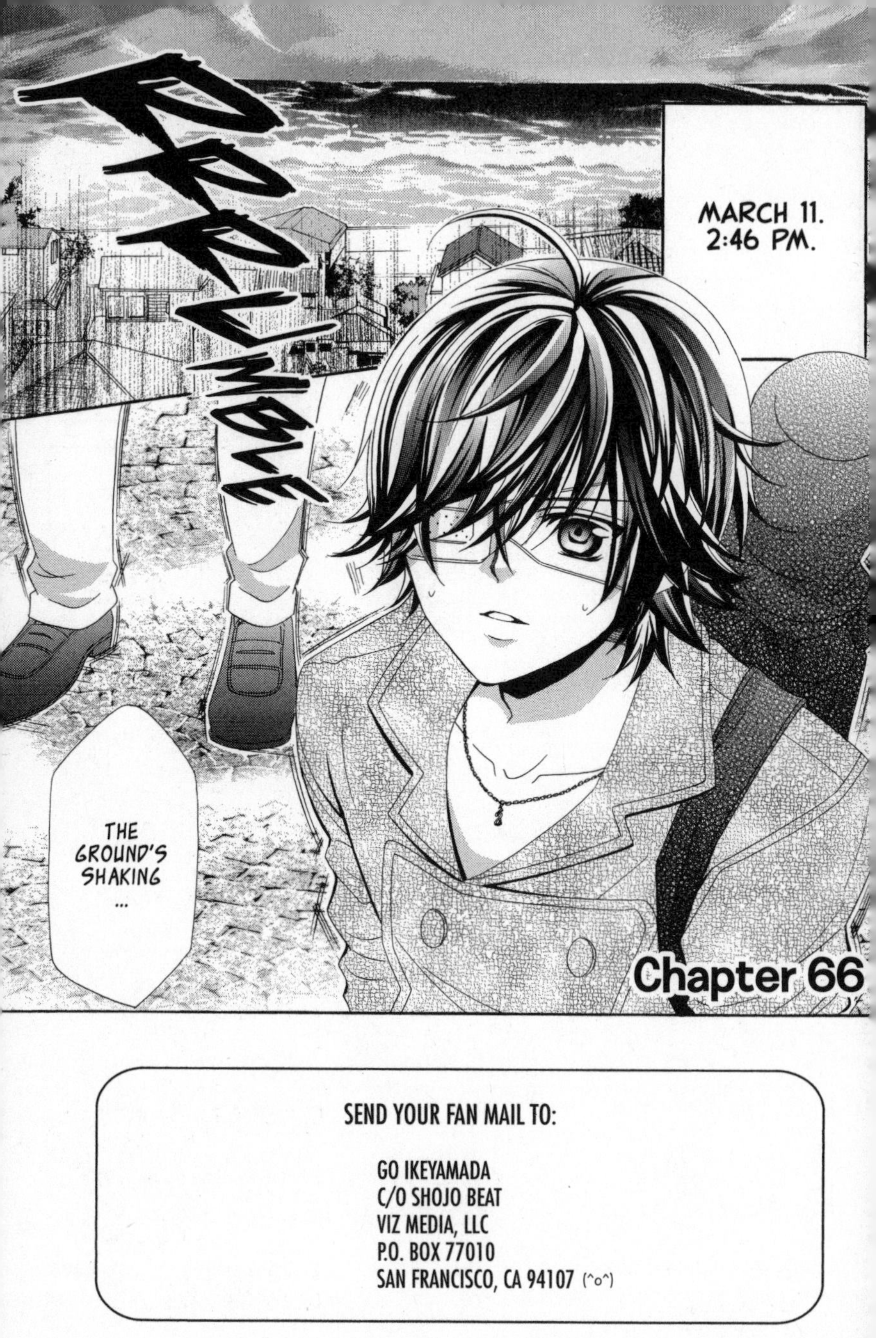
MARCH 11.
2:46 PM.
RRRUMBLE
THE GROUND'S SHAKING ...
Chapter 66

SEND YOUR FAN MAIL TO:

GO IKEYAMADA
C/O SHOJO BEAT
VIZ MEDIA, LLC
P.O. BOX 77010
SAN FRANCISCO, CA 94107 (^o^)

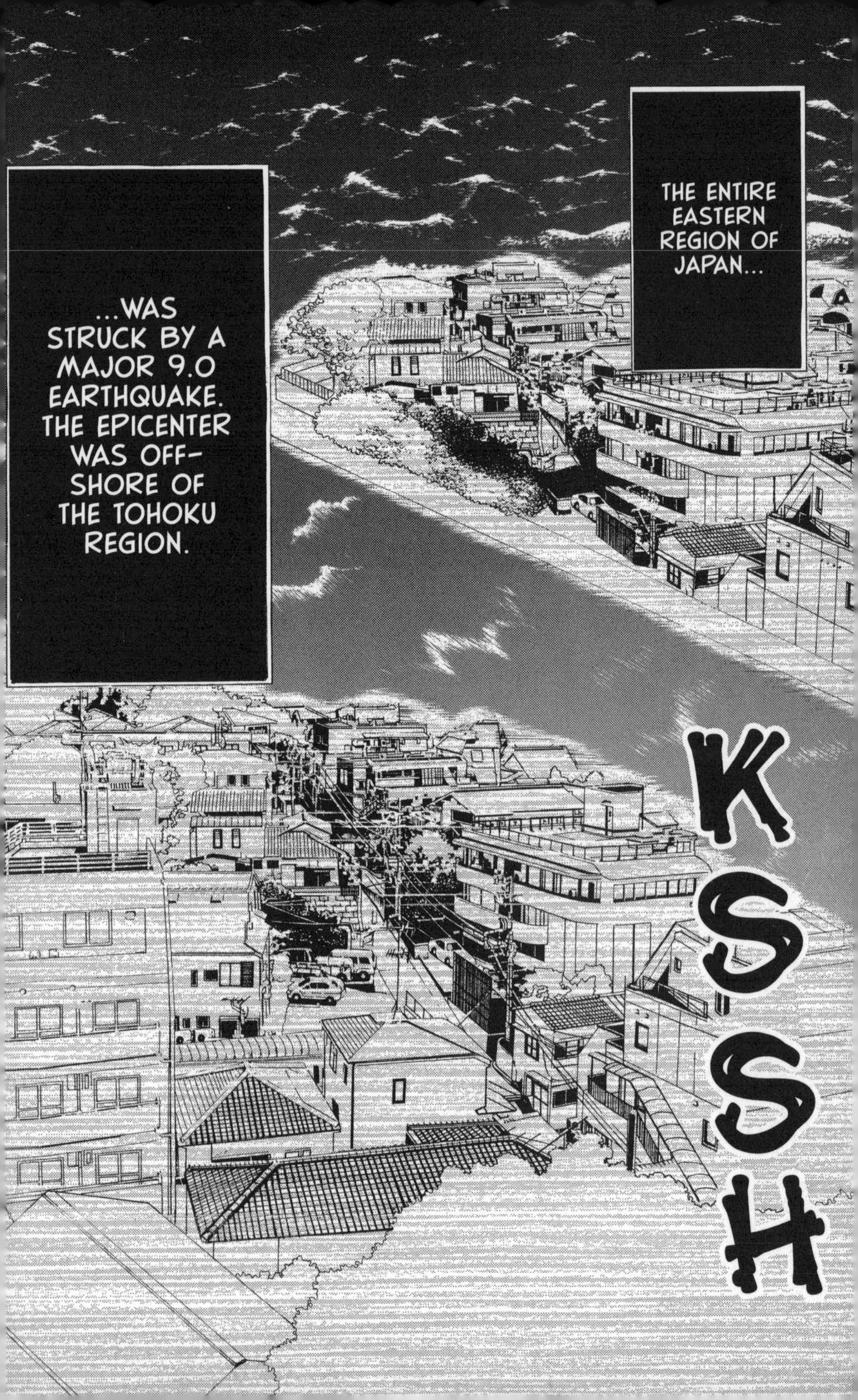
THE ENTIRE EASTERN REGION OF JAPAN...
...WAS STRUCK BY A MAJOR 9.0 EARTHQUAKE. THE EPICENTER WAS OFF-SHORE OF THE TOHOKU REGION.
KSSH

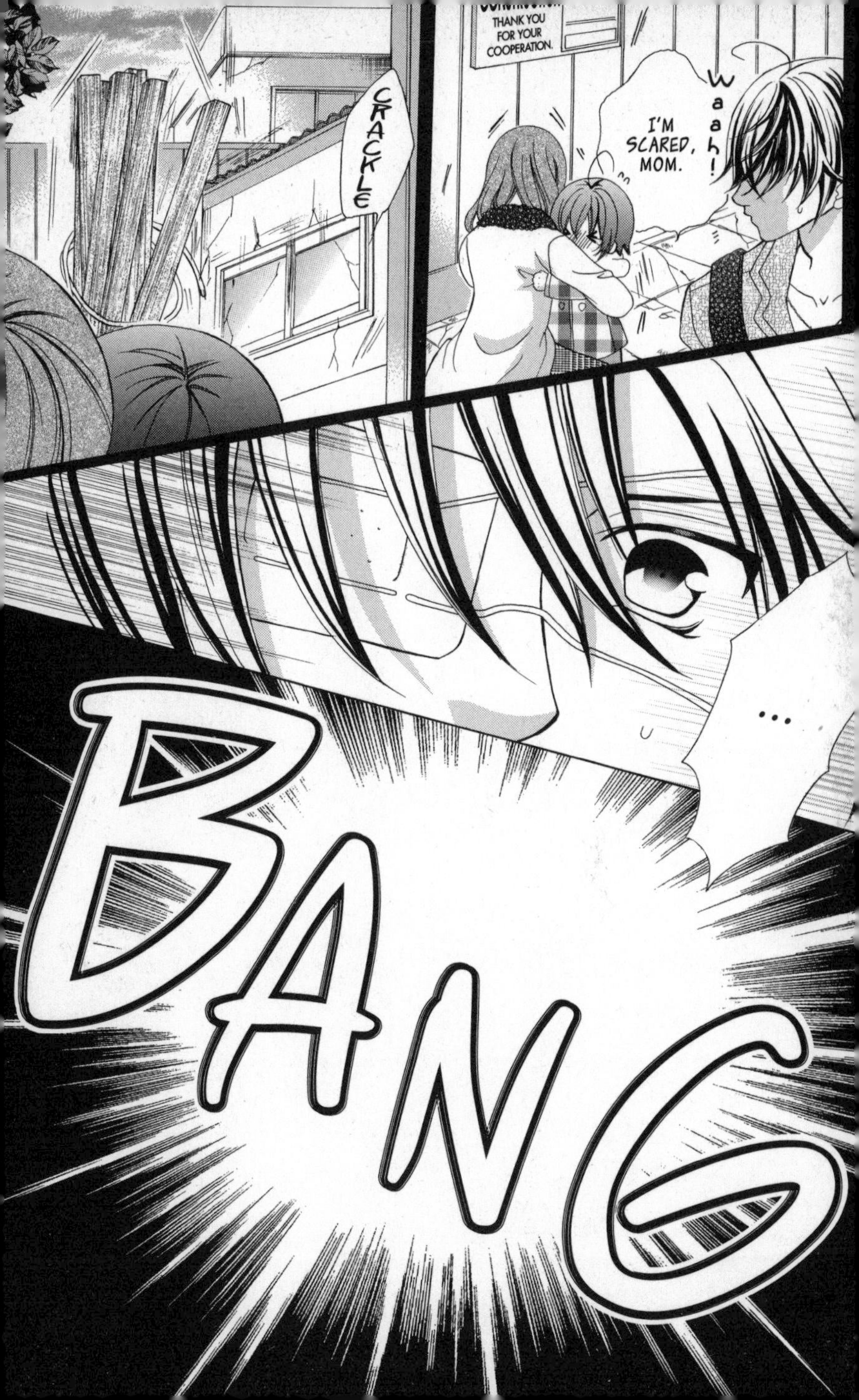
THANK YOU FOR YOUR COOPERATION.
Waah!
I'M SCARED, MOM.
CRACKLE
...
BANG

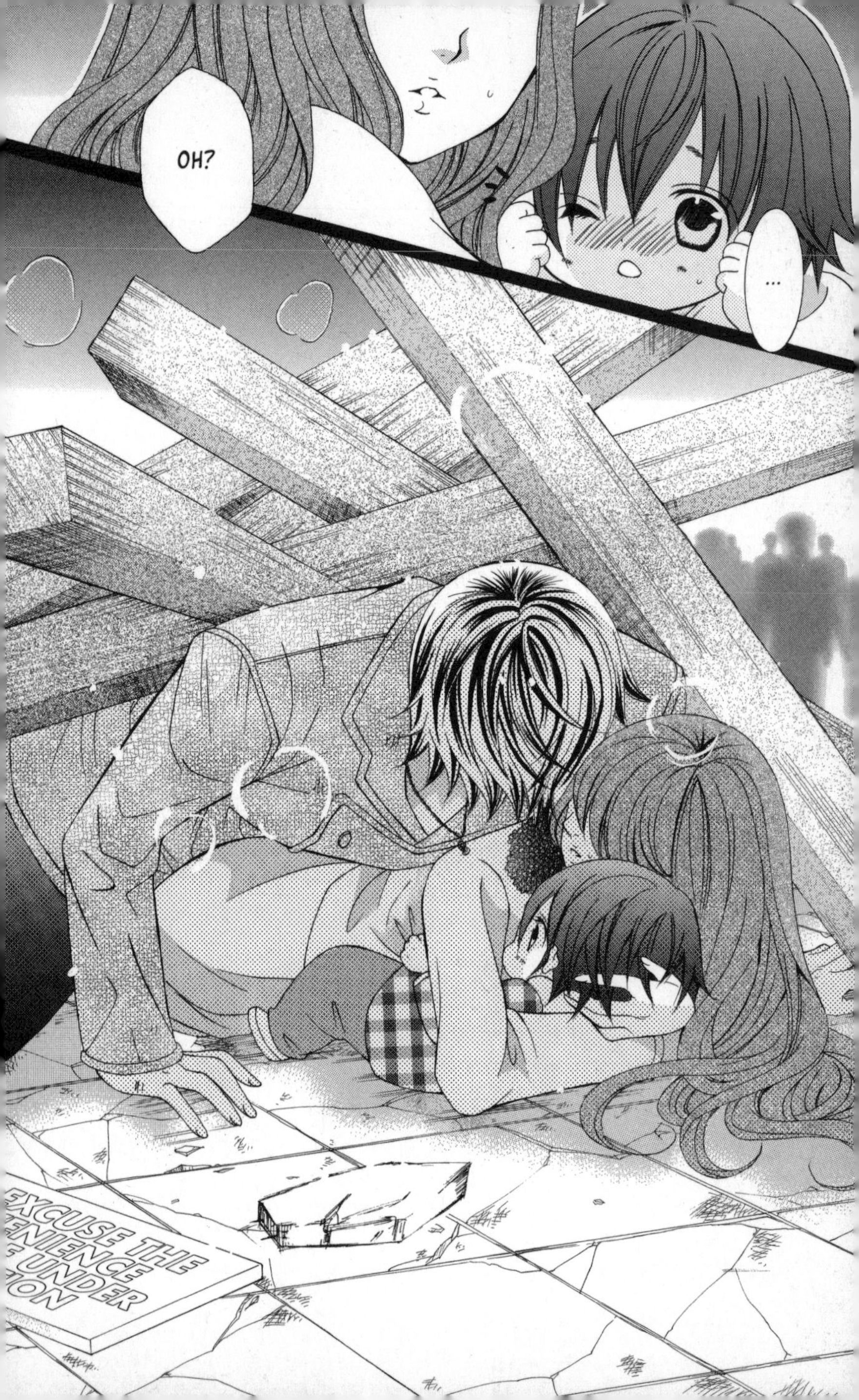
...
OH?
EXCUSE THE
ENIENCE
E UNDER
TION

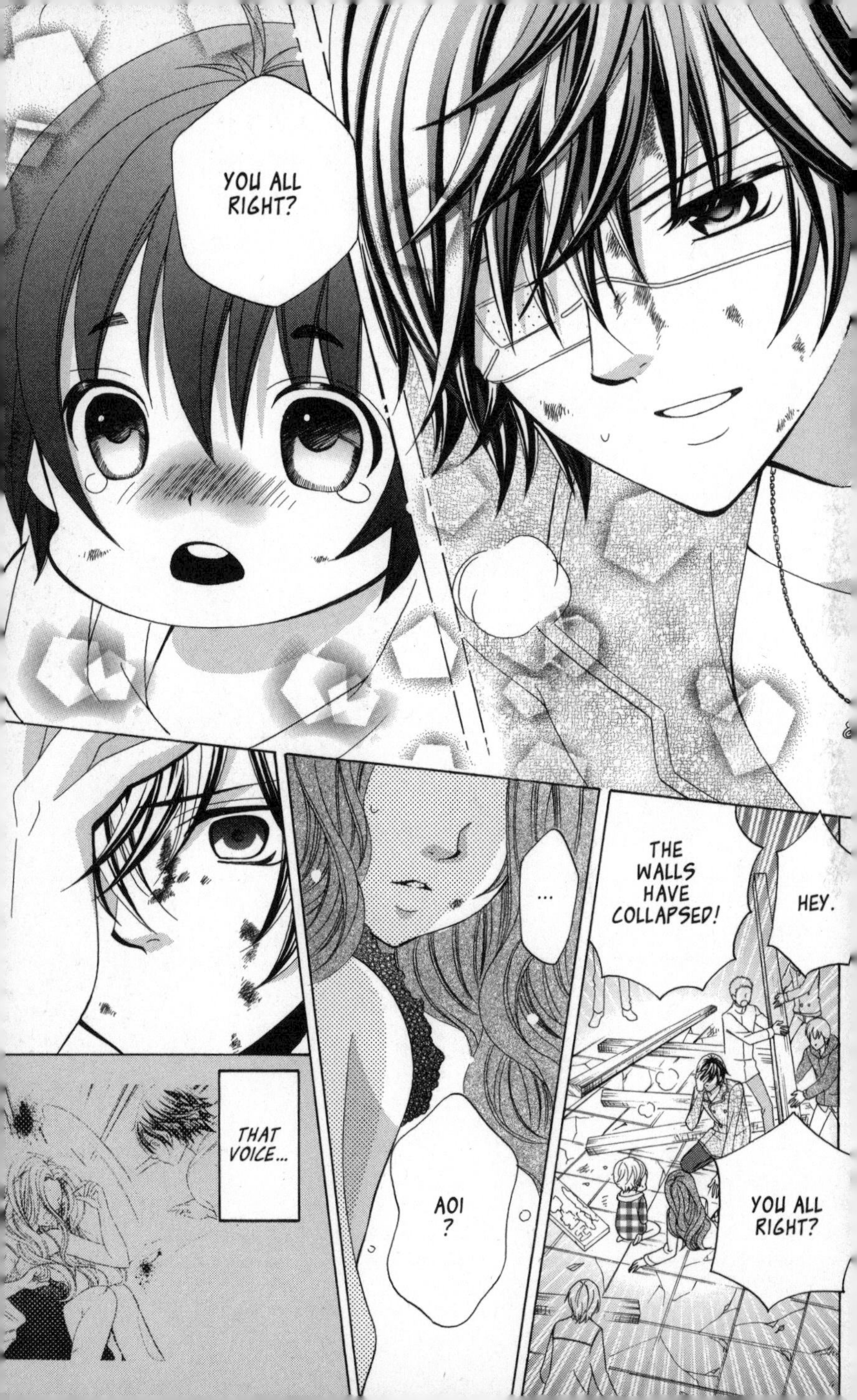
YOU ALL RIGHT?
HEY.
THE WALLS HAVE COLLAPSED!
YOU ALL RIGHT?
...
AOI?
THAT VOICE...

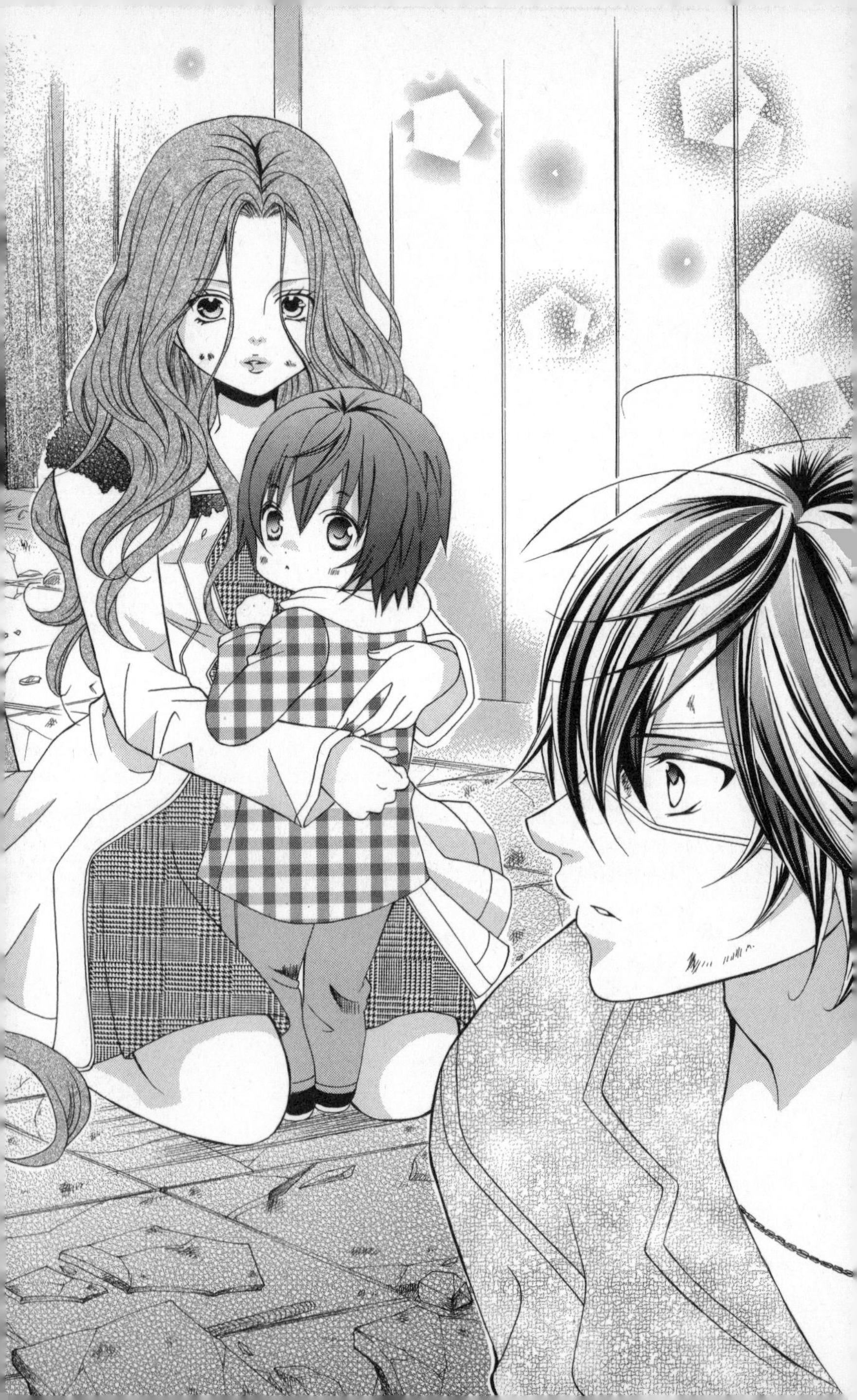

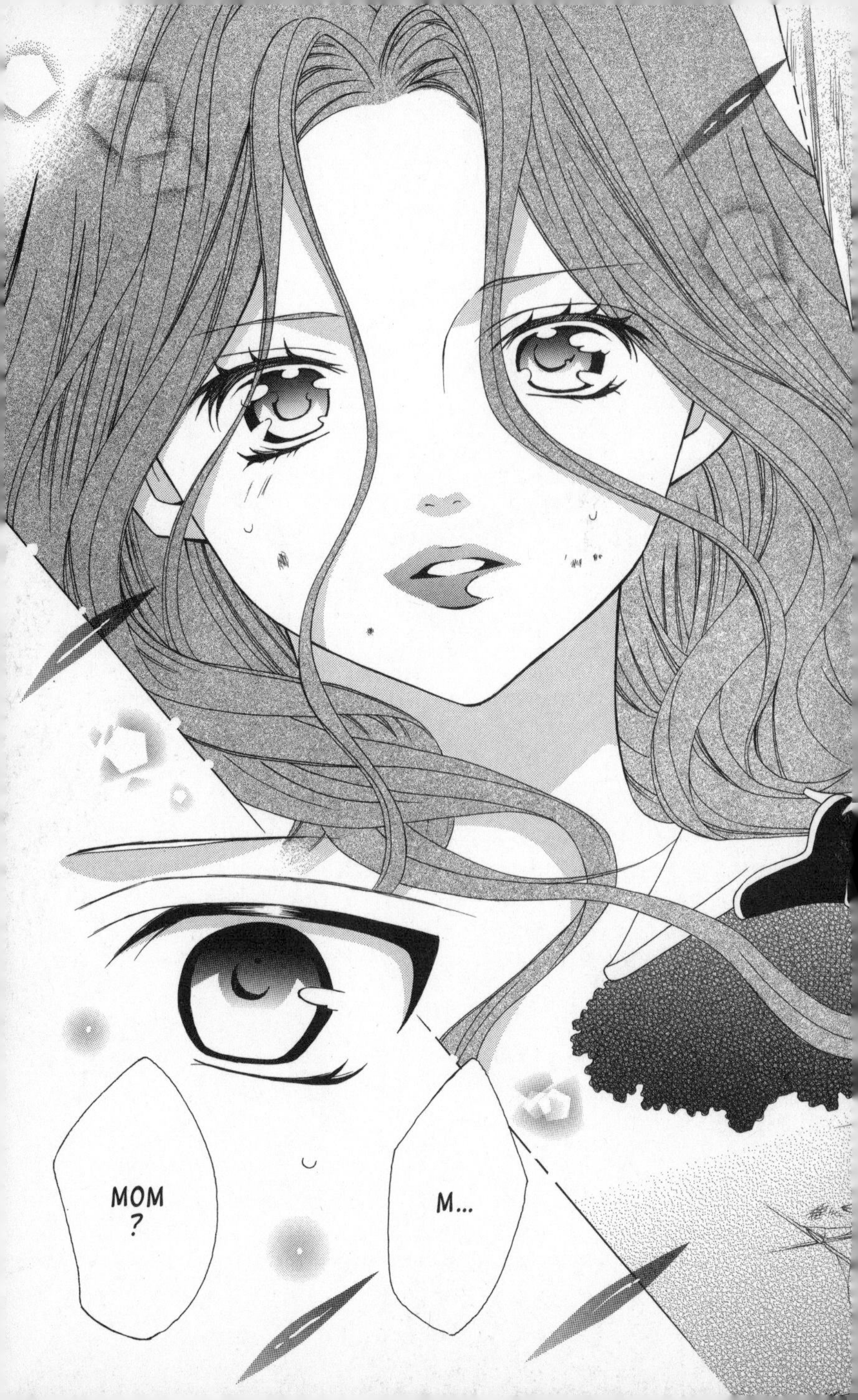
M...
MOM ?

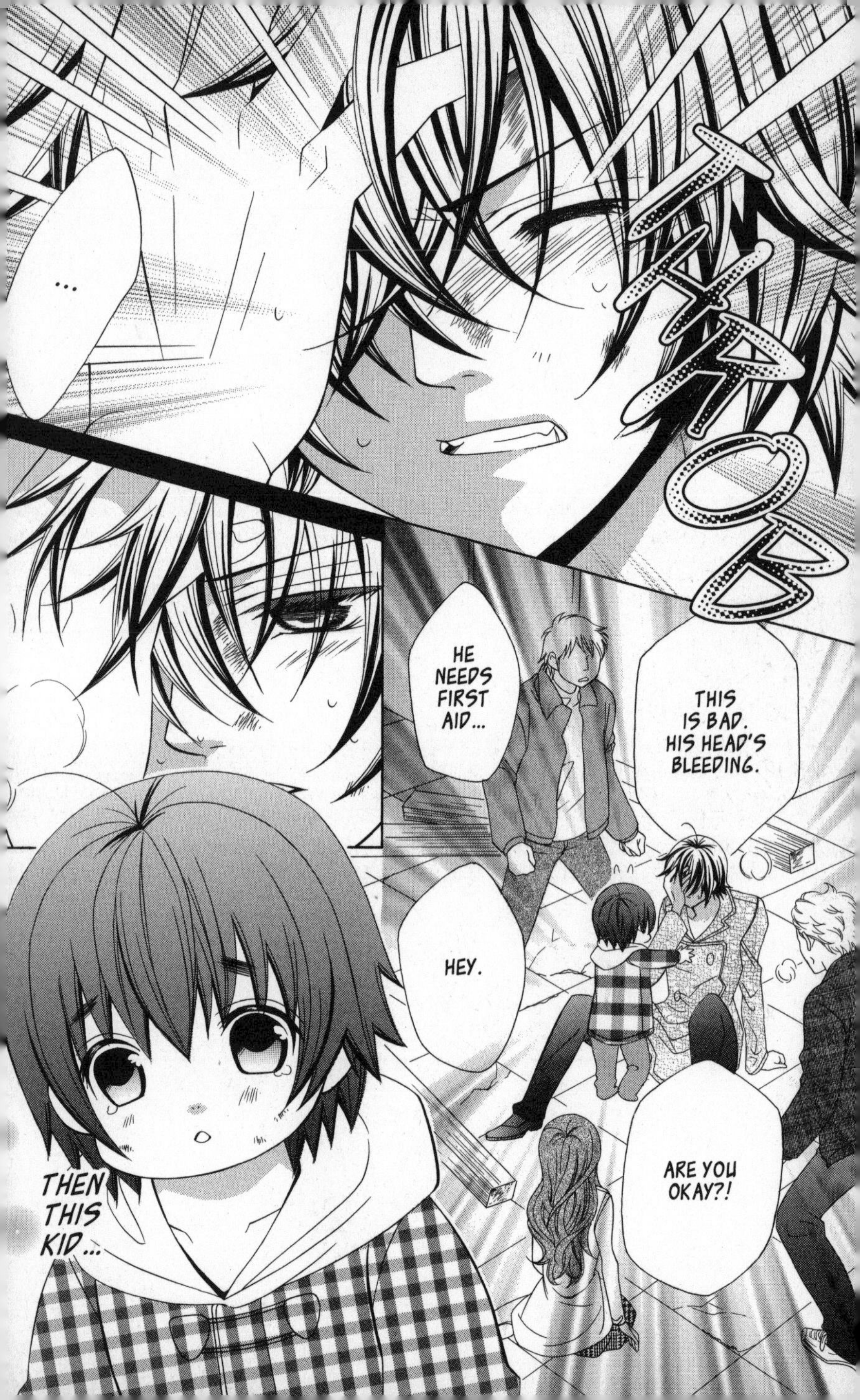
THROB
...
THIS IS BAD. HIS HEAD'S BLEEDING.
HE NEEDS FIRST AID...
HEY.
ARE YOU OKAY?!
THEN THIS KID...

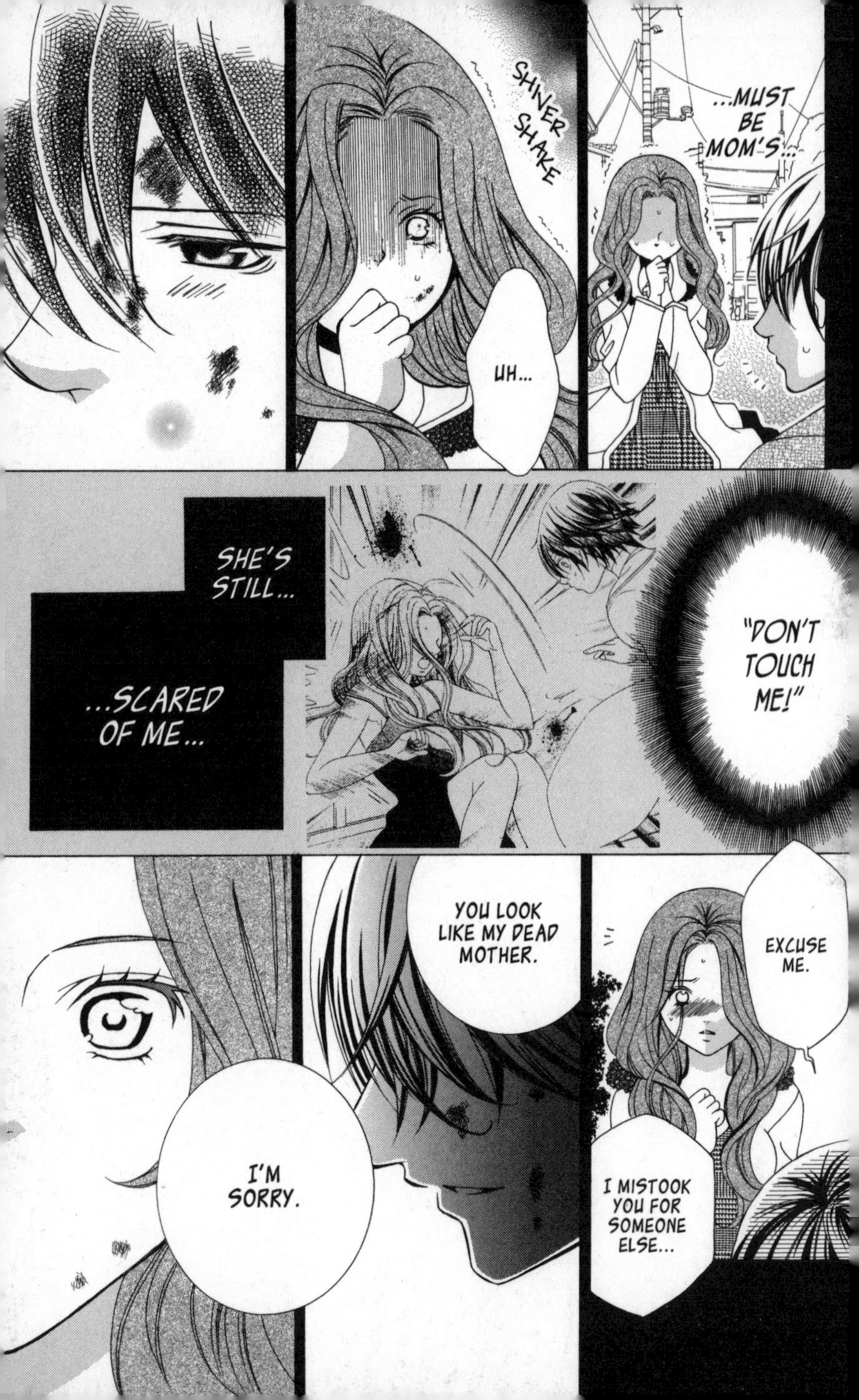
...MUST BE MOM'S...
SHIVER SHAKE
UH...
"DON'T TOUCH ME!"
SHE'S STILL...
...SCARED OF ME...
EXCUSE ME.
I MISTOOK YOU FOR SOMEONE ELSE...
YOU LOOK LIKE MY DEAD MOTHER.
I'M SORRY.

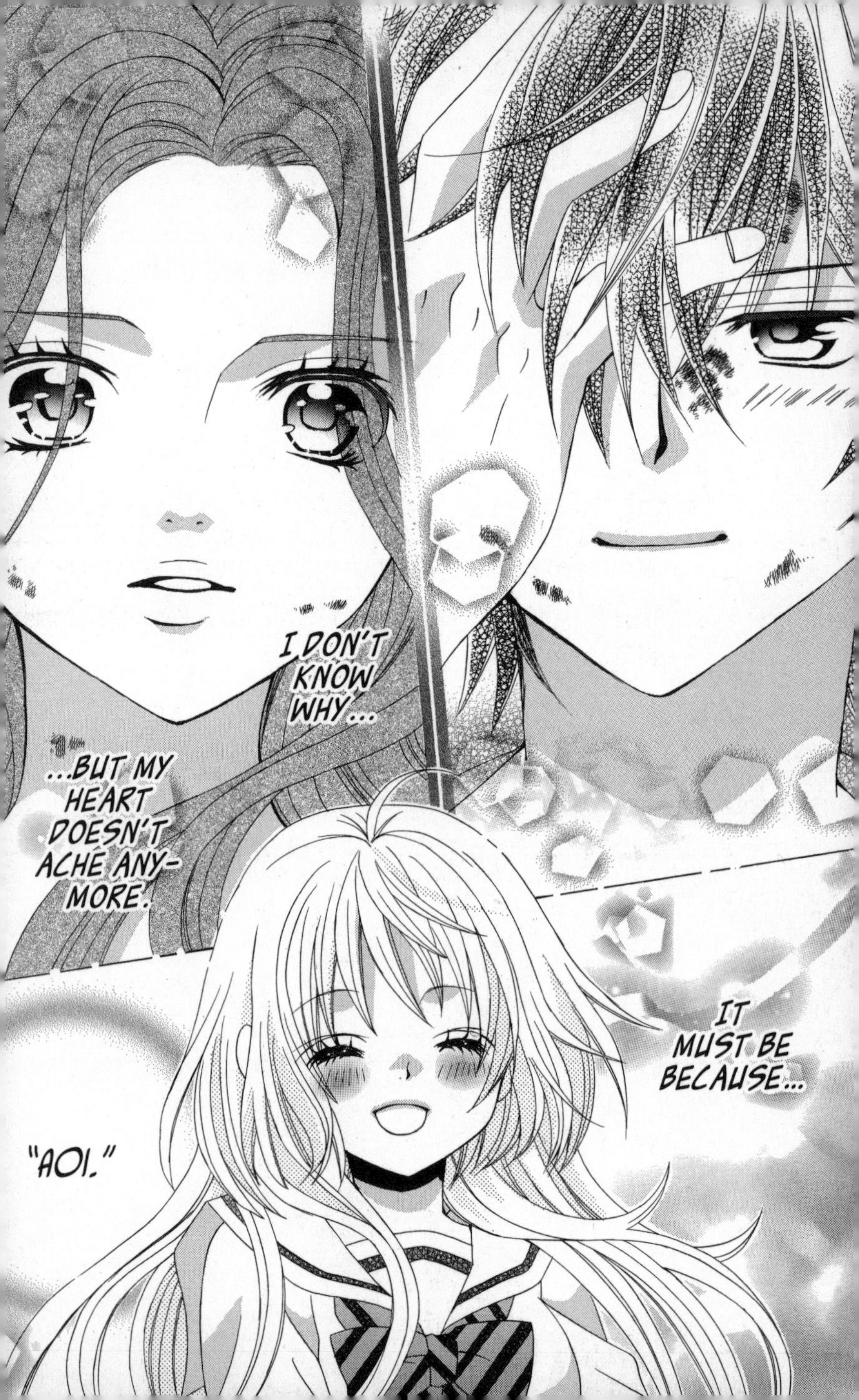
I DON'T KNOW WHY...
...BUT MY HEART DOESN'T ACHE ANY-MORE.
IT MUST BE BECAUSE...
"AOI."

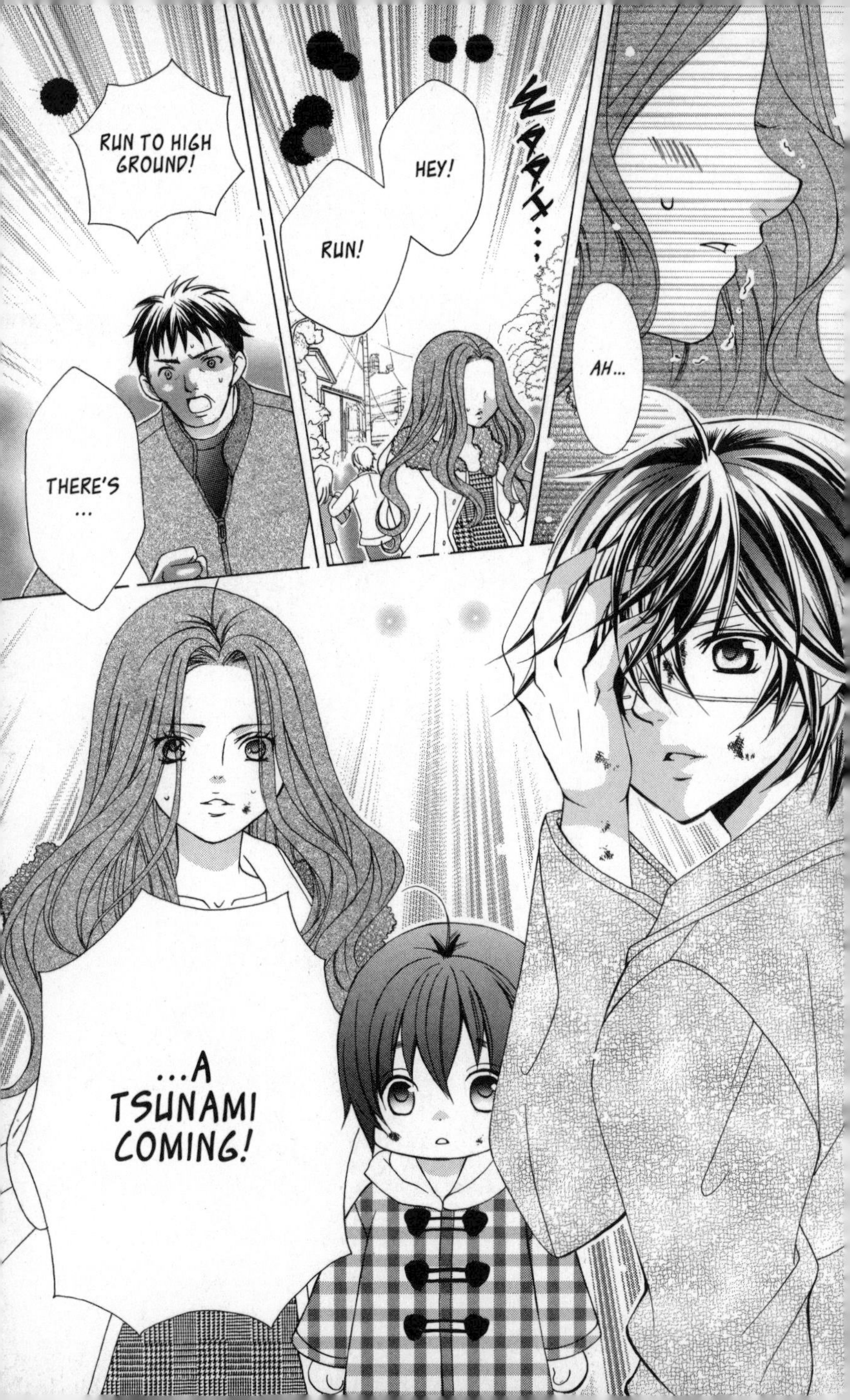
AH...
WAAH...
HEY!
RUN!
RUN TO HIGH GROUND!
THERE'S ...
...A TSUNAMI COMING!

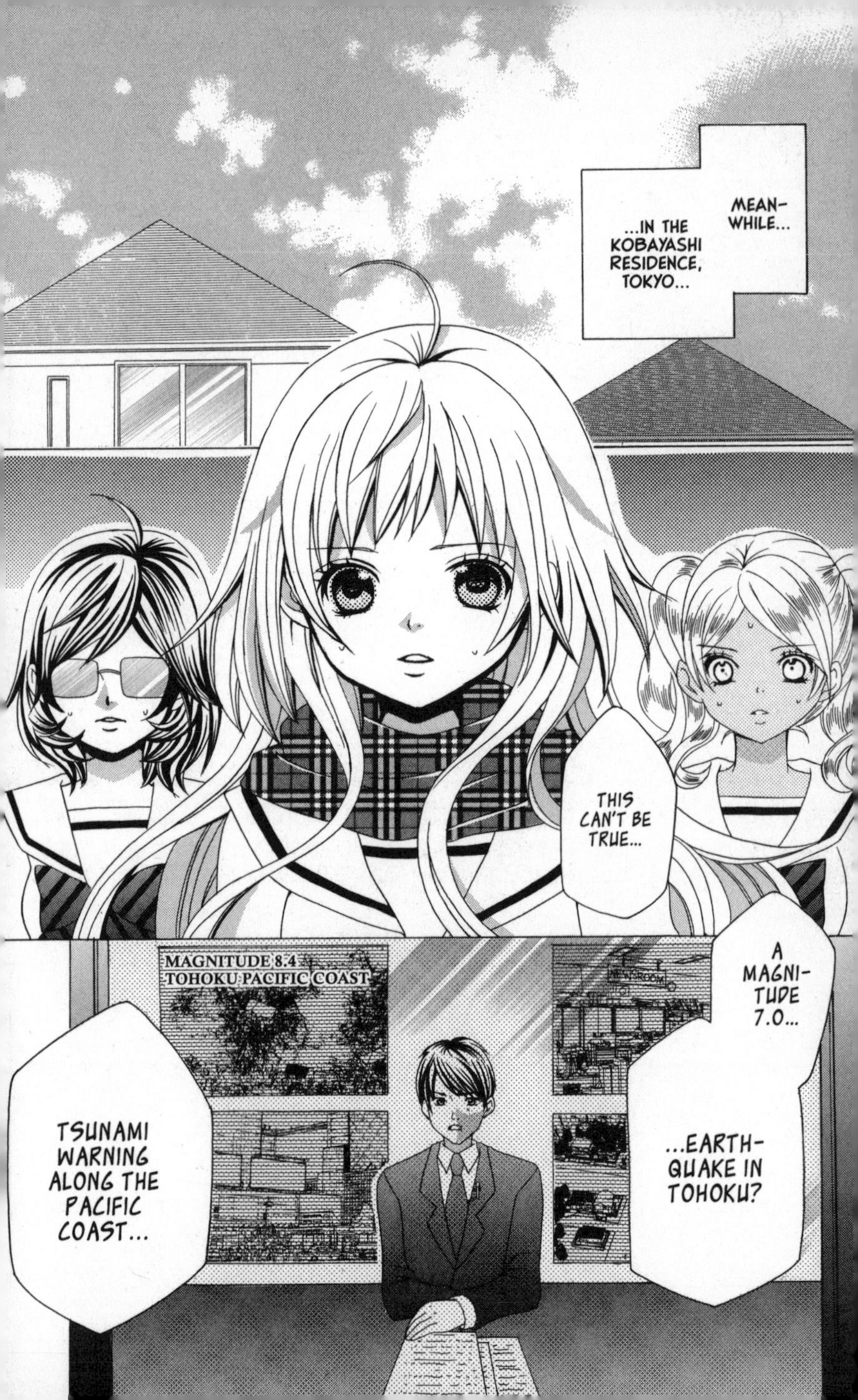
MEAN-WHILE...
...IN THE KOBAYASHI RESIDENCE, TOKYO...
THIS CAN'T BE TRUE...
A MAGNITUDE 7.0...
...EARTHQUAKE IN TOHOKU?
MAGNITUDE 8.4
TOHOKU PACIFIC COAST
TSUNAMI WARNING ALONG THE PACIFIC COAST...

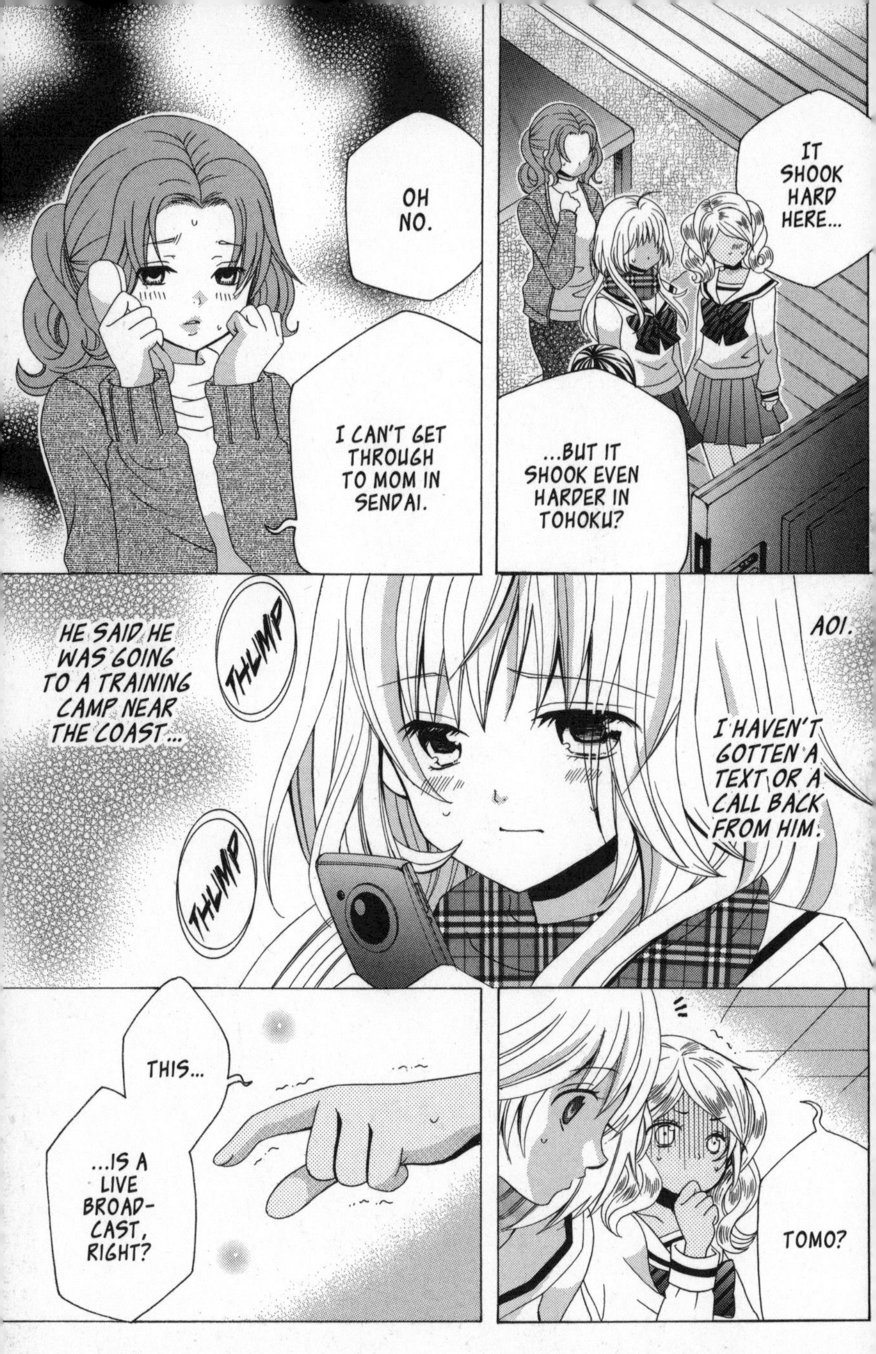
IT SHOOK HARD HERE...
...BUT IT SHOOK EVEN HARDER IN TOHOKU?
OH NO.
I CAN'T GET THROUGH TO MOM IN SENDAI.
AOI.
THUMP
HE SAID HE WAS GOING TO A TRAINING CAMP NEAR THE COAST...
I HAVEN'T GOTTEN A TEXT OR A CALL BACK FROM HIM.
THUMP
TOMO?
THIS...
...IS A LIVE BROADCAST, RIGHT?

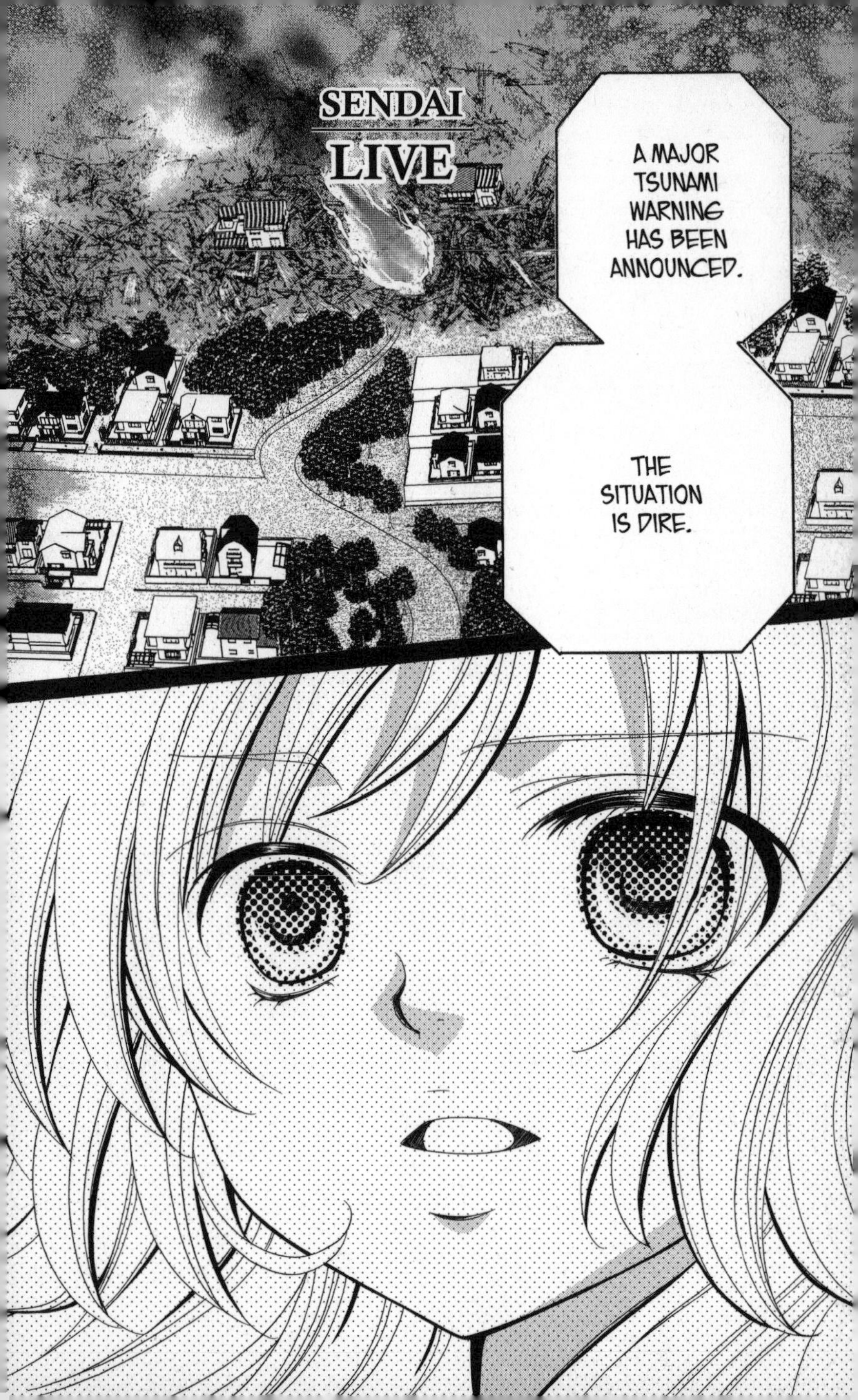
SENDAI LIVE
A MAJOR TSUNAMI WARNING HAS BEEN ANNOUNCED.
THE SITUATION IS DIRE.

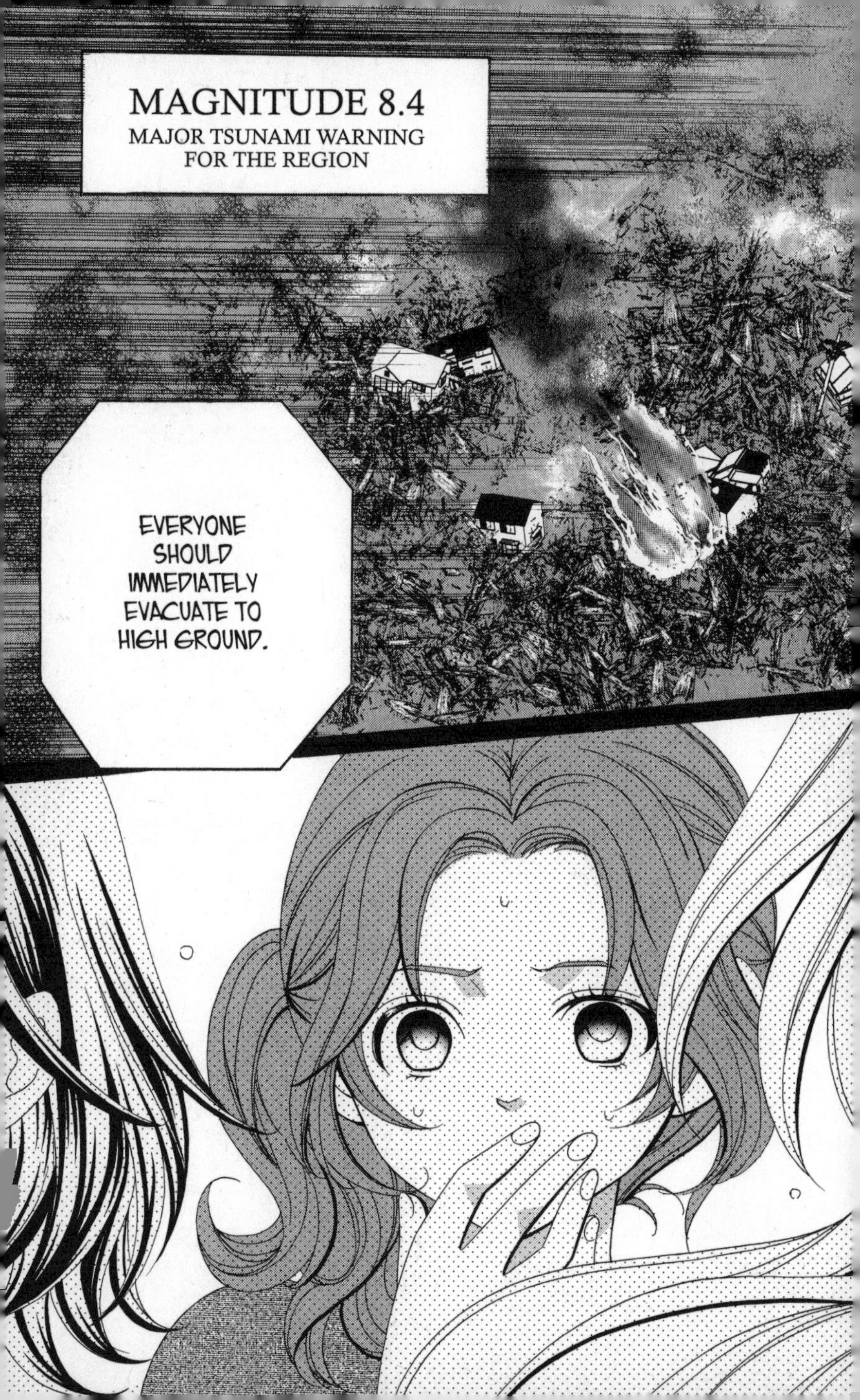
MAGNITUDE 8.4
MAJOR TSUNAMI WARNING FOR THE REGION
EVERYONE SHOULD IMMEDIATELY EVACUATE TO HIGH GROUND.

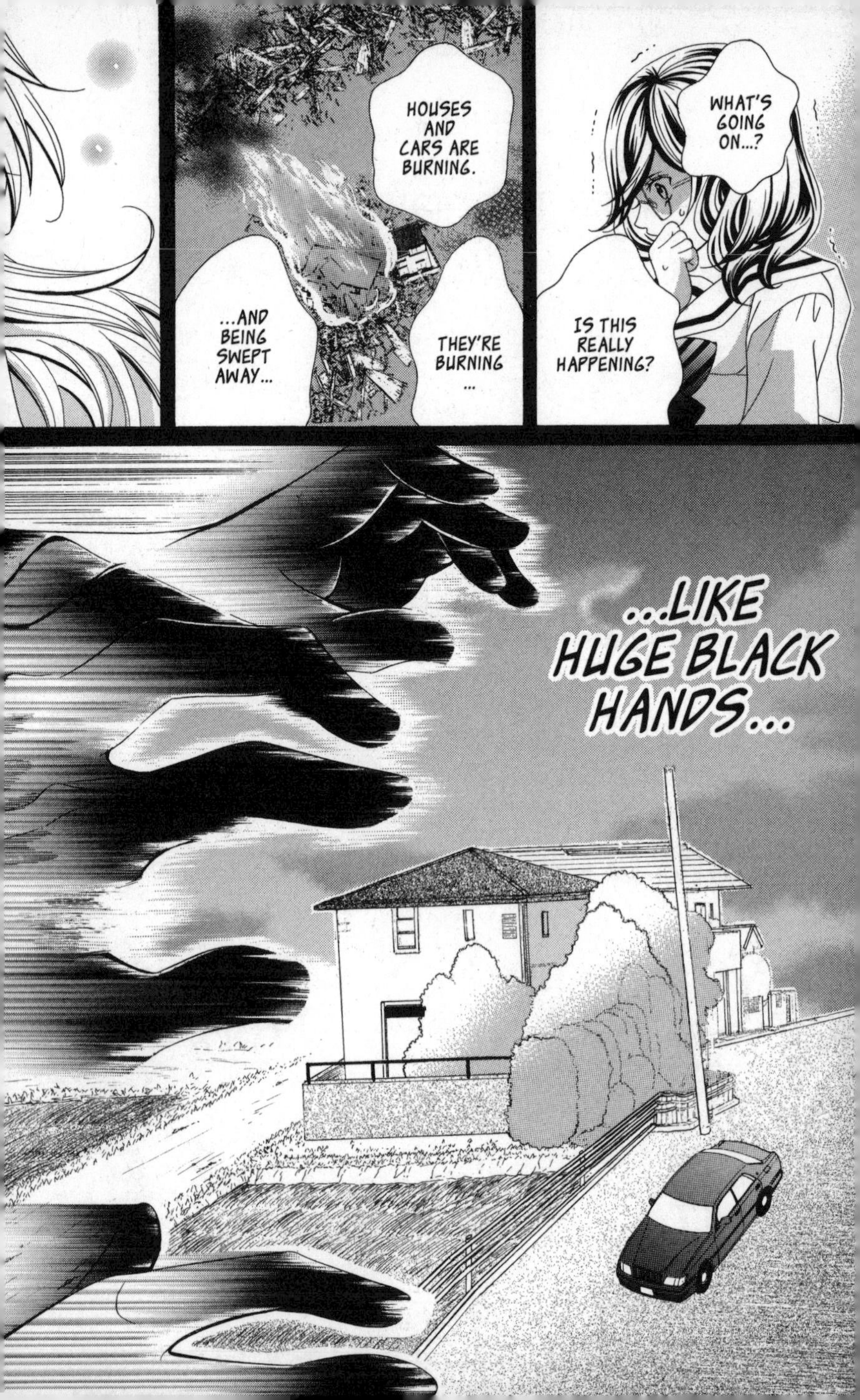
WHAT'S GOING ON...?
IS THIS REALLY HAPPENING?
HOUSES AND CARS ARE BURNING.
THEY'RE BURNING ...
...AND BEING SWEPT AWAY...
...LIKE HUGE BLACK HANDS...

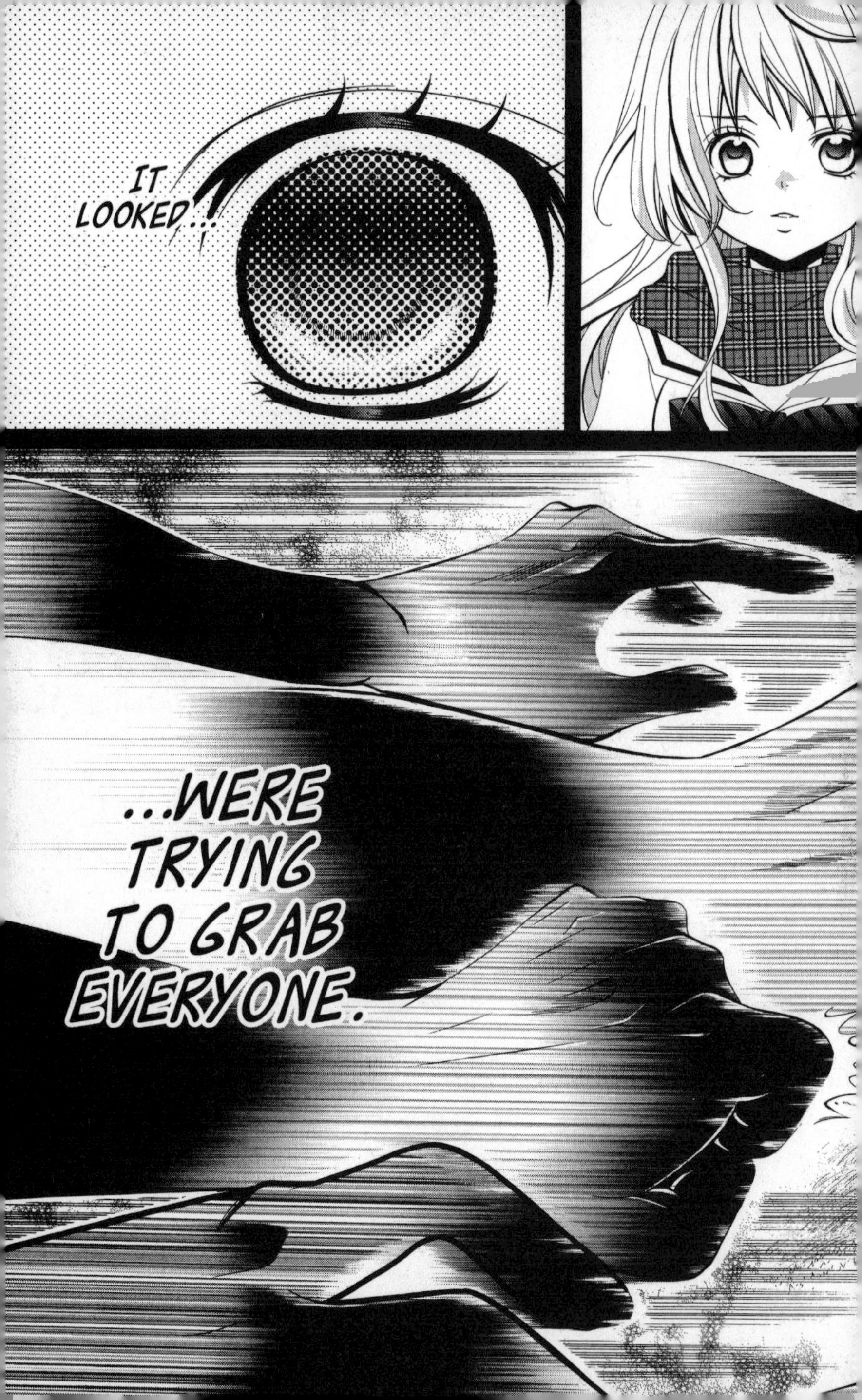
IT LOOKED...
...WERE TRYING TO GRAB EVERYONE.

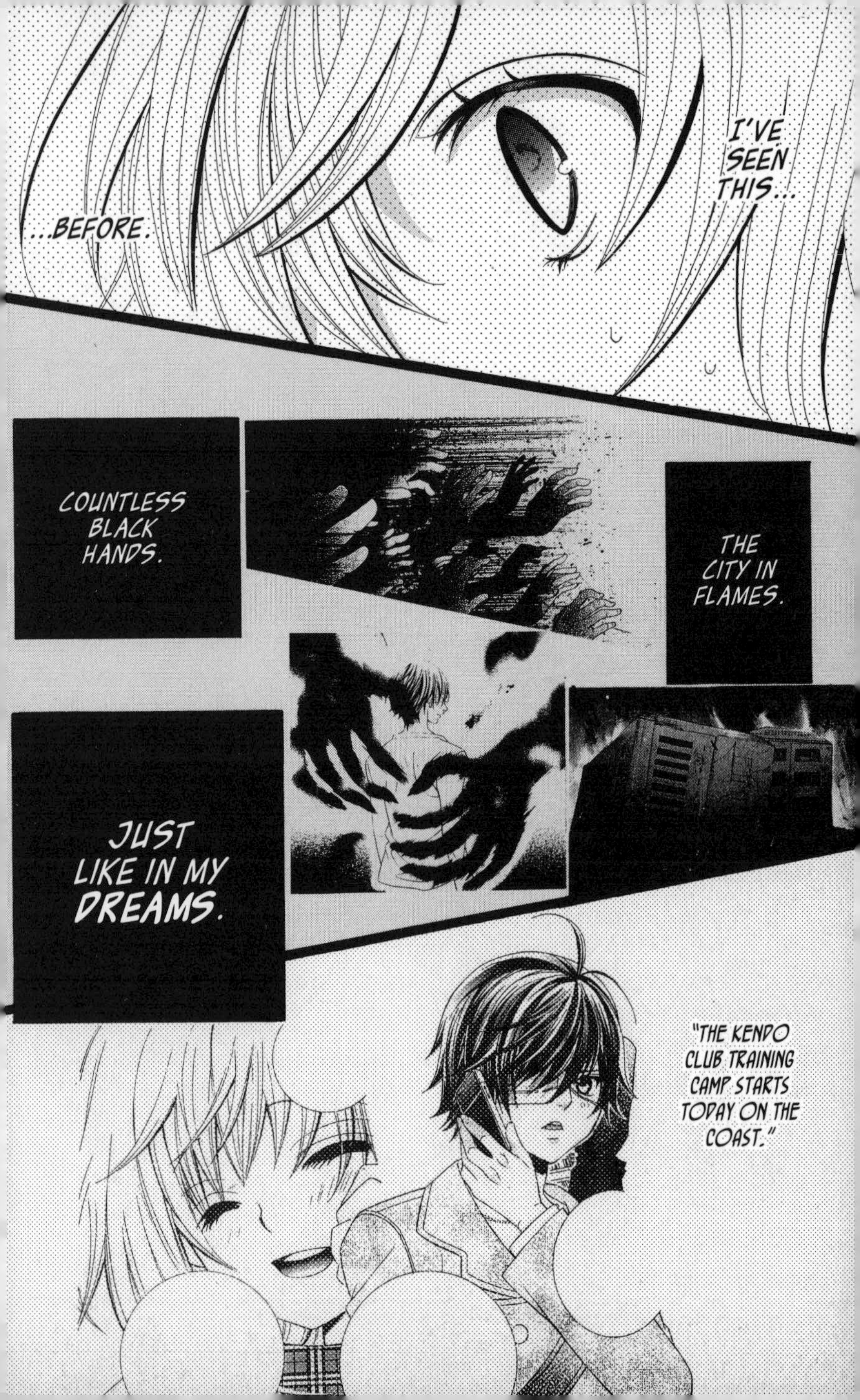
I'VE SEEN THIS...
...BEFORE.
THE CITY IN FLAMES.
COUNTLESS BLACK HANDS.
JUST LIKE IN MY DREAMS.
"THE KENDO CLUB TRAINING CAMP STARTS TODAY ON THE COAST."

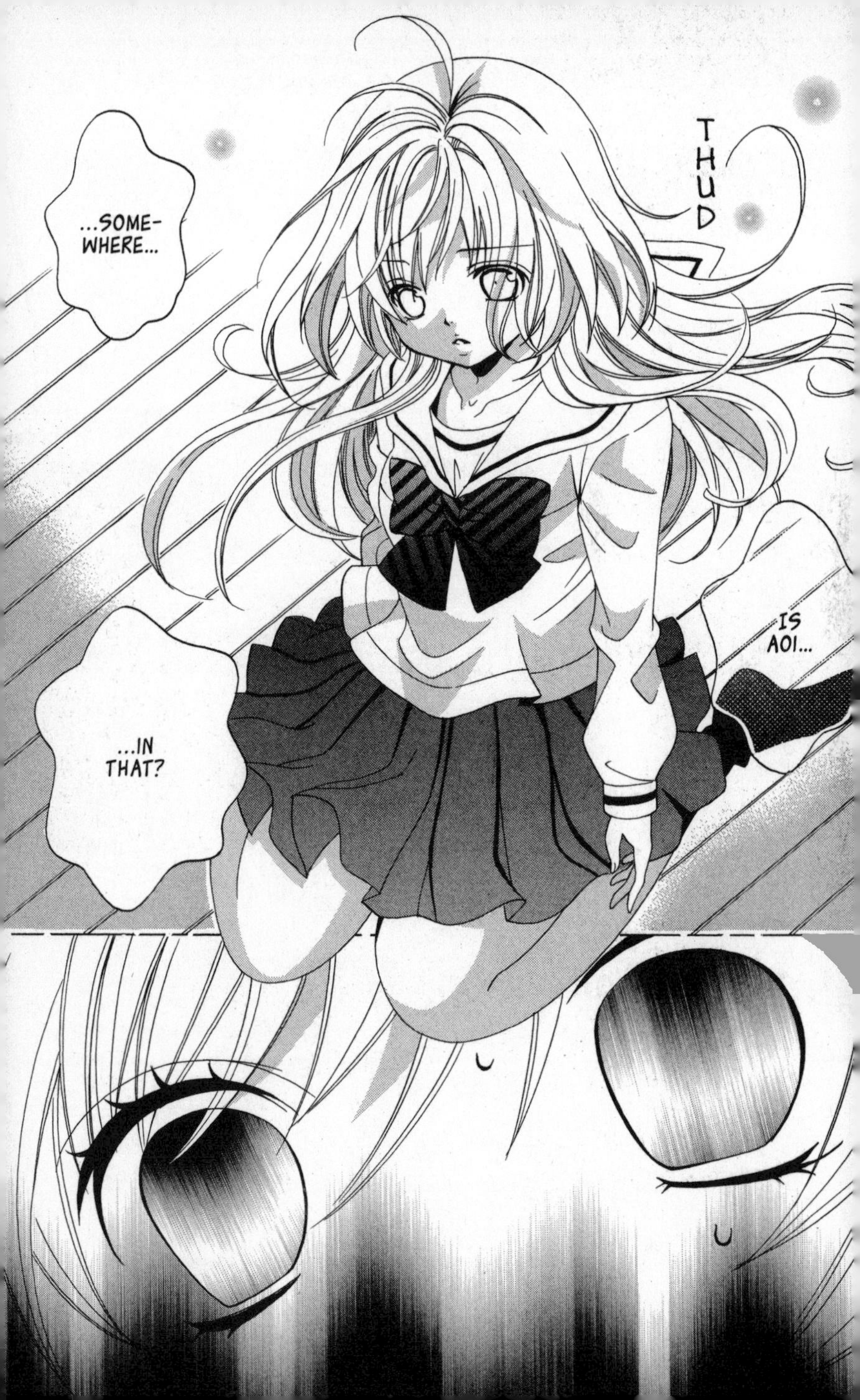
THUD
...SOME-WHERE...
IS AOI...
...IN THAT?

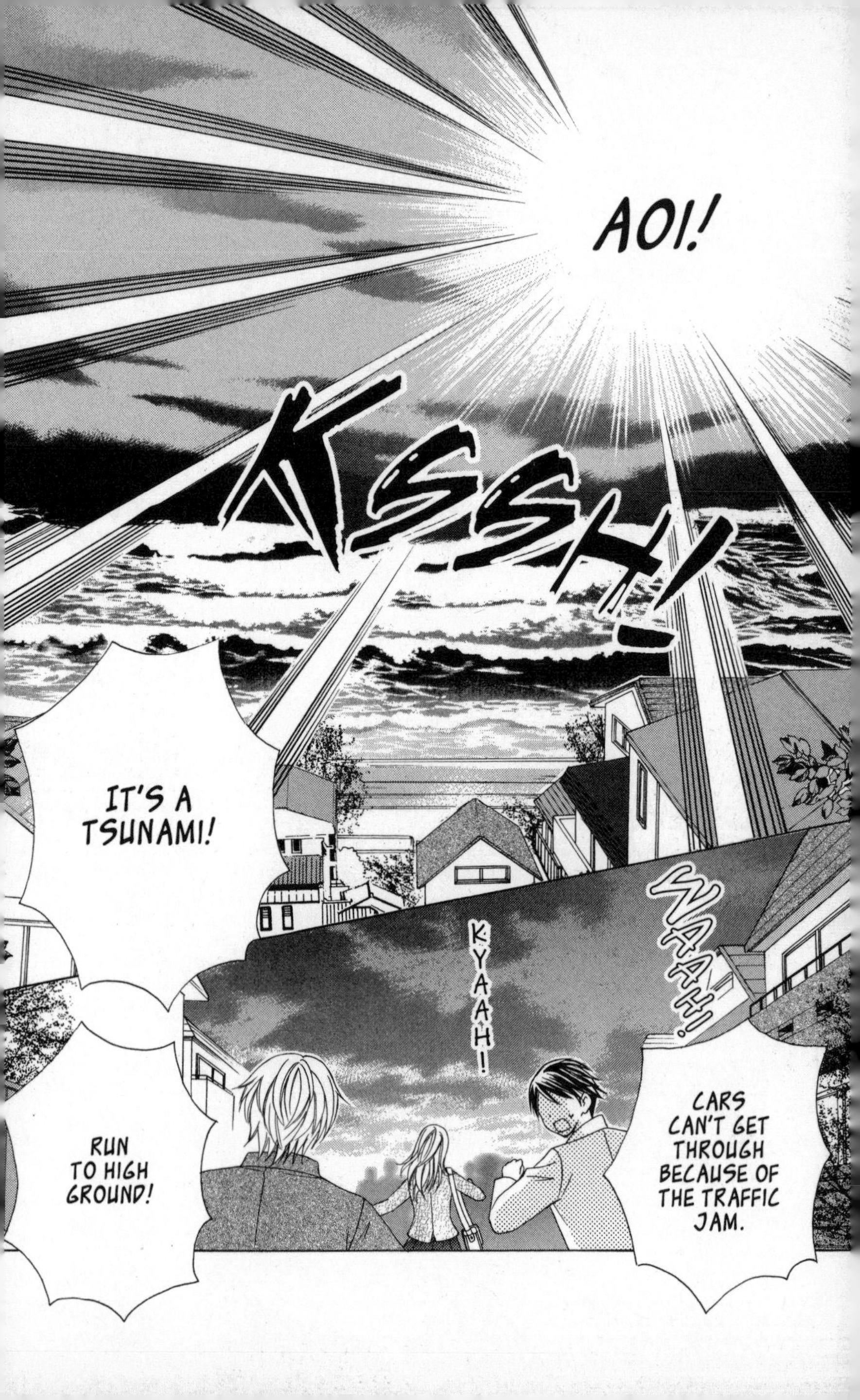
AOI!
KSSH!
IT'S A TSUNAMI!
WAAAH!
KYAAH!
CARS CAN'T GET THROUGH BECAUSE OF THE TRAFFIC JAM.
RUN TO HIGH GROUND!

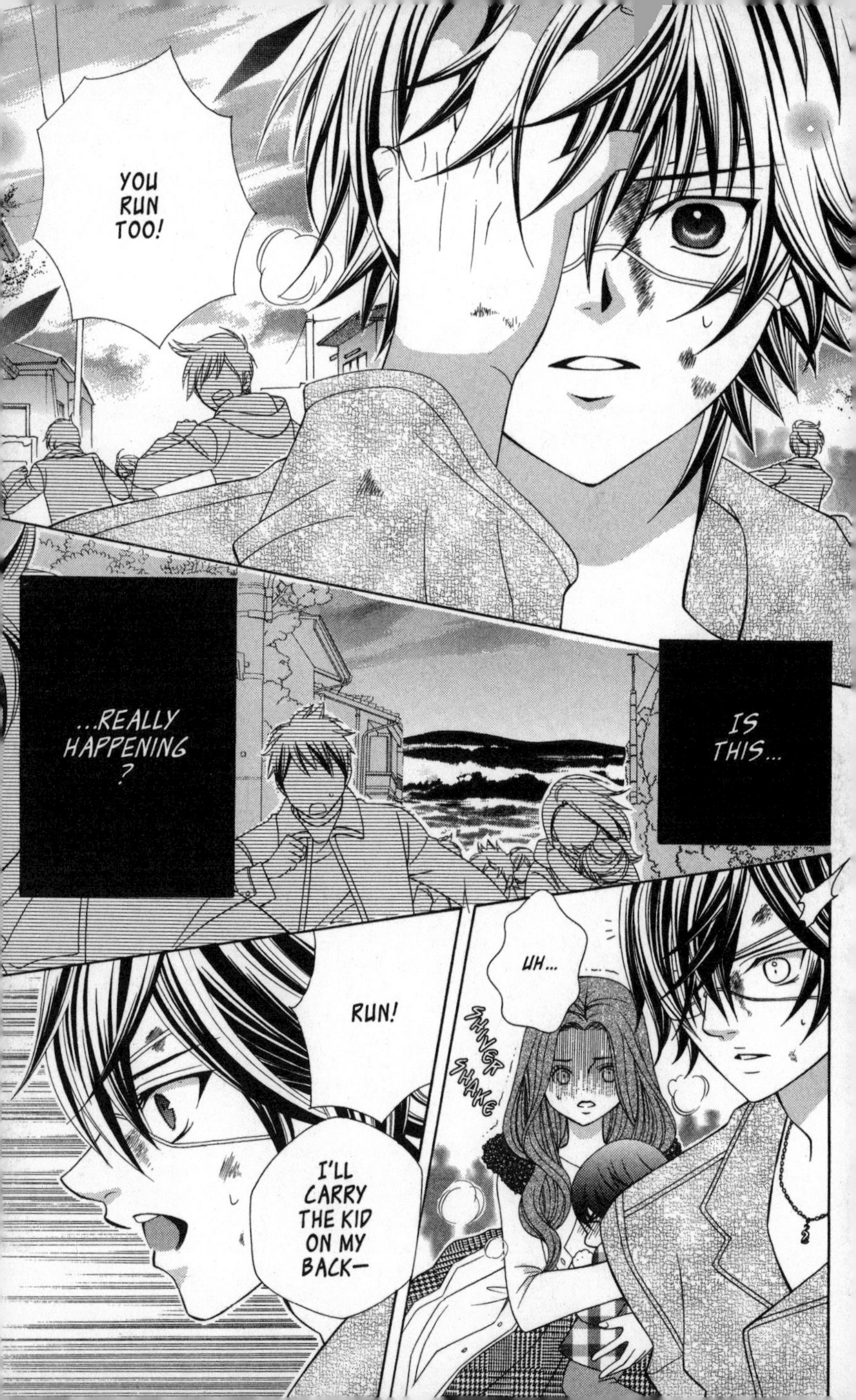
YOU RUN TOO!
IS THIS...
...REALLY HAPPENING?
UH...
SHIVER SHAKE
RUN!
I'LL CARRY THE KID ON MY BACK—

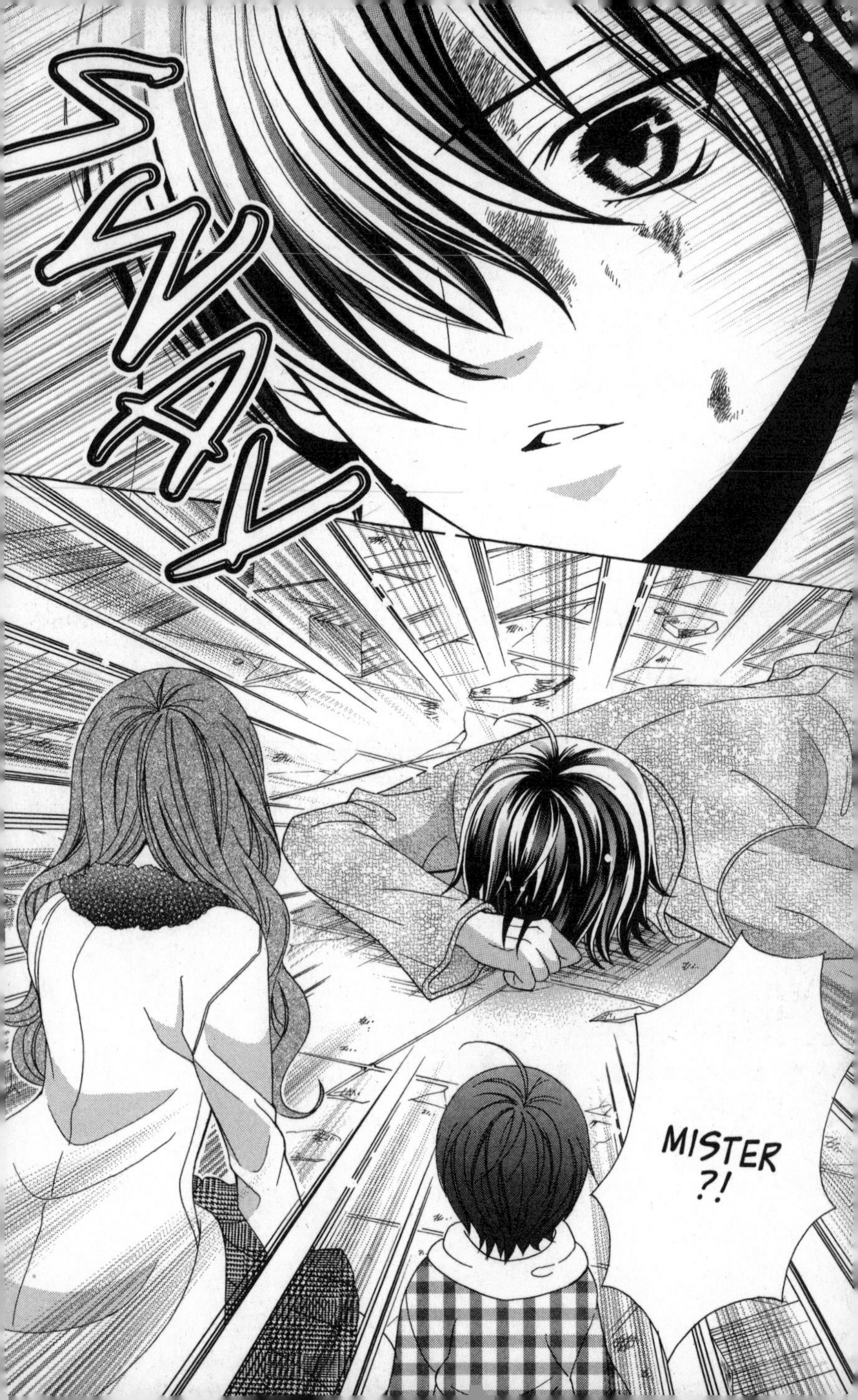
SNAP
MISTER ?!

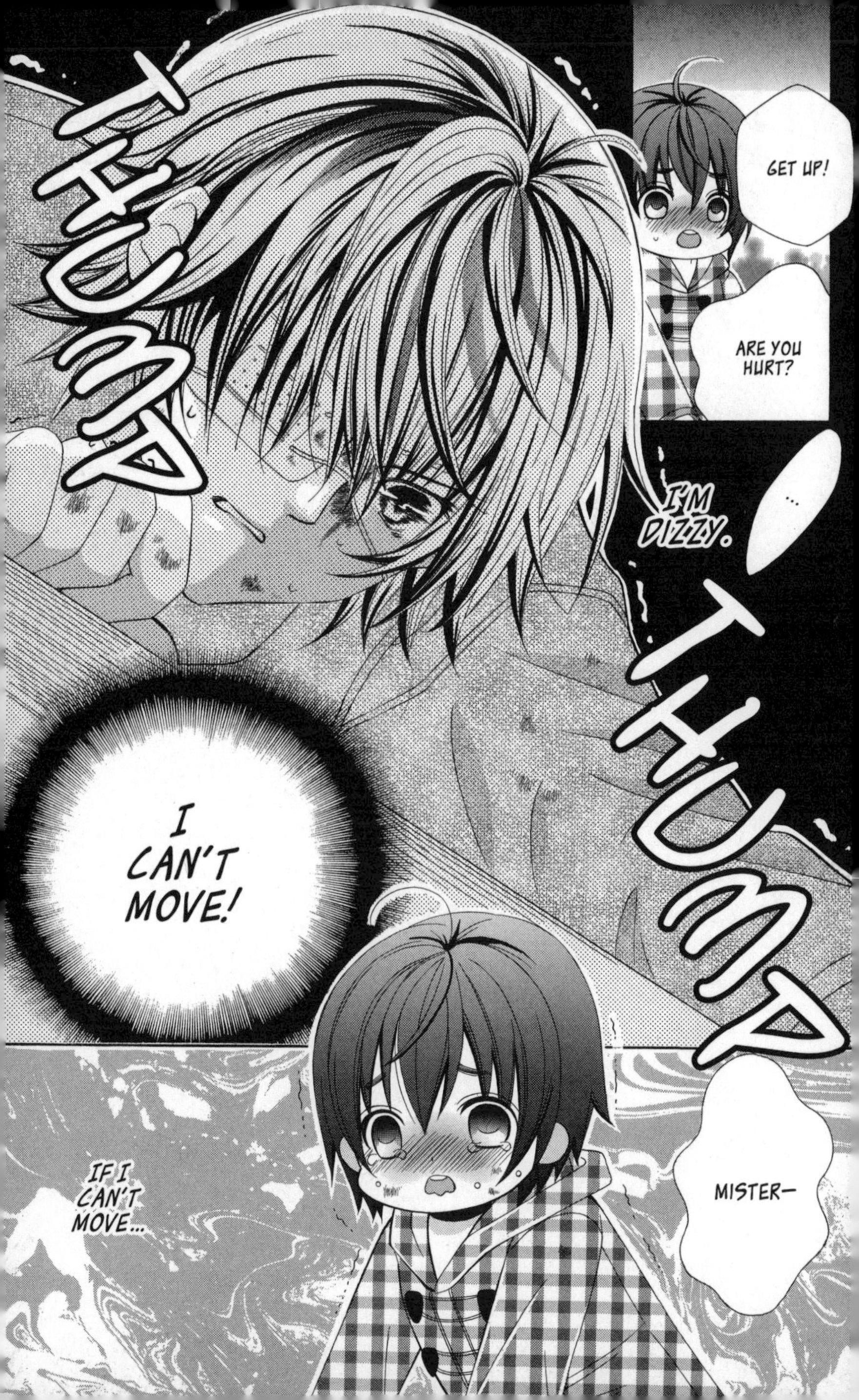
GET UP!
ARE YOU HURT?
THUMP
...
I'M DIZZY.
THUMP
I CAN'T MOVE!
MISTER—
IF I CAN'T MOVE...

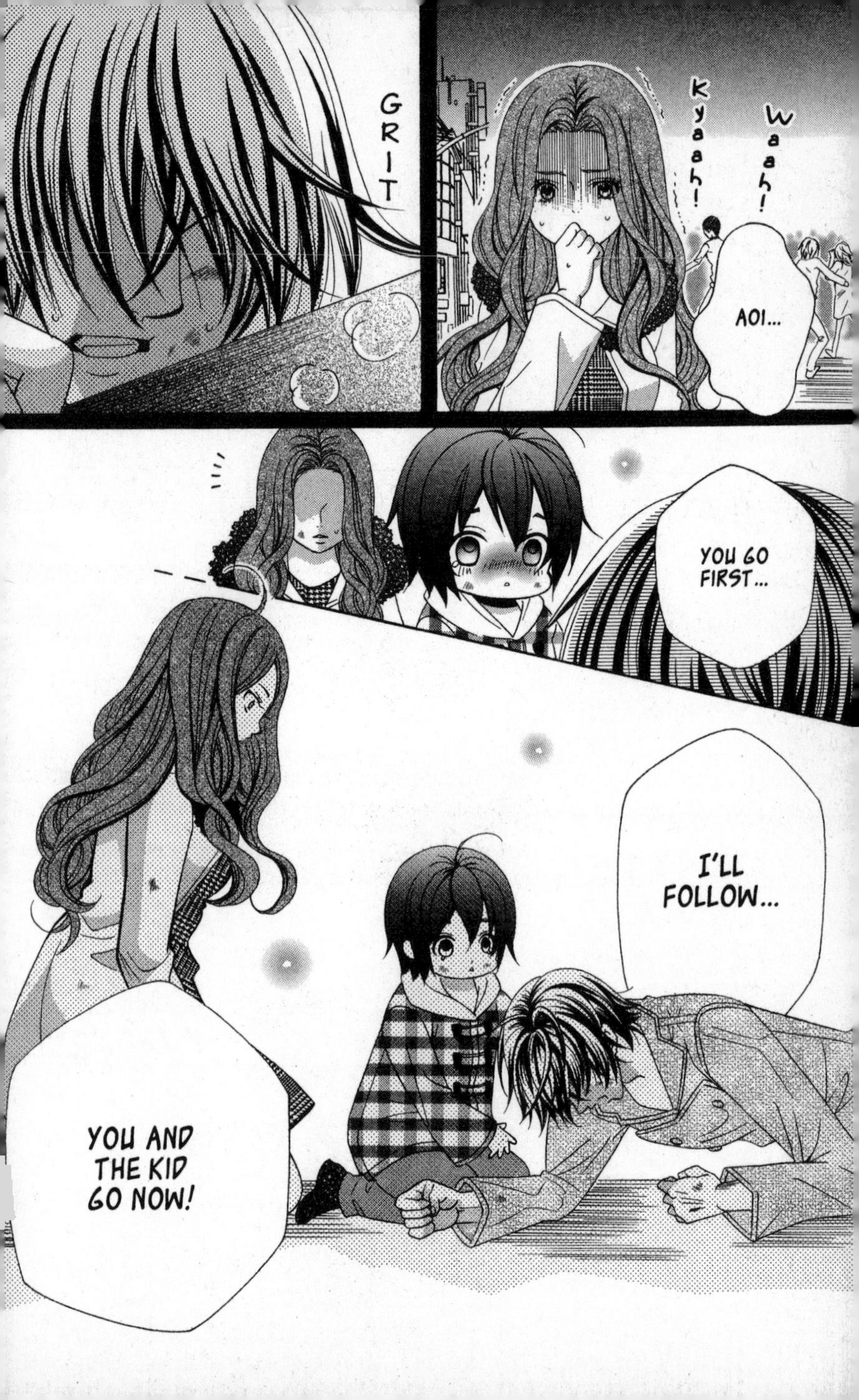
Waah!
Kyaah!
AOI...
GRIT
YOU GO FIRST...
I'LL FOLLOW...
YOU AND THE KID GO NOW!

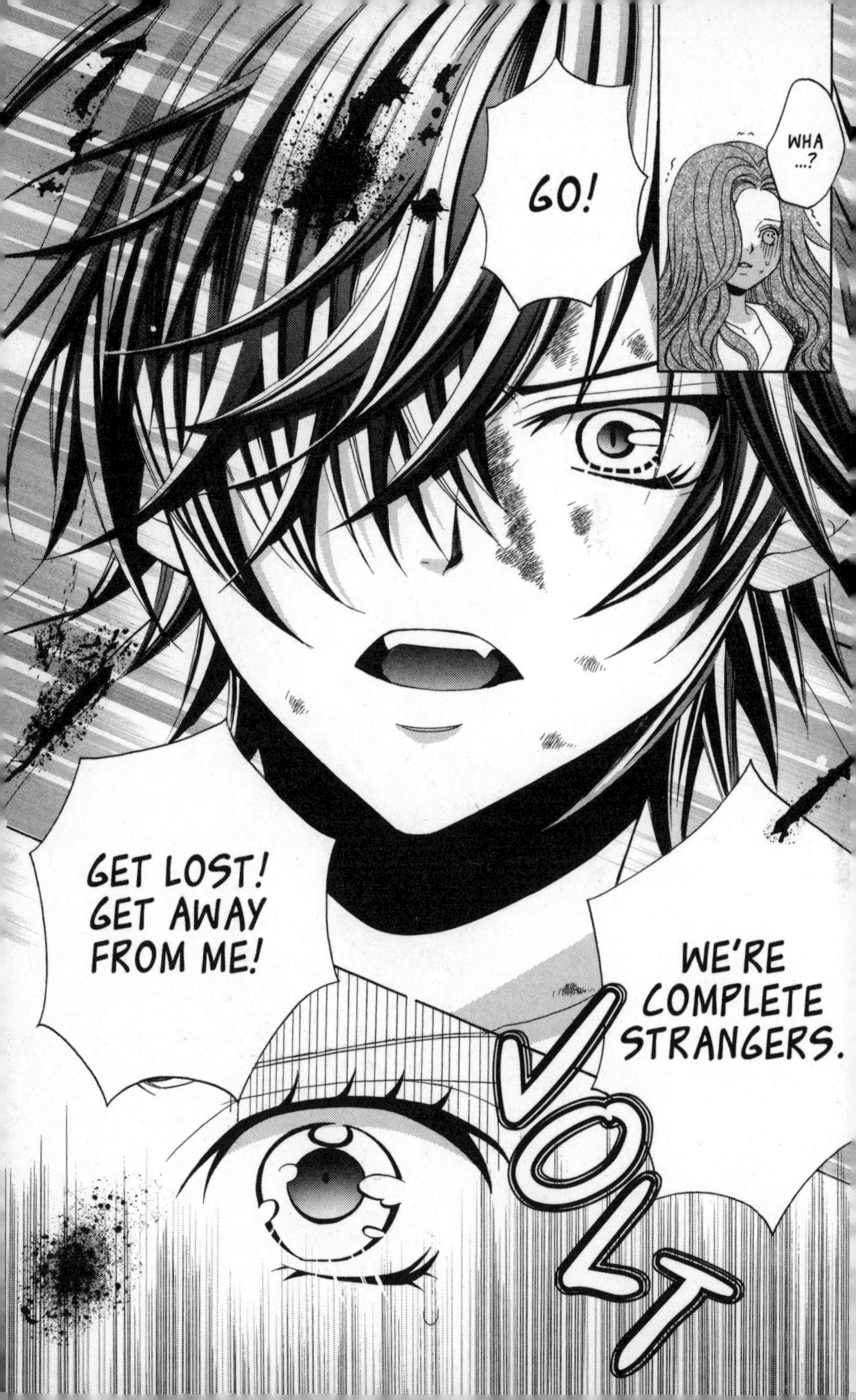
WHA ...?
GO!
GET LOST! GET AWAY FROM ME!
WE'RE COMPLETE STRANGERS.
VOLT

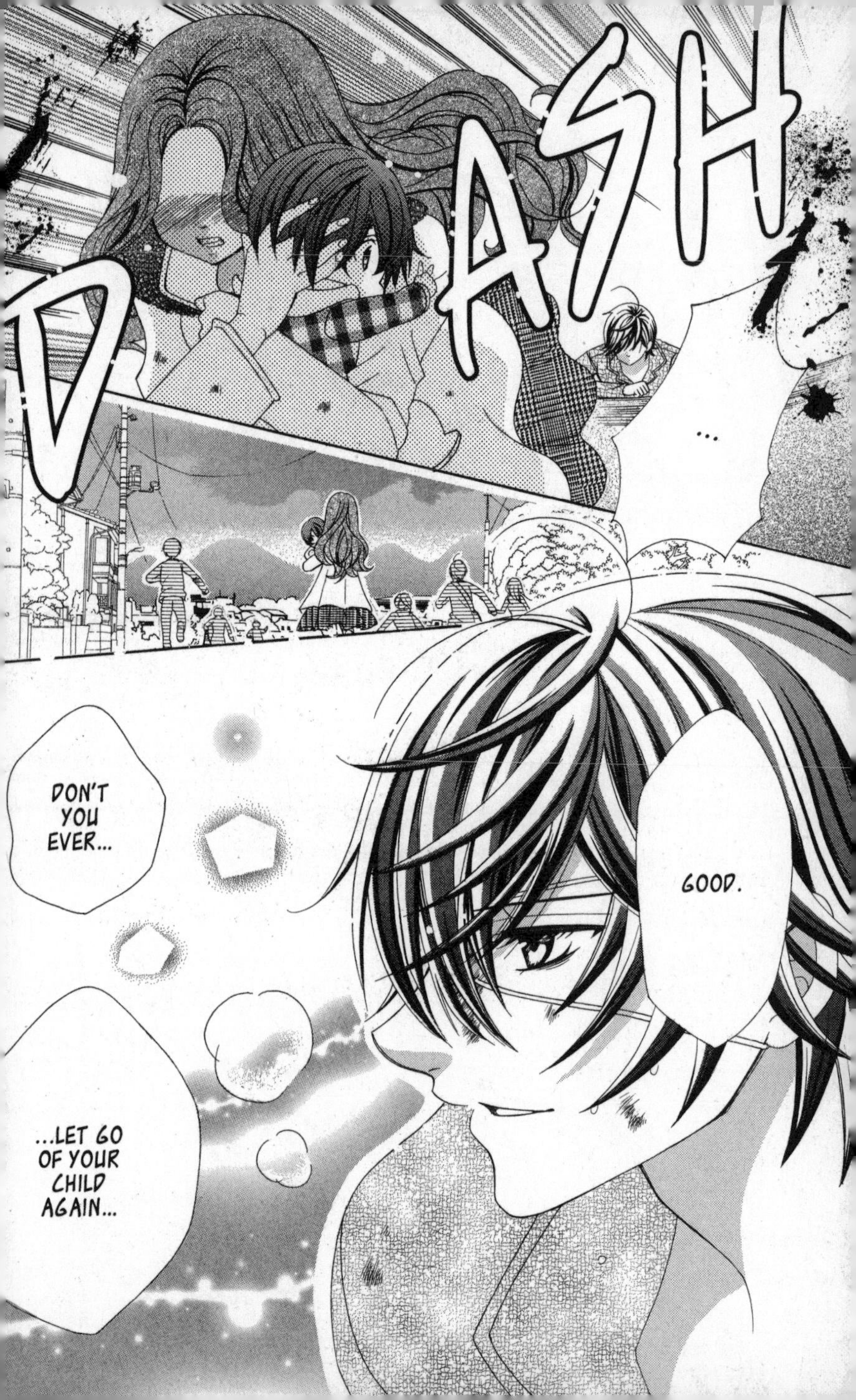
DASH
...
GOOD.
DON'T YOU EVER...
...LET GO OF YOUR CHILD AGAIN...

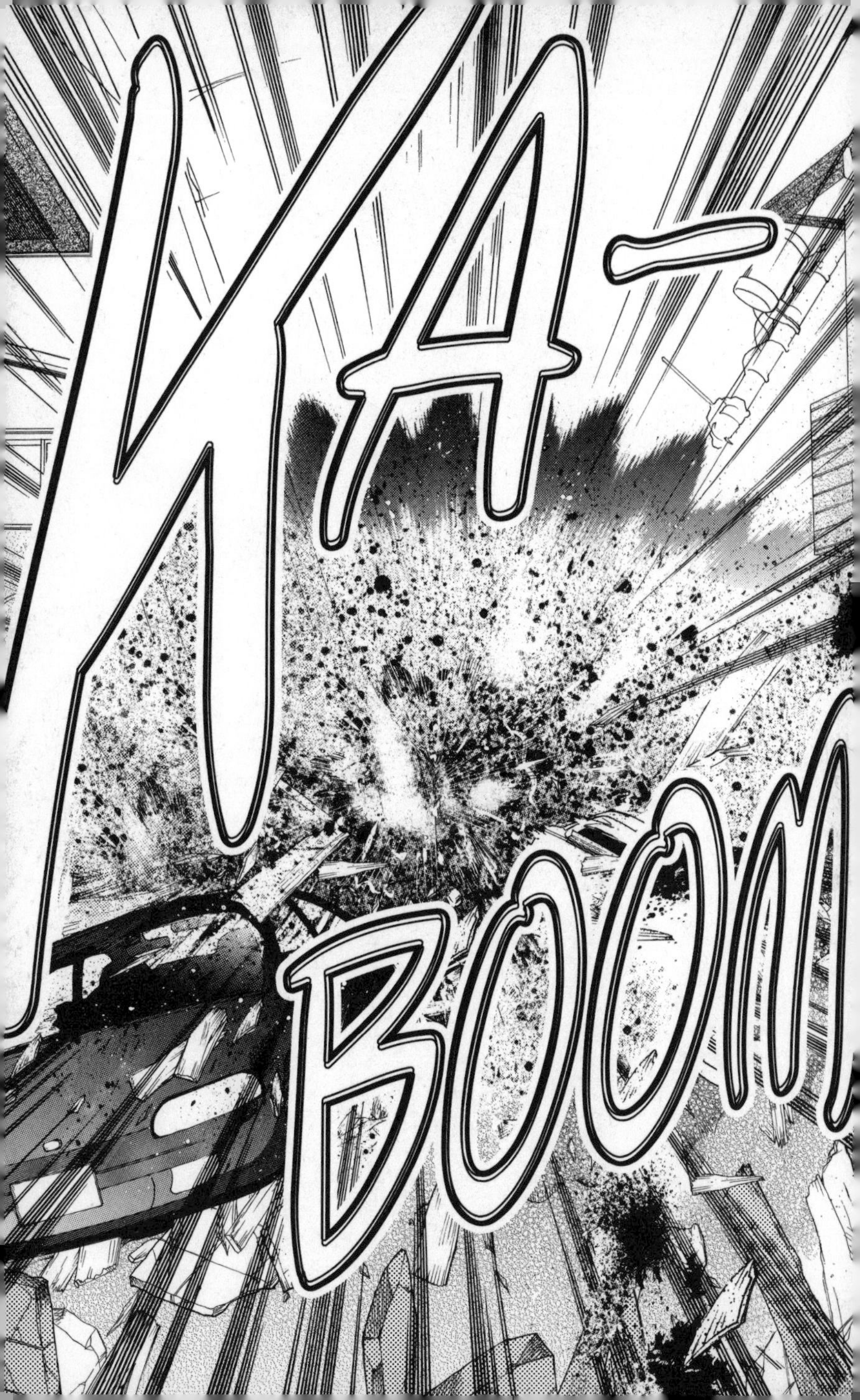
KA-BOOM

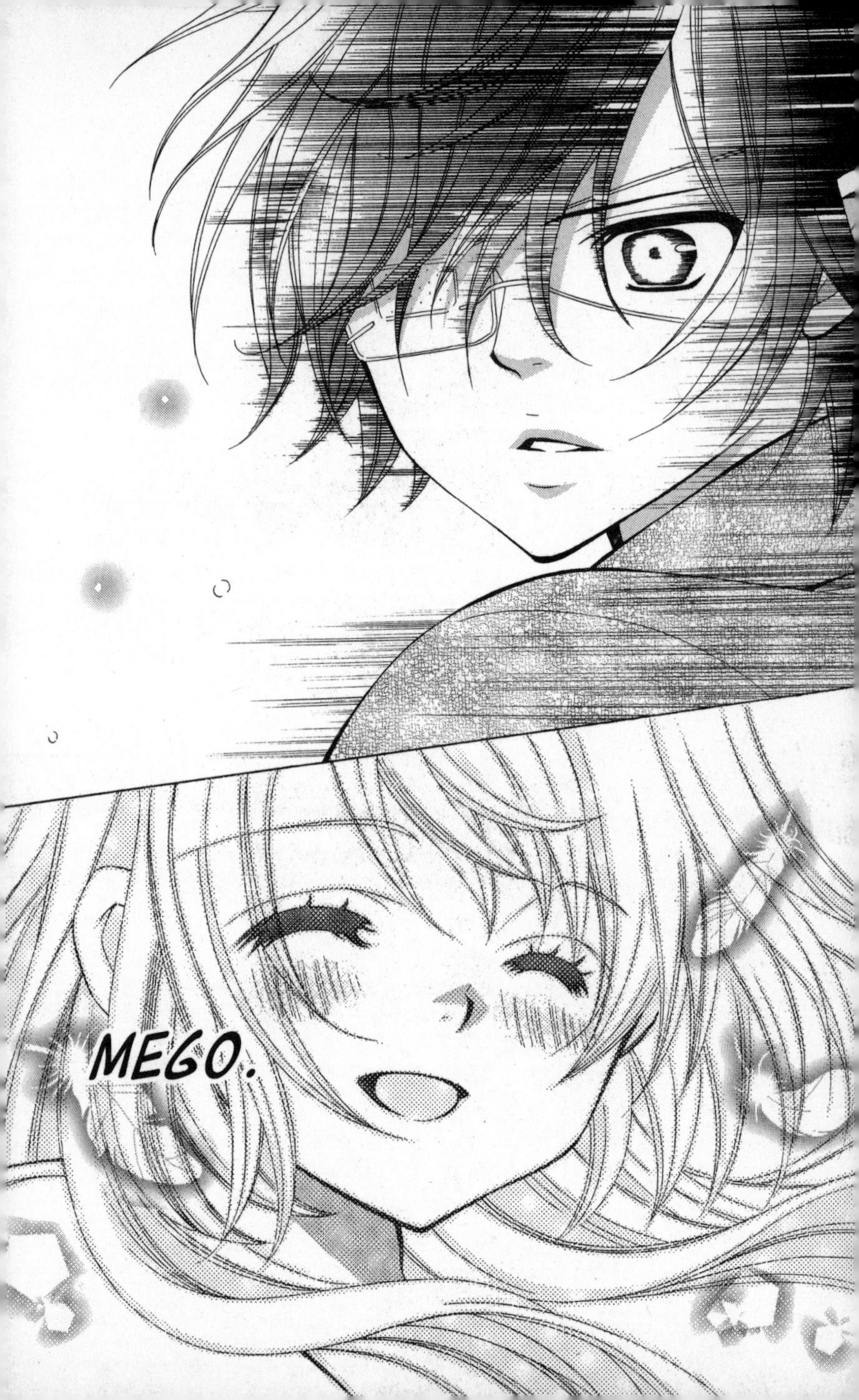
MEGO.

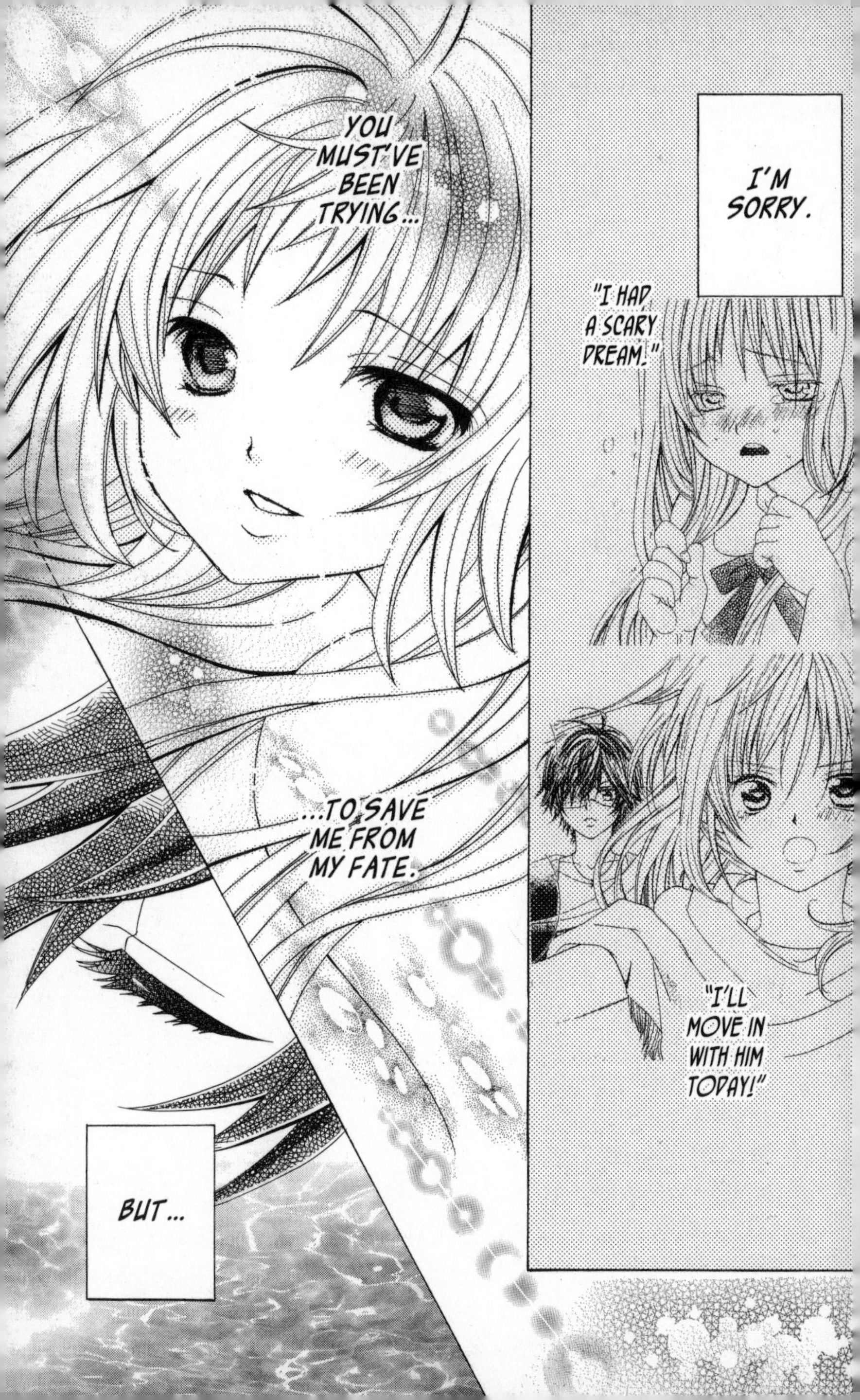
I'M SORRY.
"I HAD A SCARY DREAM!"
"I'LL MOVE IN WITH HIM TODAY!"
YOU MUST'VE BEEN TRYING...
...TO SAVE ME FROM MY FATE.
BUT...

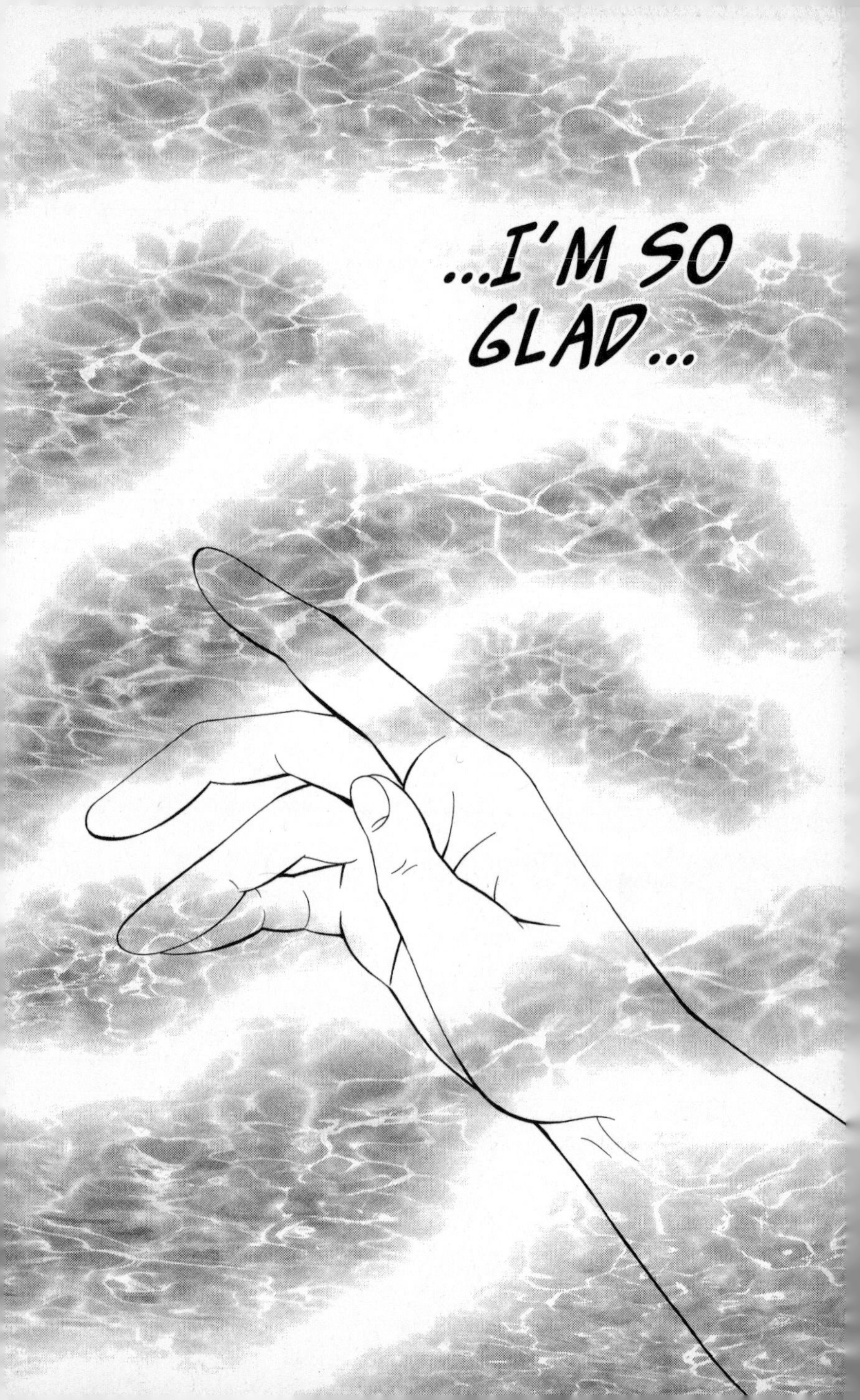
...I'M SO GLAD...

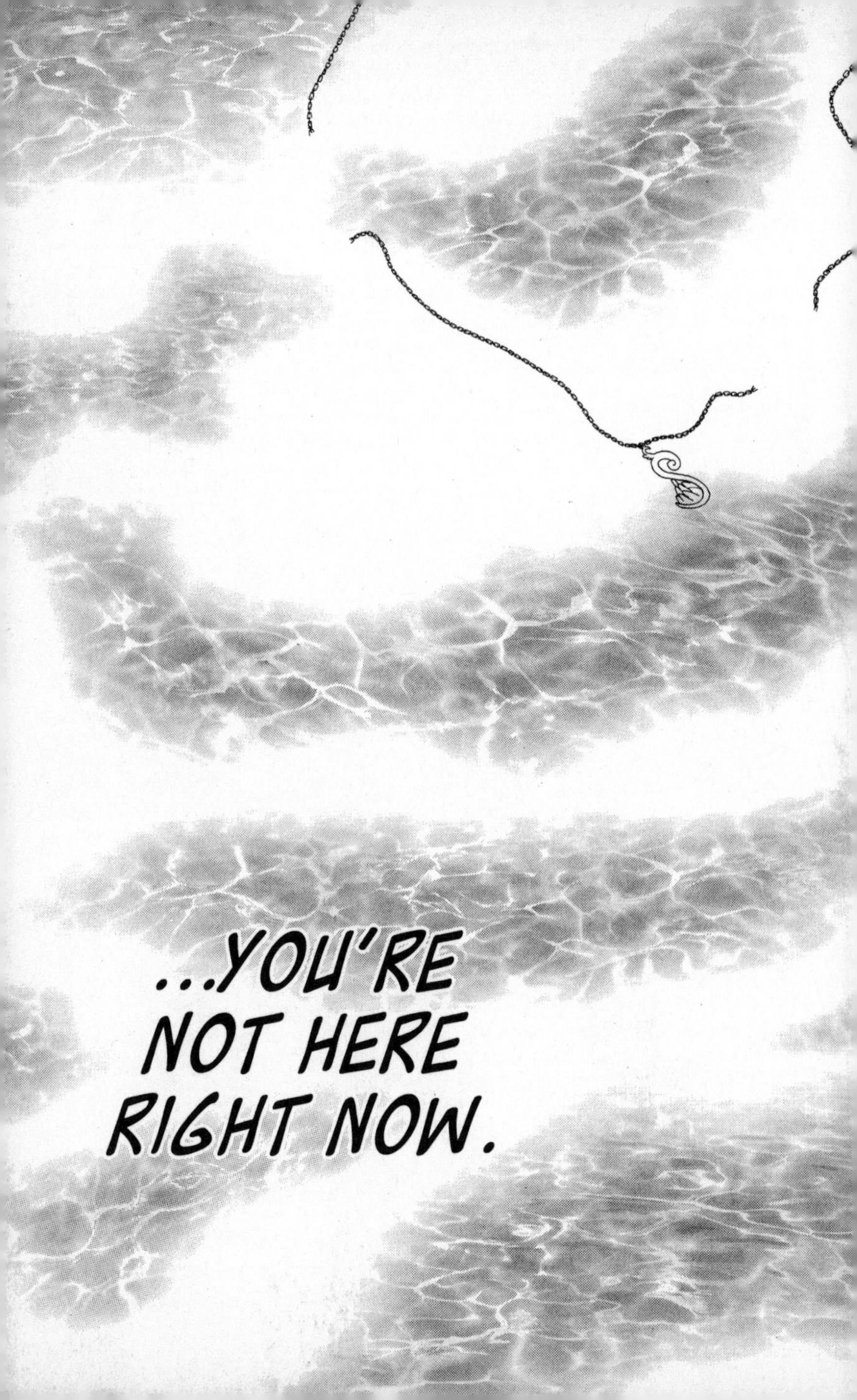
...YOU'RE NOT HERE RIGHT NOW.

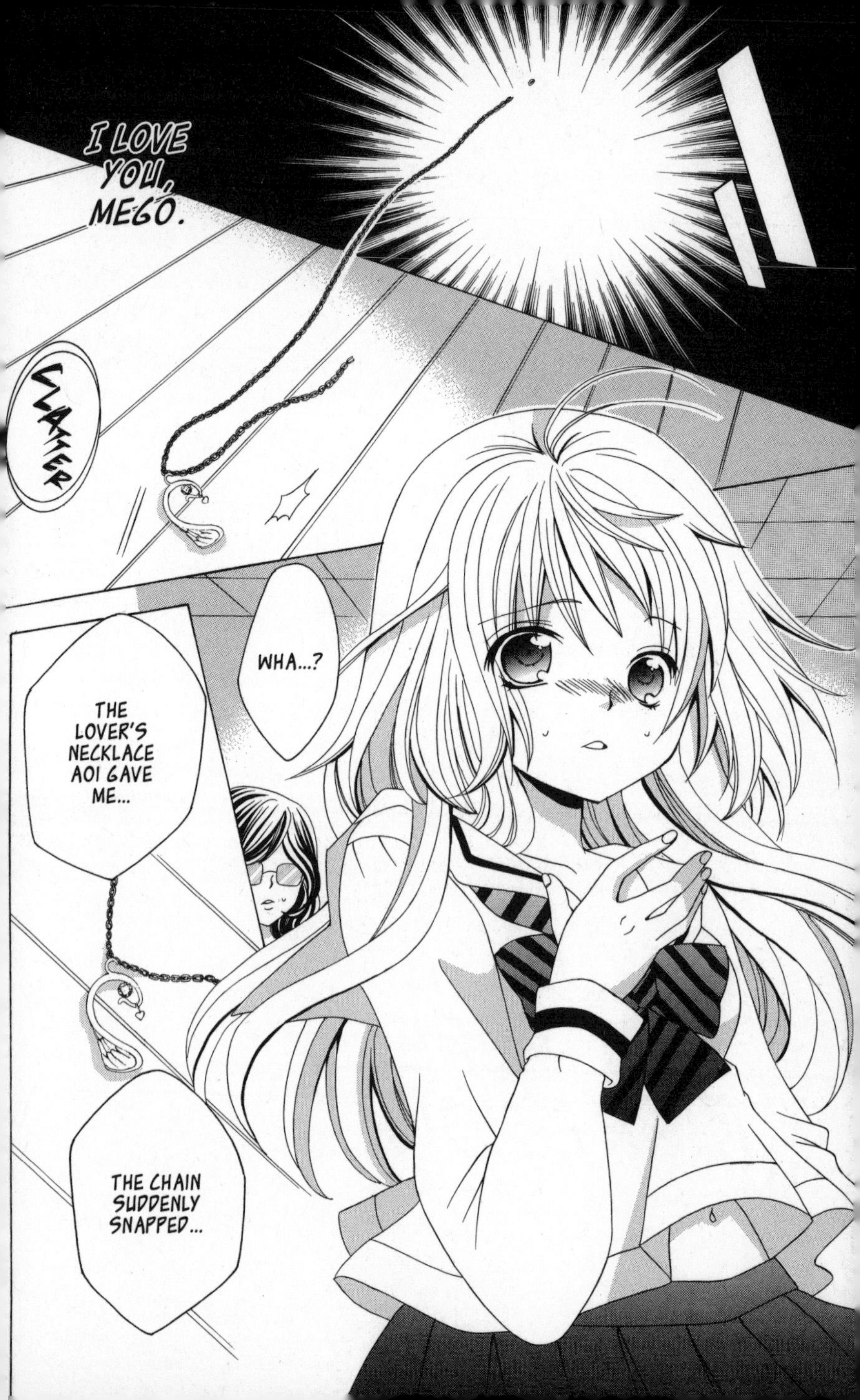
I LOVE YOU, MEGO.
CLATTER
WHA...?
THE LOVER'S NECKLACE AOI GAVE ME...
THE CHAIN SUDDENLY SNAPPED...

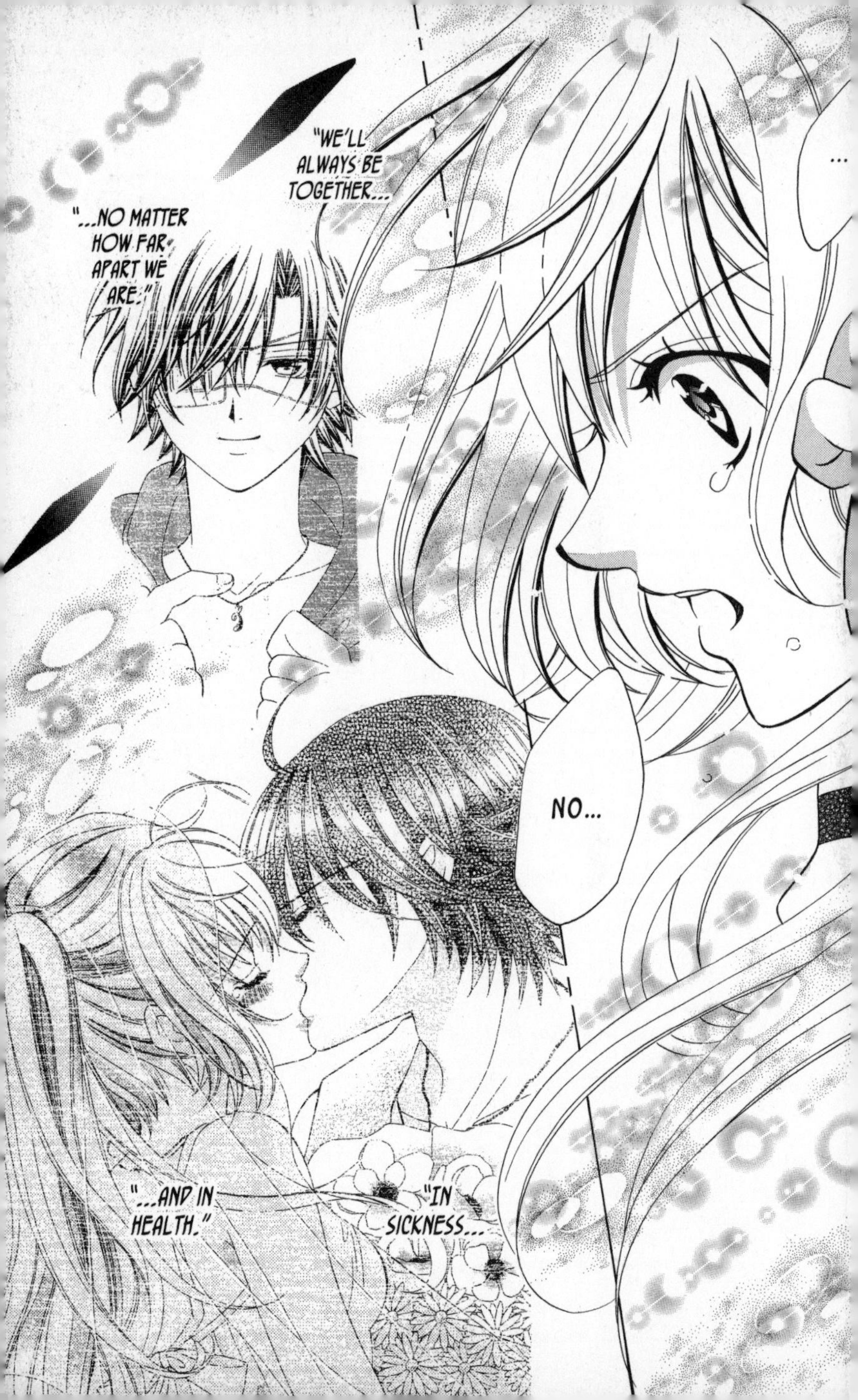
...
NO...
"WE'LL ALWAYS BE TOGETHER...
"...NO MATTER HOW FAR APART WE ARE."
"IN SICKNESS...
"...AND IN HEALTH."

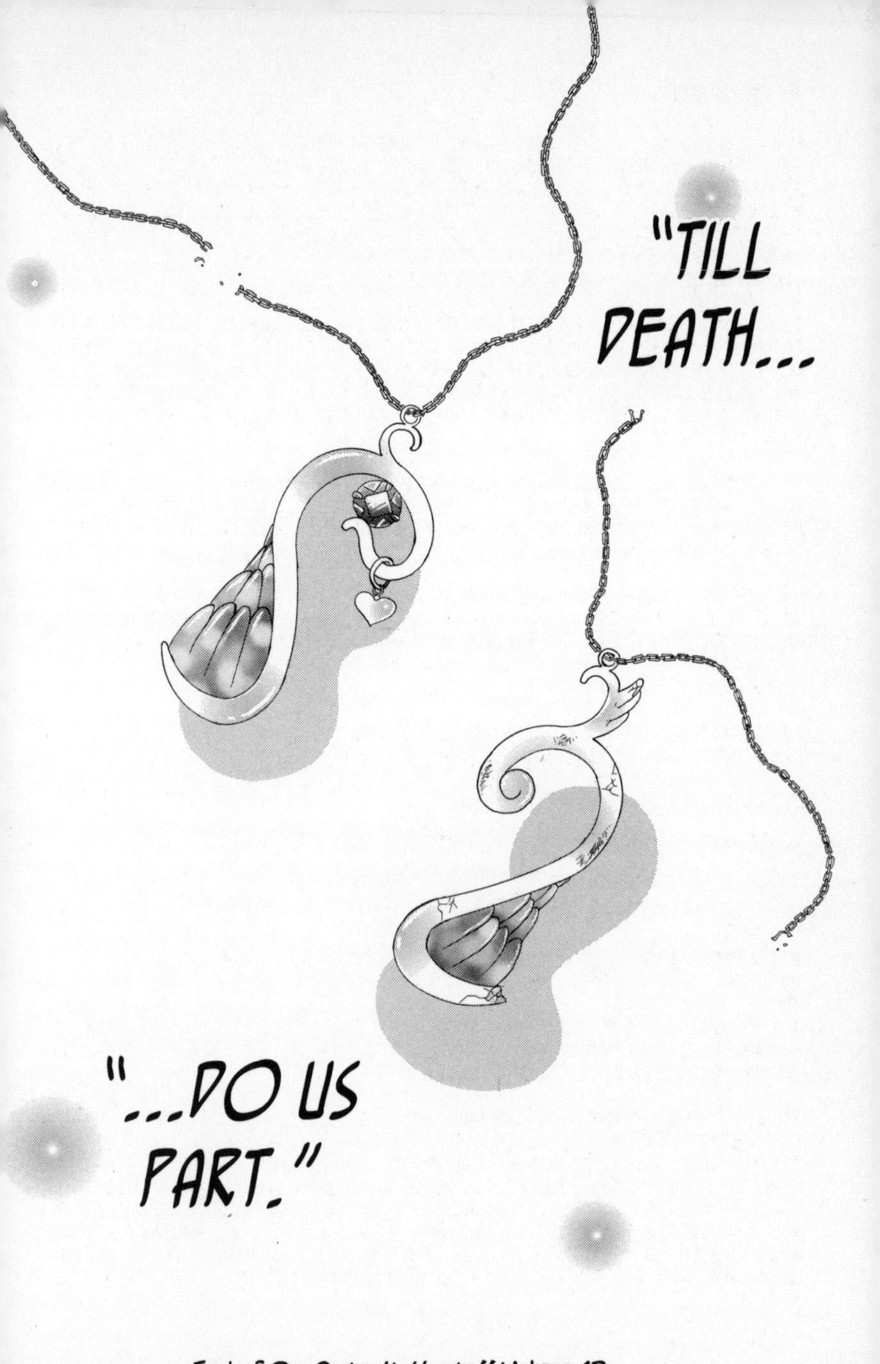
"TILL DEATH...
"...DO US PART."

End of *So Cute It Hurts!!* Volume 13

AFTERWORD

MARCH 11, 2011, 2:46 P.M. I WAS IN MY STUDIO IN TOKYO. (I WAS WORKING ON THE STORYBOARDS FOR CHAPTER 60 OF *SUKI DESU SUZUKI-KUN!!*) I REALIZED IT WAS AN EARTHQUAKE, SO I HID UNDERNEATH MY DESK AND WAS SHAKING IN FEAR. AFTER A LONG FIVE MINUTES, THE SHAKING SUBSIDED AND I NERVOUSLY TURNED ON THE TV. THAT'S WHEN I FOUND OUT THAT THE EPICENTER WAS OFFSHORE OF MY HOMETOWN, SENDAI. (WHAT'S HAPPENED TO THE PEOPLE I KNEW WHEN I WAS LITTLE? HOW'RE MY RELATIVES IN AIZU, FUKUSHIMA PREFECTURE, DOING...?)

I WAS WORRIED AND WAS WAITING FOR MORE INFORMATION ON TV WHEN I SAW THE HUGE TSUNAMI AT NATORI RIVER IN MIYAGI PREFECTURE. IT WAS A HORRIFYING SCENE THAT LOOKED LIKE HUGE BLACK HANDS SNATCHING AWAY LIVES. THAT VIDEO WAS NEVER BROADCAST AGAIN, PROBABLY BECAUSE IT WAS SO TERRIFYING, BUT I COULDN'T GET THOSE BLACK HANDS OUT OF MY HEAD, EVEN FOUR YEARS AFTER I FIRST SAW THEM.

THE TSUNAMI AT NATORI RIVER TOOK THE LIVES OF PEOPLE I KNEW WHEN I WAS YOUNG. MANY PROFESSIONAL MANGA ARTISTS WROTE MESSAGES AND DREW ILLUS-TRATIONS OF SUPPORT AFTER THE EARTHQUAKE, BUT I COULDN'T BRING MYSELF TO DRAW ANYTHING, AND I CONTINUED TO AVOID TALKING ABOUT THE EARTHQUAKE.

SUKI DESU SUZUKI-KUN!! ENDED IN JUNE 2012, AND *SO CUTE!* WAS SCHEDULED TO BEGIN IN AUGUST. I DECIDED I'D SET IT IN SENDAI, BECAUSE AS A MANGA ARTIST WHO WAS BORN IN THE TOHOKU REGION, I WANTED TO SUPPORT THE DISASTER-STRICKEN AREAS. (BY COINCIDENCE, MY THEN-EDITOR S WAS ALSO BORN IN SENDAI, AND WE FELT THIS WAS FATE.)

I HAD TO DECIDE WHETHER THE SENDAI IN *SO CUTE!* WOULD BE SENDAI BEFORE THE EARTHQUAKE OR SENDAI AFTER THE EARTHQUAKE.

I CAME UP WITH TWO POSSIBLE PLOTS:

PLOT A
BEGINS AFTER THE EARTHQUAKE AND DOESN'T MENTION THE EARTHQUAKE AT ALL.

PLOT B
BEGINS BEFORE THE EARTHQUAKE AND PORTRAYS THE EARTHQUAKE THROUGH AOI'S AND MEGO'S EYES.

AFTER TALKING IT OVER WITH MY EDITOR, WE DECIDED THAT IT WAS TOO SOON TO GO WITH PLOT B AND THAT THE THEME WAS TOO DIFFICULT TO TACKLE IN A SHOJO MANGA, AND WE DECIDED TO GO WITH PLOT A.

HOWEVER, AS 2013 AND THEN 2014 WENT BY, I BEGAN TO HEAR THE WORDS "MEMO-RIES FADING AWAY" IN THE NEWS...EVEN THOUGH IT HAD ONLY BEEN TWO OR THREE YEARS SINCE THE EARTHQUAKE. THE DISASTER-STRICKEN AREAS HADN'T EVEN STARTED TO BE REBUILT, YET PEOPLE WERE ALREADY WORRIED ABOUT FORGETTING THE EARTHQUAKE...AND I WAS SHOCKED AT THIS REALITY. I WONDERED WHETHER IT WAS TIME FOR ME TO START DEALING WITH THE EARTHQUAKE AS A MANGA ARTIST FROM THE TOHOKU REGION. I THOUGHT THINGS OVER AND TALKED TO MY EDITOR AGAIN. WE THEN DECIDED TO GO WITH THE ENDING FOR PLOT B.

I WAS SO TENSE AFTER I BEGAN WORKING ON THE FINAL CHAPTER (THE SENDAI ARC). (SHOULD I REALLY BE DRAWING THIS? THERE WILL BE PEOPLE WHO WILL READ THIS AND BE REMINDED OF WHAT THEY WENT THROUGH AND BE HURT. SOME READERS MAY BE DISMAYED AND STOP READING THE MANGA. I MYSELF AM TERRIFIED TO REMEMBER THAT DAY. WILL I REALLY BE ABLE TO DRAW THIS?)

I KEPT AGONIZING, AND I COULDN'T REACH ANY SORT OF CONCLUSION. HOWEVER, SOME PEOPLE ENCOURAGED ME. OTHERS AGREED TO LET ME TALK TO THEM ABOUT THEIR EXPERIENCES, AND I WAS FINALLY ABLE TO START DRAWING.

I AM VERY GRATEFUL THAT *SO CUTE!* IS BEING PUBLISHED OVERSEAS AS WELL. I HOPE READERS WHO DON'T KNOW MUCH ABOUT WHAT EARTHQUAKES ARE LIKE AND FUTURE READERS WHO DIDN'T EXPERIENCE THIS EARTHQUAKE WILL THINK ABOUT WHAT HAPPENED... THAT'S WHAT I WAS PRAYING FOR WHILE DRAWING THIS ARC.

MY HANDS WERE SHAKING WHEN I WAS WORKING ON THE STORYBOARDS FOR CHAPTERS 65 AND 66 AS I REMEMBERED WHAT WENT ON THAT DAY. I HADN'T BEEN ABLE TO LOOK AT THOSE "BLACK HANDS" NEWS VIDEOS SINCE THAT DAY BECAUSE I WAS TERRIFIED TO WATCH THEM AGAIN, BUT I DID WATCH THEM MANY TIMES ONLINE TO DRAW MY STORYBOARDS.

I COULDN'T STOP CRYING, BUT I WAS DRIVEN BY MY DESIRE TO DRAW THIS SO THAT PEOPLE WON'T FORGET. THE NEWS VIDEO MEGO SAW IN CHAPTER 66 IS WHAT I SAW THAT DAY. MY ASSISTANTS DID THEIR BEST TO RESEARCH ALL THOSE HORRIFYING VIDEOS AND MATERIALS TO DRAW THE BACKGROUNDS, AND THEY DREW A LOT OF VERY DIFFICULT SCENES.

SHO-COMI READERS DON'T LIKE SAD STORIES AND DEPRESSING PLOT DEVELOPMENTS, SO I WAS READY TO ACCEPT THAT READERS MIGHT NOT LIKE WHAT THEY READ FROM CHAPTER 65 ON. I KNEW I MIGHT RECEIVE LOTS OF CRITICISM THAT THE STORY DEVELOPMENT WAS INAPPROPRIATE FOR A SHOJO MANGA. BUT I STILL HAD EIGHT MORE CHAPTERS UNTIL THE END OF THE SERIES, AND I DIDN'T WANT TO REGRET NOT DRAWING WHAT I WANTED TO DRAW. (BUT TO BE HONEST, I WAS TERRIFIED OF THE READERS' REACTIONS THE DAY THE MAGAZINES WENT ON SALE.)

TO MY SURPRISE, I DIDN'T RECEIVE AS MUCH CRITICISM AS I THOUGHT I WOULD, AND THE EDITORIAL DEPARTMENT DID NOT RECEIVE A SINGLE PHONE CALL CRITICIZING THE CHAPTER. WE ACTUALLY GOT HUGE RESPONSES TO CHAPTERS 68 AND 69 (WHICH WILL BE INCLUDED IN VOLUME 14), AND BOTH MY EDITOR AND I WERE VERY SURPRISED. I COULDN'T HELP CRYING WHEN I THOUGHT OF MY READERS' WARMTH AND KINDNESS FOR SERIOUSLY RESPONDING TO MY THOUGHTS.

THERE ARE MANY READERS WHO WILL READ THESE CHAPTERS FOR THE FIRST TIME IN THE BOOK VERSION, SO I'M SURE I'LL RECEIVE ALL SORTS OF OPINIONS REGARDING VOLUMES 13 AND 14. TO BE HONEST, I'M SCARED OF THE READERS' REACTIONS. BUT THE SERIES ONLY HAS TWO MORE VOLUMES TO GO, SO I HOPE YOU'LL STICK WITH IT... THE SERIES WILL END SOON IN THE MAGAZINE, BUT I'M PUTTING MY HEART AND SOUL INTO DRAWING IT TO ITS CONCLUSION, SO I HOPE YOU'LL KEEP READING.

GO IKEYAMADA
OCTOBER 2015

lolololol

So Cute It Hurts!! (>_<)

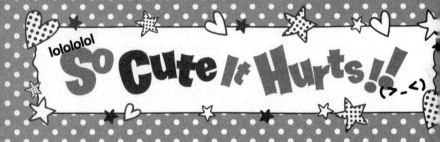

AUTHOR BIO

I finished drawing the final chapter of this series the other day for *Sho-Comi* magazine. I was able to complete all 73 chapters thanks to my editors, my assistants and everyone who's supported me. Thank you so very much!!

The story enters the climax of the final arc in this volume. This series has been the most difficult one I've ever drawn, and I really agonized over it. But I put my heart into drawing it, so I hope you keep reading until the very end.

Go Ikeyamada is a Gemini from Miyagi Prefecture whose hobbies include taking naps and watching movies. Her debut manga *Get Love!!* appeared in *Shojo Comic* in 2002, and her current work *So Cute It Hurts!!* (*Kobayashi ga Kawai Suguite Tsurai!!*) is being published by VIZ Media.

SO CUTE IT HURTS!!
Volume 13

Shojo Beat Edition

STORY AND ART BY
GO IKEYAMADA

English Translation & Adaptation/Tomo Kimura
Touch-Up Art & Lettering/Joanna Estep
Design/Izumi Evers
Editor/Pancha Diaz

KOBAYASHI GA KAWAISUGITE TSURAI!! Vol.13
by Go IKEYAMADA
© 2012 Go IKEYAMADA
All rights reserved.
Original Japanese edition published by SHOGAKUKAN.
English translation rights in the United States of America, Canada,
the United Kingdom and Ireland arranged with SHOGAKUKAN.

Printed in the U.S.A.

Published by VIZ Media, LLC
P.O. Box 77010
San Francisco, CA 94107

10 9 8 7 6 5 4 3 2 1
First printing, June 2017

www.viz.com   www.shojobeat.com

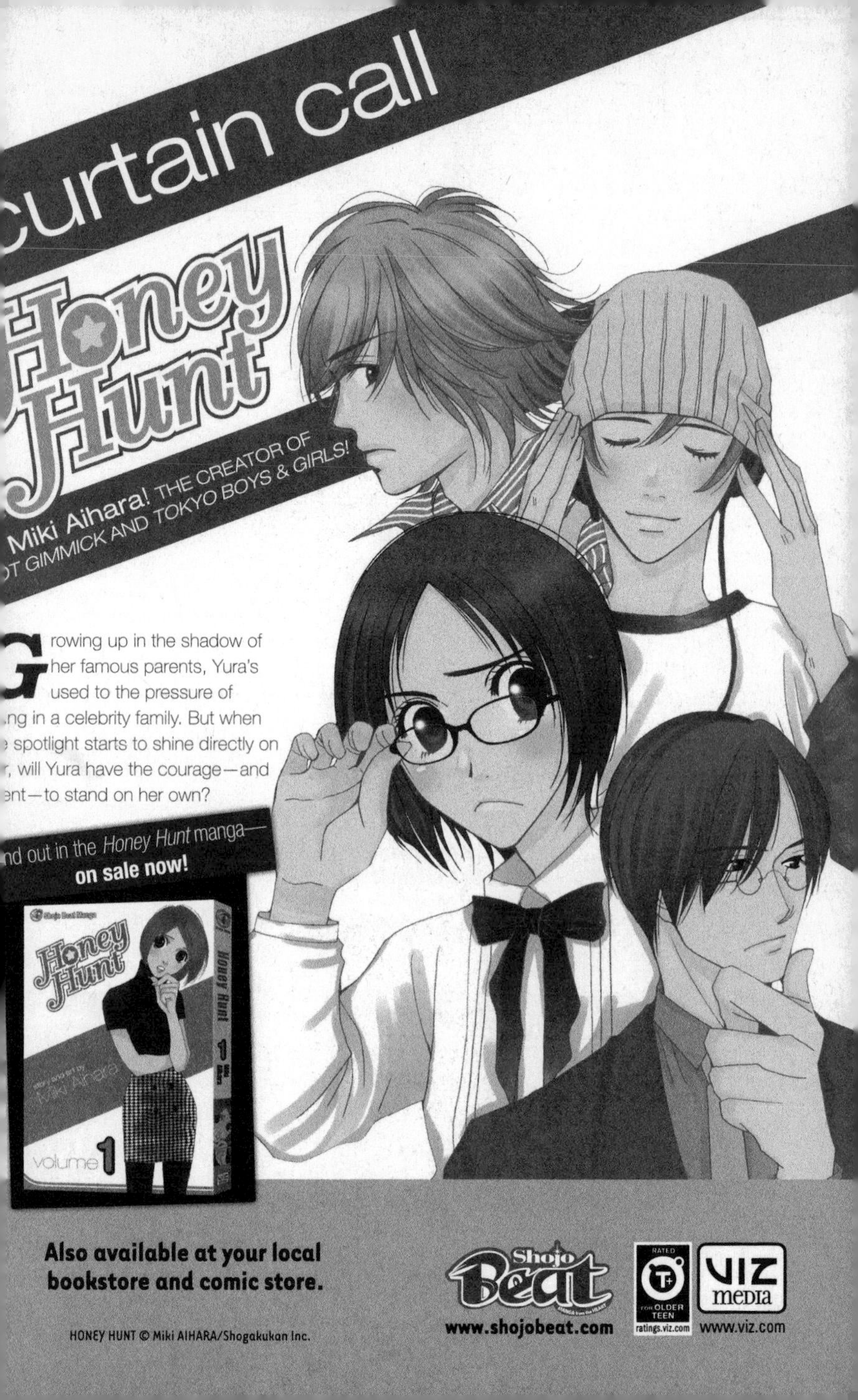
curtain call
Honey Hunt
Miki Aihara! THE CREATOR OF
DT GIMMICK AND TOKYO BOYS & GIRLS!
Growing up in the shadow of her famous parents, Yura's used to the pressure of
ng in a celebrity family. But when
spotlight starts to shine directly on
, will Yura have the courage—and
ent—to stand on her own?
nd out in the Honey Hunt manga—
on sale now!
Shojo Beat Manga
Honey Hunt
story and art by Miki Aihara
volume 1
Also available at your local
bookstore and comic store.
HONEY HUNT © Miki AIHARA/Shogakukan Inc.
Shojo Beat
www.shojobeat.com
RATED T+ FOR OLDER TEEN
ratings.viz.com
VIZ media
www.viz.com

Black Bird

STORY AND ART BY
KANOKO SAKURAKOUJI

There is a world of myth and magic that intersects ours, and only a special few can see it. Misao Harada is one such person, and she wants nothing to do with magical realms. She just wants to have a normal high school life and maybe get a boyfriend.

But she is the bride of demon prophecy, and her blood grants incredible powers, her flesh immortality. Now the demon realm is fighting over the right to her hand...or her life!

This is the last page.

In keeping with the original Japanese comic format, this book reads from right to left—so action, sound effects and word balloons are completely reversed. This preserves the orientation of the original artwork—plus, it's fun! Check out the diagram shown here to get the hang of things, and then turn to the other side of the book to get started!

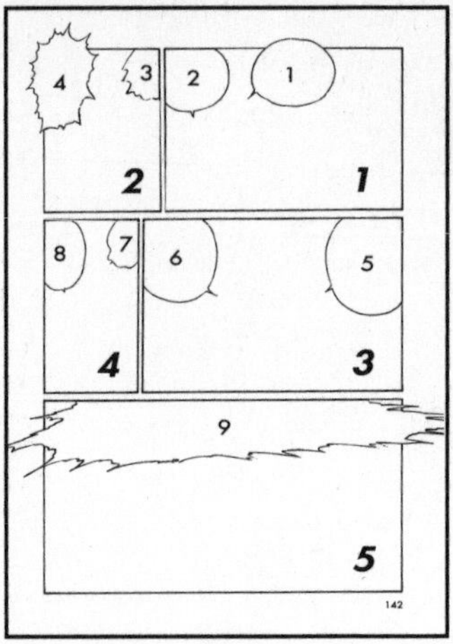
1
2
3
4
5
6
7
8
9
142

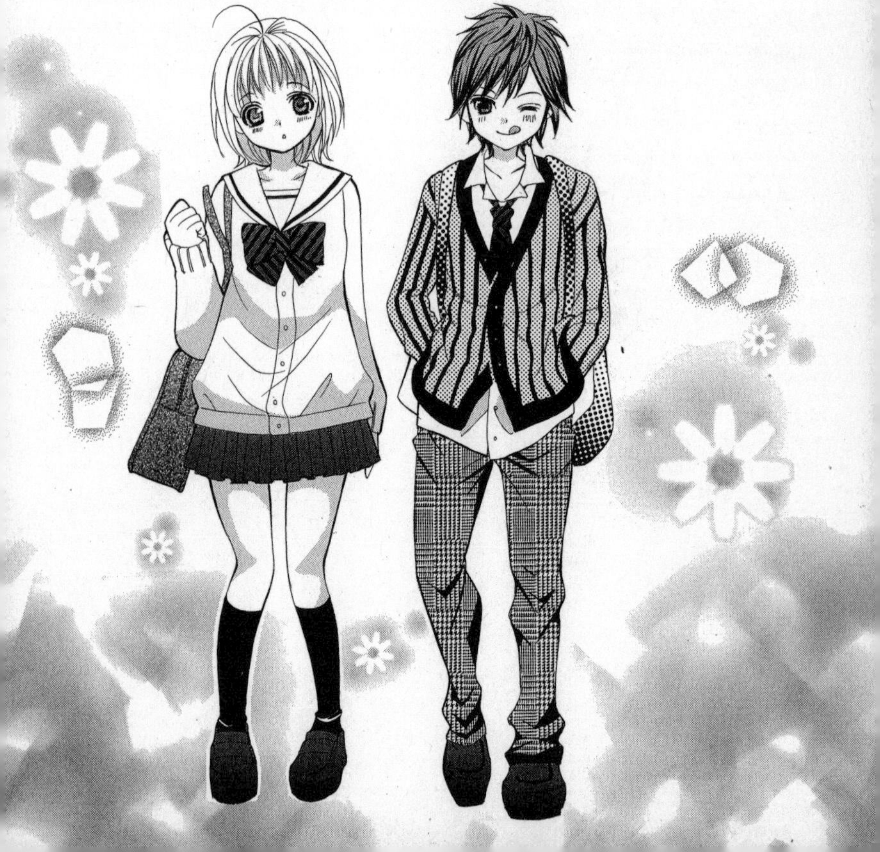